C2
51/

D0835897

Everyman, I will go with thee, and be thy guide,
In thy most need to go by thy side.

EVERYMAN'S LIBRARY

No. 492

POETRY & THE DRAMA

THE MINOR ELIZABETHAN DRAMA
INTRODUCTION BY PROFESSOR
ASHLEY THORNDYKE · IN 2 VOLS.
VOL. 2 · PRE-SHAKESPEAREAN TRAGEDIES

THE MINOR
ELIZABETHAN DRAMA

VOLUME TWO

PRE-SHAKESPEAREAN COMEDIES

LONDON: J. M. DENT & SONS LTD.
NEW YORK: E. P. DUTTON & CO. INC.

All rights reserved
Made in Great Britain
Printed by J. W. Arrowsmith Ltd.
Quay Street and Small Street Bristol
and bound by The Temple Press Letchworth
for
J. M. Dent & Sons Ltd.
Aldine House Bedford St. London
First published in this edition 1910
Last reprinted 1951

INTRODUCTION

THE term "comedy" as applied to a division of the drama was not used in England until the Renaissance had brought a knowledge of the classical drama and theatre. And the beginnings of comedy in England, in the sixteenth century, were the outcome of the breaking away from mediæval forms and an approach to the models of Plautus and Terence. Since then the term has been used loosely to include a great variety of species, some of which have only the slightest resemblance to the Greek and Latin comedies. Even in the beginning many mediæval practices and forms continued, and national conditions forbade any slavish following of ancient example. The plays in this volume illustrate several of the varieties of comedy which appeared in the sixteenth century and prepared the way for the wonderful series of romantic comedies which Shakespeare created in utter defiance of classical model or precept.

Though the term was new the thing was old. The comic spirit, which is at least older than folk games or any drama however primitive, invaded the miracle plays at an early date and flourished in the Towneley Cycle; while there were many wandering entertainers who purveyed farce and clownage. Farce elevated to the sphere of written drama appears at the beginning of the sixteenth century in the plays of John Heywood; and by that time farcical comedy had nearly captured the morality. The morality had about ceased as a long serious performance, given out of doors and lasting perhaps all day. It had become short, suited to presentation indoors, and it relieved its allegory with abundant farce. Moreover, it was enlarging its subject matter, adopting pedagogical, controversial, and other subjects for its presentation by abstractions. To the drama, reaching out on every hand for new material as well as new methods, the classical influence came not only directly through the plays of

Plautus and Terence, but also indirectly through many
continental adaptations of mediæval matter to the Latin
forms. The biblical Terentian plays, and especially those
dealing with the story of the Prodigal Son, made a species
by themselves. And, when the new spirit of endeavour
had once led men away from mediæval conventions, it was
easy to experiment in the drama as elsewhere; and all
sorts of scenic entertainments or dramatisations of story
appeared which were at least more like comedy than
tragedy.

Before the middle of the sixteenth century, conditions
governing play-acting had greatly changed from mediæval
times and had made some advance toward modern modes.
Plays, or interludes, were generally short, and capable of
being performed by a few actors wherever a platform could
be raised; and, though they might be serious in part,
they usually offered a fair share of amusement. Play-
acting, however, was still largely in the hands of amateurs,
and conformed to no settled custom or theatre. Amateur
acting of some sort was common everywhere, in villages
and schools, and by the Bottoms and their mechanics, and
the Holoferneses and their pupils; while the interest in
plays extended through every class of society from queen
to vagabond. Some of the different methods of performance are of particular influence in connection with
the development of comedy. First, the universities and
schools acted plays in both Latin and English. They
provided the main support of comedy along classical lines,
but they also ventured into other fields, and some of the
companies of school children gave public performances.
Second, the court, which constantly supported the drama,
encouraged especially all sorts of shows, pageants, and
plays that offered spectacle, music, and dancing. Third,
the custom of children acting in school and at court led to
the organisation of regular companies of children which
played both at court and in public. Their influence seems
to have been toward a lighter, more refined kind of
comedy. Fourth, the adult men's companies were constantly growing in importance. For a time they wandered
about the country, but in 1576-7 two public playhouses
were built in London, and henceforth the companies grew
in stability and reputation. They rapidly took the drama

out of the hands of amateurs, though for many years they had to contend with the children's companies. The most famous adult actors were clowns, and doubtless the public theatres in the beginning dealt largely with roaring farce, but they soon found a place for romantic story or social satire. These four kinds of performance and the varieties of drama which they encouraged are illustrated by the plays in this volume.

"Ralph Roister Doister" (1566(?), acted c. 1540) was written by Nicholas Udall, a schoolmaster, doubtless for performance by schoolboys. It is usually known as the first English comedy, but its claim to that distinction depends on the restriction of the term to a full-fledged, five-act play on the Latin model. It is an elaborate farce with a fair infusion of English manners and fun, and this sort of matter was readily adapted to Plautian characters and plot. One character, the *miles gloriosus*, was destined to have a distinguished career. Doubtless London taverns furnished many representatives of the Plautian type, and braggart soldiers are among the most lifelike figures in English comedy. Even the best of these, however, even Bobadil and Falstaff, retain some outlines of the old stage type. The close imitation of Latin drama which we find in "Ralph Roister Doister" is further exemplified by a number of other early plays: by Gascoigne's "Supposes," translated from Ariosto, by Lyly's original and clever "Mother Bombie," and by Shakespeare's "Comedy of Errors."

But the influence of Plautus and Terence was manifested not so much in elaborate copying as in innumerable borrowings. Characters like the old men, the young lovers, and the clever servants proved as well suited to the modern stage as the *miles gloriosus;* and the methods of disguise and mistaken identity became part of the stock-in-trade of Elizabethan dramatists. They were easily adapted to any kind of play or to any kind of subjects, but they proved especially suited to realistic or satirical comedies of manners. The Elizabethan age did not suffer its attraction for romantic themes to lead to a neglect of the depiction and criticism of contemporary life, and it found the Latin scheme of tricks and their exposure well fitted to the treatment of modern follies and foibles. Of the many free

developments from Latin models, Ben Jonson's plays are
the most notable; and his " Alchemist " is perhaps the
best example of a close study of the old methods resulting
in an original masterpiece of fun and social satire.

Progress away from the classical models and in new and
fortunate directions was carried on before Shakespeare by
a group of university men, of whom Lyly, Peele, and
Greene were the chief contributors to comedy. Of these
Lyly was the earliest and deserves the most praise as an
innovator. While still a young man he won a prompt and
wide success with his two novels *Euphues;* but though
this gained him a certain position at court, it brought no
large reward, and for years he wrote plays for the child
actors of St. Paul's and the queen's chapel. His eight
comedies are all, except " The Woman in the Moon,"
written in prose; and all except the Plautian " Mother
Bombie " adhere loosely to a common formula. They are
generally based on classical myths, and often introduce
pastoral elements, and they revolve about similar love
complications. The course of true love is aided or ham-
pered or participated in by gods, goddesses, nymphs, shep-
herds, foresters, philosophers, sirens, and fairies, as well as
by ordinary mortals. All of these indulge in courtly and
graceful dialogue, which is quickened to a lively word-play
and repartee from the tongues of the pages or servants,
who usually form one group of the *dramatis personæ.*
The witty page now supersedes the rude buffoon of earlier
plays as a fun-maker. The plays, though acted in public,
seem to have been written primarily for court presentation, and occasionally present an allegory of contemporary
politics. But their spectacle and music and their lively
and refined dialogue were designed above all to please.
Everything is graceful and ingenious, there is scarcely a
hint of tragedy, and all serious purpose is veiled in allegory
or relieved by merriment and song. Lyly is to be credited
with a notable extension of the court entertainments
which the children had long acted, and which are represented among extant plays by Peele's " Arraignment of
Paris " and the anonymous " Rare Triumphs of Love and
Fortune." Through Lyly comedy became a graceful
literary entertainment and a field for fancy and wit.

" Endymion " (1591, acted 1585) is one of the best and

most typical of his plays. The story of Cynthia's love for a mortal is made to symbolise the queen's affection for Leicester, and the allegory is multiplied after the fashion of "The Fairy Queen," so that Cynthia, for example, may be the moon, or Chastity, or Queen Elizabeth. But neither politics nor allegory is pressed too hard. The pert pages are always breaking in to chaff the ridiculous braggart, Sir Tophas, or to worry the stupid watch, or to join in a song. Once, indeed, some of the smallest children of the company appear as fairies. The play is a piece of theatrical confectionery suited to the precocious children, and aiming to please the court and flatter the queen. Its wit and grace are too slight to win much praise to-day except from the gentlest of readers, who may find therein many foreshadowings of Shakespeare's magic fancy. The saucy pages, the love entanglements and bewilderments, the witty dialogues, some bits of song, and even the fairies might appear as his creditors. Shakespeare's earliest comedy, "Love's Labour's Lost," is manifestly closely modelled on Lyly, and "Two Gentlemen of Verona" and "Midsummer Night's Dream" are not without considerable indebtedness. In fact, Shakespeare began where Lyly left off, and he was fortunate to find his way so well prepared. Ben Jonson was offering honest praise to his memory when he declared:

> I should commit thee surely with thy peers,
> And tell how far thou did'st our Lily outshine,
> Or sporting Kyd, or Marlowe's mighty line.

George Peele wrote plays of various kinds, tragedies, histories, and comedies, including an operatic court entertainment, "The Arraignment of Paris," somewhat in Lyly's mode, but his most original and interesting play is "The Old Wives' Tale" (1595, acted *c.* 1590). We do not know just when it was written or for what sort of presentation, but certain puzzling and perhaps archaic elements in its arrangement for the stage suggest an early date and a performance at court. It cannot be said to represent any particular species, but it is a striking illustration of the variety of ingredients which an Elizabethan playwright would often combine in one afternoon's entertainment. It begins with an induction—a mimic audience intervening between the real audience and the play proper—a device

used in Shakespeare's "Taming of the Shrew" and frequently elsewhere in the early drama.   Here lost travellers
seek refuge in a cottage, where they are entertained by
an old woman who begins a story.   This is the induction,
and presently the persons of the story appear and act it out
before old Madge and her supposed auditors.   The story
is that which Milton later borrowed and immortalised in
"Comus," but in Peele's version it is garnished with all
sorts of wonders and surprises.   A magician who is killed,
a genial ghost who goes invisible, and many magic appear-
ances and vanishings make up an amusing hodge-podge.
Such a performance could give rise to no school or historical
development, but it is very typical of the freedom of the
Elizabethan stage and of the strange medleys which entertained its audiences.   The play might easily be made over
into a children's entertainment for our theatres to-day.
The Elizabethans were children in their *naïveté*, their
delight in the wonderful, and in their quick and varied
emotional response.   This childlikeness gave a ready
welcome to extravagant romance.

The vogue of romantic themes in the early drama is
shown by the titles of many lost plays, and by "Common
Conditions" and "Sir Clyomon and Sir Clamydes" among
those extant.   It was the part of Greene to develop certain
elements usual in romantic fiction and drama, and to give
a vital poetic and dramatic presentation of sentimental
love and idealised female character.   His two best plays,
"Friar Bacon and Friar Bungay" (1594, acted *c.* 1590)
and "James IV." (1598, acted *c.* 1591), were both written
for adult companies and acted in the regular theatres.
They both attract our sympathetic interest for stories of
loyal love and for heroines who are English and lifelike as
well as idealised and charming; and they both connect
their stories with court life and with a pseudo-historical
setting.   In "Friar Bacon" there is the added interest of
the magic, doubtless suggested to Greene by the success of
Marlowe's "Dr. Faustus;" and the "glass perspective"
is used very effectively to unite the various actions.

"James IV.," if not clearly superior to "Friar Bacon"
as a play, is of more interest in illustrating dramatic conditions of the day and in its resemblance to Shakespeare's
romantic comedies.   After an induction in which Oberon

figures, we come to the main story of the guilty king, who is repulsed by the noble Ida and finally saved by his wronged but faithful queen, Dorothea. This story is from a novel by Giraldi Cinthio, who also made it into a Senecan tragi-comedy. The Elizabethan stage demanded different treatment, and Greene manufactured an elaborate historical background, some patriotic sentiments, and a pitched field for a finale, and called the whole " The Scottish Historie of James IV., slaine at Flodden." To his heroines, Ida and Dorothea, however, he gave his best efforts, and they remind us again and again of Shakespeare's women. Dorothea is a very Griselda of wifely devotion; she is driven from court; wanders disguised as a boy, accompanied only by one faithful page; she is forced to fight; she is loved by a woman, the wife of her rescuer; she remains true to her husband in spite of his attempts to kill her; and she returns at the end to forgive and save him. But it is not only these incidents which remind us of Sylvia, Viola, and Imogen; it is also her modesty, sweetness, and loyalty. Greene's characterisation is altogether sympathetic and winning. Indeed, if we compare the play with Shakespeare's " Two Gentlemen of Verona," written a year or two later, it is not certain that in this early attempt Shakespeare has greatly excelled Greene, except in his inimitable Launce. At all events, Shakespeare was there clearly following Greene's formula, and was encouraged by Greene's success in winning for his women sympathy and belief.

" James IV." might also be instanced as an example of the chronicle history plays, which were entering upon their great vogue just as Shakespeare came to the theatre. Greene's play, however, is only pseudo-history, and the history plays formed a somewhat distinct class by themselves. Some were tragical, others mingled historical scenes and royal personages with farce and comedy. These prepared the way in some measure for Shakespeare's triumphant union of history and comedy in his Falstaff plays. A more extensive survey of pre-Shakespearean comedy than the present might also dwell on the later moralities, or Wilson's satirical plays, or on the continuance of English farce, without indebtedness to Plautus, in such plays as " Two Angry Women of Abingdon." But the five plays included in this volume illustrate the most important tendencies in early comedy and those which contributed most to Shakespeare's creation of romantic comedy.

We have noted that his earliest comedies belong to the classes which we have discussed. "The Comedy of Errors" belongs with the Plautian adaptations, "Love's Labour's Lost" belongs with Lyly's plays, "The Two Gentlemen of Verona" with Greene's. The service of these predecessors was, however, more wide-reaching than can be indicated by such direct bills of indebtedness. They represent the development of comedy from rude farce to a refined, varied, and poetical form of entertainment. They prepared audience and actors for the great enchantments that were to follow, and they showed the material and some of the means whereby those enchantments might be wrought. Girls in boys' clothing, saucy pages, estranged and reuniting lovers, braggart soldiers, stupid constables, magicians, fairies, were all familiar on the stage. Courtly and witty dialogues, lovely songs, alluring descriptions, and absurd conceits, could all be heard. And the audience was accustomed to spectacle, excitement, wonders, to verbal displays, to poetry, and to the sympathetic presentation of character, and to the exaltation of virtue. The ingredients for "Twelfth Night" and "As You Like It" were all there; they only awaited the alchemist.

ASHLEY THORNDYKE.

COLUMBIA UNIVERSITY,
NEW YORK.

BIBLIOGRAPHY IN BRIEF

NORTON and SACKVILLE.—Gorboduc, first acted 1560-1, by the gentlemen of the Inner Temple; 4to, 1565; later authorised version, The Tragidie of Feerex and Porrex, 1570; reprint, 1590; edited R. Dodsley, 1736; in Dodsley's Old Plays, 1774, 1780; Hawkins, English Drama, 1773; Ancient British Drama, 1810; W. D. Cooper (Shakespeare Society), 1847; L. Toulmin Smith (Vollmoeller, Englische Sprach-ŭ Literatur Denkmale), 1883; Early English Dramatists, 1906; Tudor facsimile Texts, 1908; and in Editions of Sackville's works, 1820, 1859.

THOMAS KYD.—The Spanish Tragedie, containing the lamentable end of Don Horatio and Bel-imperia: with the pitiful death of olde Hieronimo, 4to, undated; 4to, 1594; 4to, 1599; later issues included new additions of the Painter's part and other; two entries in Henslow's Diary speak of money advanced to Ben Jonson for these additions, but a doubt is never-theless thrown on his authorship, the credit of fine passages having been given to Webster or even Shakespeare. Ed. J. Shick (Temple Dramatists), 1898.

Works.—In Dodsley's Old Plays, ed. by Hazlitt, vols. 4 and 5, 1874; by F. S. Boas (Clarendon Press), 1901.

GEORGE PEELE.—Old Wives' Tale, 4to, 1595; ed. F. B. Gummere, 1903. The Love of King David and Fair Bethsabe, with the Tragedy of Absalon, 4to, 1599.

Works.—Ed. A. Dyce, 1828, 1829-39; and with Greene's works, 1861; A. H. Bullen, 1888; Plays and Poems, with Introduction by H. Morley (Morley's Universal Library), vol. 52.

The lamentable and true tragedy of Master Arden of Feversham in Kent, doubtfully ascribed to Shakespeare, 4to, 1592; reprint, 1770; with Introduction by A. H. Bullen, 1887; 4to, 1633; ed. R. Bayne (Temple Dramatists), 1897; with Introduction by A. F. Hopkinson (Shakespeare's Doubtful Plays), 1907.

NICHOLAS UDALL.—Ralph Roister Doister, early copy undated; re-printed, 1818, 1821; published in I. White's Old English Dramas, 1830; by Shakespeare Society, 1847; in Arber's English Reprints, 1869, 1895; and in Hazlitt's edition of Dodsley's Old Plays, vol. 3, 1874; edited by W. H. Williams and P. A. Robin (Temple Dramatists), 1901; by E. Flügel, Representative English Comedies, 1903.

Works.—J. S. Farmer (Early English Dramatists), 1906; and 1907 (Museum Dramatists).

JOHN LYLY.—Endimion, The Man in the Moone, 4to, 1591; in Dodsley's Old English Plays, vol. i., 1814; edited G. P. Baker, 1894.

Works.—Edited F. W. Fairholt, 1858; by R. Warwick Bond (Clarendon Press), 3 vols. 1902.

ROBERT GREENE.—The Honorable Historie of frier Bacon and frier Bongay, 4to, 1594, 1599, etc.; The Scottish Historie of James the Fourth, slaine at Flodden, entermixed with a pleasant Comedie presented by Oboram, King of Fayeries, 4to, 1598.

Works.—Plays, edited by A. Dyce, 1831; revised edition (Dramatic and Poetical), with Peele's Works, 1861; complete works, 15 vols., edited by Dr. Grosart, 1881-6; Plays and Poems, J. Churton Collins (Clarendon Press), 1905; T. H. Dickinson (Mermaid Series), 1909.

THOMAS PRESTON.—A Lamentable Tragedie of Cambises, King of Percia, 4to, 1569 (?), 1585 (?). Reprinted in Dodsley's collection, and Hawkins's *Origin of the English Drama*, and in Manly's *Specimens of Pre-Shakesperean Drama*.

CONTENTS

RALPH ROISTER DOISTER

DRAMATIS PERSONÆ

RALPH ROISTER DOISTER.

MATHEW MERYGREEKE.

GAWYN GOODLUCK, *affianced to Dame Custance.*

TRISTRAM TRUSTIE, *his friend.*

DOBINET DOUGHTIE, *" boy " to Roister Doister.*

TOM TRUPENIE, *servant to Dame Custance.*

SYM SURESBY, *servant to Goodluck.*

SCRIVENER.

HARPAX.

DAME CHRISTIAN CUSTANCE, *a widow.*

MARGERIE MUMBLECRUST, *her nurse.*

TIBET TALKAPACE } *her maidens.*
ANNOT ALYFACE

TIME: *About two days.*

SCENE: *Not indicated. ? London.*

RALPH ROISTER DOISTER

THE PROLOGUE

What creature is in health, either young or old,
But some mirth with modesty will be glad to use?
As we in this Interlude shall now unfold,
Wherein all scurrility we utterly refuse,
Avoiding such mirth wherein is abuse:
Knowing nothing more commendable for a man's recreation
Than Mirth which is used in an honest fashion:
For Mirth prolongeth life, and causeth health,
Mirth recreates our spirits and voideth pensiveness,
Mirth increaseth amity, not hindering our wealth,   10
Mirth is to be used both of more and less,
Being mixed with virtue in decent comeliness,
As we trust no good nature can gainsay the same:
Which mirth we intend to use, avoiding all blame.
The wise Poets long time heretofore,
Under merry Comedies secrets did declare,
Wherein was contained very virtuous lore,
With mysteries and forewarnings very rare.
Such to write neither Plautus nor Terence did spare,
Which among the learned at this day bears the bell: 20
These with such other therein did excel.
Our Comedy or Interlude which we intend to play
Is named Roister Doister indeed.
Which against the vain-glorious doth inveigh,
Whose humour the roisting sort continually doth feed.
Thus by your patience we intend to proceed
In this our Interlude by God's leave and grace,
And here I take my leave for a certain space.

FINIS

3

ACT I

SCENE I

MATHEW MERYGREEKE.   *He entereth singing.*

As long liveth the merry man (they say)
As doth the sorry man, and longer by a day.
Yet the grasshopper, for all his summer piping,
Starveth in winter with hungry griping,
Therefore another said saw doth men advise,
That they be together both merry and wise.
This lesson must I practise, or else ere long,
With me, Mathew Merygreeke, it will be wrong.
Indeed men so call me, for by him that us bought,
Whatever chance betide, I can take no thought,   10
Yet wisdom would that I did myself bethink
Where to be provided this day of meat and drink:
For know ye, that for all this merry note of mine,
He might appose me now that should ask where I dine.
My living lieth here and there, of God's grace,
Sometime with this good man, sometime in that place,
Sometime Lewis Loytrer biddeth me come near,
Somewhiles Watkin Waster maketh us good cheer,
Sometime Davy Diceplayer, when he hath well cast,
Keepeth revel rout as long as it will last,   20
Sometime Tom Titivile maketh us a feast,
Sometime with Sir Hugh Pye I am a bidden guest,
Sometime at Nicol Neverthrive's I get a sop,
Sometime I am feasted with Bryan Blinkinsoppe,
Sometime I hang on Hankyn Hoddydodie's sleeve,
But this day on Ralph Roister Doister's by his leave.
For truly of all men he is my chief banker
Both for meat and money, and my chief shoot-anchor.
For, sooth Roister Doister in that he doth say,
And require what ye will ye shall have no nay.   30
But now of Roister Doister somewhat to express,
That ye may esteem him after his worthiness,
In these twenty towns and seek them throughout,
Is not the like stock, whereon to graff a lout.

All the day long is he facing and craking
Of his great acts in fighting and fraymaking:
But when Roister Doister is put to his proof,
To keep the Queen's peace is more for his behoof.
If any woman smile or cast on him an eye,
Up is he to the hard ears in love by and by,   40
And in all the hot haste must she be his wife.
Else farewell his good days, and farewell his life,
Master Ralph Roister Doister is but dead and gone
Except she on him take some compassion,
Then chief of counsel must be Mathew Merygreeke,
" What if I for marriage to such an one seek? "
Then must I sooth it, what ever it is:
For what he sayeth or doeth cannot be amiss.
Hold up his yea and nay, be his nown white son,
Praise and rouse him well, and ye have his heart won,   50
For so well liketh he his own fond fashions
That he taketh pride of false commendations.
But such sport have I with him as I would not lese,
Though I should be bound to live with bread and cheese.
For exalt him, and have him as ye lust indeed:
Yea, to hold his finger in a hole for a need.
I can with a word make him fain or loth,
I can with as much make him pleased or wroth,
I can when I will make him merry and glad,
I can when me lust make him sorry and sad,   60
I can set him in hope and eke in despair,
I can make him speak rough and make him speak fair.
But I marvel I see him not all this same day,
I will seek him out: But lo! he cometh this way.
I have yond espied him sadly coming,
And in love for twenty pound, by his gloming.

SCENE II

RALPH ROISTER DOISTER.   MATHEW MERYGREEKE.

R. Roister. Come death when thou wilt, I am weary of my life.
M. Mery. I told you, I, we should woo another wife.
R. Roister. Why did God make me such a goodly person?
M. Mery. He is in by the week, we shall have sport anon.   70
R. Roister. And where is my trusty friend, Mathew Merygreeke?

M. Mery. I will make as I saw him not, he doth me seek.

R. Roister. I have him espied me-thinketh, yond is he.

     Ho! Mathew Merygreeke, my friend, a word with thee.

M. Mery. I will not hear him, but make as I had haste,

     Farewell all my good friends, the time away doth waste.

     And the tide, they say, tarrieth for no man.

R. Roister. Thou must with thy good counsel help me if thou can.

M. Mery. God keep thee, worshipful Master Roister Doister,

     And fare well the lusty Master Roister Doister.   80

R. Roister. I must needs speak with thee a word or twain.

M. Mery. Within a month or two I will be here again.

     Negligence in great affairs, ye know, may mar all.

R. Roister. Attend upon me now, and well reward thee I shall.

M. Mery. I have take my leave, and the tide is well spent.

R. Roister. I die except thou help, I pray thee be content.

     Do thy part well now, and ask what thou wilt,

     For without thy aid my matter is all spilt.

M. Mery. Then to serve your turn I will some pains take,

     And let all mine own affairs alone for your sake.   90

R. Roister. My whole hope and trust resteth only in thee.

M. Mery. Then can ye not do amiss, whatever it be.

R. Roister. Gramercies, Merygreeke, most bound to thee I am.

M. Mery. But up with that heart, and speak out like a ram.

     Ye speak like a capon that had the cough now:

     Be of good cheer, anon ye shall do well enow.

R. Roister. Upon thy comfort, I will all things well handle.

M. Mery. So, lo! that is a breast to blow out a candle.

     But what is this great matter, I would fain know?

     We shall find remedy therefore I trow.   100

     Do ye lack money? ye know mine old offers,

     Ye have always a key to my purse and coffers.

R. Roister. I thank thee: had ever man such a friend?

M. Mery. Ye give unto me: I must needs to you lend.

R. Roister. Nay, I have money plenty all things to discharge.

M. Mery. That knew I right well when I made offer so large.

R. Roister. But it is no such matter.

M. Mery. What is it then?

     Are ye in danger of debt to any man?

     If ye be, take no thought nor be not afraid.

     Let them hardly take thought how they shall be paid.   110

R. Roister. Tut, I owe nought.

M. Mery. What then? fear ye imprisonment?

R. Roister. No.

M. Mery. No, I wist ye offend not, so to be shent.
But if ye had, the Tower could not you so hold,
But to break out at all times ye would be bold.
What is it? hath any man threatened you to beat?

R. Roister. What is he that durst have put me in that heat?
He that beateth me by his arms shall well find,
That I will not be far from him nor run behind.

M. Mery. That thing know all men ever since ye overthrew
The fellow of the lion which Hercules slew. 120
But what is it then?

R. Roister. Of love I make my moan.

M. Mery. Ah, this foolish love, wilt ne'er let us alone?
But because ye were refused the last day,
Ye said ye would ne'er more be entangled that way.
I would meddle no more, since I find all so unkind.

R. Roister. Yea, but I cannot so put love out of my mind.

M. Mery. But is your love, tell me first, in any wise,
In the way of marriage, or of merchandise?
If it may otherwise than lawful be found,
Ye get none of my help for a hundred pound. 130

R. Roister. No, by my troth, I would have her to my wife.

M. Mery. Then are ye a good man, and God save your life!
And what or who is she, with whom ye are in love?

R. Roister. A woman whom I know not by what means to move.

M. Mery. Who is it?

R. Roister. A woman yond.

M. Mery. What is her name?

R. Roister. Her yonder.

M. Mery. Whom?

R. Roister. Mistress, ah.

M. Mery. Fie, fie, for shame!
Love ye, and know not whom? but her yond, a woman,
We shall then get you a wife, I cannot tell when.

R. Roister. The fair woman, that supped with us yesternight,
And I heard her name twice or thrice, and had it right. 140

M. Mery. Yea, ye may see ye ne'er take me to good cheer with
you,
If ye had, I could have told you her name now.

R. Roister. I was to blame indeed, but the next time perchance:
And she dwelleth in this house.

M. Mery. What, Christian Custance?

R. Roister. Except I have her to my wife, I shall run mad.

M. Mery. Nay, unwise perhaps, but I warrant you for mad.

R. Roister. I am utterly dead unless I have my desire.

M. Mery. Where be the bellows that blew this sudden fire?

R. Roister. I hear she is worth a thousand pound and more.

M. Mery. Yea, but learn this one lesson of me afore: 150
    An hundred pound of marriage-money, doubtless,
    Is ever thirty pound sterling, or somewhat less,
    So that her thousand pound, if she be thrifty,
    Is much near about two hundred and fifty,
    Howbeit wooers and widows are never poor.

R. Roister. Is she a widow?   I love her better therefore.

M. Mery. But I hear she hath made promise to another.

R. Roister. He shall go without her, and he were my brother.

M. Mery. I have heard say, I am right well advised,
    That she hath to Gawyn Goodluck promised.   160

R. Roister. What is that Gawyn Goodluck?

M. Mery. A merchant-man.

R. Roister. Shall he speed afore me? nay, sir, by sweet Saint
     Anne.
    Ah, sir, *Backare*, quod Mortimer to his sow.
    I will have her mine own self I make God a vow.
    For I tell thee, she is worth a thousand pound.

M. Mery. Yet a fitter wife for your maship might be found:
    Such a goodly man as you might get one with land,
    Besides pounds of gold a thousand and a thousand,
    And a thousand, and a thousand, and a thousand,
    And so to the sum of twenty hundred thousand,   170
    Your most goodly personage is worthy of no less.

R. Roister. I am sorry God made me so comely, doubtless.
    For that maketh me each where so highly favoured,
    And all women on me so enamoured.

M. Mery. Enamoured, quod you? have ye spied out that?
    Ah, sir, marry, now, I see you know what is what.
    Enamoured, ka? marry, sir, say that again,
    But I thought not ye had marked it so plain.

R. Roister. Yes, each where they gaze all upon me and stare.

M. Mery. Yea, malkyn, I warrant you as much as they dare.
    And ye will not believe what they say in the street,   181
    When your maship passeth by, all such as I meet,
    That sometimes I can scarce find what answer to make.
    Who is this (saith one) Sir Launcelot du Lake?

    Who is this, great Guy of Warwick, saith another?
    No (say I) it is the thirteenth Hercules brother.
    Who is this? noble Hector of Troy, saith the third?
    No, but of the same nest (say I) it is a bird.
    Who is this? great Goliah, Sampson, or Colbrand?
    No (say I) but it is a Brute of the Alie land.   190
    Who is this? great Alexander? or Charles le Maigne?
    No, it is the tenth worthy, say I to them again:
    I know not if I said well.
R. Roister. Yes, for so I am.
M. Mery. Yea, for there were but nine worthies before ye came.
    To some others, the third Cato I do you call.
    And so as well as I can I answer them all.
    " Sir, I pray you, what lord or great gentleman is this? "
    Master Ralph Roister Doister, dame (say I), ywis.
    O Lord (saith she then) what a goodly man it is,
    Would Christ I had such a husband as he is!   200
    O Lord (say some) that the sight of his face we lack:
    It is enough for you (say I) to see his back.
    His face is for ladies of high and noble parages,
    With whom he hardly 'scapeth great marriages.
    With much more than this, and much otherwise.
R. Roister. I can thee thank that thou canst such answers devise:
    But I perceive thou dost me throughly know.
M. Mery. I mark your manners for mine own learning, I trow.
    But such is your beauty, and such are your acts,
    Such is your personage, and such are your facts,   210
    That all women fair and foul, more and less,
    That eye you, they lub you, they talk of you doubtless.
    Your p[l]easant look maketh them all merry,
    Ye pass not by, but they laugh till they be weary,
    Yea, and money could I have, the truth to tell,
    Of many, to bring you that way where they dwell.
R. Roister. Merygreeke, for this thy reporting well of me—
M. Mery. What should I else, sir? it is my duty, pardee.
R. Roister. I promise thou shalt not lack, while I have a groat.
M. Mery. Faith, sir, and I ne'er had more need of a new coat.
R. Roister. Thou shalt have one to-morrow, and gold for to
    spend.   221
M. Mery. Then I trust to bring the day to a good end.
    For as for mine own part having money enow,
    I could live only with the remembrance of you.

But now to your widow whom you love so hot.

R. Roister. By Cock, thou sayest truth, I had almost forgot.

M. Mery. What if Christian Custance will not have you, what?

R. Roister. Have me? yes, I warrant you, never doubt of that,
    I know she loveth me, but she dare not speak.

M. Mery. Indeed, meet it were some body should it break. 230

R. Roister. She looked on me twenty times yesternight,
    And laughed so.

M. Mery. That she could not sit upright.

R. Roister. No, faith, could she not.

M. Mery. No, even such a thing I cast.

R. Roister. But for wooing, thou knowest, women are shamefast.
    But and she knew my mind, I know she would be glad,
    And think it the best chance that ever she had.

M. Mery. To her then like a man, and be bold forth to start,
    Wooers never speed well, that have a false heart.

R. Roister. What may I best do?

M. Mery. Sir, remain ye awhile here.
    Ere long one or other of her house will appear.   240
    Ye know my mind.

R. Roister. Yea, now hardly let me alone.

M. Mery. In the meantime, sir, if you please, I will home,
    And call your musicians, for in this your case
    It would set you forth, and all your wooing grace.
    Ye may not lack your instruments to play and sing.

R. Roister. Thou knowest I can do that.

M. Mery. As well as anything.
    Shall I go call your folks, that ye may show a cast?

R. Roister. Yea, run, I beseech thee, in all possible haste.

M. Mery. I go.   [*Exeat.*

R. Roister. Yea, for I love singing out of measure,
    It comforteth my spirits and doth me great pleasure.   250
    But who cometh forth yond from my sweetheart Custance?
    My matter frameth well, this is a lucky chance.

SCENE III

MADGE MUMBLECRUST, *spinning on the distaff.* TIBET TALKA-
PACE, *sewing.* ANNOT ALYFACE, *knitting.* R. ROISTER.

M. Mumble. If this distaff were spun, Margerie Mumblecrust—

Tib. Talk. Where good stale ale is will drink no water I trust.

M. Mumble. Dame Custance hath promised us good ale and
    white bread.
Tib. Talk. If she keep not promise, I will beshrew her head:
    But it will be stark night before I shall have done.
R. Roister. I will stand here awhile, and talk with them anon.
    I hear them speak of Custance, which doth my heart good.
    To hear her name spoken doth even comfort my blood. 260
M. Mumble. Sit down to your work, Tibet, like a good girl.
Tib. Talk. Nurse, meddle you with your spindle and your whirl,
    No haste but good, Madge Mumblecrust, for whip and
        whur,
    The old proverb doth say, never made good fur.
M. Mumble. Well, ye will sit down to your work anon, I trust.
Tib. Talk. Soft fire maketh sweet malt, good Madge Mumble-
    crust.
M. Mumble. And sweet malt maketh jolly good ale for the
    nones.
Tib. Talk. Which will slide down the lane without any bones.
                                       [*Cantet.*
    Old brown bread crusts must have much good mumbling.
    But good ale down your throat hath good easy tumbling.
R. Roister. The jolliest wench that ere I heard, little mouse,
    May I not rejoice that she shall dwell in my house?   272
Tib. Talk. So, sirrah, now this gear beginneth for to frame.
M. Mumble. Thanks to God, though your work stand still, your
    tongue is not lame.
Tib. Talk. And though your teeth be gone, both so sharp and so
    fine,
    Yet your tongue can renne on patins as well as mine.
M. Mumble. Ye were not for nought named Tib Talkapace.
Tib. Talk. Doth my talk grieve you?   Alack, God save your
    grace.
M. Mumble. I hold a groat, ye will drink anon for this gear.
Tib. Talk. And I will pray you the stripes for me to bear.   280
M. Mumble. I hold a penny, ye will drink without a cup.
Tib. Talk. Wherein so e'er ye drink, I wot ye drink all up.

Enter ANNOT.

An. Alyface. By Cock, and well sewed, my good Tibet Talk-
    apace.
Tib. Talk. And e'en as well knit, my nown Annot Alyface.

R. Roister. See what a sort she keepeth that must be my wife.
　　Shall not I, when I have her, lead a merry life?
Tib. Talk. Welcome, my good wench, and sit here by me just.
An. Alyface. And how doth our old beldame here, Madge
　　Mumblecrust?
Tib. Talk. Chide, and find faults, and threaten to complain.
An. Alyface. To make us poor girls shent to her is small gain.
M. Mumble. I did neither chide, nor complain, nor threaten. 291
R. Roister. It would grieve my heart to see one of them beaten.
M. Mumble. I did nothing but bid her work and hold her peace.
Tib. Talk. So would I, if you could your clattering cease:
　　But the devil cannot make old trot hold her tongue.
An. Alyface. Let all these matters pass, and we three sing a song,
　　So shall we pleasantly both the time beguile now,
　　And eke dispatch all our works ere we can tell how.
Tib. Talk. I shrew them that say nay, and that shall not be I.
M. Mumble. And I am well content.
Tib. Talk. Sing on then, by and by.   300
R. Roister. And I will not away, but listen to their song,
　　Yet Merygreeke and my folks tarry very long.

　　　TIB., AN., *and* MARGERIE, *do sing here.*

　　　　Pipe merry Annot, etc.
　　Trilla, trilla, trillarie.
　　Work Tibet, work Annot, work Margerie.
　　Sew Tibet, knit Annot, spin Margerie.
　　Let us see who shall win the victory.

Tib. Talk. This sleeve is not willing to be sewed, I trow.
　　A small thing might make me all in the ground to throw.

　　　　Then they sing again.

　　　　Pipe merry Annot, etc.   310
　　Trilla, trilla, trillarie.
　　What Tibet, what Annot, what Margerie.
　　Ye sleep, but we do not, that shall we try.
　　Your fingers be numbed, our work will not lie.

Tib. Talk. If ye do so again, well I would advise you nay.
　　In good sooth one stop more, and I make holy day.

　　　　They sing the third time.

　　　　Pipe merry Annot, etc.
　　Trilla, trilla, trillarie.
　　Now Tibet, now Annot, now Margerie.
　　Now whippet apace for the maistry,
　　But it will not be, our mouth is so dry.   320

Tib. Talk. Ah, each finger is a thumb to-day methink,
  I care not to let all alone, choose it swim or sink.

They sing the fourth time.

Pipe merry Annot, etc.
Trilla, trilla, trillarie.
When Tibet, when Annot, when Margerie.
I will not, I cannot, no more can I.
Then give we all over, and there let it lie.
        [Let her cast down her work.

Tib. Talk. There it lieth, the worst is but a curried coat,
  Tut, I am used thereto, I care not a groat.   330
An. Alyface. Have we done singing since? then will I in again,
  Here I found you, and here I leave both twain.   *[Exeat.*
M. Mumble. And I will not be long after. Tib Talkapace!
Tib. Talk. What is the matter?
M. Mumble. Yond stood a man all this space
  And hath heard all that ever we spake together.
Tib. Talk. Marry, the more lout he for his coming hither.
  And the less good he can to listen maidens talk.
  I care not and I go bid him hence for to walk:
  It were well done to know what he maketh here away.
R. Roister. Now might I speak to them, if I wist what to say.
M. Mumble. Nay, we will go both off, and see what he is. 341
R. Roister. One that hath heard all your talk and singing i-wis.
Tib. Talk. The more to blame you, a good thrifty husband
  Would elsewhere have had some better matters in hand.
R. Roister. I did it for no harm, but for good love I bear
  To your dame mistress Custance, I did your talk hear.
  And, mistress nurse, I will kiss you for acquaintance.
M. Mumble. I come anon, sir.
Tib. Talk. Faith, I would our dame Custance
  Saw this gear.   350
M. Mumble. I must first wipe all clean, yea, I must.
Tib. Talk. Ill 'chieve it, doting fool, but it must be cust.
M. Mumble. God yelde you, sir; chad not so much, i-chotte
    not when,
  Ne'er since chwas bore chwine, of such a gay gentleman.
R. Roister. I will kiss you too, maiden, for the good will I bear
    you.
Tib. Talk. No, forsooth, by your leave, ye shall not kiss me.
R. Roister. Yes, be not afeard, I do not disdain you a whit.

Tib. Talk. Why should I fear you? I have not so little wit,
    Ye are but a man I know very well.

R. Roister. Why then?

Tib. Talk. Forsooth for I will not, I use not to kiss men.   360

R. Roister. I would fain kiss you too, good maiden, if I might.

Tib. Talk. What should that need?

R. Roister. But to honour you by this light.
    I use to kiss all them that I love, to God I vow.

Tib. Talk. Yea, sir? I pray you, when did ye last kiss your
    cow?

R. Roister. Ye might be proud to kiss me, if ye were wise.

Tib. Talk. What promotion were therein?

R. Roister. Nurse is not so nice.

Tib. Talk. Well, I have not been taught to kissing and licking.

R. Roister. Yet I thank you, mistress nurse, ye made no sticking.

M. Mumble. I will not stick for a kiss with such a man as you.

Tib. Talk. They that lust: I will again to my sewing now. 370

Enter ANNOT.

An. Alyface. Tidings, ho! tidings! dame Custance greeteth you
    well.

R. Roister. Whom? me?

An. Alyface. You, sir? No, sir! I do no such tale tell.

R. Roister. But and she knew me here.

An. Alyface. Tibet Talkapace,
    Your mistress Custance and mine, must speak with your
    grace.

Tib. Talk. With me?

An. Alyface. Ye must come in to her, out of all doubts.

Tib. Talk. And my work not half done? A mischief on all
    louts.   [*Ex. am.*

R. Roister. Ah, good sweet nurse!

M. Mumble. A good sweet gentleman.

R. Roister. What?

M. Mumble. Nay, I cannot tell, sir, but what thing would you?

R. Roister. How doth sweet Custance, my heart of gold, tell me
    how?

M. Mumble. She doth very well, sir, and command me to you.

R. Roister. To me?

M. Mumble. Yea, to you, sir.

R. Roister. To me? Nurse, tell me plain,   381
    To me?

M. Mumble. Ye.

R. Roister. That word maketh me alive again.

M. Mumble. She command me to one last day, whoe'er it was.

R. Roister. That was e'en to me and none other, by the Mass.

M. Mumble. I cannot tell you surely, but one it was.

R. Roister. It was I and none other: this cometh to good pass.
    I promise thee, nurse, I favour her.

M. Mumble. E'en so, sir.

R. Roister. Bid her sue to me for marriage.

M. Mumble. E'en so, sir.

R. Roister. And surely for thy sake she shall speed.

M. Mumble. E'en so, sir.

R. Roister. I shall be contented to take her.

M. Mumble. E'en so, sir.   390

R. Roister. But at thy request and for thy sake.

M. Mumble. E'en so, sir.

R. Roister. And, come, hark in thine ear what to say.

M. Mumble. E'en so, sir.

    [Here let him tell her a great long tale in her ear.

SCENE IV

MATHEW MERYGREEKE. DOBINET DOUGHTIE. HARPAX.
RALPH ROISTER. MARGERIE MUMBLECRUST.

M. Mery. Come on, sirs, apace, and quit yourselves like men,
    Your pains shall be rewarded.

D. Dough. But I wot not when.

M. Mery. Do your master worship as ye have done in time past.

D. Dough. Speak to them: of mine office he shall have a cast.

M. Mery. Harpax, look that thou do well too, and thy fellow.

Harpax. I warrant, if he will mine example follow.

M. Mery. Curtsy, whoresons, douk you and crouch at every
    word.

D. Dough. Yes, whether our master speak earnest or bord. 400

M. Mery. For this lieth upon his preferment indeed.

D. Dough. Oft is he a wooer, but never doth he speed.

M. Mery. But with whom is he now so sadly rounding yond?

D. Dough. With *Nobs nicebecetur miserere* fond.

M. Mery. God be at your wedding, be ye sped already?
    I did not suppose that your love was so greedy.
    I perceive now ye have chose of devotion,

    And joy have ye, lady, of your promotion.

R. Roister. Tush, fool, thou art deceived, this is not she.

M. Mery. Well, mock much of her, and keep her well, I 'vise ye.
    I will take no charge of such a fair piece keeping.   411

M. Mumble. What aileth this fellow? he driveth me to weeping.

M. Mery. What, weep on the wedding day? Be merry, woman,
    Though I say it, ye have chose a good gentleman.

R. Roister. Kocks nowns, what meanest thou, man? tut, a whistle.

M. Mery. Ah, sir, be good to her; she is but a gristle.
    Ah, sweet lamb and coney!

R. Roister. Tut, thou art deceived.

M. Mery. Weep no more, lady, ye shall be well received.
    Up with some merry noise, sirs, to bring home the bride.

R. Roister. Gogs arms, knave, art thou mad?
    I tell thee thou art wide.   420

M. Mery. Then ye intend by night to have her home brought.

R. Roister. I tell thee no.

M. Mery. How then?

R. Roister. 'Tis neither meant ne thought.

M. Mery. What shall we then do with her?

R. Roister. Ah, foolish harebrain,
    This is not she.

M. Mery. No, is? why then unsaid again.
    And what young girl is this with your maship so bold?

R. Roister. A girl?

M. Mery. Yea. I dare say, scarce yet three score year old.

R. Roister. This same is the fair widow's nurse, of whom ye wot.

M. Mery. Is she but a nurse of a house? hence home, old trot,
    Hence at once.

R. Roister. No, no.

M. Mery. What, an please your maship,
    A nurse talk so homely with one of your worship?   430

R. Roister. I will have it so: it is my pleasure and will.

M. Mery. Then I am content. Nurse, come again, tarry still.

R. Roister. What, she will help forward this my suit for her part.

M. Mery. Then is't mine own pigs nie, and blessing on my heart.

R. Roister. This is our best friend, man.

M. Mery. Then teach her what to say,

M. Mumble. I am taught already.

M. Mery. Then go, make no delay.

R. Roister. Yet hark, one word in thine ear.

M. Mery. Back, sirs, from his tail.

R. Roister. Back, villains, will ye be privy of my counsel?

M. Mery. Back, sirs, so: I told you afore ye would be shent.

R. Roister. She shall have the first day a whole peck of argent.

M. Mumble. A peck? *Nomine patris*, have ye so much spare?

R. Roister. Yea, and a cart-load thereto, or else were it bare,   442
     Besides other movables, household stuff, and land.

M. Mumble. Have ye lands too?

R. Roister. An hundred marks.

M. Mery. Yea, a thousand.

M. Mumble. And have ye cattle too? and sheep too?

R. Roister. Yea, a few.

M. Mery. He is ashamed the number of them to show.
     E'en round about him, as many thousand sheep goes,
     As he and thou, and I too, have fingers and toes.

M. Mumble. And how many years old be you?

R. Roister. Forty at least.

M. Mery. Yea, and thrice forty to them.

R. Roister. Nay, now thou dost jest.   450
     I am not so old, thou misreckonest my years.

M. Mery. I know that: but my mind was on bullocks and
     steers.

M. Mumble. And what shall I show her your mastership's name
     is?

R. Roister. Nay, she shall make suit ere she know that, i-wis.

M. Mumble. Yet let me somewhat know.

M. Mery. This is he, understand,
     That killed the blue spider in Blanchepowder land.

M. Mumble. Yea, Jesus, William zee law, did he zo law?

M. Mery. Yea, and the last elephant that ever he saw,
     As the beast passed by, he start out of a busk,
     And e'en with pure strength of arms plucked out his great
     tusk.   460

M. Mumble. Jesus, *nomine patris*, what a thing was that?

R. Roister. Yea, but, Merygreeke, one thing thou hast forgot.

M. Mery. What?

R. Roister. Of th' other elephant.

M. Mery. Oh, him that fled away.

R. Roister. Yea.

M. Mery. Yea, he knew that his match was in place that day.
     Tut, he bet the king of crickets on Christmas day,

That he crept in a hole, and not a word to say.

M. Mumble. A sore man, by zembletee.

M. Mery. Why, he wrung a club
 Once in a fray out of the hand of Belzebub.

R. Roister. And how when Mumfision?

M. Mery. Oh, your coustreling
 Bore the lantern a-field so before the gozeling. 470
 Nay that is too long a matter now to be told:
 Never ask his name, nurse, I warrant thee, be bold.
 He conquered in one day from Rome to Naples,
 And won towns, nurse, as fast as thou canst make apples.

M. Mumble. O Lord, my heart quaketh for fear: he is too sore.

R. Roister. Thou makest her too much afeard, Merygreeke, no
  more.
 This tale would fear my sweetheart Custance right evil.

M. Mery. Nay, let her take him, nurse, and fear not the devil.
 But thus is our song dashed.   Sirs, ye may home again.

R. Roister. No, shall they not.   I charge you all here to remain:
 The villain slaves, a whole day ere they can be found. 481

M. Mery. Couch on your marybones, whoresons, down to the
  ground.
 Was it meet he should tarry so long in one place
 Without harmony of music, or some solace?
 Whoso hath such bees as your master in his head,
 Had need to have his spirits with music to be fed.
 By your mastership's licence.

R. Roister. What is that? a mote?

M. Mery. No, it was a fowl's feather had light on your coat.

R. Roister. I was nigh no feathers since I came from my bed.

M. Mery. No, sir, it was a hair that was fall from your head.

R. Roister. My men come when it please them.

M. Mery. By your leave.

R. Roister. What is that? 491

M. Mery. Your gown was foul spotted with the foot of a gnat.

R. Roister. Their master to offend they are nothing afeard. 101
 What now?

M. Mery. A lousy hair from your mastership's beard.

Omnes famuli. And sir, for nurse's sake, pardon this one offence.
 We shall not after this show the like negligence.

R. Roister. I pardon you this once, and come, sing ne'er the
  worse.

M. Mery. How like you the goodness of this gentleman, nurse?

M. Mumble. God save his mastership that so can his men forgive,
 And I will hear them sing ere I go, by his leave.   500
R. Roister. Marry and thou shalt, wench: come, we two will
  dance.
M. Mumble. Nay, I will by mine own self foot the song per-
  chance.
R. Roister. Go to it, sirs, lustily.
M. Mumble. Pipe up a merry note,
 Let me hear it played, I will foot it for a groat. [*Cantent.*
R. Roister. Now, nurse, take this same letter here to thy mis-
  tress.
 And as my trust is in thee, ply my business.
M. Mumble. It shall be done.
M. Mery. Who made it?
R. Roister. I wrote it each whit.
M. Mery. Then needs it no mending.
R. Roister. No, no.
M. Mery. No, I know your wit.
 I warrant it well.
M. Mumble. It shall be delivered.
 But if ye speed, shall I be considered?   510
M. Mery. Whough! dost thou doubt of that?
Madge. What shall I have?
M. Mery. An hundred times more than thou canst devise to
  crave.
M. Mumble. Shall I have some new gear? for my old is all spent.
M. Mery. The worst kitchen wench shall go in ladies' raiment.
M. Mumble. Yea?
M. Mery. And the worst drudge in the house shall go better
 Than your mistress doth now.
Mar. Then I trudge with your letter.
R. Roister. Now, may I repose me: Custance is mine own.
 Let us sing and play homeward that it may be known.
M. Mery. But are you sure that your letter is well enough?
R. Roister. I wrote it myself.
M. Mery. Then sing we to dinner.   520
     [*Here they sing, and go out singing.*

SCENE V

CHRISTIAN CUSTANCE.   MARGERIE MUMBLECRUST.

C. Custance. Who took thee this letter, Margerie Mumblecrust?
M. Mumble. A lusty gay bachelor took it me of trust,
  And if ye seek to him he will love your doing.
C. Custance. Yea, but where learned he that manner of wooing?
M. Mumble. If to sue to him, you will any pains take,
  He will have you to his wife (he saith) for my sake.
C. Custance. Some wise gentleman, belike. I am bespoken:
  And I thought verily this had been some token
  From my dear spouse Gawin Goodluck, whom when him
    please,
  God luckily send home to both our hearts' ease.   10
M. Mumble. A joyly man it is, I wot well by report,
  And would have you to him for marriage resort;
  Best open the writing, and see what it doth speak.
C. Custance. At this time, nurse, I will neither read ne break.
M. Mumble. He promised to give you a whole peck of gold.
C. Custance. Perchance, lack of a pint when it shall be all told.
M. Mumble. I would take a gay rich husband, and I were you.
C. Custance. In good sooth, Madge, e'en so would I, if I were
    thou.
  But no more of this fond talk now, let us go in,
  And see thou no more move me folly to begin.   20
  Nor bring me no more letters for no man's pleasure,
  But thou know from whom.
M. Mumble. I warrant ye shall be sure.

ACT II

SCENE I

DOBINET DOUGHTIE.

D. Dough. Where is the house I go to, before or behind?
    I know not where nor when nor how I shall it find.
    If I had ten men's bodies and legs and strength,
    This trotting that I have must needs lame me at length.
    And now that my master is new set on wooing,
    I trust there shall none of us find lack of doing:
    Two pair of shoes a day will now be too little
    To serve me, I must trot to and fro so mickle.
    " Go bear me this token, carry me this letter,
    Now this is the best way, now that way is better.   10
    Up before day, sirs, I charge you, an hour or twain,
    Trudge, do me this message, and bring word quick again."
    If one miss but a minute, then, " His arms and wounds,
    I would not have slacked for ten thousand pounds.
    Nay, see, I beseech you, if my most trusty page
    Go not now about to hinder my marriage."
    So fervent hot wooing, and so far from wiving,
    I trow, never was any creature living.
    With every woman is he in some love's pang,
    Then up to our lute at midnight, twangledom twang,   20
    Then twang with our sonnets, and twang with our dumps,
    And heigho from our heart, as heavy as lead lumps;
    Then to our recorder with toodleloodle poop,
    As the howlet out of an ivy bush should hoop.
    Anon to our gittern, thrumpledum, thrumpledum thrum,
    Thrumpledum, thrumpledum, thrumpledum, thrumple
        dum, thrum.
    Of songs and ballads also he is a maker,
    And that can he as finely do as Jack Raker;
    Yea, and extempore will he ditties compose,
    Foolish Marsias ne'er made the like, I suppose,   30
    Yet must we sing them, as good stuff I undertake,

As for such a pen-man is well fitting to make.
"Ah, for these long nights! heigho! when will it be day?
I fear ere I come she will be wooed away."
Then when answer is made that it may not be,
"O death, why comest thou not?" (by and by saith he)
But then, from his heart to put away sorrow,
He is as far in with some new love next morrow.
But in the mean season, we trudge and we trot,
From dayspring to midnight, I sit not, nor rest not.   40
And now am I sent to dame Christian Custance:
But I fear it will end with a mock for pastance.
I bring her a ring, with a token in a clout,
And by all guess this same is her house out of doubt.
I know it now perfect, I am in my right way.
And lo! yond the old nurse that was with us last day.

SCENE II

MADGE MUMBLECRUST.   DOBINET DOUGHTIE.

M. Mumble. I was ne'er so shoke up afore, since I was born.
    That our mistress could not have chid, I would have sworn:
    And I pray God I die, if I meant any harm,
    But for my life-time this shall be to me a charm.   50
D. Dough. God you save and see, nurse, and how is it with you?
M. Mumble. Marry, a great deal the worse it is for such as thou.
D. Dough. For me? Why so?
M. Mumble. Why, were not thou one of them, say,
    That sang and played here with the gentleman last day?
D. Dough. Yes, and he would know if you have for him spoken,
    And prays you to deliver this ring and token.
M. Mumble. Now by the token that God tokened, brother,
    I will deliver no token, one nor other.
    I have once been so shent for your master's pleasure,
    As I will not be again for all his treasure.   60
D. Dough. He will thank you, woman.
M. Mumble. I will none of his thank.   [*Ex.*
D. Dough. I ween I am a prophet, this gear will prove blank:
    But what, should I home again without answer go?
    It were better go to Rome on my head than so.
    I will tarry here this month, but some of the house
    Shall take it of me, and then I care not a louse.

But yonder cometh forth a wench or a lad,
If he have not one Lombard's touch, my luck is bad.

SCENE III

TRUPENIE.   D. DOUGHTIE.   TIBET TALKAPACE.
ANNOT ALYFACE.

Trupenie. I am clean lost for lack of merry company,
  We 'gree not half well within, our wenches and I: 70
  They will command like mistresses, they will forbid,
  If they be not served, Trupenie must be chid.
  Let them be as merry now as ye can desire,
  With turning of a hand, our mirth lieth in the mire.
  I cannot skill of such changeable mettle,
  There is nothing with them but in dock out nettle.
D. Dough. Whether is it better that I speak to him first,
  Or he first to me? it is good to cast the worst.
  If I begin first, he will smell all my purpose,
  Otherwise I shall not need anything to disclose.   80
Trupenie. What boy have we yonder?   I will see what he is.
D. Dough. He cometh to me.   It is hereabout, i-wis.
Trupenie. Wouldest thou ought, friend, that thou lookest so
    about?
D. Dough. Yea, but whether ye can help me or no, I doubt.
  I seek to one mistress Custance house here dwelling.
Trupenie. It is my mistress ye seek too, by your telling.
D. Dough. Is there any of that name here but she?
Trupenie. Not one in all the whole town that I know, pardee.
D. Dough. A widow she is, I trow.
Trupenie. And what and she be?
D. Dough. But ensured to an husband.
Trupenie. Yea, so think we.   90
D. Dough. And I dwell with her husband that trusteth to be.
Trupenie. In faith, then must thou needs be welcome to me,
  Let us for acquaintance shake hands together,
  And whate'er thou be, heartily welcome hither.

Enter TIBET *and* ANNOT.

Tib. Talk. Well, Trupenie, never but flinging?
An. Alyface. And frisking?

Trupenie. Well, Tibet and Annot, still swinging and whisking?
Tib. Talk. But ye roil abroad.
An. Alyface. In the street everywhere.
Trupenie. Where are ye twain, in chambers when ye meet me
　　there?
　　But come hither, fools, I have one now by the hand,
　　Servant to him that must be our mistress' husband,　　100
　　Bid him welcome.
An. Alyface. To me truly is he welcome.
Tib. Talk. Forsooth, and as I may say, heartily welcome.
D. Dough. I thank you, mistress maids.
An. Alyface. I hope we shall better know.
Tib. Talk. And when will our new master come?
D. Dough. Shortly, I trow.
Tib. Talk. I would it were to-morrow: for till he resort,
　　Our mistress, being a widow, hath small comfort,
　　And I heard our nurse speak of an husband to-day
　　Ready for our mistress, a rich man and a gay.
　　And we shall go in our French hoods every day,
　　In our silk cassocks (I warrant you) fresh and gay,　　110
　　In our trick ferdegews and billiments of gold;
　　Brave in our suits of change, seven double fold
　　Then shall ye see Tibet, sirs, tread the moss so trim.
　　Nay, why said I tread? ye shall see her glide and swim,
　　Not lumperdee clumperdee like our spaniel Rig.
Trupenie. Marry, then, prick-me-dainty, come toast me a fig,
　　Who shall then know our Tib Talkapace, trow ye?
An. Alyface. And why not Annot Alyface as fine as she?
Trupenie. And what had Tom Trupenie, a father or none?
An. Alyface. Then our pretty new come man will look to be one.
Trupenie. We four, I trust, shall be a joyly merry knot.　　121
　　Shall we sing a fit to welcome our friend, Annot?
An. Alyface. Perchance he cannot sing.
D. Dough. I am at all essays.
Tib. Talk. By Cock, and the better welcome to us always.

Here they sing.

A thing very fit
For them that have wit
And are fellows knit,
Servants in one house to be,

> Is fast for to sit,
> And not oft to flit,　　　　　　　　130
> Nor vary a whit,
> But lovingly to agree.
>
> No man complaining,
> No other disdaining,
> For loss or for gaining,
> But fellows or friends to be.
> No grudge remaining,
> No work refraining,
> Nor help restraining,
> But lovingly to agree.　　　　　　　140
>
> No man for despite,
> By word or by write
> His fellow to twite,
> But further in honesty,
> No good turns entwite,
> Nor old sores recite,
> But let all go quite,
> And lovingly to agree.
>
> After drudgery,
> When they be weary,
> Then to be merry,　　　　　　　　150
> To laugh and sing they be free;
> With chip and cherie
> Heigh derie derie,
> Trill on the berie,
> And lovingly to agree.

Finis.

Tib. Talk. Will you now in with us unto our mistress go?
D. Dough. I have first for my master an errand or two.
　　But I have here from him a token and a ring,
　　They shall have most thank of her that first doth it bring.
Tib. Talk. Marry, that will I.
Trupenie. See, and Tibet snatch not now.　　　161
Tib. Talk. And why may not I, sir, get thanks as well as you?
　　　　　　　　　　　　　　　　　　[*Exeat.*
An. Alyface. Yet get ye not all, we will go with you both,
　　And have part of your thanks, be ye never so loth.
　　　　　　　　　　　　　　　　　[*Exeant omnes.*
D. Dough. So my hands are rid of it: I care for no more.
　　I may now return home: so durst I not afore.　[*Exeat.*

SCENE IV

C. CUSTANCE. TIBET. ANNOT ALYFACE. TRUPENIE.

C. Custance. Nay, come forth all three: and come hither, pretty
    maid:
    Will not so many forewarnings make you afraid?
Tib. Talk. Yes, forsooth.
C. Custance. But still be a runner up and down,
    Still be a bringer of tidings and tokens to town. 170
Tib. Talk. No, forsooth, mistress.
C. Custance. Is all your delight and joy
    In whisking and ramping abroad like a Tom-boy?
Tib. Talk. Forsooth, these were there too, Annot and Trupenie.
Trupenie. Yea, but ye alone took it, ye cannot deny.
An. Alyface. Yea, that ye did.
Tibet. But if I had not, ye twain would.
C. Custance. You great calf, ye should have more wit, so ye
    should:
    But why should any of you take such things in hand?
Tibet. Because it came from him that must be your husband.
C. Custance. How do ye know that?
Tibet. Forsooth, the boy did say so.
C. Custance. What was his name?
An. Alyface. We asked not.
C. Custance. No, did? 180
An. Alyface. He is not far gone, of likelihood.
Trupenie. I will see.
C. Custance. If thou canst find him in the street, bring him to me.
Trupenie. Yes. [*Exeat.*
C. Custance. Well, ye naughty girls, if ever I perceive
    That henceforth you do letters or tokens receive,
    To bring unto me from any person or place,
    Except ye first show me the party face to face,
    Either thou or thou, full truly abye thou shalt.
Tibet. Pardon this, and the next time powder me in salt.
C. Custance. I shall make all girls by you twain to beware.
Tibet. If ever I offend again, do not me spare. 190
    But if ever I see that false boy any more
    By your mistresship's licence, I tell you afore,
    I will rather have my coat twenty times swinged,

Than on the naughty wag not to be avenged.

C. Custance. Good wenches would not so ramp abroad idly.
  But keep within doors, and ply their work earnestly.
  If one would speak with me that is a man likely,
  Ye shall have right good thank to bring me word quickly.
  But otherwise with messages to come in post
  From henceforth, I promise you, shall be to your cost. 200
  Get you in to your work.

Tibet. Yes, forsooth.

C. Custance. Hence, both twain.
  And let me see you play me such a part again.

Re-enter TRUPENIE.

Trupenie. Mistress, I have run past the far end of the street,
  Yet can I not yonder crafty boy see nor meet.

C. Custance. No?

Trupenie, Yet I looked as far beyond the people,
  As one may see out of the top of Paul's steeple.

C. Custance. Hence, in at doors, and let me no more be vexed.

Trupenie. Forgive me this one fault, and lay on for the next.
                                              [*Exeat.*

C. Custance. Now will I in too, for I think, so God me mend,
  This will prove some foolish matter in the end.   210
                                              [*Exeat.*

ACT III

SCENE I

Mathew Merygreeke.

M. Mery. Now say this again: he hath somewhat to doing
    Which followeth the trace of one that is wooing,
    Specially that hath no more wit in his head,
    Than my cousin Roister Doister withal is led.
    I am sent in all haste to espy and to mark
    How our letters and tokens are likely to wark.
    Master Roister Doister must have answer in haste,
    For he loveth not to spend much labour in waste.
    Now as for Christian Custance, by this light,
    Though she had not her troth to Gawin Goodluck plight, 10
    Yet rather than with such a loutish dolt to marry,
    I daresay would live a poor life solitary.
    But fain would I speak with Custance, if I wist how,
    To laugh at the matter: yond cometh one forth now.

SCENE II

Tibet. M. Merygreeke. Christian Custance.

Tib. Talk. Ah, that I might but once in my life have a sight
    Of him that made us all so ill shent: by this light,
    He should never escape if I had him by the ear,
    But even from his head I would it bite or tear.
    Yea, and if one of them were not enow,
    I would bite them both off, I make God avow.   20
M. Mery. What is he, whom this little mouse doth so threaten?
Tib. Talk. I would teach him, I trow, to make girls shent or
    beaten.
M. Mery. I will call her: Maid, with whom are ye so hasty?
Tib. Talk. Not with you, sir, but with a little wagpasty,
    A deceiver of folks by subtle craft and guile.

28

M. Mery. I know where she is: Dobinet hath wrought some wile.
Tib. Talk. He brought a ring and token which he said was sent
　　From our dame's husband, but I wot well I was shent:
　　For it liked her as well, to tell you no lies,
　　As water in her ship, or salt cast in her eyes:　　　　30
　　And yet whence it came neither we nor she can tell.
M. Mery. We shall have sport anon: I like this very well.
　　And dwell ye here with mistress Custance, fair maid?
Tib. Talk. Yea, marry do I, sir: what would ye have said?
M. Mery. A little message unto her by word of mouth.
Tib. Talk. No messages, by your leave, nor tokens forsooth.
M. Mery. Then help me to speak with her.
Tib. Talk. With a good will that.
　　Here she cometh forth.　Now speak ye know best what.
C. Custance. None other life with you, maid, but abroad to skip?
Tib. Talk. Forsooth, here is one would speak with your mistress-
　　　ship.　　　　40
C. Custance. Ah, have ye been learning of mo messages now?
Tib. Taly. I would not hear his mind, but bade him show it to
　　　you.
C. Custance. In at doors.
Tib. Talk. I am gone.　　　　　　　　　　　[*Ex.*
M. Mery. Dame Custance, God ye save.
C. Custance. Welcome, friend Merygreeke: and what thing
　　would ye have?
M. Mery. I am come to you a little matter to break.
C. Custance. But see it be honest, else better not to speak.
M. Mery. How feel ye yourself affected here of late?
C. Custance. I feel no manner change but after the old rate.
　　But whereby do ye mean?
M. Mery. Concerning marriage.
　　Doth not love lade you?
C. Custance. I feel no such carriage.　　　　50
M. Mery. Do ye feel no pangs of dotage? answer me right.
C. Custance. I dote so, that I make but one sleep all the night.
　　But what need all these words?
M. Mery. Oh, Jesus, will ye see
　　What dissembling creatures these same women be?
　　The gentleman ye wot of, whom ye do so love,
　　That ye would fain marry him, if ye durst it move,
　　Among other rich widows, which are of him glad,
　　Lest ye for lesing of him perchance might run mad,

Is now contented that upon your suit making,
Ye be as one in election of taking.   60
C. Custance. What a tale is this? that I wote of? whom I love?
M. Mery. Yea, and he is as loving a worm again as a dove.
E'en of very pity he is willing you to take,
Because ye shall not destroy yourself for his sake.
C. Custance. Marry, God yeld his maship whatever he be.
It is gentmanly spoken.
M. Mery. Is it not, trow ye?
If ye have the grace now to offer yourself, ye speed.
C. Custance. As much as though I did, this time it shall not need.
But what gentman is it, I pray you tell me plain,
That wooeth so finely?
M. Mery. Lo, where ye be again,   70
As though ye knew him not.
C. Custance. Tush, ye speak in jest.
M. Mery. Nay sure, the party is in good knacking earnest,
And have you he will (he saith), and have you he must.
C. Custance. I am promised during my life, that is just.
M. Mery. Marry, so thinketh he, unto him alone.
C. Custance. No creature hath my faith and troth but one,
That is Gawyn Goodluck: and if it be not he,
He hath no title this way whatever he be,
Nor I know none to whom I have such word spoken.
M. Mery. Ye know him not you by his letter and token.   80
C. Custance. Indeed true it is, that a letter I have,
But I never read it yet, as God me save.
M. Mery. Ye a woman? and your letter so long unread.
C. Custance. Ye may thereby know what haste I have to wed.
But now who it is, for my hand I know by guess.
M. Mery. Ah, well I say.
C. Custance. It is Roister Doister, doubtless.
M. Mery. Will ye never leave this dissimulation?
Ye know him not.
C. Custance. But by imagination,
For no man there is but a very dolt and lout
That to woo a widow would so go about.   90
He shall never have me his wife while he do live.
M. Mery. Then will he have you if he may, so mote I thrive,
And he biddeth you send him word by me,
That ye humbly beseech him, ye may his wife be,
And that there shall be no let in you nor mistrust,

But to be wedded on Sunday next if he lust,
And biddeth you to look for him.

C. Custance. Doth he bid so?

M. Mery. When he cometh, ask him whether he did or no.

C. Custance. Go say, that I bid him keep him warm at home,
 For if he come abroad, he shall cough me a mome. 100
 My mind was vexed, I shrew his head, sottish dolt.

M. Mery. He hath in his head—

C. Custance. As much brain as a burbolt.

M. Mery. Well, dame Custance, if he hear you thus play chop-
 loge—

C. Custance. What will he?

M. Mery. Play the devil in the horologe.

C. Custance. I defy him, lout.

M. Mery. Shall I tell him what ye say?

C. Custance. Yea, and add whatsoever thou canst, I thee pray.
 And I will avouch it, whatsoever it be.

M. Mery. Then let me alone; we will laugh well, ye shall see,
 It will not be long ere he will hither resort.

C. Custance. Let him come when him lust, I wish no better sport.
 Fare ye well, I will in, and read my great letter. 111
 I shall to my wooer make answer the better. [*Exeat.*

SCENE III

Mathew Merygreeke. Roister Doister.

M. Mery. Now that the whole answer in my devise doth rest,
 I shall paint out our wooer in colours of the best.
 And all that I say shall be on Custance's mouth,
 She is author of all that I shall speak forsooth.
 But yond cometh Roister Doister now in a trance.

R. Roister. Juno send me this day good luck and good chance.
 I cannot but come see how Merygreeke doth speed.

M. Mery. I will not see him, but give him a jut indeed. 120
 I cry your mastership mercy.

R. Roister. And whither now?

M. Mery. As fast as I could run, sir, in post against you.
 But why speak ye so faintly, or why are ye so sad?

R. Roister. Thou knowest the proverb, because I cannot be had,
 Hast thou spoken with this woman?

M. Mery. Yea, that I have.

R. Roister. And what will this gear be?

M. Mery. No, so God me save.

R. Roister. Hast thou a flat answer?

M. Mery. Nay, a sharp answer.

R. Roister. What?

M. Mery. Ye shall not (she saith) by her will marry her cat.
    Ye are such a calf, such an ass, such a block,
    Such a lilburn, such a hoball, such a lobcock,   130
    And because ye should come to her at no season,
    She despised your maship out of all reason.
    Beware what ye say (ko I) of such a gentman,
    Nay, I fear him not (ko she), do the best he can.
    He vaunteth himself for a man of prowess great,
    Whereas a good gander, I daresay, may him beat.
    And where he is louted and laughed to scorn,
    For the veriest dolt that ever was born,
    And veriest lover, sloven and beast,
    Living in this world from the west to the east: 140
    Yet of himself hath he such opinion,
    That in all the world is not the like minion.
    He thinketh each woman to be brought in dotage
    With the only sight of his goodly personage:
    Yet none that will have him: we do him lout and flock,
    And make him among us our common sporting stock,
    And so would I now (ko she), save only because
    Better nay (ko I), I lust not meddle with daws.
    Ye are happy (ko I) that ye are a woman,
    This would cost you your life in case ye were a man.   150

R. Roister. Yea, an hundred thousand pound should not save
    her life.

M. Mery. No, but that ye woo her to have her to your wife.
    But I could not stop her mouth.

R. Roister. Heigh ho, alas!

M. Mery. Be of good cheer, man, and let the world pass.

R. Roister. What shall I do or say now that it will not be?

M. Mery. Ye shall have choice of a thousand as good as she,
    And ye must pardon her, it is for lack of wit.

R. Roister. Yea, for were not I an husband for her fit?
    Well, what should I now do?

M. Mery. In faith I cannot tell.

R. Roister. I will go home and die.

M. Mery. Then shall I bid toll the bell?   160

R. Roister. No.

M. Mery. God have mercy on your soul, ah, good gentleman,
  That e'er ye should th[u]s die for an unkind woman.
  Will ye drink once ere ye go?

R. Roister. No, no, I will none.

M. Mery. How feel your soul to God?

R. Roister. I am nigh gone.

M. Mery. And shall we hence straight?

R. Roister. Yea.

M. Mery. *Placebo dilexi.*   [*ut infra.*
  Master Roister Doister will straight go home and die.

R. Roister. Heigh-how! alas, the pangs of death my heart do
  break.

M. Mery. Hold your peace for shame, sir, a dead man may not
  speak.
    Nequando. What mourners and what torches shall we
  have?

R. Roister. None.

M. Mery. Dirige. He will go darkling to his grave,   170
  Neque lux, neque crux, neque mourners, *neque* clink,
  He will steal to heaven, unknowing to God, I think.
  A porta inferi. Who shall your goods possess?

R. Roister. Thou shalt be my sectour, and have all more and less.

M. Mery. Requiem æternam. Now, God reward your master-
  ship.
  And I will cry halfpenny-dole for your worship.
  Come forth, sirs, hear the doleful news I shall you tell.
                          [*Evocat servos militis.*
  Our good master here will no longer with us dwell,
  But in spite of Custance, which hath him wearied,
  Let us see his maship solemnly buried.   180
  And while some piece of his soul is yet him within,
  Some part of his funerals let us here begin.
  Audivi vocem. All men take heede by this one gentleman,
  How you set your love upon an unkind woman.
  For these women be all such mad peevish elves,
  They will not be won except it please themselves.
  But in faith, Custance, if ever ye come in hell,
  Master Roister Doister shall serve you as well.
  And will ye needs go from us thus in very deed?

R. Roister. Yea, in good sadness.

M. Mery. Now, Jesus Christ be your speed.   190

Good-night, Roger old knave; farewell, Roger old knave.
Good-night, Roger old knave, knave, knap.   [*ut infra.*
Pray for the late master Roister Doister's soul,
And come forth, parish clerk, let the passing bell toll.

                         [*Ad servos militis.*

Pray for your master, sirs, and for him ring a peal.
He was your right good master while he was in heal.
Qui Lazarum.

R. Roister. Heigh-how!

M. Mery. Dead men go not so fast
     In Paradisum.

R. Roister. Heihow!

M. Mery. Soft, hear what I have cast.

R. Roister. I will hear nothing, I am past.

M. Mery. Whough, wellaway.
     Ye may tarry one hour, and hear what I shall say,   200
     Ye were best, sir, for a while to revive again,
     And quite them ere ye go.

R. Roister. Trowest thou so?

M. Mery. Ye, plain.

R. Roister. How may I revive, being now so far past?

M. Mery. I will rub your temples, and fet you again at last.

R. Roister. It will not be possible.

M. Mery. Yes, for twenty pound.

R. Roister. Arms, what dost thou?

M. Mery. Fet you again out of your sound.
     By this cross ye were nigh gone indeed, I might feel
     Your soul departing within an inch of your heel.
     Now follow my counsel.

R. Roister. What is it?

M. Mery. If I were you,
     Custance should eft seek to me, ere I would bow.   210

R. Roister. Well, as thou wilt have me, even so will I do.

M. Mery. Then shall ye revive again for an hour or two.

R. Roister. As thou wilt, I am content for a little space.

M. Mery. Good hap is not hasty: yet in space com[e]th grace.
     To speak with Custance yourself should be very well,
     What good thereof may come, nor I nor you can tell.
     But now the matter standeth upon your marriage,
     Ye must now take unto you a lusty courage,
     Ye may not speak with a faint heart to Custance,
     But with a lusty breast and countenance,   220

That she may know she hath to answer to a man.

R. Roister. Yes, I can do that as well as any can.

M. Mery. Then because ye must Custance face to face woo,
Let us see how to behave yourself ye can do.
Ye must have a portly brag after your estate.

R. Roister. Tush, I can handle that after the best rate.

M. Mery. Well done! so lo, up man with your head and chin,
Up with that snout, man! so lo, now ye begin!
So, that is somewhat like, but pranky cote, nay whan?
That is a lusty brute; hands under your side, man.   230
So lo, now is it even as it should be,
That is somewhat like, for a man of your degree.
Then must ye stately go, jetting up and down.
Tut, can ye no better shake the tail of your gown?
There, lo, such a lusty brag it is ye must make.

R. Roister. To come behind, and make curtesy, thou must some
    pains take.

M. Mery. Else were I much to blame, I thank your mastership.
The lord one day all to begrime you with worship,
Back, sir sauce, let gentlefolks have elbow room,
'Void, sirs, see ye not master Roister Doister come?   240
Make place, my masters.

R. Roister. Thou jostlest now too nigh.

M. Mery. Back, all rude louts.

R. Roister. Tush!

M. Mery. I cry your maship mercy.
Hoighdagh, if fair fine mistress Custance saw you now,
Ralph Roister Doister were her own, I warrant you.

R. Roister. Near an M by your girdle?

M. Mery. Your good mastership's
Mastership, were her own mistress-ship's mistress-ships,
Ye were take up for hawks, ye were gone, ye were gone,
But now one other thing more yet I think upon.

R. Roister. Show what it is.

M. Mery. A wooer, be he never so poor,
Must play and sing before his best-beloved's door,   250
How much more than you?

R. Roister. Thou speakest well, out of doubt.

M. Mery. And perchance that would make her the sooner come
    out.

R. Roister. Go call my musicians, bid them hie apace.

M. Mery. I will be here with them ere ye can say *trey ace.*

[Exeat.

R. Roister. This was well said of Merygreeke, I 'low his wit.
    Before my sweetheart's door we will have a fit,
    That if my love come forth, that I may with her talk,
    I doubt not but this gear shall on my side walk.
    But lo, how well Merygreeke is returned sence.

Re-enter MERYGREEKE.

M. Mery. There hath grown no grass on my heel since I went
    hence,   260
    Lo, here have I brought that shall make you pastance.
R. Roister. Come, sirs, let us sing to win my dear love Custance.

Cantent.

M. Mery. Lo, where she cometh, some countenance to her make,
    And ye shall hear me be p'ain with her for your sake.

SCENE IV

CUSTANCE. MERYGREEKE. ROISTER DOISTER.

C. Custance. What gauding and fooling is this afore my door?
M. Mery. May not folks be honest, pray you, though they be
    poor?
C. Custance. As that thing may be true, so rich folks may be
    fools.
R. Roister. Her talk is as fine as she had learned in schools.
M. Mery. Look partly toward her, and draw a little near.
C. Custance. Get ye home, idle folks.
M. Mery. Why, may not we be here?   270
    Nay, and ye will haze, haze: otherwise, I tell you plain,
    And ye will not haze, then give us our gear again.
C. Custance. Indeed I have of yours much gay things, God save
    all.
R. Roister. Speak gently unto her, and let her take all.
M. Mery. Ye are too tender-hearted: shall she make us daws?
    Nay, dame, I will be plain with you in my friend's cause.
R. Roister. Let all this pass, sweetheart, and accept my service.
C. Custance. I will not be served with a fool in no wise,
    When I choose an husband I hope to take a man.
M. Mery. And where will ye find one which can do that he can?
    Now this man toward you being so kind,   281

You not to make him an answer somewhat to his mind.

C. Custance. I sent him a full answer by you, did I not?

M. Mery. And I reported it.

C. Custance. Nay, I must speak it again.

R. Roister. No, no, he told it all.

M. Mery. Was I not metely plain?

R. Roister. Yes.

M. Mery. But I would not tell all; for faith, if I had,
 With you, dame Custance, ere this hour it had been bad,
 And not without cause: for this goodly personage
 Meant no less than to join with you in marriage.

C. Custance. Let him waste no more labour nor suit about me.

M. Mery. Ye know not where your preferment lieth, I see, 291
 He sending you such a token, ring and letter.

C. Custance. Marry, here it is; ye never saw a better.

M. Mery. Let us see your letter.

C. Custance. Hold, read it if ye can.
 And see what letter it is to win a woman.

M. Mery. " To mine own dear coney bird, sweetheart, and
   pigsny,
 Good Mistress Custance, present these by and by."
 Of this superscription do ye blame the style?

C. Custance. With the rest as good stuff as ye read a great while.

M. Mery. " Sweet mistress, where as I love you nothing at all,
 Regarding your substance and richesse chief of all, 301
 For your personage, beauty, demeanour and wit,
 I commend me unto you never a whit.
 Sorry to hear report of your good welfare,
 For (as I hear say) such your conditions are,
 That ye be worthy favour of no living man,
 To be abhorred of every honest man.
 To be taken for a woman inclined to vice.
 Nothing at all to virtue giving her due price.
 Wherefore, concerning marriage, ye are thought 310
 Such a fine paragon, as ne'er honest man bought.
 And now by these presents I do you advertise
 That I am minded to marry you in no wise.
 For your goods and substance, I could be content
 To take you as ye are. If ye mind to be my wife,
 Ye shall be assured for the time of my life,
 I will keep you right well, from good raiment and fare,
 Ye shall not be kept but in sorrow and care.

Ye shall in no wise live at your own liberty,
Do and say what ye lust, ye shall never please me,   320
But when ye are merry, I will be all sad;
When ye are sorry, I will be very glad.
When ye seek your heart's ease, I will be unkind.
At no time in me shall ye much gentleness find.
But all things contrary to your will and mind,
Shall be done: otherwise I will not be behind
To speak.   And as for all them that would do you wrong
I will so help and maintain, ye shall not live long.
Nor any foolish dolt shall cumber you but I.
I, whoe'er say nay, will stick by you till I die,
Thus, good mistress Custance, the Lord you save and keep,
From me, Roister Doister, whether I wake or sleep.   330
Who favoureth you no less (ye may be bold)
Than this letter purporteth, which ye have unfold."

C. Custance. How by this letter of love? is it not fine?

R. Roister. By the arms of Caleys it is none of mine.

M. Mery. Fie, you are foul to blame, this is your own hand.

C. Custance. Might not a woman be proud of such an husband?

M. Mery. Ah, that ye would in a letter show such despite.   339

R. Roister. Oh, I would I had him here, the which did it endite.

M. Mery. Why, ye made it yourself, ye told me by this light.

R. Roister. Yea, I meant I wrote it mine own self yesternight.

C. Custance. I-wis, sir, I would not have sent you such a mock.

R. Roister. Ye may so take it, but I meant it not so, by Cock.

M. Mery. Who can blame this woman to fume and fret and
        rage?
    Tut, tut! yourself now have marred your own marriage.
    Well, yet mistress Custance, if ye can this remit,
    This gentleman otherwise may your love requit.

C. Custance. No, God be with you both, and seek no more to me.
                                                                [Exeat.

R. Roister. Wough! she is gone for ever, I shall her no more see.

M. Mery. What, weep? fie, for shame, and blubber?   For man-
        hood's sake,   351
    Never let your foe so much pleasure of you take.
    Rather play the man's part, and do love refrain.
    If she despise you, e'en despise ye her again.

R. Roister. By Goss, and for thy sake I defy her indeed.

M. Mery. Yea, and perchance that way ye shall much sooner
        speed,

For one mad property these women have in fey,
When ye will, they will not: will not ye, then will they.
Ah, foolish woman! ah, most unlucky Custance!
Ah, unfortunate woman! ah, peevish Custance!   360
Art thou to thine harms so obstinately bent,
That thou canst not see where lieth thine high preferment?
Canst thou not lub dis man, which could lub dee so well?
Art thou so much thine own foe?

R. Roister. Thou dost the truth tell.

M. Mery. Well I lament.

R. Roister. So do I.

M. Mery. Wherefore?

R. Roister. For this thing
Because she is gone.

M. Mery. I mourn for another thing.

R. Roister. What is it, Merygreeke, wherefore thou dost grief
take?

M. Mery. That I am not a woman myself for your sake,
I would have you myself, and a straw for yond Gill,
And mock much of you though it were against my will.
I would not, I warrant you, fall in such a rage,   371
As so to refuse such a goodly personage.

R. Roister. In faith, I heartily thank thee, Merygreeke.

M. Mery. And I were a woman——

R. Roister. Thou wouldest to me seek.

M. Mery. For, though I say it, a goodly person ye be.

R. Roister. No, no.

M. Mery. Yes, a goodly man as e'er I did see.

R. Roister. No, I am a poor homely man, as God made me.

M. Mery. By the faith that I owe to God, sir, but ye be,
Would I might for your sake, spend a thousand pound land.

R. Roister. I dare say thou wouldest have me to thy husband.

M. Mery. Yea: and I were the fairest lady in the shire,   381
And knew you as I know you, and see you now here.
Well, I say no more.

R. Roister. Gramercies, with all my heart.

M. Mery. But since that cannot be, will ye play a wise part?

R. Roister. How should I?

M. Mery. Refrain from Custance a while now,
And I warrant her soon right glad to seek to you.
Ye shall see her anon come on her knees creeping,
And pray you to be good to her, salt tears weeping.

R. Roister. But what and she come not?

M. Mery. In faith, then, farewell she.
Or else if ye be wroth, ye may avenged be.   390

R. Roister. By Cock's precious potstick, and e'en so I shall.
I will utterly destroy her, and house and all.
But I would be avenged in the mean space,
On that vile scribbler, that did my wooing disgrace.

M. Mery. Scribbler (ko you), indeed he is worthy no less,
I will call him to you, and ye bid me doubtless.

R. Roister. Yes, for although he had as many lives,
As a thousand widows, and a thousand wives,
As a thousand lions, and a thousand rats,
A thousand wolves, and a thousand cats,   400
A thousand bulls, and a thousand calves,
And a thousand legions divided in halves,
He shall never 'scape death on my sword's point,
Though I should be torn therefore joint by joint.

M. Mery. Nay, if ye will kill him, I will not bet him,
I will not in so much extremity set him;
He may yet amend, sir, and be an honest man,
Therefore pardon him, good soul, as much as ye can.

R. Roister. Well, for thy sake, this once with his life he shall pass,
But I will hew him all to pieces, by the Mass.   410

M. Mery. Nay, faith, ye shall promise that he shall no harm have,
Else I will not bet him.

R. Roister. I shall so, God me save.
But I may chide him a good.

M. Mery. Yea, that do hardly.

R. Roister. Go, then.

M. Mery. I return, and bring him to you by and by.   [*Ex.*

SCENE V

ROISTER DOISTER. MATHEW MERYGREEKE. SCRIVENER.

R. Roister. What is a gentleman but his word and his promise?
I must now save this villain's life in any wise,
And yet at him already my hands do tickle,
I shall uneth hold them, they will be so fickle.
But lo, and Merygreeke have not brought him sens.

M. Mery. Nay, I would I had of my purse paid forty pens. 420

Scrivener. So would I too: but it needed not that stound.

M. Mery. But the gentman had rather spent five thousand
   pound,

  For it disgraced him at least five times so much.

Scrivener. He disgraced himself, his loutishness is such.

R. Roister. How long they stand prating! Why comest thou
   not away?

M. Mery. Come now to himself, and hark what he will say.

Scrivener. I am not afraid in his presence to appear.

R. Roister. Art thou come, fellow?

Scrivener. How think you? am I not here?

R. Roister. What hindrance hast thou done me, and what
   villainy?

Scrivener. It hath come of thyself, if thou hast had any.   430

R. Roister. All the stock thou comest of later or rather,
  From thy first father's grandfather's father's father,
  Nor all that shall come of thee to the world's end,
  Though to threescore generations they descend,
  Can be able to make me a just recompense,
  For this trespass of thine and this one offence.

Scrivener. Wherein?

R. Roister. Did not you make me a letter, brother?

Scrivener. Pay the like hire, I will make you such another.

R. Roister. Nay, see and these whoreson Pharisees and Scribes
  Do not get their living by polling and bribes.   440

  If it were not for shame——

Scrivener. Nay, hold thy hands still.

M. Mery. Why, did ye not promise that ye would not him spill?

Scrivener. Let him not spare me.

R. Roister. Why wilt thou strike me again?

Scrivener. Ye shall have as good as ye bring of me, that is plain.

M. Mery. I cannot blame him, sir, though your blows would
   him grieve.

  For he knoweth present death to ensue of all ye give.

R. Roister. Well, this man for once hath purchased thy pardon.

Scrivener. And what say ye to me? or else I will be gone.

R. Roister. I say the letter thou madest me was not good.

Scrivener. Then did ye wrong copy it, of likelihood.   450

R. Roister. Yes, out of thy copy word for word I wrote.

Scrivener. Then was it as ye prayed to have it, I wot,
  But in reading and pointing there was made some fault.

R. Roister. I wot not, but it made all my matter to halt.

Scrivener. How say you, is this mine original or no?

R. Roister. The self same that I wrote out of, so mote I go.

Scrivener. Look you on your own fist, and I will look on this,
And let this man be judge whether I read amiss.
    " To mine own dear coney bird, sweetheart, and pigsny,
    Good Mistress Custance, present these by and by."   460
    How now? doth not this superscription agree?

R. Roister. Read that is within, and there ye shall the fault see.

Scrivener. " Sweet mistress, whereas I love you, nothing at all
    Regarding your richesse and substance: chief of all
    For your personage, beauty, demeanour, and wit
    I commend me unto you: never a whit
    Sorry to hear report of your good welfare.
    For (as I hear say) such your conditions are,
    That ye be worthy of favour: of no living man
    To be abhorred: of every honest man   470
    To be taken for a woman inclined to vice
    Nothing at all: to virtue giving her due price.
    Wherefore concerning marriage, ye are thought
    Such a fine paragon, as ne'er honest man bought.
    And now by these presents I do you advertise,
    That I am minded to marry you: in no wise
    For your goods and substance: I can be content
    To take you as you are: if ye will be my wife,
    Ye shall be assured for the time of my life,
    I will keep you right well: from good raiment and fare, 480
    Ye shall not be kept: but in sorrow and care
    Ye shall in no wise live: at your own liberty,
    Do and say what ye lust: ye shall never please me
    But when ye are merry: I will be all sad
    When ye are sorry: I will be very glad
    When ye seek your heart's ease: I will be unkind
    At no time: in me shall ye much gentleness find.
    But all things contrary to your will and mind
    Shall be done otherwise: I will not be behind
    To speak: and as for all them that would do you wrong, 490
    (I will so help and maintain ye) shall not live long.
    Nor any foolish dolt shall cumber you, but I,
    I, whoe'er say nay, will stick by you till I die.
    Thus, good mistress Custance, the Lord you save and keep,
    From me, Roister Doister, whether I wake or sleep,

Who favoureth you no less (ye may be bold),
Than this letter purporteth, which ye have unfold."
Now, sir, what default can ye find in this letter?

R. Roister. Of truth, in my mind there cannot be a better.

Scrivener. Then was the fault in reading, and not in writing, 500
No, nor I dare say in the form of enditing.
But who read this letter, that it sounded so naught?

M. Mery. I read it, indeed.

Scrivener. Ye read it not as ye ought.

R. Roister. Why, thou wretched villain, was all this same fault
   in thee?

M. Mery. I knock your costard if ye offer to strike me.

R. Roister. Strikest thou, indeed? and I offer but in jest?

M. Mery. Yea, and rap you again except ye can sit in rest.
And I will no longer tarry here, me believe.

R. Roister. What, wilt thou be angry, and I do thee forgive?
Fare thou well, scribbler, I cry thee mercy indeed.   510

Scrivener. Fare ye well, bibbler, and worthily may ye speed.

R. Roister. If it were another but thou, it were a knave.

M. Mery. Ye are another yourself, sir, the Lord us both save.
Albeit in this matter I must your pardon crave.
Alas, would ye wish in me the wit that ye have?
But as for my fault I can quickly amend,
I will show Custance it was I that did offend.

R. Roister. By so doing her anger may be reformed.

M. Mery. But if by no entreaty she will be turned,
Then set light by her and be as testy as she,   520
And do your force upon her with extremity.

R. Roister. Come on, therefore, let us go home in sadness.

M. Mery. That if force shall need all may be in a readiness,
And as for this letter hardly let all go,
We will know where she refuse you for that or no.

         [Exeant am.

ACT IV

SCENE I

Sym Suresby.

Sym Sure. Is there any man but I, Sym Suresby, alone,
 That would have taken such an enterprise him upon,
 In such an outrageous tempest as this was,
 Such a dangerous gulf of the sea to pass?
 I think, verily, Neptune's mighty godship
 Was angry with some that was in our ship,
 And but for the honesty which in me he found,
 I think for the others' sake we had been drowned.
 But fie on that servant which for his master's wealth
 Will stick for to hazard both his life and his health. 10
 My master, Gawyn Goodluck, after me a day,
 Because of the weather, thought best his ship to stay,
 And now that I have the rough surges so well past,
 God grant I may find all things safe here at last.
 Then will I think all my travail well spent.
 Now the first point wherefore my master hath me sent
 Is to salute dame Christian Custance, his wife
 Espoused, whom he tendereth no less than his life.
 I must see how it is with her, well or wrong,
 And whether for him she doth not now think long: 20
 Then to other friends I have a message or tway,
 And then so to return and meet him on the way.
 Now will I go knock that I may despatch with speed,
 But lo, forth cometh herself happily indeed.

SCENE II

Christian Custance. Sym Suresby.

C. Custance. I come to see if any more stirring be here,
 But what stranger is this which doth to me appear?
Sym Sure. I will speak to her: Dame, the Lord you save and
 see.

C. Custance. What, friend Sym Suresby? Forsooth, right
    welcome ye be,
  How doth mine own Gawyn Goodluck, I pray thee tell?
Sym Sure. When he knoweth of your health he will be perfect
    well.   30
C. Custance. If he have perfect health, I am as I would be.
Sym Sure. Such news will please him well, this is as it should be.
C. Custance. I think now long for him.
Sym Sure. And he as long for you.
C. Custance. When will he be at home?
Sym Sure. His heart is here e'en now,
  His body cometh after.
C. Custance. I would see that fain.
Sym Sure. As fast as wind and sail can carry it amain.
  But what two men are yond coming hitherward?
C. Custance. Now I shrew their best Christmas cheeks both
    togetherward.

SCENE III

CHRISTIAN CUSTANCE. SYM SURESBY. RALPH ROISTER.
    MATHEW MERYGREEKE. TRUPENIE.

C. Custance. What mean these lewd fellows thus to trouble me
    still?
  Sym Suresby here perchance shall thereof deem some ill.   40
  And shall suspect in me some point of naughtiness,
  And they come hitherward.
Sym Sure. What is their business?
C. Custance. I have nought to them; nor they to me in sadness.
Sym Sure. Let us hearken them; somewhat there is, I fear it.
R. Roister. I will speak out aloud best, that she may hear it.
M. Mery. Nay, alas, ye may so fear her out of her wit.
R. Roister. By the cross of my sword, I will hurt her no whit.
M. Mery. Will ye do no harm indeed? shall I trust your word?
R. Roister. By Roister Doister's faith, I will speak but in borde.
Sym Sure. Let us hearken them; somewhat there is, I fear it. 50
R. Roister. I will speak out aloud, I care not who hear it:
  Sirs, see that my harness, my target, and my shield,
  Be made as bright now, as when I was last in field,
  As white as I should to war again to-morrow:
  For sick shall I be, but I work some folk sorrow.

Therefore see that all shine as bright as Saint George,
Or as doth a key newly come from the smith's forge,
I would have my sword and harness to shine so bright,
That I might therewith dim mine enemies' sight,
I would have it cast beams as fast, I tell you plain,   60
As doth the glittering grass after a shower of rain.
And see that in case I should need to come to arming,
All things may be ready at a minute's warning,
For such chance may chance in an hour, do ye hear?

M. Mery. As perchance shall not chance again in seven year.

R. Roister. Now draw we near to her, and hear what shall be
    said.

M. Mery. But I would not have you make her too much afraid.

R. Roister. Well found, sweet wife (I trust), for all this your sour
    look.

C. Custance. Wife, why call ye me wife?

Sym Sure. Wife? this gear goeth acrook.

M. Mery. Nay, mistress Custance, I warrant you, our letter 70
Is not as we read e'en now, but much better,
And where ye half stomached this gentleman afore,
For this same letter, ye will love him now therefore,
Nor it is not this letter, though ye were a queen,
That should break marriage between you twain, I ween.

C. Custance. I did not refuse him for the letter's sake.

R. Roister. Then ye are content me for your husband to take?

C. Custance. You for my husband to take? nothing less truly.

R. Roister. Yea, say so, sweet spouse, afore strangers hardly.

M. Mery. And though I have here his letter of love with me, 80
Yet his ring and tokens he sent, keep safe with ye.

C. Custance. A mischief take his tokens, and him and thee too.
But what prate I with fools? have I naught else to do?
Come in with me, Sym Suresby, to take some repast.

Sym Sure. I must ere I drink, by your leave, go in all haste,
To a place or two, with earnest letters of his.

C. Custance. Then come drink here with me.

Sym Sure. I thank you!

C. Custance. Do not miss.
You shall have a token to your master with you.

Sym Sure. No tokens this time, gramercies, God be with you.
                                  [Exeat.

C. Custance. Surely this fellow misdeemeth some ill in me. 90
Which thing but God help, will go near to spill me.

R. Roister. Yea, farewell, fellow, and tell thy master Goodluck
  That he cometh too late of this blossom to pluck.
  Let him keep him there still, or at leastwise make no haste,
  As for his labour hither he shall spend in waste.
  His betters be in place now.
M. Mery. As long as it will hold.
C. Custance. I will be even with thee, thou beast, thou mayst be
    bold.
R. Roister. Will ye have us then?
C. Custance. I will never have thee.
R. Roister. Then will I have you?
C. Custance. No, the devil shall have thee.
  I have gotten this hour more shame and harm by thee, 100
  Than all thy life days thou canst do me honesty.
M. Mery. Why now may ye see what it cometh to, in the end,
  To make a deadly foe of your most loving friend:
  And i-wis this letter, if ye would hear it now——
C. Custance. I will hear none of it.
M. Mery. In faith, would ravish you.
C. Custance. He hath stained my name for ever, this is clear.
R. Roister. I can make all as well in an hour.
M. Mery. As ten year.
  How say ye, will ye have him?
C. Custance. No.
M. Mery. Will ye take him?
C. Custance. I defy him.
M. Mery. At my word?
C. Custance. A shame take him.
  Waste no more wind, for it will never be. 110
M. Mery. This one fault with twain shall be mended, ye shall see.
  Gentle mistress Custance, now, good mistress Custance!
  Honey mistress Custance, now, sweet mistress Custance!
  Golden mistress Custance, now, white mistress Custance!
  Silken mistress Custance, now, fair mistress Custance!
C. Custance. Faith, rather than to marry with such a doltish
    lout,
  I would match myself with a beggar, out of doubt.
M. Mery. Then I can say no more; to speed we are not like,
  Except ye rap out a rag of your rhetoric. 119
C. Custance. Speak not of winning me: for it shall never be so.
R. Roister. Yes, dame, I will have you, whether ye will or no.
  I command you to love me, wherefore should ye not?

Is not my love to you chafing and burning hot?

M. Mery. To her, that is well said.

R. Roister. Shall I so break my brain
　　To dote upon you, and ye not love us again?

M. Mery. Well said yet.

C. Custance. Go to, you goose.

R. Roister. I say, Kit Custance,
　　In case ye will not haze, well, better yes perchance.

C. Custance. Avaunt, lozel! pick thee hence.

M. Mery. Well, sir, ye perceive,
　　For all your kind offer, she will not you receive.

R. Roister. Then a straw for her, and a straw for her again, 130
　　She shall not be my wife, would she never so fain;
　　No, and though she would be at ten thousand pound cost.

M. Mery. Lo, dame, ye may see what an husband ye have lost.

C. Custance. Yea, no force, a jewel much better lost than found.

M. Mery. Ah, ye will not believe how this doth my heart wound.
　　How should a marriage between you be toward,
　　If both parties draw back, and become so froward?

R. Roister. Nay, dame, I will fire thee out of thy house,
　　And destroy thee and all thine, and that by and by.

M. Mery. Nay, for the passion of God, sir, do not so.　　140

R. Roister. Yes, except she will say yea to that she said no.

C. Custance. And what, be there no officers, trow we, in town
　　To check idle loiterers, bragging up and down?
　　Where be they, by whom vacabunds should be represt?
　　That poor silly widows might live in peace and rest.
　　Shall I never rid thee out of my company?
　　I will call for help: what ho, come forth Trupenie!

Enter Trupenie.

Trupenie. Anon.　What is your will, mistress? did ye call me?

C. Custance. Yea; go run apace, and as fast as may be,
　　Pray Tristram Trustie, my most assured friend,　　150
　　To be here by and by, that he may me defend.

Trupenie. That message so quickly shall be done, by God's grace,
　　That at my return ye shall say, I went apace.　　[*Exeat*

C. Custance. Then shall we see, I trow, whether ye shall do me
　　harm.

R. Roister. Yes, in faith, Kit, I shall thee and thine so charm,
　　That all women incarnate by thee may beware.

C. Custance. Nay, as for charming me, come hither if thou dare,
　　I shall clout thee till thou stink, both thee and thy train,
　　And coil thee mine own hands, and send thee home again.
R. Roister. Yea, sayest thou me that, dame? dost thou me
　　　　threaten? 160
　　Go we, I still see whether I shall be beaten.
M. Mery. Nay, for the paishe of God, let me now treat peace,
　　For bloodshed will there be in case this strife increase.
　　Ah, good dame Custance, take better way with you.
C. Custance. Let him do his worst.
M. Mery. Yield in time.
R. Roister. Come hence, thou.　　　　*[Exeant Roister et Mery.*

SCENE IV

Christian Custance. Annot Alyface. Tibet T.
M. Mumblecrust.

C. Custance. So, sirrah, if I should not with him take this way,
　　I should not be rid of him, I think, till doom's day.
　　I will call forth my folks, that without any mocks,
　　If he come again we may give him raps and knocks.
　　Madge Mumblecrust, come forth, and Tibet Talkapace. 170
　　Yea, and come forth too, mistress Annot Alyface.
An. Alyface. I come.
Tibet. And I am here.
M. Mumble. And I am here too, at length.
C. Custance. Like warriors, if need be, ye must show your
　　　　strength.
　　The man that this day hath thus beguiled you,
　　Is Ralph Roister Doister, whom ye know well inowe,
　　The most lout and dastard that ever on ground trod.
Tib. Talk. I see all folk mock him when he goeth abroad.
C. Custance. What, pretty maid? will ye talk when I speak?
Tib. Talk. No, forsooth, good mistress.
C. Custance. Will ye my tale break? 179
　　He threateneth to come hither with all his force to fight,
　　I charge you, if he come, on him with all your might.
M. Mumble. I with my distaff will reach him one rap.
Tib. Talk. And I with my new broom will sweep him one swap,
　　And then with our great club I will reach him one rap.

An. Alyface. And I with our skimmer will fling him one flap.
Tib. Talk. Then Trupenie's firefork will him shrewdly fray,
    And you with the spit may drive him quite away.
C. Custance. Go, make all ready, that it may be even so.
Tib. Talk. For my part I shrew them that last about it go.
                                [*Exeant.*

SCENE V

CHRISTIAN CUSTANCE.   TRUPENIE.   TRISTRAM TRUSTIE.

C. Custance. Trupenie did promise me to run a great pace, 180
    My friend Tristram Trustie to fet into this place.
    Indeed he dwelleth hence a good start, I confess:
    But yet a quick messenger might twice since, as I guess,
    Have gone and come again.   Ah, yond I spy him now.
Trupenie. Ye are a slow goer, sir, I make God avow.
    My mistress Custance will in me put all the blame,
    Your legs be longer than mine: come apace for shame.
C. Custance. I can thee thank, Trupenie, thou hast done right
      well.
Trupenie. Mistress, since I went no grass hath grown on my heel,
    But master Tristram Trustie here maketh no speed.   190
C. Custance. That he came at all, I thank him in very deed,
    For now have I need of the help of some wise man.
T. Trustie. Then may I be gone again, for none such I [a]m.
Trupenie. Ye may be by your going: for no Alderman
    Can go I dare say a sadder pace than ye can.
C. Custance. Trupenie, get thee in, thou shalt among them know,
    How to use thyself, like a proper man I trow.
Trupenie. I go.   [*Exeant.*
C. Custance. Now, Tristram Trustie, I thank you right much.
    For at my first sending to come ye never grutch.
T. Trustie. Dame Custance, God ye save, and while my life shall
      last,   200
    For my friend Goodluck's sake ye shall not send in wast.
C. Custance. He shall give you thanks.
T. Trustie. I will do much for his sake.
C. Custance. But alack, I fear, great displeasure shall be take.
T. Trustie. Wherefore?
C. Custance. For a foolish matter.
T. Trustie. What is your cause?

C. Custance. I am ill accombred with a couple of daws.

T. Trustie. Nay, weep not, woman: but tell me what your cause
is.

As concerning my friend is anything amiss?

C. Custance. No, not on my part: but here was Sym Suresby.

T. Trustie. He was with me and told me so.

C. Custance. And he stood by

While Ralph Roister Doister with help of Merygreeke, 210

For promise of marriage did unto me seek.

T. Trustie. And had ye made any promise before them twain?

C. Custance. No, I had rather be torn in pieces and slain,

No man hath my faith and troth, but Gawyn Goodluck,

And that before Suresby did I say, and there stuck,

But of certain letters there were such words spoken.

T. Trustie. He told me that too.

C. Custance. And of a ring and token.

That Suresby I spied did more than half suspect,

That I my faith to Gawyn Goodluck did reject.

T. Trustie. But there was no such matter, dame Custance,
indeed?   220

C. Custance. If ever my head thought it, God send me ill speed.

Wherefore, I beseech you, with me to be a witness,

That in all my life I never intended thing less,

And what a brainsick fool Ralph Roister Doister is,

Yourself know well enough.

T. Trustie. Ye say full true, i-wis.

C. Custance. Because to be his wife I ne grant nor apply,

Hither will he come, he sweareth, by and by,

To kill both me and mine, and beat down my house flat.

Therefore I pray your aid.

T. Trustie. I warrant you that.

C. Custance. Have I so many years lived a sober life,   230

And showed myself honest, maid, widow, and wife,

And now to be abused in such a vile sort?

Ye see how poor widows live all void of comfort.

T. Trustie. I warrant him do you no harm nor wrong at all.

C. Custance. No, but Mathew Merygreeke doth me most appall,

That he would join himself with such a wretched lout.

T. Trustie. He doth it for a jest, I know him out of doubt,

And here cometh Merygreeke.

C. Custance. Then shall we hear his mind.

SCENE VI

MERYGREEKE.   CHRISTIAN CUSTANCE.   TRIST. TRUSTIE.

M. Mery. Custance and Trustie both, I do you here well find.

C. Custance. Ah, Mathew Merygreeke, ye have used me well.

M. Mery. Now for altogether ye must your answer tell.   241
> Will ye have this man, woman? or els will ye not?
> Else will he come never boar so brim nor toast so hot.

Tris. and Cus. But why join ye with him?

T. Trustie. For mirth?

C. Custance. Or else in sadness?

M. Mery. The more fond of you both hardly that matter guess.

T. Trustie. Lo, how say ye, dame?

M. Mery. Why do ye think, dame Custance,
> That in this wooing I have meant ought but pastance?

C. Custance. Much things ye spake, I wot, to maintain his
> dotage.

M. Mery. But well might ye judge I spake it all in mockage.
> For why? Is Roister Doister a fit husband for you?   250

T. Trustie. I daresay ye never thought it.

M. Mery. No, to God I vow.
> And did not I know afore of the insurance
> Between Gawyn Goodluck and Christian Custance?
> And did not I for the nonce, by my conveyance,
> Read his letter in a wrong sense for dalliance?
> That if you could have take it up at the first bound,
> We should thereat such a sport and pastime have found,
> That all the whole town should have been the merrier.

C. Custance. Ill ache your heads both! I was never wearier,
> Nor never more vexed since the first day I was born.   260

T. Trustie. But very well I wist he here did all in scorn.

C. Custance. But I feared thereof to take dishonesty.

M. Mery. This should both have made sport and showed your
> honesty,
> And Goodluck, I dare swear, your wit therein would low.

T. Trustie. Yea, being no worse than we know it to be now.

M. Mery. And nothing yet too late; for when I come to him,
> Hither will he repair with a sheep's look full grim,
> By plain force and violence to drive you to yield.

C. Custance. If ye two bid me, we will with him pitch a field,

　　　I and my maids together.

M. Mery. Let us see, be bold.　　　　　　　　　　　　　270

C. Custance. Ye shall see women's war.

T. Trustie. That fight will I behold.

M. Mery. If occasion serve, taking his part full brim,
　　　I will strike at you, but the rap shall light on him,
　　　When we first appear.

C. Custance. Then will I run away
　　　As though I were afeard.

T. Trustie. Do you that part well play
　　　And I will sue for peace.

M. Mery. And I will set him on.
　　　Then will he look as fierce as a Cotsold lion.

T. Trustie. But when goest thou for him?

M. Mery. That do I very now.

C. Custance. Ye shall find us here.

M. Mery. Well, God have mercy on you.　　　　　　[*Ex.*

T. Trustie. There is no cause of fear; the least boy in the
　　　street——　　　　　　　　　　　　　　　　280

C. Custance. Nay, the least girl I have, will make him take his
　　　feet.
　　　But hark! methink they make preparation.

T. Trustie. No force, it will be a good recreation.

C. Custance. I will stand within, and step forth speedily,
　　　And so make as though I ran away dreadfully.

SCENE VII

R. Roister.　M. Merygreeke.　C. Custance.　D. Doughtie.
　　　　Harpax.　Tristram Trustie.

R. Roister. Now, sirs, keep your ray, and see your hearts be
　　　stout.
　　　But where be these caitiffs? methink they dare not rout.
　　　How sayest thou, Merygreeke? What doth Kit Custance
　　　say?

M. Mery. I am loth to tell you.

R. Roister. Tush, speak, man: yea or nay?

M. Mery. Forsooth, sir, I have spoken for you all that I can.
　　　But if ye win her, ye must e'en play the man,　　　291
　　　E'en to fight it out, ye must a man's heart take.

R. Roister. Yes, they shall know, and thou knowest I have a
　　　stomach.

[*M. Mery.*] A stomach (quod you), yea, as good as e'er man had.

R. Roister. I trow they shall find and feel that I am a lad.

M. Mery. By this cross, I have seen you eat your meat as well
　　　As any that e'er I have seen of or heard tell.
　　　A stomach, quod you? he that will that deny,
　　　I know, was never at dinner in your company.

R. Roister. Nay, the stomach of a man it is that I mean.　　300

M. Mery. Nay, the stomach of a horse or a dog, I ween.

R. Roister. Nay, a man's stomach with a weapon, mean I.

M. Mery. Ten men can scarce match you with a spoon in a pie.

R. Roister. Nay, the stomach of a man to try in strife.

M. Mery. I never saw your stomach cloyed yet in my life.

R. Roister. Tush, I mean in strife or fighting to try.

M. Mery. We shall see how ye will strike now, being angry.

R. Roister. Have at thy pate then, and save thy head if thou
　　　may.

M. Mery. Nay, then have at your pate again by this day.

R. Roister. Nay, thou mayst not strike at me again in no wise.

M. Mery. I cannot in fight make to you such warrantise:　311
　　　But as for your foes, here let them the bargain bie.

R. Roister. Nay, as for they, shall every mother's child die.
　　　And in this my fume a little thing might make me
　　　To beat down house and all, and else the devil take me.

M. Mery. If I were as ye be, by Gog's dear mother,
　　　I would not leave one stone upon another,
　　　Though she would redeem it with twenty thousand pounds.

R. Roister. It shall be even so, by his lily wounds.

M. Mery. Be not at one with her upon any amends.　　320

R. Roister. No, though she make to me never so many friends.
　　　Nor if all the world for her would undertake,
　　　No, not God himself neither, shall not her peace make,
　　　On, therefore, march forward, soft, stay a while yet.

M. Mery. On.

R. Roister. Tarry.

M. Mery. Forth.

R. Roister. Back.

M. Mery. On.

R. Roister. Soft. Now forward set.

C. Custance. What business have we here? Out! alas, alas!

R. Roister. Ha, ha, ha, ha, ha!

Didst thou see that, Merygreeke, how afraid she was?
Didst thou see how she fled apace out of my sight?
Ah, good sweet Custance, I pity her by this light.

M. Mery. That tender heart of yours will mar altogether,   330
Thus will ye be turned with wagging of a feather.

R. Roister. On, sirs, keep your ray.

M. Mery. On, forth, while this gear is hot.

R. Roister. Soft, the arms of Caleys, I have one thing forgot.

M. Mery. What lack we now?

R. Roister. Retire, or else we be all slain.

M. Mery. Back, for the pash of God! back, sirs, back again!
What is the great matter?

R. Roister. This hasty forthgoing
Had almost brought us all to utter undoing,
It made me forget a thing most necessary.

M. Mery. Well remembered of a captain, by Saint Mary.

R. Roister. It is a thing must be had.

M. Mery. Let us have it then.   340

R. Roister. But I wot not where nor how.

M. Mery. Then wot not I when.
But what is it?

R. Roister. Of a chief thing I am to seek.

M. Mery. Tut, so will ye be, when ye have studied a week.
But tell me what it is?

R. Roister. I lack yet an headpiece.

M. Mery. The kitchen collocavit, the best hens to grece,
Run, fet it, Dobinet, and come at once withal,
And bring with thee my potgun, hanging by the wall.

                       [Exit Dobinet.

I have seen your head with it full many a time,
Covered as safe as it had been with a skrine:
And I warrant it save your head from any stroke,   350
Except perchance to be amazed with the smoke:
I warrant your head therewith, except for the mist,
As safe as if it were fast locked up in a chest:
And lo, here our Dobinet cometh with it now.

                     [Re-enter Dobinet.

D. Doughtie. It will cover me to the shoulders well enow.

M. Mery. Let me see it on.

R. Roister. In faith, it doth metely well.

M. Mery. There can be no fitter thing. Now ye must us tell
What to do.

R. Roister. Now forth in ray, sirs, and stop no more.

M. Mery. Now, Saint George to borrow, drum dub-a-dub afore.

T. Trustie. What mean you to do, sir, commit manslaughter?

R. Roister. To kill forty such is a matter of laughter.   361

T. Trustie. And who is it, sir, whom ye intend thus to spill?

R. Roister. Foolish Custance here forceth me against my will.

T. Trustie. And is there no mean your extreme wrath to slake?
    She shall some amends unto your good maship make.

R. Roister. I will none amends.

T. Trustie. Is her offence so sore?

M. Mery. And he were a lout she could have done no more.
    She hath called him fool, and dressed him like a fool,
    Mocked him like a fool, used him like a fool.

T. Trustie. Well, yet the sheriff, the justice, or constable,   370
    Her misdemeanour to punish might be able.

R. Roister. No, sir, I mine own self will, in this present cause,
    Be sheriff, and justice, and whole judge of the laws,
    This matter to amend, all officers be I shall,
    Constable, bailiff, sergeant.

M. Mery. And hangman and all.

T. Trustie. Yet a noble courage, and the heart of a man,
    Should more honour win by bearing with a woman.
    Therefore take the law, and let her answer thereto.

R. Roister. Merygreeke, the best way were even so to do.
    What honour should it be with a woman to fight?   380

M. Mery. And what then, will ye thus forgo and lese your right?

R. Roister. Nay, I will take the law on her withouten grace.

T. Trustie. Or if your maship could pardon this one trespace,
    I pray you forgive her.

R. Roister. Hoh!

M. Mery. Tush, tush, sir, do not.
    Be good, master, to her.

R. Roister. Hoh!

M. Mery. Tush, I say, do not.
    And what, shall your people here return straight home?

T. Trustie. Yea; levy the camp, sirs, and hence again each one.

R. Roister. But be still in readiness, if I hap to call,
    I cannot tell what sudden chance may befall.

M. Mery. Do not off your harness, sirs, I you advise,   390
    At the least for this fortnight in no manner wise,
    Perchance in an hour when all ye think least,
    Our master's appetite to fight will be best.

    But soft, ere ye go, have one at Custance house.

R. Roister. Soft, what wilt thou do?

M. Mery. Once discharge my harquebouse,
    And, for my heart's ease, have once more with my potgun.

R. Roister. Hold thy hands, else is all our purpose clean fordone.

M. Mery. And it cost me my life.

R. Roister. I say, thou shalt not.

M. Mery. By the matte, but I will.   Have once more with hail
    shot.

    I will have some pennyworth, I will not lese all.   400

SCENE VIII

M. Merygreeke. C. Custance. R. Roister. Tib. Talk.
An. Alyface. M. Mumblecrust. Trupenie. Dobinet
Doughtie. Harpax. *Two drums with their ensigns.*

C. Custance. What caitiffs are those that so shake my house
    wall?

M. Mery. Ah, sirrah! now Custance, if ye had so much wit,
    I would see you ask pardon, and yourselves submit.

C. Custance. Have I still this ado with a couple of fools?

M. Mery. Hear ye what she saith?

C. Custance. Maidens come forth with your tools.

R. Roister. In a ray.

M. Mery. Dubba dub, sirrah.

R. Roister. In a ray.
    They come suddenly on us.

M. Mery. Dubbadub.

R. Roister. In a ray.
    That ever I was born, we are taken tardy.

M. Mery. Now, sirs, quit ourselves like tall men and hardy.

C. Custance. On afore, Trupenie; hold thine own, Annot;   410
    On toward them, Tibet, for 'scape us they cannot.
    Come forth, Madge Mumblecrust, to stand fast together.

M. Mery. God send us a fair day.

R. Roister. See, they march on hither.

Tib. Talk. But, mistress——

C. Custance. What sayest you?

Tib. Talk. Shall I go fet our goose?

C. Custance. What to do?

Tib. Talk. To yonder captain I will turn her loose,

And she gape and hiss at him, as she doth at me,
I durst jeopard my hand she will make him flee.

C. Custance. On forward.

R. Roister. They come.

M. Mery. Stand.

R. Roister. Hold.

M. Mery. Keep.

R. Roister. There.

M. Mery. Strike.

R. Roister. Take heed.

C. Custance. Well said, Trupenie.

Trupenie. Ah, whoresons.

C. Custance. Well done, indeed.

M. Mery. Hold thine own, Harpax; down with them, Dobinet.

C. Custance. Now Madge, there Annot: now stick them, Tibet.

Tib. Talk. All my chief quarrel is to this same little knave, 422
        That beguiled me last day, nothing shall him save.

D. Doughtie. Down with this little quean, that hath at me such
                spite;
        Save you from her, master, it is a very sprite.

C. Custance. I myself will mounsire grand captain undertake.

R. Roister. They win ground.

M. Mery. Save yourself, sir, for God's sake.

R. Roister. Out, alas! I am slain, help!

M. Mery. Save yourself.

R. Roister. Alas!

M. Mery. Nay, then, have at you, mistress.

R. Roister. Thou hittest me, alas!

M. Mery. I will strike at Custance here.

R. Roister. Thou hittest me.

M. Mery. So I will.   430
        Nay, mistress Custance.

R. Roister. Alas! thou hittest me still.
        Hold.

M. Mery. Save yourself, sir.

R. Roister. Help! out, alas! I am slain.

M. Mery. Truce, hold your hands; truce for a pissing while or
                twain:
        Nay, how say you, Custance, for saving of your life,
        Will ye yield and grant to be this gentman's wife?

C. Custance. Ye told me he loved me; call ye this love?

M. Mery. He loved a while even like a turtle-dove.

C. Custance. Gay love, God save it: so soon hot, so soon cold.

M. Mery. I am sorry for you: he could love you yet, so he could.

R. Roister. Nay, by Cock's precious, she shall be none of mine.

M. Mery. Why so?   441

R. Roister. Come away, by the matte she is mankine.
    I durst adventure the loss of my right hand,
    If she did not slee her other husband:
    And see if she prepare not again to fight.

M. Mery. What then? Saint George to borrow, our ladies'
    knight.

R. Roister. Slee else whom she will, by gog she shall not slee me.

M. Mery. How then?

R. Roister. Rather than to be slain, I will flee.

C. Custance. To it again, my knightesses; down with them all.

R. Roister. Away, away, away! she will else kill us all.

M. Mery. Nay, stick to it, like an hardy man and a tall.   450

R. Roister. Oh bones, thou hittest me! Away, or else die we
    shall.

M. Mery. Away, for the pashe of our sweet Lord Jesus Christ.

C. Custance. Away, lout and lubber, or I shall be thy priest.

                            [Exeant om.
    So this field is ours, we have driven them all away.

Tib. Talk. Thanks to God, mistress, ye have had a fair day.

C. Custance. Well, now go ye in, and make yourself some good
    cheer.

Omnes pariter. We go.

T. Trustie. Ah, sir, what a field we have had here!

C. Custance. Friend Tristram, I pray you be a witness with me.

T. Trustie. Dame Custance, I shall depose for your honesty,
    And now fare ye well, except something else ye would. 460

C. Custance. Not now, but when I need to send I will be bold.
    I thank you for these pains. *[Exeat.]* And now I will get
    me in.
    Now Roister Doister will no more wooing begin.   *[Exeat.*

ACT V

SCENE I

GAWYN GOODLUCK. SYM SURESBY.

G. Good. Sym Suresby, my trusty man, now advise thee well,
    And see that no false surmises thou me tell,
    Was there such ado about Custance of a truth?
Sym Sure. To report that I heard and saw, to me is ruth,
    But both my duty and name and property
    Warneth me to you to show fidelity.
    It may be well enough, and I wish it so to be,
    She may herself discharge and try her honesty.
    Yet their claim to her methought was very large,
    For with letters, rings and tokens, they did her charge. 10
    Which when I heard and saw I would none to you bring.
G. Good. No, by Saint Marie, I allow thee in that thing.
    Ah, sirrah, now I see truth in the proverb old,
    All things that shineth is not by and by pure gold.
    If any do live a woman of honesty,
    I would have sworn Christian Custance had been she.
Sym Sure. Sir, though I to you be a servant true and just,
    Yet do not ye therefore your faithful spouse mistrust.
    But examine the matter, and if ye shall it find
    To be all well, be not ye for my words unkind. 20
G. Good. I shall do that is right, and as I see cause why.
    But here cometh Custance forth, we shall know by and by.

SCENE II

C. CUSTANCE. GAWY GOODLUCK. SYM SURESBY.

C. Custance. I come forth to see and hearken for news good,
    For about this hour is the time of likelihood,
    That Gawyn Goodluck by the sayings of Suresby
    Would be at home, and lo, yond I see him, I.
    What! Gawyn Goodluck, the only hope of my life!
    Welcome home, and kiss me your true espoused wife.

G. Good. Nay, soft, dame Custance; I must first, by your licence,

　　See whether all things be clear in your conscience.   30

　　I hear of your doings to me very strange.

C. Custance. What fear ye, that my faith towards you should change?

G. Good. I must needs mistrust ye be elsewhere entangled,

　　For I hear that certain men with you have wrangled

　　About the promise of marriage by you to them made.

C. Custance. Could any man's report your mind therein persuade?

G. Good. Well, ye must therein declare yourself to stand clear,

　　Else I and you, dame Custance, may not join this year.

C. Custance. Then would I were dead, and fair laid in my grave.

　　Ah, Suresby, is this the honesty that ye have?   40

　　To hurt me with your report, not knowing the thing.

Sym Sure. If ye be honest my words can hurt you nothing.

　　But what I heard and saw, I might not but report.

C. Custance. Ah, Lord, help poor widows, destitute of comfort!

　　Truly, most dear spouse, nought was done but for pastance.

G. Good. But such kind of sporting is homely dalliance.

C. Custance. If ye knew the truth, ye would take all in good part.

G. Good. By your leave, I am not half well skilled in that art.

C. Custance. It was none but Roister Doister, that foolish mome.

G. Good. Yea, Custance, better (they say) a bad 'scuse than none.

C. Custance. Why, Tristram Trustie, sir, your true and faithful friend,   51

　　Was privy both to the beginning and the end.

　　Let him be the judge, and for me testify.

G. Good. I will the more credit that he shall verify,

　　And because I will the truth know e'en as it is,

　　I will to him myself, and know all without miss.

　　Come on, Sym Suresby, that before my friend thou may

　　Avouch the same words, which thou didst to me say.

　　　　　　　　　　　　　　　　　　　　　　[*Exeant.*

SCENE III

Christian Custance.

C. Custance. O Lord! how necessary it is now of days,

　　That each body live uprightly all manner ways;   60

　　For let never so little a gap be open,

And be sure of this, the worst shall be spoken.
How innocent stand I in this for deed or thought!
And yet see what mistrust towards me it hath wrought.
But thou, Lord, knowest all folks' thoughts and eke intents,
And thou art the deliverer of all innocents.
Thou didst help the advoutress, that she might be amended,
Much more then help, Lord, that never ill intended.
Thou didst help Susanna, wrongfully accused,
And no less dost thou see, Lord, how I am now abused. 70
Thou didst help Hester, when she should have died,
Help also, good Lord, that my truth may be tried.
Yet if Gawyn Goodluck with Tristram Trustie speak,
I trust of ill report the force shall be but weak.
And lo, yond they come, sadly talking together,
I will abide, and not shrink for their coming hither.

SCENE IV

GAWYN GOODLUCK. TRISTRAM TRUSTIE. C. CUSTANCE.
SYM SURESBY.

G. Good. And was it none other than ye to me report?
Tristram. No, and here were ye wished to have seen the sport.
G. Good. Would I had, rather than half of that in my purse.
Sym Sure. And I do much rejoice the matter was no worse, 80
　　And like as to open it I was to you faithful,
　　So of dame Custance honest truth I am joyful.
　　For God forfend that I should hurt her by false report.
G. Good. Well, I will no longer hold her in discomfort.
C. Custance. Now come they hitherward, I trust all shall be well.
G. Good. Sweet Custance, neither heart can think nor tongue tell,
　　How much I joy in your constant fidelity.
　　Come now, kiss me, the pearl of perfect honesty.
C. Custance. God let me no longer to continue in life,
　　Than I shall towards you continue a true wife.   90
G. Good. Well, now to make you for this some part of amends,
　　I shall desire first you, and then such of our friends
　　As shall to you seem best, to sup at home with me,
　　Where at your fought field we shall laugh and merry be.
Sym Sure. And mistress, I beseech you, take with me no grief,
　　I did a true man's part, not wishing you reprief.

C. Custance. Though hasty reports through surmises growing
    May of poor innocents be utter overthrowing,
    Yet because to thy master thou hast a true heart,
    And I know mine own truth, I forgive thee for my part.
G. Good. Go we all to my house, and of this gear no more.   101
    Go, prepare all things, Sym Suresby; hence, run afore.
Sym Sure. I go.   *[Ex.*
G. Good. But who cometh yond, M. Merygreeke?
C. Custance. Roister Doister's champion, I shrew his best cheek.
T. Trustie. Roister Doister self, your wooer, is with him too.
    Surely some thing there is with us they have to do.

SCENE V

M. Merygreeke. Ralph Roister. Gawyn Goodluck.
Tristram Trustie. C. Custance.

M. Mery. Yond I see Gawyn Goodluck, to whom lieth my
    message;
    I will first salute him after his long voyage,
    And then make all thing well concerning your behalf.
R. Roister. Yea, for the pash of God.
M. Mery. Hence out of sight, ye calf,   110
    Till I have spoke with them, and then I will you fet.
R. Roister. In God's name.   *[Exit R. Roister.*
M. Mery. What, master Gawyn Goodluck, well met!
    And from your long voyage I bid you right welcome home.
G. Good. I thank you.
M. Mery. I come to you from an honest mome.
G. Good. Who is that?
M. Mery. Roister Doister, that doughty kite.
C. Custance. Fie! I can scarcely abide ye should his name recite.
M. Mery. Ye must take him to favour, and pardon all past,
    He heareth of your return, and is full ill aghast.
G. Good. I am right well content he have with us some cheer.
C. Custance. Fie upon him, beast! then will not I be there. 120
G. Good. Why, Custance, do ye hate him more than ye love me?
C. Custance. But for your mind, sir, where he were would I
    not be.
T. Trustie. He would make us all laugh.
M. Mery. Ye ne'er had better sport.
G. Good. I pray you, sweet Custance, let him to us resort.

C. Custance. To your will I assent.

M. Mery. Why, such a fool it is,
    As no man for good pastime would forgo or miss.

G. Good. Fet him to go with us.

M. Mery. He will be a glad man.   [*Ex.*

T. Trustie. We must to make us mirth, maintain him all we can.
    And lo, yond he cometh, and Merygreeke with him.

C. Custance. At his first entrance ye shall see I will him trim.
    But first let us hearken the gentleman's wise talk.   131

T. Trustie. I pray you, mark, if ever ye saw crane so stalk.

SCENE VI

R. Roister. M. Merygreeke. C. Custance.
G. Goodluck. T. Trustie. D. Doughtie. Harpax.

R. Roister. May I then be bold?

M. Mery. I warrant you on my word,
    They say they shall be sick, but ye be at their board.

R. Roister. They were not angry, then?

M. Mery. Yes, at first, and made strange,
    But when I said your anger to favour should change,
    And therewith had commended you accordingly,
    They were all in love with your maship by and by,
    And cried you mercy that they had done you wrong.

R. Roister. For why, no man, woman, nor child can hate me
    long.   140

M. Mery. We fear (quod they) he will be avenged one day,
    Then for a penny give all our lives we may.

R. Roister. Said they so indeed?

M. Mery. Did they? yea, even with one voice.
    He will forgive all (quod I).   Oh, how they did rejoice.

R. Roister. Ha, ha, ha.

M. Mery. Go fet him (say they) while he is in good mood,
    For have his anger who lust, we will not, by the Rood.

R. Roister. I pray God that it be all true, that thou hast me told
    And that she fight no more.

M. Mery. I warrant you, be bold.
    To them, and salute them.

R. Roister. Sirs, I greet you all well.

Omnes. Your mastership is welcome.

C. Custance. Saving my quarrel.   150

For sure I will put you up into the Exchequer.

M. Mery. Why so? better nay: wherefore?

C. Custance. For an usurer.

R. Roister. I am no usurer, good mistress, by his arms.

M. Mery. When took he gain of money to any man's harms?

C. Custance. Yes, a foul usurer he is, ye shall see else.

R. Roister. Didst not thou promise she would pick no mo
    quarrels?

C. Custance. He will lend no blows, but he have in recompense
    Fifteen for one, which is too much of conscience.

R. Roister. Ah, dame, by the ancient law of arms, a man
    Hath no honour to foil his hands on a woman.   160

C. Custance. And where other usurers take their gains yearly,
    This man is angry but he have his by and by.

G. Good. Sir, do not for her sake bear me your displeasure.

M. Mery. Well, he shall with you talk thereof more at leisure.
    Upon your good usage, he will now shake your hand.

R. Roister. And much heartily welcome from a strange land.

M. Mery. Be not afeard, Gawyn, to let him shake your fist.

G. Good. Oh, the most honest gentleman that e'er I wist.
    I beseech your maship to take pain to sup with us.

M. Mery. He shall not say you nay, and I too, by Jesus,   170
    Because ye shall be friends, and let all quarrels pass.

R. Roister. I will be as good friends with them as ere I was.

M. Mery. Then let me fet your quire that we may have a song.

R. Roister. Go.   *[Exit M. Mery.*

G. Good. I have heard no melody all this year long.

Re-enter M. Mery.

M. Mery. Come on, sirs, quickly.

R. Roister. Sing on, sirs, for my friends' sake.

D. Dough. Call ye these your friends?

R. Roister. Sing on, and no mo words make.   *[Here they sing.*

G. Good. The Lord preserve our most noble Queen of renown,
    And her virtues reward with the heavenly crown.

C. Custance. The Lord strengthen her most excellent Majesty,
    Long to reign over us in all prosperity.   180

T. Trustie. That her godly proceedings the faith to defend,
    He may 'stablish and maintain through to the end.

M. Mery. God grant her, as she doth, the Gospel to protect,
    Learning and virtue to advance, and vice to correct.

R. Roister. God grant her loving subjects both the mind and
 grace,
 Her most godly proceedings worthily to embrace.
Harpax. Her highness' most worthy counsellors, God prosper
 With honour and love of all men to minister.
Omnes. God grant the nobility her to serve and love,
 With all the whole commonty as doth them behove. 190

AMEN.

CERTAIN SONGS TO BE SUNG BY THOSE WHICH SHALL USE
THIS COMEDY OR INTERLUDE

The Second Song.

Whoso to marry a minion wife,
 Hath had good chance and hap,
Must love her and cherish her all his life,
 And dandle her in his lap.

If she will fare well, if she will go gay,
 A good husband ever still,
Whatever she lust to do, or to say,
 Must let her have her own will.

About what affairs soever he go,
 He must show her all his mind. 10
None of his counsel she may be kept fro,
 Else is he a man unkind.

The Fourth Song.

I mun be married a Sunday,
I mun be married a Sunday,
Whosoever shall come that way,
I mun be married a Sunday.

Roister Doister is my name,
Roister Doister is my name,
A lusty brute I am the same,
I mun be married a Sunday.

Christian Custance have I found,
Christian Custance have I found,   10
A widow worth a thousand pound,
I mun be married a Sunday.

Custance is as sweet as honey,
Custance is as sweet as honey,
I her lamb and she my coney,
I mun be married a Sunday.

When we shall make our wedding feast,
When we shall make our wedding feast,
There shall be cheer for man and beast,
I mun be married a Sunday.   20
    I mun be married a Sunday, etc.

The Psalmody.

Placebo dilexi,
Master Roister Doister will straight go home and die,
Our Lord Jesus Christ his soul have mercy upon:
Thus you see to-day a man, to-morrow John.
    Yet saving for a woman's extreme cruelty,
He might have lived yet a month or two or three,
But in spite of Custance which hath him wearied,
His maship shall be worshipfully buried.
And while some piece of his soul is yet him within,
Some part of his funerals let us here begin.
    Dirige. He will go darkling to his grave.   10
Neque lux, neque crux, nisi solum clink,
Never gentman so went toward heaven, I think.

Yet, sirs, as ye will the bliss of heaven win,
When he cometh to the grave lay him softly in,
And all men take heed by this one gentleman,
How you set your love upon an unkind woman:
For these women be all such mad peevish elves,
They will not be won except it please themselves,
But in faith, Custance, if ever ye come in hell,
Master Roister Doister shall serve you as well.   20
Good night, Roger old knave; farewell, Roger old knave.
Good night, Roger old knave, knave, knap.
    Nequando. Audivi vocem. Requiem æternam.

THE PEAL OF BELLS RUNG BY THE PARISH CLERK AND ROISTER
DOISTER'S FOUR MEN

The first Bell a Triple. When died he?   When died he?
The second. We have him, we have him.
The third. Roister Doister, Roister Doister.
The fourth Bell. He cometh, he cometh.
The great Bell. Our own, our own.

ENDIMION
THE MAN IN THE MOONE

PLAYED BEFORE THE QUEEN'S MAJESTY AT GREENWICH
ON NEW YEAR'S DAY AT NIGHT BY THE
CHILDREN OF PAUL'S

DRAMATIS PERSONÆ

ENDIMION, *in love with Cynthia.*
EUMENIDES, *his friend; in love with Semele.*
CORSITES,
PANTALION, } *Lords of Cynthia's Court.*
ZONTES,
PYTHAGORAS, } *Philosophers.*
GYPTES,
GERON, *an old man, husband to Dipsas.*
SIR TOPHAS, *a bragging Soldier.*
SAMIAS, *Page to Endimion.*
DARES, *Page to Eumenides.*
EPITON, *Page to Sir Tophas.*

Master Constable.
Watchmen.
Fairies.
Characters in Dumb Show.

CYNTHIA.
TELLUS, *enamoured of Endimion.*
FLOSCULA, *her confidant.*
SEMELE,
SCINTILLA, } *Ladies of Cynthia's Court.*
FAVILLA,
DIPSAS, *an Enchantress.*
BAGOA, *her Servant.*

ENDIMION

THE PROLOGUE

MOST high and happy Princess, we must tell you a tale of the Man in the Moon, which if it seem ridiculous for the method, or superfluous for the matter, or for the means incredible, for three faults we can make but one excuse. It is a tale of the Man in the Moon.

It was forbidden in old time to dispute of Chimera, because it was a fiction, we hope in our times none will apply pastimes, because they are fancies; for there liveth none under the sun, that knows what to make of the Man in the Moon. We present neither comedy, nor tragedy, nor story, nor anything, but that whosoever heareth may say this, Why, here is a tale of the Man in the Moon.

ACT I

SCENE I

ENDIMION. EUMENIDES.

End. I find, Eumenides, in all things both variety to content, and satiety to glut, saving only in my affections: which are so stayed, and withal so stately, that I can neither satisfy my heart with love, nor mine eyes with wonder. My thoughts, Eumenides, are stitched to the stars, which being as high as I can see, thou mayst imagine how much higher they are than I can reach.

Eum. If you be enamoured of anything above the Moon, your thoughts are ridiculous, for that things immortal are not subject to affections; if allured or enchanted with these transitory things under the Moon, you show yourself senseless, to attribute such lofty titles to such love trifles.

End. My love is placed neither under the Moon nor above.

Eum. I hope you be not sotted upon the Man in the Moon.

End. No, but settled, either to die, or possess the Moon herself.

Eum. Is Endimion mad, or do I mistake? do you love the Moon, Endimion?

End. Eumenides, the Moon.

Eum. There was never any so peevish to imagine *the Moon* either capable of affection, or shape of a Mistress: for as impossible it is to make love sit to her humour, which no man knoweth, as a coat to her form, which continueth not in one bigness whilst she is measuring. Cease off, Endimion, to feed so much upon fancies. That melancholy blood must be purged, which draweth you to a dotage no less miserable than monstrous.

End. My thoughts have no veins, and yet unless they be let blood, I shall perish.

Eum. But they have vanities, which being reformed, you may be restored.

End. O fair Cynthia, why do others term thee inconstant, whom I have ever found unmovable? Injurious time, corrupt manners, unkind men, who finding a constancy not to be matched in my sweet Mistress, have christened her with the name of wavering, waxing, and waning. Is she inconstant that keepeth a settled course, which since her first creation altereth not one minute in her moving? There is nothing thought more admirable, or commendable in the sea, than the ebbing and flowing; and shall the Moon, from whom the sea taketh this virtue, be accounted fickle for increasing and decreasing? Flowers in their buds, are nothing worth till they be blown; nor blossoms accounted till they be ripe fruit; and shall we then say they be changeable, for that they grow from seeds to leaves, from leaves to buds, from buds to their perfection? then, why be not twigs that become trees, children that become men, and mornings that grow to evenings, termed wavering, for that they continue not at one stay? Ay, but Cynthia being in her fullness decayeth, as not delighting in her greatest beauty, or withering when she should be most honoured. When malice cannot object anything, folly will; making that a vice, which is the greatest virtue. What thing (my mistress excepted) being in the pride of her beauty, and latter minute of her age, that waxeth young again? Tell me, Eumenides, what is he that having a mistress of ripe years, and infinite virtues, great honours, and unspeakable beauty, but would wish that she might grow tender again? getting youth by years, and never-decaying beauty by time; whose fair face, neither the summer's blaze can scorch, nor winter's blast chap, nor the numbering of years breed altering of colours. Such is my sweet Cynthia, whom time cannot touch, because she is divine, nor will offend because she is delicate.   O Cynthia, if thou shouldest always continue at thy fullness, both Gods and men would conspire to ravish thee.   But thou to abate the pride of our affections, dost detract from thy perfections; thinking it sufficient, if once in a month we enjoy a glimpse of thy majesty; and then, to increase our griefs, thou dost decrease thy gleams; coming out of thy royal robes, wherewith thou dazzlest our eyes, down into thy swathy clouts, beguiling our eyes; and then—

Eum. Stay there, Endimion, thou that committest idolatry, wilt straight blaspheme, if thou be suffered. Sleep would do thee more good than speech: the Moon heareth thee not, or if she do, regardeth thee not.

End. Vain Eumenides, whose thoughts never grow higher than the crown of thy head. Why troublest thou me, having neither head to conceive the cause of my love, or a heart to receive the impressions? follow thou thine own fortunes, which creep on the earth, and suffer me to fly to mine, whose fall though it be desperate, yet shall it come by daring. Farewell.

Eum. Without doubt Endimion is bewitched, otherwise in a man of such rare virtues there could not harbour a mind of such extreme madness.   I will follow him, lest in this fancy of the moon he deprive himself of the sight of the sun.

[*Exit.*

SCENE II

Tellus.   Floscula.

Tellus. Treacherous and most perjured Endimion, is Cynthia the sweetness of thy life, and the bitterness of my death? What revenge may be devised so full of shame, as my thoughts are replenished with malice?   Tell me, Floscula, if falseness in love can possibly be punished with extremity of hate.   As long as sword, fire, or poison may be hired, no

traitor to my love shall live unrevenged. Were thy oaths
without number, thy kisses without measure, thy sighs
without end, forged to deceive a poor credulous virgin whose
simplicity had been worth thy favour and better fortune?
If the Gods sit unequal beholders of injuries, or laughers
at lovers' deceits; then let mischief be as well forgiven in
women, as perjury winked at in men.

Flosc. Madam, if you would compare the state of Cynthia with
your own, and the height of Endimion his thoughts, with
the meanness of your fortune, you would rather yield than
contend, being between you and her no comparison; and
rather wonder than rage at the greatness of his mind, being
affected with a thing more than mortal.

Tellus. No comparison, Floscula? and why so? is not my beauty
divine, whose body is decked with fair flowers; and veins
are vines, yielding sweet liquor to the dullest spirits; whose
ears are corn, to bring strength; and whose hairs are grass
to bring abundance? Doth not frankincense and myrrh
breathe out of my nostrils, and all the sacrifice of the Gods
breed in my bowels? Infinite are my creatures, without
which neither thou nor Endimion, nor any could love, or
live.

Flosc. But know you not, fair lady, that Cynthia governeth all
things? Your grapes would be but dry husks, your corn
but chaff, and all your virtues vain, were it not Cynthia
that preserveth the one in the bud, and nourisheth the other
in the blade, and by her influence both comforteth all things,
and by her authority commandeth all creatures; suffer
then Endimion to follow his affections, though to obtain
her be impossible, and let him flatter himself in his own
imaginations, because they are immortal.

Tellus. Loath I am, Endimion, thou shouldest die, because I love
thee well; and that shouldest live it grieveth me, because
thou lovest Cynthia too well. In these extremities what
shall I do? Floscula, no more words, I am resolved. He
shall neither live, nor die.

Flosc. A strange practice if it be possible.

Tellus. Yes, I will entangle him in such a sweet net, that he
shall neither find the means to come out, nor desire it. All
allurements of pleasure will I cast before his eyes, insomuch
that he shall slake that love which he now voweth to Cynthia
and burn in mine, of which he seemeth careless. In this

languishing, between my amorous devices, and his own loose desires, there shall such dissolute thoughts take root in his head, and over his heart grow so thick a skin, that neither hope of preferment, nor fear of punishment, nor counsel of the wisest, nor company of the worthiest, shall alter his humour, nor make him once to think of his honour.

Flosc. A revenge incredible, and if it may be, unnatural.

Tellus. He shall know the malice of a woman, to have neither mean, nor end; and of a woman deluded in love, to have neither rule nor reason. I can do it, I must; I will! All his virtues will I shadow with vices; his person (ah, sweet person) shall he deck with such rich robes, as he shall forget it is his own person; his sharp wit (ah, wit too sharp, that hath cut off all my joys) shall he use, in flattering of my face, and devising sonnets in my favour. The prime of his youth and pride of his time shall be spent in melancholy passions, careless behaviour, untamed thoughts, and un-bridled affections.

Flosc. When this is done, what then; shall it continue till his death, or shall he dote for ever in this delight?

Tellus. Ah Floscula, thou rendest my heart in sunder in putting me in remembrance of the end.

Flosc. Why if this be not the end, all the rest is to no end.

Tellus. Yet suffer me to imitate Juno, who would turn Jupiter's lovers to beasts on the earth though she knew afterwards they should be stars in heaven.

Flosc. Affection that is bred by enchantment is like a flower that is wrought in silk, in colour and form most like, but nothing at all in substance or savour.

Tellus. It shall suffice me if the world talk that I am favoured of Endimion.

Flosc. Well, use your own will; but you shall find that love gotten with witchcraft is as unpleasant as fish taken with medicines unwholesome.

Tellus. Floscula, they that be so poor that they have neither net nor hook will rather poison do than pine with hunger: and she that is so oppressed with love, that she is neither able with beauty nor wit to obtain her friend, will rather use unlawful means than try intolerable pains. I will do it. [*Exit.*

Flosc. Then about it. Poor Endimion, what traps are laid for thee, because thou honourest one that all the world wondreth

at; and what plots are cast to make thee unfortunate,
that studiest of all men to be the faithfullest.   [*Exit.*

SCENE III

DARES. SAMIAS. SIR TOPHAS. EPITON.

Dares. Now our masters are in love up to the ears, what have
we to do but to be in knavery up to the crowns.

Samias. O that we had Sir Tophas that brave squire in the midst
of our mirth, *et ecce autem*, will you see the devil?

Enter SIR TOPHAS.

Top. Epi.

Epi. Here, sir.

Top. I brook not this idle humour of love, it tickleth not my
liver, from whence the love-mongers in former age seemed
to infer they should proceed.

Epi. Love, sir, may lie in your lungs, and I think it doth; and
that is the cause you blow and are so pursie.

Top. Tush, boy! I think it but some device of the poet to get
money.

Epi. A poet? what's that?

Top. Dost thou not know what a poet is?

Epi. No.

Top. Why, fool, a poet is as much as one should say, a poet.
But soft, yonder be two wrens, shall I shoot at them?

Epi. They are two lads.

Top. Larks or wrens, I will kill them.

Epi. Larks? are you blind? they are two little boys.

Top. Birds, or boys, they are both but a pittance for my breakfast; therefore have at them, for their brains must as it
were embroider my bolts.

Sam. Stay your courage, valiant knight, for your wisdom is so
weary that it stayeth itself.

Dar. Why, Sir Tophas, have you forgotten your old friends?

Top. Friends? *Nego argumentum.*

Sam. And why not friends?

Top. Because Amicitia (as in old annals we find) is *inter pares*,
now my pretty companions you shall see how unequal you
be to me; but I will not cut you quite off, you shall be my

half friends; for reaching to my middle, so far as from the ground to the waist I will be your friend.

Dar. Learnedly. But what shall become of the rest of your body, from the waist to the crown?

Top. My children, *quod supra vos nihil ad vos*, you must think the rest immortal, because you cannot reach it.

Epi. Nay, I tell ye my master is more than a man.

Dar. And thou less than a mouse.

Top. But what be you two?

Sam. I am Samias, page to Endimion.

Dar. And I Dares, page to Eumenides.

Top. Of what occupation are your masters?

Dar. Occupation, you clown, why they are honourable, and warriors.

Top. Then they are my prentices.

Dar. Thine, and why so?

Top. I was the first that ever devised war, and therefore by Mars himself had given me for my arms a whole armoury; and thus I go as you see, clothed with artillery; it is not silks (*milksops*) nor tissues, nor the fine wool of Ceres, but iron, steel, swords, flame, shot, terror, clamour, blood, and ruin, that rocks asleep my thoughts, which never had any other cradle but cruelty. Let me see, do you not bleed?

Dar. Why so?

Top. Commonly my words wound.

Sam. What then do your blows?

Top. Not only wound, but also confound.

Sam. How darest thou come so near thy master, Epi? Sir Tophas, spare us.

Top. You shall live. You, Samias, because you are little; you, Dares, because you are no bigger; and both of you, because you are but two; for commonly I kill by the dozen, and have for every particular adversary a peculiar weapon.

Sam. May we know the use for our better skill in war?

Top. You shall. Here is a bird-bolt for the ugly beast the blackbird.

Dar. A cruel sight.

Top. Here is the musket for the untamed (or as the vulgar sort term it) the wild mallard.

Sam. O desperate attempt!

Epi. Nay, my master will match them.

Dar. Ay, if he catch them.

Top. Here is a spear and shield, and both necessary; the one
to conquer, the other to subdue or overcome the terrible
trout, which although he be under the water, yet tying a
string to the top of my spear and an engine of iron to the
end of my line, I overthrow him; and then herein I put him.

Sam. O wonderful war! Dares, didst thou ever hear such a dolt?

Dar. All the better, we shall have good sport hereafter, if we can
get leisure.

Sam. Leisure? I will rather lose my master's service than his
company! look how he *strowtes;* but what is this, call you
it your sword?

Top. No, it is my *simiter;* which I, by construction often study-
ing to be compendious, call my smiter.

Dar. What, are you also learned, sir?

Top. Learned? I am all Mars and Ars.

Sam. Nay, you are all mass and ass.

Top. Mock you me? You shall both suffer, yet with such
weapons, as you shall make choice of the weapon wherewith
you shall perish. Am I all a mass or lump, is there no
proportion in me? Am I all ass? is there no wit in me.
Epi, prepare them to the slaughter.

Sam. I pray, sir, hear us speak! we call you mass, which your
learning doth well understand is all man, for *Mas maris*
is a man. Then *As* (as you know) is a weight, and we for
your virtues account you a weight.

Top. The Latin hath saved your lives, the which a world of
silver could not have ransomed. I understand you, and
pardon you.

Dar. Well, Sir Tophas, we bid you farewell, and at our next
meeting we will be ready to do you service.

Top. Samias, I thank you;—Dares, I thank you; but especially
I thank you both.

Sam. Wisely. Come, next time we'll have some pretty gentlewomen with us to walk, for without doubt with them he
will be very dainty.

Dar. Come, let us see what our masters do, it is high time.

[*Exeunt.*

Top. Now will I march into the field, where if I cannot encounter
with my foul enemies, I will withdraw myself to the river,
and there fortify for fish: for there resteth no minute free
from fight.   [*Exit.*

SCENE IV

Tellus. Floscula. Dipsas.

Tellus. Behold, Floscula, we have met with the woman by chance
that we sought for by travel; I will break my mind to her
without ceremony or circumstance, lest we lose that time
in advice that should be spent in execution.

Flosc. Use your discretion, I will in this case neither give counsel
nor consent, for there cannot be a thing more monstrous
than to force affection by sorcery, neither do I imagine
anything more impossible.

Tellus. Tush, Floscula! in obtaining of love, what impossibilities
will I not try? and for the winning of Endimion, what
impieties will I not practise? Dipsas, whom as many
honour for age, as wonder at for cunning; listen in few
words to my tale, and answer in one word to the purpose; for that neither my burning desire can afford long
speech, nor the short time I have to stay many delays. Is it
possible by herbs, stones, spells, incantation, enchantment,
exorcisms, fire, metals, planets, or any practice, to plant
affection where it is not, and to supplant it where it is?

Dipsas. Fair lady, you may imagine that these hoary hairs are
not void of experience, nor the great name that goeth of
my cunning to be without cause. I can darken the sun by
my skill, and remove the moon out of her course; I can
restore youth to the aged, and make hills without bottoms;
there is nothing that I cannot do, but that only which you
would have me do; and therein I differ from the Gods, that
I am not able to rule hearts; for were it in my power to
place affection by appointment, I would make such evil
appetites, such inordinate lusts, such cursed desires, as all
the world should be filled both with superstitious heats,
and extreme love.

Tellus. Unhappy Tellus, whose desires are so desperate that they
are neither to be conceived of any creature, nor to be cured
by any art.

Dipsas. This I can, breed slackness in love, though never root
it out. What is he whom you love, and what she that he
honoureth?

Tellus. Endimion, sweet Endimion is he that hath my heart;

and Cynthia, too, too fair Cynthia, the miracle of nature, of time, of fortune, is the lady that he delights in; and dotes on every day, and dies for ten thousand times a day.

Dipsas. Would you have his love, either by absence or sickness aslaked? Would you that Cynthia should mistrust him, or be jealous of him without colour?

Tellus. It is the only thing I crave, that seeing my love to Endimion unspotted, cannot be accepted, his truth to Cynthia (though it be unspeakable) may be suspected.

Dipsas. I will undertake it, and overtake him, that all his love shall be doubted of, and therefore become desperate: but this will wear out with time, that treadeth all things down but truth.

Tellus. Let us go.

Dipsas. I follow. [*Exeunt.*

ACT II

SCENE I

ENDIMION, TELLUS.

End. O fair Cynthia! O unfortunate Endimion! Why was not thy birth as high as thy thoughts, or her beauty less than heavenly? or why are not thine honours as rare as her beauty? or thy fortunes as great as thy deserts? Sweet Cynthia, how wouldst thou be pleased, how possessed? will labours (patient of all extremities) obtain thy love? There is no mountain so steep that I will not climb, no monster so cruel that I will not tame, no action so desperate that I will not attempt. Desirest thou the passions of love, the sad and melancholy moods of perplexed minds, the not-to-be-expressed torments of racked thoughts? Behold my sad tears, my deep sighs, m y hollow eyes, my broken sleeps, my heavy countenance. Wouldst thou have me vowed only to thy beauty, and consume every minute of time in thy service? remember my solitary life, almost these seven years, whom have I entertained but mine own thoughts, and thy virtues? What company have I used but contemplation? Whom have I wondered at but thee? Nay, whom have I not contemned, for thee? Have I not crept to those on whom I might have trodden, only because thou didst shine upon them? Have not injuries been sweet to me, if thou vouchsafest I should bear them? Have I not spent my golden years in hopes, waxing old with wishing, yet wishing nothing but thy love. With Tellus, fair Tellus, have I dissembled, using her but as a cloak for mine affections, that others, seeing my mangled and disordered mind, might think it were for one that loveth me, not for Cynthia, whose perfection alloweth no companion, nor comparison. In the midst of these distempered thoughts of mine thou art not only jealous of my truth, but careless, suspicious, and secure: which strange humour maketh my mind as desperate as thy conceits are doubtful. I am none of those wolves that bark most, when thou shinest brightest, but that fish (thy fish, Cynthia, in the flood Aranis) which at thy waxing is as white as the driven snow, and at thy waning, as black as deepest darkness. I am that Endimion (sweet Cynthia) that have carried my thoughts in equal balance with my actions, being always as free from imagining ill as enterprising; that Endimion, whose eyes never esteemed anything fair but thy face, whose tongue termed nothing rare but thy virtues, and whose heart imagined nothing miraculous but thy government. Yea, that Endimion who, divorcing himself from the amiableness of all ladies, the bravery of all courts, the company of all men, hath chosen in a solitary cell to live, only by feeding on thy favour, accounting in the world (but thyself) nothing excellent, nothing immortal; thus mayst thou see every vein, sinew, muscle, and artery of my love, in which there is no flattery nor deceit, error nor art. But soft, here cometh Tellus, I must turn my other face to her like Janus, lest she be as suspicious as Juno.

Enter TELLUS.

Tellus. Yonder I espy Endimion. I will seem to suspect nothing, but soothe him, that seeing I cannot obtain the depth of his love, I may learn the height of his dissembling; Floscula and Dipsas, withdraw yourselves out of our sight, yet be within the hearing of our saluting. How now, Endimion, always solitary? no company but your own thoughts? no friend but melancholy fancies?

End. You know (fair Tellus) that the sweet remembrance of your love is the only companion of my life, and thy presence my paradise: so that I am not alone when nobody is with me, and in heaven itself when thou art with me.

Tellus. Then you love me, Endimion.

End. Or else I live not, Tellus.

Tellus. Is it not possible for you, Endimion, to dissemble?

End. Not, Tellus, unless I could make me a woman.

Tellus. Why, is dissembling joined to their sex inseparable? as heat to fire, heaviness to earth, moisture to water, thinness to air?

End. No, but found in their sex, as common as spots upon doves, moles upon faces, caterpillars upon sweet apples, cobwebs upon fair windows.

Tellus. Do they all dissemble?

End. All but one.

Tellus. Who is that?

End. I dare not tell. For if I should say you, then would you imagine my flattery to be extreme; if another, then would you think my love to be but indifferent.

Tellus. You will be sure I shall take no vantage of your words. But in sooth, Endimion, without more ceremonies, is it not Cynthia?

End. You know, Tellus, that of the gods we are forbidden to dispute, because their deities come not within the compass of our reasons; and of Cynthia we are allowed not to talk but to wonder, because her virtues are not within the reach of our capacities.

Tellus. Why, she is but a woman.

End. No more was Venus.

Tellus. She is but a virgin.

End. No more was Vesta.

Tellus. She shall have an end.

End. So shall the world.

Tellus. Is not her beauty subject to time?

End. No more than time is to standing still.

Tellus. Wilt thou make her immortal?

End. No, but incomparable.

Tellus. Take heed, Endimion, lest like the wrestler, in Olympia, that striving to lift an impossible weight caught an incurable strain, thou, by fixing thy thoughts above thy reach, fall into a disease without all recure? But I see thou art now in love with Cynthia.

End. No, Tellus; thou knowest that the stately cedar, whose top reacheth unto the clouds, never boweth his head to the shrubs that grow in the valley; nor ivy, that climbeth up by the elm, can ever get hold of the beams of the sun; Cynthia I honour in all humility, whom none ought, or dare adventure to love; whose affections are immortal, and virtues infinite. Suffer me therefore to gaze on the Moon, at whom, were it not for thyself, I would die with wondering. [*Exeunt.*

SCENE II

DARES. SAMIAS. SCINTILLA. FAVILLA.

Dar. Come, Samias, diddest thou ever hear such a sighing, the one for Cynthia, the other for Semele, and both for moonshine in the water?

Sam. Let them sigh, and let us sing; how say you, gentlewomen, are not our masters too far in love?

Scint. Their tongues happily are dipped to the root in amorous words and sweet discourses, but I think their hearts are scarce tipped on the side with constant desires.

Dar. How say you, Favilla, is not love a lurcher, that taketh men's stomachs away that they cannot eat; their spleen that they cannot laugh; their hearts that they cannot fight; their eyes that they cannot sleep; and leaveth nothing but livers to make nothing but lovers?

Favil. Away, peevish boy, a rod were better under thy girdle, than love in thy mouth: it will be a forward cock that croweth in the shell.

Dar. Alas! good old gentlewoman, how it becometh you to be grave.

Scint. Favilla though she be but a spark, yet is she fire.

Favil. And you, Scintilla, be not much more than a spark, though you would be esteemed a flame.

Sam. It were good sport to see the fight between two sparks.

Dar. Let them to it, and we will warm us by their words.

Scint. You are not angry, Favilla?

Favil. That is, Scintilla, as you list to take it.

Sam. That, that.

Scint. This it is to be matched with girls, who coming but yesterday from making of babies, would before to-morrow be accounted matrons.

Favil. I cry your matronship mercy; because your pantables be higher with cork, therefore your feet must needs be higher in the insteps: you will be mine elder, because you stand upon a stool, and I on the floor.

Sam. Good, good.

Dar. Let them love, and see with what countenance they will become friends.

Scint. Nay, you think to be the wiser, because you mean to have the last word.

Sam. Step between them lest they scratch. In faith, gentlewomen, seeing we came out to be merry, let not your jarring
mar our jests: be friends, how say you?

Scint. I am not angry, but it spited me to see how short she was.

Favil. I meant nothing, till she would needs cross me.

Dar. Then so let it rest.

Scint. I am agreed.

Favil. And I, yet I never took anything so unkindly in my life.

Scint. 'Tis I have the cause, that never offered the occasion.

Dar. Excellent and right like a woman.

Sam. A strange sight to see water come out of fire.

Dar. It is their property, to carry in their eyes fire and water,
tears and torches, and in their mouths, honey and gall.

Scint. You will be a good one if you live; but what is yonder
formal fellow?

Enter Sir Tophas.

Dar. Sir Tophas, Sir Tophas, of whom we told you: if you be
good wenches make as though you love him, and wonder
at him.

Favil. We will do our parts.

Dar. But first let us stand aside, and let him use his garb, for
all consisteth in his gracing.

Top. Epi.

Epi. At hand, sir.

Top. How likest thou this martial life, where nothing but blood
besprinkleth our bosoms? Let me see, be our enemies fat?

Epi. Passing fat: and I would not change this life to be a lord;
and yourself passeth all comparison, for other captains kill
and beat, and there is nothing you kill, but you also eat.

Top. I will draw out their guts out of their bellies, and tear the
flesh with my teeth, so mortal is my hate, and so eager my
unstanched stomach.

Epi. My master thinks himself the valiantest man in the world
if he kill a wren: so warlike a thing he accounteth to take
away life, though it be from a lark.

Top. Epi, I find my thoughts to swell, and my spirit to take
wings, in so much that I cannot continue within the compass of so slender combats.

Favil. This passeth!

Scint. Why, is he not mad?

Sam. No, but a little vainglorious.

Top. Epi.

Epi. Sir.

Top. I will encounter that black and cruel enemy that beareth rough and untewed locks upon his body, whose sire throweth down the strongest walls, whose legs are as many as both ours, on whose head are placed most horrible horns by nature, as a defence from all harm.

Epi. What mean you, master, to be so desperate?

Top. Honour inciteth me, and very hunger compelleth me.

Epi. What is that monster?

Top. The monster Ovis. I have said,—let thy wits work.

Epi. I cannot imagine it; yet let me see,—a black enemy with rough locks? it may be a sheep, and Ovis is a sheep; his sire so strong, a ram is a sheep's sire, that being also an engine of war; horns he hath, and four legs,—so hath a sheep: without doubt this monster is a black sheep. Is it not a sheep that you mean?

Top. Thou hast hit it, that monster will I kill and sup with.

Sam. Come, let us take him off. Sir Tophas, all hail.

Top. Welcome, children. I seldom cast mine eyes so low as to the crowns of your heads, and therefore pardon me that I spake not all this while.

Dar. No harm done; here be fair ladies come to wonder at your person, your valour, your wit, the report whereof hath made them careless of their own honours, to glut their eyes and hearts upon yours.

Top. Report cannot but injure me, for that not knowing fully what I am, I fear she hath been a niggard in her praises.

Scint. No, gentle knight, Report hath been prodigal; for she hath left you no equal, nor herself credit, so much hath she told, yet no more than we now see.

Dar. A good wench.

Favil. If there remain as much pity toward women, as there is in you courage against your enemies, then shall we be happy, who hearing of your person, came to see it, and seeing it, are now in love with it.

Top. Love me, ladies? I easily believe it, but my tough heart receiveth no impression with sweet words. Mars may pierce it, Venus shall not paint on it.

Favil. A cruel saying.

Sam. There's a girl.

Dar. Will you cast these ladies away, and all for a little love?
do but speak kindly.

Top. There cometh no soft syllable within my lips, custom hath
made my words bloody, and my heart barbarous: that
pelting word love, how waterish it is in my mouth, it
carrieth no sound; hate, horror, death, are speeches that
nourish my spirits. I like honey but I care not for the
bees, I delight in music but I love not to play on the bag-
pipes, I can vouchsafe to hear the voice of women, but to
touch their bodies I disdain it, as a thing childish, and fit
for such men as can digest nothing but milk.

Scint. A hard heart! shall we die for your love, and find no
remedy.

Top. I have already taken a surfeit.

Epi. Good master, pity them.

Top. Pity them, Epi? no, I do not think that this breast shall
be pestered with such a foolish passion. What is that the
gentlewoman carrieth in a chain?

Epi. Why it is a squirrel.

Top. A squirrel? O Gods, what things are made for money!

Dar. Is not this gentleman otherwise?

Favil. I could stay all day with him, if I feared not to be shent.

Scint. Is it not possible to meet again?

Dar. Yes, at any time.

Favil. Then let us hasten home.

Scint. Sir Tophas, the God of war deal better with you than
you do with the God of love.

Favil. Our love we may dissemble, digest we cannot; but I
doubt not but time will hamper you, and help us.

Top. I defy time, who hath no interest in my heart: come, Epi,
let me to the battle with that hideous beast; love is pap
and hath no relish in my taste, because it is not terrible.

Dar. Indeed a black sheep is a perilous beast, but let us in till
another time.

Favil. I shall long for that time.　　　　　　　　　*[Exeunt.*

SCENE III

ENDIMION. DIPSAS. BAGOA.

End. No rest, Endimion? still uncertain how to settle thy steps
by day, or thy thoughts by night? thy truth is measured

by thy fortune, and thou art judged unfaithful because thou art unhappy. I will see if I can beguile myself with sleep, and if no slumber will take hold in my eyes, yet will I embrace the golden thoughts in my head, and wish to melt by musing: that as ebony, which no fire can scorch, is yet consumed with sweet savours; so my heart, which cannot be bent by the hardness of fortune, may be bruised by amorous desires. On yonder bank never grew anything but lunary, and hereafter I will never have any bed but that bank. O Endimion, Tellus was fair, but what availeth beauty without wisdom? Nay, Endimion, she was wise, but what availeth wisdom without honour? She was honourable, Endimion, belie her not, ay but how obscure is honour without fortune? Was she not fortunate whom so many followed? Yes, yes, but base is fortune without majesty: thy majesty, Cynthia, all the world knoweth and wondereth at, but not one in the world that can imitate it, or comprehend it. No more, Endimion, sleep or die; nay die, for to sleep it is impossible, and yet I know not how it cometh to pass, I feel such a heaviness both in mine eyes and heart that I am suddenly benumbed, yea, in every joint; it may be weariness, for when did I rest? it may be deep melancholy, for when did I not sigh? Cynthia, ay so, I say Cynthia.   [*He falls asleep.*

Dipsas. Little dost thou know, Endimion, when thou shalt wake, for hadst thou placed thy heart as low in love as thy head lieth now in sleep, thou mightest have commanded Tellus whom now instead of a mistress, thou shalt find a tomb. These eyes must I seal up by art, not nature, which are to be opened neither by art nor nature. Thou that layest down with golden locks, shalt not awake until they be turned to silver hairs: and that chin, on which scarcely appeareth soft down, shall be filled with bristles as hard as broom: thou shalt sleep out thy youth and flowering time, and become dry hay before thou knewest thyself green grass; and ready by age to step into the grave when thou wakest, that was youthful in the court when thou laidst thee down to sleep. The malice of Tellus hath brought this to pass, which if she could not have entreated of me by fair means, she would have commanded by menacing, for from her gather we all our simples to maintain our sorceries. Fan with this hemlock over his face, and sing

the enchantment for sleep, whilst I go in and finish those
ceremonies that are required in our art: take heed ye touch
not his face, for the fan is so seasoned that who so it
toucheth with a leaf shall presently die, and over whom the
wind of it breatheth, he shall sleep for ever.   [*Exit.*

Bagoa. Let me alone, I will be careful. What hap hadst thou,
Endimion, to come under the hands of Dipsas. O fair
Endimion! how it grieveth me that that fair face must be
turned to a withered skin, and taste the pains of death
before it feel the reward of love. I fear Tellus will repent
that which the heavens themselves seemed to rue; but I
hear Dipsas coming, I dare not repine, lest she make me
pine, and rock me into such a deep sleep, that I shall not
awake to my marriage.

Enter Dipsas.

Dipsas. How now, have you finished?
Bagoa. Yea.
Dipsas. Well then, let us in, and see that you do not so much as
whisper that I did this, for if you do, I will turn thy hairs
to adders, and all thy teeth in thy head to tongues; come
away, come away.   [*Exeunt.*

A Dumb Show.

Music sounds.

Three ladies enter; one with a knife and a looking-glass, who
by the procurement of one of the other two, offers to stab
Endimion as he sleeps, but the third wrings her hands,
lamenteth, offering still to prevent it, but dares not.
At last, the first lady looking in the glass, casts down the knife.
          [*Exeunt.*

Enters an ancient Man *with books with three leaves, offers
the same twice.*

Endimion refuseth, he readeth two and offers the third, where
he stands awhile, and then Endimion offers to take it.
          [*Exit.*

ACT III

SCENE I

CYNTHIA. Three Lords. TELLUS.

Cynth. Is the report true, that Endimion is stricken into such
a dead sleep, that nothing can either wake him or move him?

Eum. Too true, madam, and as much to be pitied as wondered at.

Tellus. As good sleep and do no harm, as wake and do no good.

Cynth. What maketh you, Tellus, to be so short; the time was
Endimion only was.

Eum. It is an old saying, madam, that a waking dog doth afar
off bark at a sleeping lion.

Sem. It were good, Eumenides, that you took a nap with your
friend, for your speech beginneth to be heavy.

Eum. Contrary to your nature, Semele, which hath been always
accounted light.

Cynth. What have we here before my face, these unseemly and
malapert overthwarts? I will take your tongues, and your
thoughts, and make your speeches answerable to your duties
and your conceits fit for my dignity, else will I banish you
both my person and the world.

Eum. Pardon I humbly ask: but such is my unspotted faith to
Endimion, that whatsoever seemeth a needle to prick his
finger, is a dagger to wound my heart.

Cynth. If you be so dear to him, how happeneth it you neither
go to see him, nor search for remedy for him?

Eum. I have seen him to my grief, and sought recure with
despair, for that I cannot imagine who should restore him
that is the wonder to all men: your highness, on whose hands
the compass of the earth is at command (though not in
possession) may show yourself both worthy your sex, your
nature, and your favour, if you redeem that honourable
Endimion, whose ripe years foretell rare virtues, and those
unmellowed conceits promise ripe counsel.

Cynth. I have had trial of Endimion, and conceive greater
assurance of his age, than I could hope of his youth.

Tellus. But timely, madam, crooks that tree that will be a cammock; and young it pricks that will be a thorn: and therefore he that began without care to settle his life, it is a sign without amendment he will end it.

Cynth. Presumptuous girl, I will make thy tongue an example of unrecoverable displeasure; Corsites, carry her to the castle in the desert, there to remain and weave.

Cors. Shall she work stories or poetries?

Cynth. It skilleth not which, go to, in both, for she shall find examples infinite in either what punishment long tongues have. Eumenides, if either the soothsayers in Egypt, or the enchanters in Thessaly, or the philosophers in Greece, or all the sages of the world, can find remedy, I will procure it; therefore dispatch with all speed: you, Eumenides, into Thessaly: You, Zontes, into Greece (because you are acquainted in Athens). You, Pantalion, to Egypt, saying that Cynthia sendeth, and if you will, commandeth.

Eum. On bowed knee I give thanks, and with wings on my legs I fly for remedy.

Zon. We are ready at your highness' command, and hope to return to your full content.

Cynth. It shall never be said that Cynthia, whose mercy and goodness filleth the heavens with joys, and the world with marvel, will suffer either Endimion or any to perish, if he may be protected.

Eum. Your majesty's words have been always deeds, and your deeds virtues.   [*Exeunt.*

SCENE II

Corsites. Tellus.

Cors. Here is the castle (fair Tellus) in which you must weave, till either time end your days, or Cynthia her displeasure. I am sorry so fair a face should be subject to so hard a fortune, and that the flower of beauty, which is honoured in courts, should here wither in prison.

Tellus. Corsites, Cynthia may restrain the liberty of my body, of my thoughts she cannot, and therefore do I esteem myself most free, though I am in greatest bondage.

Cors. Can you then feed on fancy, and subdue the malice of envy by the sweetness of imagination.

Tellus. Corsites, there is no sweeter music to the miserable than despair; and therefore the more bitterness I feel, the more sweetness I find; for so vain were liberty, and so unwelcome the following of higher fortune, that I choose rather to pine in this castle than to be a prince in any other court.

Cors. A humour contrary to your years, and nothing agreeable to your sex: the one commonly allured with delights, the other always with sovereignty.

Tellus. I marvel, Corsites, that you being a captain, who should sound nothing but terror, and suck nothing but blood, can find in your heart to talk such smooth words, for that it agreeth not with your calling to use words so soft, as that of love.

Cors. Lady, it were unfit of wars to discourse with women, into whose minds nothing can sink but smoothness; besides, you must not think that soldiers be so rough hewn, or of such knotty mettle, that beauty cannot allure, and you being beyond perfection enchant.

Tellus. Good Corsites, talk not of love, but let me to my labour: the little beauty I have shall be bestowed on my loom, which I now mean to make my lover.

Cors. Let us in, and what favour Corsites can show, Tellus shall command.

Tellus. The only favour I desire is now and then to walk.

[*Exeunt.*

SCENE III

Sir Tophas *and* Epi.

Top. Epi.

Epi. Here sir.

Top. Unrig me. Hey ho!

Epi. What's that?

Top. An interjection, whereof some are of mourning: as *eho, vah.*

Epi. I understand you not.

Top. Thou seest me?

Epi. Ay.

Top. Thou hearest me?

Epi. Ay.

Top. Thou feelst me?

Epi. Ay.

Top. And not understandest me?

Epi. No.

Top. Then am I but three-quarters of a noun substantive. But alas, Epi, to tell thee the truth, I am a noun adjective.

Epi. Why?

Top. Because I cannot stand without another.

Epi. Who is that?

Top. Dipsa.

Epi. Are you in love?

Top. No: but love hath as it were milked my thoughts, and drained from my heart the very substance of my accustomed courage; it worketh in my head like new wine, so as I must hoop my sconce with iron, lest my head break, and so I bewray my brain: but I pray thee first discover me in all parts, that I may be like a lover, and then will I sigh and die. Take my gun, and give me a gown: *Cædant arma togæ.*

Epi. Here.

Top. Take my sword and shield, and give me beard, brush, and scissors: *bella gerant alii, tu pari emper ama.*

Epi. Will you be trimmed, sir?

Top. Not yet: for I feel a contention within me, whether I shall frame the bodkin beard or the bush. But take my pike and give me pen: *dicere quæ puduit, scribere jussit amor.*

Epi. I will furnish you, sir.

Top. Now for my bow and bolts, give me ink and paper; for my scimitar a pen-knife: for *Scalpellum, calami, atramentum, charta, libelli, sint semper studiis arma parata meis.*

Epi. Sir, will you give over wars, and play with that bauble called love?

Top. Give over wars? No, Epi, *Militat omnis amans, et habet sua castra Cupido.*

Epi. Love hath made you very eloquent, but your face is nothing fair.

Top. *Non formosus erat, sederat facundus Ulisses.*

Epi. Nay, I must seek a new master if you can speak nothing but verses.

Top. *Quicquid conabar dicere versus erat.* Epi, I feel all *Ovid de arte amandi* lie as heavy at my heart as a load of logs. O what a fine thin hair hath Dipsas! What a pretty low forehead! What a tall and stately nose! What little hollow eyes! What great and goodly lips! How harmless she is being toothless! her fingers fat and short, adorned with long nails like a bittern! In how sweet a proportion her cheeks hang down to her breasts like dugs, and her paps to her

waist like bags! What a low stature she is, and yet what a
great foot she carrieth! How thrifty must she be in whom
there is no waist! How virtuous is she like to be, over
whom no man can be jealous!

Epi. Stay, master, you forget yourself.

Top. O Epi, even as a dish melteth by the fire so doth my wit
increase by love.

Epi. Pithily, and to the purpose, but what? begin you to nod?

Top. Good Epi, let me take a nap: for as some man may better
steal a horse, than another look over the hedge: so divers
shall be sleepy when they would fainest take rest. [*He sleeps.*

Epi. Who ever saw such a woodcock, love Dipsas! without
doubt all the world will now account him valiant, that
ventureth on her, whom none durst undertake. But here
cometh two wags.

Enter DARES *and* SAMIAS.

Sam. Thy master hath slept his share.

Dar. I think he doth it because he would not pay me my board
wages.

Sam. It is a thing most strange, and I think mine will never
return, so that we must both seek new masters, for we shall
never live by our manners.

Epi. If you want masters, join with me, and serve Sir Tophas,
who must needs keep more men, because he is toward
marriage.

Sam. What, Epi, where's thy master?

Epi. Yonder sleeping in love.

Dar. Is it possible?

Epi. He hath taken his thoughts a hole lower, and saith, seeing
it is the fashion of the world, he will vail bonnet to beauty.

Sam. How is he attired?

Epi. Lovely.

Dar. Whom loveth this amorous knight?

Epi. Dipsas.

Sam. That ugly creature? Why she is a fool, a scold, fat,
without fashion, and quite without favour.

Epi. Tush, you be simple, my master hath a good marriage.

Dar. Good? as how?

Epi. Why, in marrying Dipsas, he shall have every day twelve dishes of meat to his dinner, though there be none but Dipsas with him. Four of flesh, four of fish, four of fruit.

Sam. As how Epi?

Epi. For flesh these; woodcock, goose, bittern, and rail.

Dar. Indeed he shall not miss, if Dipsas be there.

Epi. For fish these; crab, carp, lump, and pouting.

Sam. Excellent, for of my word she is both crabbish, lumpish, and carping.

Epi. For fruit these; fritters, meddlers, artichokes, and lady longings. Thus you see he shall fare like a king, though he be but a beggar.

Dar. Well, Epi, dine thou with him, for I had rather fast than see her face. But see, thy master is asleep, let us have a song to wake this amorous knight.

Epi. Agreed.

Sam. Content.

THE FIRST SONG.

Epi. Here snores Tophas,
 That amorous ass,
 Who loves Dipsas,
 With face so sweet,
 Nose and chin meet.
All three { At sight of her each fury skips
      And flings into her lap their whips.
Dar. Holla, holla in his ear.
Sam. The witch sure thrust her fingers there.
Epi. Cramp him, or wring the fool by th' nose.
Dar. Or clap some burning flax to his toes.
Sam. What music's best to wake him?
Epi. Baw wow, let bandogs shake him.
Dar. Let adders hiss in's ear.
Sam. Else earwigs wriggle there.
Epi. No, let him batten, when his tongue
 Once goes, a cat is not worse strung.
All three { But if he ope nor mouth, nor eyes,
      He may in time sleep himself wise.

Top. Sleep is a binding of the senses, love a loosing.

Epi. Let us hear him awhile.

Top. There appeared in my sleep a goodly owl, who sitting upon my shoulder, cried twit, twit, and before mine eyes presented herself the express image of Dipsas. I marvelled what the owl said, till at the last, I perceived twit, twit, to it, to it: only by contraction admonished by this vision, to make account of my sweet Venus.

Sam. Sir Tophas, you have over-slept yourself.

Top. No, youth, I have but slept over my love.

Dar. Love? Why it is impossible that into so noble and un-
conquered a courage love should creep, having first a head
as hard to pierce as steel, then to pass to a heart armed with
a shirt of mail.

Epi. Ay, but my master yawning one day in the sun, Love crept
into his mouth before he could close it, and there kept such
a tumbling in his body that he was glad to untruss the points
of his heart, and entertain Love as a stranger.

Top. If there remain any pity in you, plead for me to Dipsas.

Dar. Plead? Nay, we will press her to it. Let us go with him
to Dipsas, and there shall we have good sport. But, Sir
Tophas, when shall we go? for I find my tongue voluble,
and my heart venturous, and all myself like myself.

Sam. Come, Dares, let us not loose him till we find our masters,
for as long as he liveth, we shall lack neither mirth nor meat.

Epi. We will traverse. Will you go, sir?

Top. *I præ, sequar.* [*Exeunt.*

SCENE IV

EUMENIDES. GERON.

Eum. Father, your sad music being tuned on the same key that
my hard fortune is, hath so melted my mind, that I wish to
hang at your mouth's end till life end.

Ger. These tunes, gentleman, have I been accustomed with these
fifty winters, having no other house to shroud myself but
the broad heavens, and so familiar with me hath use made
misery, that I esteem sorrow my chiefest solace. And
welcomest is that guest to me, that can rehearse the saddest
tale, or the bloodiest tragedy.

Eum. A strange humour, might I inquire the cause?

Ger. You must pardon me if I deny to tell it, for knowing that the
revealing of griefs is as it were a renewing of sorrow, I have
vowed therefore to conceal them, that I might not only feel
the depth of everlasting discontentment, but despair of
remedy. But whence are you? What fortune hath thrust
you to this distress?

Eum. I am going to Thessaly, to seek remedy for Endimion my
dearest friend, who hath been cast into a dead sleep, almost
these twenty years, waxing old, am ready for the grave,
being almost but newly come forth of the cradle.

Ger. You need not for recure travel far, for who so can clearly see the bottom of this fountain shall have remedy for anything.

Eum. That me thinketh is impossible; why, what virtue can there be in water?

Ger. Yes, whosoever can shed the tears of a faithful lover shall obtain anything he would; read these words engraven about the brim.

Eum. Have you known this by experience, or is it placed here of purpose to delude men?

Ger. I only would have experience of it, and then should there be an end of my misery. And then would I tell the strangest discourse that ever yet was heard.

Eum. Ah, Eumenides!

Ger. What lack you, gentleman, are you not well?

Eum. Yes, father, but a qualm that often cometh over my heart doth now take hold of me; but did never any lovers come hither?

Ger. Lusters, but not lovers; for often have I seen them weep, but never could I hear they saw the bottom.

Eum. Came there women also?

Ger. Some.

Eum. What did they see?

Ger. They all wept that the fountain overflowed with tears, but so thick became the water with their tears, that I could scarce discern the brim, much less behold the bottom.

Eum. Be faithful lovers so scant?

Ger. It seemeth so, for yet heard I never of any.

Eum. Ah, Eumenides, how art thou perplexed? call to mind the beauty of thy sweet mistress, and the depth of thy never dying affections: how oft hast thou honoured her, not only without spot, but suspicion of falsehood? And how hardly hath she rewarded thee, without cause or colour of despite. How secret hast thou been these seven years, that hast not, nor once darest not to name her, for discontenting her. How faithful! that hath offered to die for her, to please her. Unhappy Eumenides!

Ger. Why, gentleman, did you once love?

Eum. Once? Ay, father, and ever shall.

Ger. Was she unkind, and you faithful?

Eum. She of all women the most froward, and I of all creatures the most fond.

Ger. You doted then, not loved: for affection is grounded on
virtue, and virtue is never peevish: or on beauty, and
beauty loveth to be praised.

Eum. Ay, but if all virtuous ladies should yield to all that be
loving, or all amiable gentlewomen entertain all that be
amorous, their virtues would be accounted vices, and
beauties deformities; for that love can be but between
two, and that not proceeding of him that is most faithful,
but most fortunate.

Ger. I would you were so faithful, that your tears might make
you fortunate.

Eum. Yea, father, if that my tears clear not this fountain, then
may you swear it is but a mere mockery.

Ger. So saith every one yet, that wept.

Eum. Ah, I faint, I die! Ah, sweet Semele, let me alone, and
dissolve by weeping into water.

Ger. This affection seemeth strange, if he see nothing, without
doubt this dissembling passeth, for nothing shall draw me
from the belief.

Eum. Father, I plainly see the bottom, and there in white
marble engraven these words, *Ask one for all, and but one
thing at all.*

Ger. O fortunate Eumenides (for so have I heard thee call thyself), let me see. I cannot discern any such thing. I
think thou dreamest.

Eum. Ah, father, thou art not a faithful lover, and therefore
canst not behold it.

Ger. Then ask, that I may be satisfied by the event, and thyself
blessed.

Eum. Ask? so I will: and what shall I do but ask, and whom
should I ask but Semele, the possessing of whose person is a
pleasure that cannot come within the compass of comparison;
whose golden locks seem most curious, when they seem most
careless; whose sweet looks seem most alluring, when they are
most chaste; and whose words the more virtuous they are,
the more amorous they be accounted. I pray thee, fortune,
when I shall first meet with fair Semele, dash my delight
with some light disgrace, lest embracing sweetness beyond
measure, I take a surfeit without recure: let her practise
her accustomed coyness, that I may diet myself upon my
desires: otherwise the fullness of my joys will diminish the
sweetness, and I shall perish by them before I possess them.

Why do I trifle the time in words? The least minute being spent in the getting of Semele is more worth than the whole world: therefore let me ask, What now, Eumenides? Whither art thou drawn? Hast thou forgotten both friendship and duty? Care of Endimion, and the commandment of Cynthia? Shall he die in a leaden sleep, because thou sleepest in a golden dream? Ay, let him sleep ever, so I slumber but one minute with Semele. Love knoweth neither friendship nor kindred. Shall I not hazard the loss of a friend, for the obtaining of her for whom I would often lose myself? Fond Eumenides, shall the enticing beauty of a most disdainful lady be of more force than the rare fidelity of a tried friend? The love of men to women is a thing common, and of course: the friendship of man to man infinite and immortal. Tush, Semele doth possess my love. Ay, but Endimion hath deserved it. I will help Endimion. I found Endimion unspotted in his truth. Ay, but I shall find Semele constant in her love. I will have Semele. What shall I do? Father, thy grey hairs are ambassadors of experience. Which shall I ask?

Ger. Eumenides, release Endimion, for all things (friendship excepted) are subject to fortune: love is but an eye-worm, which only tickleth the head with hopes, and wishes: friendship the image of eternity, in which there is nothing movable, nothing mischievous. As much difference as there is between beauty and virtue, bodies and shadows, colours and life—so great odds is there between love and friendship. Love is a cameleon, which draweth nothing into the mouth but air, and nourisheth nothing in the body but lungs: believe me, Eumenides, desire dies in the same moment that beauty sickens, and beauty fadeth in the same instant that it flourisheth. When adversities flow, then love ebbs: but friendship standeth stiffly in storms. Time draweth wrinkles in a fair face, but addeth fresh colours to a fast friend, which neither heat, nor cold, nor misery, nor place, nor destiny, can alter or diminish. O friendship! of all things the most rare, and therefore most rare because most excellent, whose comfort in misery is always sweet, and whose counsels in prosperity are ever fortunate. Vain love, that only coming near to friendship in name, would seem to be the same, or better, in nature.

Eum. Father, I allow your reasons, and will therefore conquer mine own. Virtue shall subdue affections, wisdom lust, friendship beauty. Mistresses are in every place, and as common as hares in Atho, bees in Hybla, fowls in the air: but friends to be found are like the Phœnix in Arabia, but one, or the Philadelphi in Arays, never above two. I will have Endimion: sacred fountain, in whose bowels are hidden divine secrets, I have increased your waters with the tears of unspotted thoughts and therefore let me receive the reward you promise: Endimion, the truest friend to me, and faithfullest lover to Cynthia, is in such a dead sleep that nothing can wake or move him.

Ger. Dost thou see anything?

Eum. I see in the same pillar these words: *When she whose figure of all is the perfectest, and never to be measured: always one, yet never the same: still inconstant, yet never wavering: shall come and kiss Endimion in his sleep, he shall then rise, else never.* This is strange.

Ger. What see you else?

Eum. There cometh over mine eyes either a dark mist, or upon the fountain a deep thickness: for I can perceive nothing. But how am I deluded? or what difficult, nay, impossible thing is this?

Ger. Methinketh it easy.

Eum. Good father, and how?

Ger. Is not a circle of all figures the perfectest?

Eum. Yes.

Ger. And is not Cynthia of all circles the most absolute?

Eum. Yes.

Ger. Is it not impossible to measure her, who still worketh by her influence, never standing at one stay?

Eum. Yes.

Ger. Is she not always Cynthia, yet seldom in the same bigness; always wavering in her waxing or waning, that our bodies might the better be governed, our seasons the daylier give their increase; yet never to be removed from her course as long as the heavens continue theirs?

Eum. Yes.

Ger. Then who can it be but Cynthia, whose virtues being all divine, must needs bring things to pass that be miraculous? Go, humble thyself to Cynthia, tell her the success of which myself shall be a witness. And this assure thyself, that she that sent to find means for his safety will now work her cunning.

Eum. How fortunate am I if Cynthia be she that may do it.

Ger. How silly art thou if thou do not believe it?

Eum. I will hasten thither that I may intreat on my knees for succour, and embrace in mine arms my friend.

Ger. I will go with thee, for unto Cynthia must I discover all my sorrows, who also must work in me a contentment.

Eum. May I now know the cause?

Ger. That shall be as we walk, and I doubt not but the strangeness of my tale will take away the tediousness of our journey.

Eum. Let us go.

Ger. I follow. [*Exeunt.*

ACT IV

SCENE I

Tellus. Corsites.

Tellus. I marvel Corsites giveth me so much liberty: all the
world knowing his charge to be so high, and his nature to
be most strange; who hath so ill intreated ladies of great
honour that he hath not suffered them to look out of
windows, much less to walk abroad: it may be he is in love
with me, for (Endimion, hard-hearted Endimion, excepted)
what is he that is not enamoured of my beauty? But
what respectest thou the love of all the world? Endimion
hates thee. Alas, poor Endimion, my malice hath exceeded
my love: and thy faith to Cynthia quenched my affections. Quenched, Tellus? nay kindled them afresh; insomuch that I find scorching flames for dead embers, and
cruel encounters of war in my thoughts, instead of sweet
parleys. Ah, that I might once again see Endimion:
accursed girl, what hope hast thou to see Endimion: on
whose head already are grown grey hairs, and whose life
must yield to nature, before Cynthia end her displeasure.
Wicked Dipsas, and more devilish Tellus, the one for
cunning too exquisite, the other for hate too intolerable. Thou wast commanded to weave the stories and
poetries wherein were showed both examples and punish-
ments of tattling tongues, and thou hast only embroidered
the sweet face of Endimion, devices of love, melancholy
imaginations, and what not, out of thy work, that thou
shouldest study to pick out of thy mind. But here cometh
Corsites, I must seem yielding and stout, full of mildness,
yet tempered with a majesty: for if I be too flexible, I shall
give him more hope than I mean; if too forward, enjoy
less liberty than I would; love him I cannot, and therefore
will practise that which is most contrary to our sex to
dissemble.

Enter CORSITES.

Cor. Fair Tellus, I perceive you rise with the lark, and to your
self sing with the nightingale.

Tellus. My lord, I have no playfellow but fancy, being barred of
all company I must question with myself, and make my
thoughts my friends.

Cor. I would you would account my thoughts also your friends,
for they be such as are only busied in wondering at your
beauty and wisdom; and some such as have esteemed your
fortune too hard; and divers of that kind that offer to set
you free, if you will set them free.

Tellus. There are no colours so contrary as white and black, nor
elements so disagreeing as fire and water, nor anything so
opposite as men's thoughts and their words.

Cor. He that gave Cassandra the gift of prophecying, with the
curse that spake she never so true she should never be
believed, hath I think poisoned the fortune of men, that
uttering the extremities of their inward passions are always
suspected of outward perjuries.

Tellus. Well, Corsites, I will flatter myself and believe you.
What would you do to enjoy my love?

Cor. Set all the ladies of the castle free, and make you the
pleasure of my life: more I cannot do, less I will not.

Tellus. These be great words, and fit for your calling: for
captains must promise things impossible. But will you do
one thing for all.

Cor. Anything, sweet Tellus, that am ready for all.

Tellus. You know that on the lunary bank sleepeth Endimion.

Cor. I know it.

Tellus. If you will remove him from that place by force, and
convey him into some obscure cave by policy, I give you
here the faith of an unspotted virgin that you only shall
possess me as a lover, and in spite of malice, have me for a
wife.

Cor. Remove him, Tellus? Yes, Tellus, he shall be removed,
and that so soon, as thou shalt as much commend my
diligence as my force. I go.

Tellus. Stay, will yourself attempt it?

Cor. Ay, Tellus: as I would have none partaker of my sweet love,
so shall none be partners of my labours: but I pray thee go

at your best leisure, for Cynthia beginneth to rise, and if she discover our love we both perish, for nothing pleaseth her but the fairness of virginity. All things must be not only without lust, but without suspicion of lightness.

Tellus. I will depart, and go you to Endimion.

Cor. I fly, Tellus, being of all men the most fortunate. [*Exit.*

Tellus. Simple Corsites, I have set thee about a task being but a man, the gods themselves cannot perform: for little dost thou know how heavy his head lies, how hard his fortune: but such shifts must women have to deceive men, and under colour of things easy, entreat that which is impossible: otherwise we should be cumbered with importunities, oaths, sighs, letters, and all implements of love, which to one resolved to the contrary, are most loathsome. I will in, and laugh with the other ladies at Corsites' sweating. [*Exit.*

SCENE II

SAMIAS. DARES. EPITON.

Sam. Will thy master never awake?

Dar. No, I think he sleeps for a wager: but how shall we spend the time? Sir Tophas is so far in love that he pineth in his bed, and cometh not abroad?

Sam. But here cometh Epi, in a pelting chafe.

Epi. A pox of all false proverbs, and were a proverb a page, I would have him by the ears.

Sam. Why art thou angry?

Epi. Why? you know it is said, the tide tarrieth no man.

Sam. True.

Epi. A monstrous lie; for I was tied two hours, and tarried for one to unloose me.

Dar. Alas, poor Epi.

Epi. Poor? No, no, you base, conceited slaves, I am a most complete gentleman, although I be in disgrace with Sir Tophas.

Dar. Art thou out with him?

Epi. Ay, because I cannot get him a lodging with Endimion; he would fain take a nap for forty or fifty years.

Dar. A short sleep, considering our long life.

Sam. Is he still in love?

Epi. In love? why he doth nothing but make sonnets.

Sam. Canst thou remember any one of his poems?

Epi. Ay, this is one.

> The beggar Love that knows not where to lodge:
> At last within my heart when I slept,
> He crept.
> I waked, and so my fancies began to fodge.

Sam. That's a very long verse.

Epi. Why, the other was short, the first is called from the thumb to the little finger, the second from the little finger to the elbow, and some he made to reach to the crown of his head, and down again to the sole of his foot: it is set to the tune of the black Saunce, *ratio est*, because Dipsas is a black saint.

Dar. Very wisely, but pray thee, Epi, how art thou complete, and being from thy master what occupation wilt thou take?

Epi. No, my harts, I am an absolute *Microcosmus*, a petty world of myself, my library is my head, for I have no other books but my brains: my wardrobe on my back, for I have no more apparel than is on my body; my armoury at my finger ends, for I use no other artillery than my nails; my treasure in my purse. *Sic omnia mea mecum porto.*

Dar. Good!

Epi. Now, sirs, my palace is paved with grass, and tiled with stars: for *cælo tegitur qui non habet urnam*, he that hath no house must lie in the yard.

Sam. A brave resolution. But how wilt thou spend thy time?

Epi. Not in any melancholy sort, for mine exercise I will walk horses, Dares.

Dar. Too bad.

Epi. Why, is it not said: It is good walking when one hath his horse in his hand?

Sam. Worse, and worse, but how wilt thou live?

Epi. By angling; O 'tis a stately occupation to stand four hours in a cold morning, and to have his nose bitten with frost before his bait be mumbled with a fish.

Dar. A rare attempt, but wilt thou never travel?

Epi. Yes, in a western barge, when with a good wind and lusty pugs one may go ten miles in two days.

Sam. Thou art excellent at thy choice, but what pastime wilt thou use, none?

Epi. Yes, the quickest of all.

Sam. What! dice?

Epi. No, when I am in haste, one and twenty games at chess to pass a few minutes.

Dar. A life for a little lord, and full of quickness.

Epi. Tush, let me alone! but I must needs see if I can find where Endimion lieth; and then go to a certain fountain hard by, where they say faithful lovers shall have all things they will ask. If I can find out any of these, *ego et magister meus erimus in tuto*, I and my master shall be friends. He is resolved to weep some three or four pailfuls to avoid the rheum of love that wambleth in his stomach.

Enter the WATCH.

Sam. Shall we never see thy master, Dares?

Dar. Yes, let us go now, for to-morrow Cynthia will be there.

Epi. I will go with you. But how shall we see for the Watch?

Sam. Tush, let me alone! I'll begin to them. Masters, God speed you.

1 *Watch.* Sir boy, we are all sped already.

Epi. So methinks, for they smell all of drink like a beggar's beard.

Dar. But I pray, sirs, may we see Endimion?

2 *Watch.* No, we are commanded in Cynthia's name that no man shall see him.

Sam. No man? Why, we are but boys.

1 *Watch.* Mass neighbours he says true, for if I swear I will never drink my liquor by the quart, and yet call for two pints, I think with a safe conscience I may carouse both.

Dar. Pithily, and to the purpose.

2 *Watch.* Tush, tush, neighbours, take me with you.

Sam. This will grow hot.

Dar. Let them alone.

2 *Watch.* If I say to my wife, Wife, I will have no raisins in my pudding, she puts in currants, small raisins are raisins, and boys are men. Even as my wife should have put no raisins in my pudding, so shall there no boys see Endimion.

Dar. Learnedly.

Epi. Let Master Constable speak: I think he is the wisest among you.

Mast. Const. You know, neighbours, 'tis an old said saw, *Children and fools speak true.*

All say. True.

Mast. Const. Well, there you see the men be the fools, because it is provided from the children.

Dar. Good.

Mast. Const. Then say I, neighbours, that children must not see Endimion, because children and fools speak true.

Epi. O wicked application!

Sam. Scurvily brought about!

1 *Watch.* Nay, he says true, and therefore till Cynthia have been here he shall not be uncovered.   Therefore away!

Dar. A watch quoth you? a man may watch seven years for a wise word, and yet go without it.   Their wits are all as rusty as their bills.   But come on, Master Constable, shall we have a song before we go?

Const. With all my heart.   [*Exeunt.*

THE SECOND SONG.

> *Watch.* Stand: Who goes there?
> We charge you appear
> Fore our Constable here.
> (In the name of the Man in the Moon)
> To us Billmen relate,
> Why you stagger so late,
> And how you come drunk so soon.
> *Pages.* What are ye, scabs?
> *Watch.* The Watch:
> This the Constable.
> *Pages.* A patch.
> *Const.* Knock 'em down unless they all stand.
> If any run away,
> 'Tis the old watchman's play,
> To reach him a bill of his hand.
> *Pages.* O gentlemen, hold,
> Your gowns freeze with cold,
> And your rotten teeth dance in your head;
> *Epi.* Wine, nothing shall cost ye.
> *Sam.* Nor huge fires to roast ye.
> *Dares.* Then soberly let us be led.
> *Const.* Come, my brown bills, we'll roar,
> Bounce loud at tavern door,
> *Omnes.* And i' th' morning steal all to bed.

SCENE III

CORSITES *solus.*

Cors. I am come in sight of the Lunary bank; without doubt Tellus doteth upon me, and cunningly that I might not perceive her love, she hath set me to a task that is done before it is begun.   Endimion, you must change your pillow, and if you be not weary of sleep I will carry you where at ease you shall sleep your fill. It were good that without more ceremonies I took him, lest being espied I be entrapped and so incur the displeasure of Cynthia, who commonly setteth watch that Endimion have no wrong. [*He tries to lift Endimion.*] What now, is your mastership so heavy? or are you nailed to the ground? Not stir one whit? then use all thy force though he feel it and wake. What stone still? turned I think to earth, with lying so long on the earth. Didst thou not, Corsites, before Cynthia pull up a tree, that forty years was fastened with roots and wreathed in knots to the ground? Didst not thou with main force pull open the iron gates, which no ram or engine could move? Have my weak thoughts made brawn-fallen my strong arms? or is it the nature of love or the quintessence of the mind to breed mumness, or lytherness, or I know not what languishing in my joints and sinews, being but the base strings of my body? Or doth the remembrance of Tellus so refine my spirits into a matter so subtle and divine, that the other fleshy parts cannot work whilst they muse? Rest thyself, rest thyself; nay, rend thyself in pieces, Corsites, and strive in spite of love, fortune, and nature, to lift up this dulled body, heavier than dead, and more senseless than death.

Enter Fairies.

But what are these so fair fiends that cause my hairs to stand upright, and spirits to fall down? Hags, out alas, Nymphs, I crave pardon. Aye me, but what do I hear.

[*The Fairies dance, and with a Song pinch him, and he falleth asleep, they kiss Endimion, and depart.*

THE THIRD SONG BY FAIRIES.

Omnes. Pinch him, pinch him, black and blue,
　　　Saucy mortals must not view
　　　What the Queen of Stars is doing,
　　　Nor pry into our fairy wooing.
1 *Fairy.* Pinch him blue.
2 *Fairy.* And pinch him black.
3 *Fairy.* Let him not lack
　　　Sharp nails to pinch him blue and red,
　　　Till sleep has rock'd his addle head.
4 *Fairy.* For the trespass he hath done,
　　　Spots o'er all his flesh shall run.
　　　Kiss Endimion, kiss his eyes,
　　　Then to our midnight heidegyes.　　　[*Exeunt.*

Cynthia. Floscula. Semele. Panelion. Zonte.
Pythagoras. Gyptes. Corsites.

Cynth. You see, Pythagoras, what ridiculous opinions you hold,
and I doubt not but you are now of another mind. .

Pyth. Madam, I plainly perceive that the perfection of your
brightness hath pierced through the thickness that covered
my mind; in so much that I am no less glad to be reformed
than ashamed to remember my grossness.

Gyptes. They are thrice fortunate that live in your palace, where
truth is not in colours, but life; virtues not in imagination,
but execution.

Cynth. I have always studied to have rather living virtues than
painted Gods; the body of truth, than the tomb. But let
us walk to Endimion; it may be it lieth in your arts to deliver
him: as for Eumenides, I fear he is dead.

Pyth. I have alleged all the natural reasons I can for such a
long sleep.

Gyptes. I can do nothing till I see him.

Cynth. Come, Floscula, I am sure you are glad that you shall
behold Endimion.

Flosc. I were blessed if I might have him recovered.

Cynth. Are you in love with his person?

Flosc. No, but with his virtue.

Cynth. What say you, Semele?

Sem. Madam, I dare say nothing for fear I offend.

Cynth. Belike you cannot speak except you be spiteful. But
as good be silent as saucy. Panelion, what punishment
were fit for Semele, in whose speech and thoughts is only
contempt and sourness?

Panel. I love not, madam, to give any judgment. Yet since
your highness commandeth, I think, to commit her tongue
close prisoner to her mouth.

Cynth. Agreed; Semele, if thou speak this twelvemonth thou
shalt forfeit thy tongue. Behold Endimion! alas, poor
gentleman, hast thou spent thy youth in sleep that once
vowed all to my service. Hollow eyes? grey hairs?
wrinkled cheeks? and decayed limbs? Is it destiny or
deceit that hath brought this to pass? If the first, who
could prevent thy wretched stars? If the latter, I would I
might know thy cruel enemy. I favoured thee, Endimion,

for thy honour, thy virtues, thy affections: but to bring thy thoughts within the compass of thy fortunes I have seemed strange, that I might have thee stayed, and now are thy days ended before my favour begin. But whom have we here, is it not Corsites?

Zon. It is, but more like a leopard than a man.

Cynth. Awake him. How now, Corsites, what make you here? How came you deformed? Look on thy hands, and then thou seest the picture of thy face.

Cors. Miserable wretch, and accursed. How am I deluded? Madame, I ask pardon for my offence, and you see my fortune deserveth pity.

Cynth. Speak on, thy offence cannot deserve greater punishment: but see thou rehearse the truth, else shalt thou not find me as thou wishest me.

Cors. Madam, as it is no offence to be in love being a man mortal, so I hope can it be no shame to tell with whom, my lady being heavenly. Your majesty committed to my charge the fair Tellus, whose beauty in the same moment took my heart captive that I undertook to carry her body prisoner. Since that time have I found such combats in my thoughts between love and duty, reverence and affection, that I could neither endure the conflict, nor hope for the conquest.

Cynth. In love? A thing far unfitting the name of a captain, and (as I thought) the tough and unsmoothed nature of Corsites. But forth.

Cors. Feeling this continual war, I thought rather by parley to yield, than by certain danger to perish. I unfolded to Tellus the depth of my affections, and framed my tongue to utter a sweet tale of love, that was wont to sound nothing but threats of war. She too fair to be true, and too false for one so fair, after a nice denial, practised a notable deceit; commanding me to remove Endimion from this cabin, and carry him to some dark cave; which I, seeking to accomplish, found impossible; and so by fairies or fiends have been thus handled.

Cynth. How say you, my lords, is not Tellus always practising of some deceits? In sooth, Corsites, thy face is now too foul for a lover, and thine heart too fond for a soldier. You may see when warriors become wantons how their manners alter with their faces. Is it not a shame, Corsites, that having lived so long in Mars his camp thou shouldst now be rocked in Venus' cradle. Dost thou wear Cupid's quiver at thy girdle, and make lances of looks? Well, Corsites, rouse thyself, and be as thou hast been, and let Tellus, who is made all of love, melt herself in her own looseness.

Cors. Madam, I doubt not but to recover my former state; for Tellus' beauty never wrought such love in my mind, as now her deceit hath despite; and yet to be revenged of a woman were a thing that love itself more womanish.

Gyptes. These spots, gentlemen, are to be worn out, if you rub them over with this lunary; so that in place where you received this maim, you shall find a medicine.

Cors. I thank you for that. The gods bless me from love, and these pretty ladies that haunt this green.

Flosc. Corsites, I would Tellus saw your amiable face.

Zon. How spitefully Semele laugheth, that dare not speak.

Cynth. Could you not stir Endimion with that doubled strength of yours?

Cors. Not so much as his finger with all my force.

Cynth. Pythagoras and Gyptes, what think you of Endimion? what reason is to be given, what remedy?

Pyth. Madam, it is impossible to yield reason for things that happen not in compass of nature. It is most certain that some strange enchantment hath bound all his senses.

Cynth. What say you, Gyptes?

Gyptes. With Pythagoras, that it is enchantment, and that so strange that no art can undo it, for that heaviness argueth a malice unremovable in the enchantress, and that no power can end it, till she die that did it, or the heavens show some means more miraculous.

Flosc. O Endimion, could spite itself devise a mischief so monstrous as to make thee dead with life, and living being altogether dead? Where others number their years, their hours, their minutes, and step to age by stairs, thou only hast thy years and times in a cluster, being old before thou rememberest thou wast young.

Cynth. No more, Floscula, pity doth him no good; I would anything else might, and I vow by the unspotted honour of a lady he should not miss it: but is this all, Gyptes, that is to be done?

Gyptes. All as yet. It may be that either the enchantress shall die, or else be discovered: if either happen I will then practise the utmost of my art. In the mean season, about this grove would I have a watch, and the first living thing that toucheth Endimion to be taken.

Cynth. Corsites, what say you, will you undertake this?

Cors. Good madam, pardon me! I was overtaken too late, I should rather break into the midst of a main battle than again fall into the hands of those fair babies.

Cynth. Well, I will provide others. Pythagoras and Gyptes, you shall yet remain in my court, till I hear what may be done in this matter.

Pyth. We attend.

Cynth. Let us go in.   [*Exeunt.*

ACT V

SCENE I

SAMIAS. DARES.

Sam. Eumenides hath told such strange tales as I may well wonder at them, but never believe them.

Dar. The other old man, what a sad speech used he, that caused us almost all to weep. Cynthia is so desirous to know the experiment of her own virtue, and so willing to ease Endimion's hard fortune, that she no sooner heard the discourse, but she made herself in readiness to try the event.

Sam. We will also see the event; but whist! here cometh Cynthia with all her train: let us sneak in amongst them.

Enter CYNTHIA, FLOSCULA, SEMELE, PANELION, etc.

Cynth. Eumenides, it cannot sink into my head that I should be signified by that sacred fountain, for many things there are in the world to which those words may be applied.

Eum. Good madam, vouchsafe but to try, else shall I think myself most unhappy that I asked not my sweet mistress.

Cynth. Will you not yet tell me her name?

Eum. Pardon me, good madam, for if Endimion awake, he shall: myself have sworn never to reveal it.

Cynth. Well, let us to Endimion. I will not be so stately (good Endimion) not to stoop to do thee good: and if thy liberty consist in a kiss from me, thou shalt have it. And although my mouth hath been heretofore as untouched as my thoughts, yet now to recover thy life (though to restore thy youth it be impossible) I will do that to Endimion which yet never mortal man could boast of heretofore, nor shall ever hope for hereafter.   [*She kisseth him.*

Eum. Madam, he beginneth to stir.

Cynth. Soft, Eumenides, stand still.

Eum. Ah, I see his eyes almost open.

Cynth. I command thee once again stir not: I will stand behind him.

Pan. What do I see, Endimion almost awake?

Eum. Endimion, Endimion, art thou deaf or dumb? or hath this long sleep taken away thy memory? Ah, my sweet Endimion, seest thou not Eumenides? thy faithful friend, thy faithful Eumenides, who for thy safety hath been careless of his own content. Speak Endimion, Endimion, Endimion.

End. Endimion? I call to mind such a name.

Eum. Hast thou forgotten thyself, Endimion? then do I not marvel thou rememberest not thy friend. I tell thee thou art Endimion, and I Eumenides: behold also Cynthia, by whose favour thou art awaked, and by whose virtue thou shalt continue thy natural course.

Cynth. Endimion, speak sweet Endimion, knowest thou not Cynthia?

End. O heavens, whom do I behold, fair Cynthia, divine Cynthia.

Cynth. I am Cynthia, and thou Endimion.

End. Endimion, What do I here? What a grey beard? hollow eyes? withered body? decayed limbs? and all in one night?

Eum. One night? thou hast here slept forty years, by what enchantress as yet it is not known: and behold the twig to which thou layest thy head is now become a tree; callest thou not Eumenides to remembrance?

End. Thy name I do remember by the sound, but thy favour I do not yet call to mind: only divine Cynthia, to whom time, fortune, destiny, and death, are subject, I see and remember; and in all humility, I regard and reverence.

Cynth. You have good cause to remember Eumenides, who hath for thy safety forsaken his own solace.

End. Am I that Endimion who was wont in court to lead my life; and in jousts, tourneys, and arms, to exercise my youth? am I that Endimion?

Eum. Thou art that Endimion, and I Eumenides, wilt thou not yet call me to remembrance?

End. Ah, sweet Eumenides, I now perceive thou art he, and that myself have the name of Endimion; but that this should be my body I doubt, for how could my curled locks be turned to grey hairs, and my strong body to dying weakness, having waxed old and not knowing it.

Cynth. Well, Endimion, arise, a while sit down, for that thy limbs are stiff, and not able to stay thee, and tell what hast thou seen in thy sleep all this while? What dreams, visions, thoughts, and fortunes? For it is impossible, but in so long time, thou shouldest see things strange.

End. Fair Cynthia, I will rehearse what I have seen, humbly desiring that when I exceed in length you give me warning, that I may end: for to utter all I have to speak would be troublesome, although happily the strangeness may somewhat abate the tediousness.

Cynth. Well, Endimion, begin.

End. Methought I saw a lady passing fair, but very mischievous; who in the one hand carried a knife with which she ordered to cut my throat, and in the other a looking-glass, wherein seeing how ill anger became ladies, she refrained from intended violence. She was accompanied with other damsels, one of which with a stern countenance, and as it were with a settled malice engraven in her eyes, provoked her to execute mischief: another visage sad and constant only in sorrow, with her arms crossed, and watery eyes seemed to lament my fortune, but durst not offer to prevent the force. I started in my sleep, feeling my very veins to swell, and my sinews to stretch with fear, and such a cold sweat bedewed all my body, that death itself could not be so terrible as the vision.

Cynth. A strange sight. Gyptes at our better leisure shall expound it.

End. After long debating with herself, mercy overcame anger; and there appeared in her heavenly face such a divine majesty, mingled with a sweet mildness, that I was ravished with the sight above measure: and wished that I might have enjoyed the sight without end; and so she departed with the other ladies, of which the one retained still an unmovable cruelty, the other a constant pity.

Cynth. Poor Endimion, how wast thou affrighted? What else?

End. After her immediately appeared an aged man with a beard as white as snow, carrying in his hand a book with three leaves, and speaking as I remember these words. *Endimion, receive this book with three leaves, in which are contained counsels, policies, and pictures:* and with that he offered me the book, which I rejected: wherewith moved with a disdainful pity, he rent the first leaf in a thousand shivers; the second time he offered it, which I refused also; at which bending his brows, and pitching his eyes fast to

the ground, as though they were fixed to the earth, and not
again to be removed—then suddenly casting them up to the
heavens, he tore in a rage the second leaf, and offered the
book only with one leaf. I know not whether fear to
offend, or desire to know some strange thing, moved me, I
took the book, and so the old man vanished.

Cynth. What didst thou imagine was in the last leaf?

End. There portrayed to life, with a cold quaking in every joint,
I beheld many wolves barking at thee, Cynthia, who having
ground their teeth to bite, did with striving bleed themselves to death. There might I see ingratitude with an
hundred eyes, gazing for benefits, and with a thousand teeth,
gnawing on the bowels wherein she was bred. Treachery
stood all clothed in white, with a smiling countenance, but
both her hands bathed in blood. Envy with a pale and
meagre face (whose body was so lean, that one might tell
all her bones, and whose garment was so tattered, that it
was easy to number every thread) stood shooting at stars,
whose darts fell down again on her own face. There might
I behold drones or beetles, I know not how to term them,
creeping under the wings of a princely eagle, who being
carried into her nest, sought there to suck that vein, that
would have killed the eagle. I mused that things so base
should attempt a fact so barbarous, or durst imagine a
thing so bloody. And many other things, madam, the
repetition whereof may at your better leisure seem more
pleasing; for bees surfeit sometimes with honey, and the
gods are glutted with harmony, and your highness may be
dulled with delight.

Cynth. I am content to be dieted, therefore let us in. Eumenides,
see that Endimion be well tended, lest either eating im-
moderately, or sleeping again too long, he fall into a deadly
surfeit, or into his former sleep. See this also be proclaimed,
that whosoever will discover this practice shall have of
Cynthia infinite thanks, and no small rewards.   [*Exit.*

Flosc. Ah, Endimion, none so joyful as Floscula, of thy restoring.

Eum. Yes, Floscula, let Eumenides be somewhat gladder, and
do not that wrong to the settled friendship of a man, as to
compare it with the light affection of a woman. Ah, my
dear friend Endimion, suffer me to die, with gazing at thee.

End. Eumenides, thy friendship is immortal, and not to be
conceived; and thy good will, Floscula, better than I have

deserved. But let us all wait on Cynthia: I marvel Semele
speaketh not a word.

Eum. Because if she do, she loseth her tongue.

End. But how prospereth your love?

Eum. I never yet spake word since your sleep.

End. I doubt not but your affection is old, and your appetite
cold.

Eum. No, Endimion, thine hath made it stronger, and now are
my sparks grown to flames, and my fancies almost to
frenzies: but let us follow, and within we will debate all
this matter at large. [*Exeunt*.

SCENE II

Sir Tophas. Epiton.

Top. Epi, love hath jostled my liberty from the wall, and taken
the upper hand of my reason.

Epi. Let me then trip up the heels of your affection, and thrust
your good will into the gutter.

Top. No, Epi; love is a lord of misrule, and keepeth Christmas
in my corpse.

Epi. No doubt there is good cheer: what dishes of delight doth
his lordship feast you with withal?

Top. First, with a great platter of plum-porridge of pleasure,
wherein is stewed the mutton of mistrust.

Epi. Excellent love lap.

Top. Then cometh a pie of patience, a hen of honey, a goose of
gall, a capon of care, and many other viands; some sweet,
and some sour; which proveth love to be as it was said of,
in old years, *Dulce venenum*.

Epi. A brave banquet.

Top. But Epi. I pray thee feel on my chin, something pricketh
me. What dost thou feel or see.

Epi. There are three or four little hairs.

Top. I pray thee call it my beard; how shall I be troubled when
this young spring shall grow to a great wood!

Epi. Oh, sir, your chin is but a quiller yet; you will be most
majestical when it is full fledge. But I marvel that you
love Dipsas, that old crone.

Top. *Agnosco veteris vestigia flammæ*, I love the smoke of an
old fire.

Epi. Why she is so cold, that no fire can thaw her thoughts.

Top. It is an old goose, Epi, that will eat no oats; old kine will kick, old rats gnaw cheese, and old sacks will have much patching: I prefer an old cony before a rabbit sucker, and an ancient hen before a young chicken peeper.

Epi. Argumentum ab antiquitate, My master loveth antique work.

Top. Give me a pippin that is withered like an old wife.

Epi. Good sir.

Top. Then, *à contrario sequitur argumentum.* Give me a wife that looks like an old pippin.

Epi. Nothing hath made my master a fool, but flat scholarship.

Top. Knowest thou not that old wine is best?

Epi. Yes.

Top. And thou knowest that like will to like?

Epi. Ay.

Top. And thou knowest that Venus loved the best wine.

Epi. So.

Top. Then I conclude, that Venus was an old woman in an old cup of wine. For, *est* Venus *in vinis, ignis in igne fuit.*

Epi. O lepidum caput, O madcap master! You were worthy to win Dipsas, were she as old again, for in your love you have worn the nap of your wit quite off, and made it threadbare. But soft, who comes here?

Top. My solicitors.

Sam. All hail, Sir Tophas, how feel you yourself?

Top. Stately in every joint, which the common people term stiffness. Doth Dipsas stoop? will she yield? will she bend?

Dar. Oh, sir, as much as you would wish, for her chin almost toucheth her knees.

Epi. Master, she is bent I warrant you.

Top. What conditions doth she ask?

Sam. She hath vowed she will never love any that hath not a tooth in his head less than she.

Top. How many hath she?

Dar. One.

Epi. That goeth hard, master, for then you must have none.

Top. A small request, and agreeable to the gravity of her years. What should a wise man do with his mouth full of bones like a charnel house? The turtle true hath ne'er a tooth.

Sam. Thy master is in a notable vein, that will lose his teeth to be like a turtle.

Epi. Let him lose his tongue too, I care not.

Dar. Nay, you must also have no nails, for she long since hath cast hers.

Top. That I yield to, what a quiet life shall Dipsas and I lead when we can neither bite nor scratch? You may see, youths, how age provides for peace.

Sam. How shall we do to make him leave his love, for we never spake to her?

Dar. Let me alone. She is a notable witch, and hath turned her maid Bagoa to an aspen tree for betraying her secrets.

Top. I honour her for her cunning, for now when I am weary of walking on two legs, what a pleasure may she do me to turn me to some goodly ass, and help me to four.

Dar. Nay, then I must tell you the truth; her husband Geron is come home, who this fifty years hath had her to wife.

Top. What do I hear? Hath she an husband? Go to the sexton, and tell him desire is dead, and will him to dig his grave. O heavens, an husband? What death is agreeable to my fortune?

Sam. Be not desperate, and we will help you to find a young lady.

Top. I love no grissels; they are so brittle they will crack like glass, or so dainty that if they be touched they are straight of the fashion of wax: *animus majoribus instat.* I desire old matrons. What a sight would it be to embrace one whose hair were as orient as the pearl! whose teeth shall be so pure a watchet that they shall stain the truest turkis! whose nose shall throw more beams from it than the fiery carbuncle! whose eyes shall be environed about with redness exceeding the deepest coral! And whose lips might compare with silver for the paleness! Such a one if you can help me to, I will by piecemeal curtail my affections towards Dipsas, and walk my swelling thoughts till they be cold.

Epi. Wisely provided. How say you, my friends, will you angle for my master's cause?

Sam. Most willingly.

Dar. If we speed him not shortly I will burn my cap, we will serve him of the spades, and dig an old wife out of the grave that shall be answerable to his gravity.

Top. Youths, adieu; he that bringeth me first news shall
possess mine inheritance.

Dar. What, is thy master landed?

Epi. Know you not that my master is *liber tenens ?*

Sam. What's that?

Epi. A free-holder.   But I will after him.

Sam. And we to hear what news of Endimion for the conclusion.
[*Exeunt.*

SCENE III

PANELION.   ZONTES.

Pan. Who would have thought that Tellus, being so fair by
nature, so honourable by birth, so wise by education, would
have entered into a mischief to the gods so odious, to men
so detestable, and to her friend so malicious.

Zon. If Bagoa had not bewrayed it, how then should it have
come to light?   But we see that gold and fair words, are of
force to corrupt the strongest men; and therefore able to
work silly women like wax.

Pan. I marvel what Cynthia will determine in this cause.

Zon. I fear as in all causes, hear of it in justice, and then judge
of it in mercy: for how can it be that she that is unwilling
to punish her deadliest foes with disgrace, will revenge
injuries of her train with death.

Pan. That old witch Dipsas, in a rage, having understood her
practice to be discovered, turned poor Bagoa to an aspen
tree; but let us make haste and bring Tellus before Cynthia,
for she was coming out after us.

Zon. Let us go.   [*Exeunt.*

CYNTHIA.   SEMELE.   FLOSCULA.   DIPSAS.   ENDIMION.
EUMENIDES.

Cynth. Dipsas, thy years are not so many as thy vices; yet
more in number than commonly nature doth afford, or
justice should permit.   Hast thou almost these fifty years
practised that detested wickedness of witchcraft?   Wast
thou so simple, as for to know the nature of simples, of all
creatures to be most sinful?   Thou hast threatened to
turn my course awry, and alter by thy damnable art the

government that I now possess by the eternal gods. But know thou, Dipsas, and let all the enchanters know, that Cynthia being placed for light on earth is also protected by the powers of heaven. Breathe out thou mayest words, gather thou mayest herbs, find out thou mayest stones agreeable to thine art, yet of no force to appal my heart, in which courage is so rooted, and constant persuasion of the mercy of the gods so grounded, that all thy witchcraft I esteem as weak as the world doth thy case wretched. This noble gentleman, Geron (once thy husband, but now thy mortal hate), didst thou procure to live in a desert, almost desperate. Endimion, the flower of my court and the hope of succeeding time, hast thou bewitched by art, before thou wouldst suffer him to flourish by nature.

Dipsas. Madam, things past may be repented, not recalled: there is nothing so wicked that I have not done, nor any thing so wished for as death. Yet among all the things that I committed, there is nothing so much tormenteth my rented and ransacked thoughts, as that in the prime of my husband's youth I divorced him by my devilish art; for which, if to die might be amends, I would not live till to-morrow. If to live and still be more miserable would better content him, I would wish of all creatures to be oldest and ugliest.

Ger. Dipsas, thou hast made this difference between me and Endimion, that being both young, thou hast caused me to wake in melancholy, losing the joys of my youth; and him to sleep, not remembering youth.

Cynth. Stay, here cometh Tellus, we shall now know all.

Enter Corsites, Tellus, Panelion, etc.

Cors. I would too, Cynthia, thou couldest make as good an excuse in truth, as to me thou hast done by wit.

Tellus. Truth shall be mine answer, and therefore I will not study for an excuse.

Cynth. Is it possible, Tellus, that so few years should harbour so many mischiefs? Thy swelling pride have I borne, because it is a thing that beauty maketh blameless, which the more it exceedeth fairness in measure, the more it stretcheth itself in disdain. Thy devices against Corsites I smile at; for that wits, the sharper they are, the shrewder they are. But this unacquainted and most unnatural practice with a vile enchantress against so noble a gentleman as Endimion, I abhor as a thing most malicious, and will revenge as a deed most monstrous. And as for you, Dipsas, I will send you into the desert amongst wild beasts, and try whether you can cast lions, tigers, boars, and bears, into as dead a sleep as you did Endimion; or turn them to trees, as you have done Bagoa. But tell me, Tellus, what was the cause of this cruel part, far unfitting thy sex, in which nothing should be but simpleness: and much disagreeing from thy face, in which nothing seemed to be but softness.

Tellus. Divine Cynthia, by whom I receive my life, and am content to end it, I can neither excuse my fault without lying, nor confess it without shame; yet were it possible that in so heavenly thoughts as yours, there could fall such earthly motions as mine, I would then hope, if not to be pardoned without extreme punishment, yet to be heard without great marvel.

Cynth. Say, on Tellus, I cannot imagine anything that can colour such a cruelty.

Tellus. Endimion, that Endimion in the prime of his youth, so ravished my heart with love, that to obtain my desires I could not find means, nor to recite them reason. What was she that favoured not Endimion, being young, wise, honourable, and virtuous; besides, what metal was she made of (be she mortal) that is not affected with the spice, nay, infected with the poison of that (not to be expressed, yet always to be felt) love? which breaketh the brains, and never bruiseth the brow: consumeth the heart, and never toucheth the skin: and maketh a deep scar to be seen, before any wound at all be felt. My heart, too tender to withstand such a divine fury, yielded to love. Madam, I, not without blushing confess, yielded to love.

Cynth. A strange effect of love, to work such an extreme hate. How say you, Endimion, all this was for love?

End. I say, madam, then the gods send me a woman's hate.

Cynth. That were as bad, for then by contrary you should never sleep. But on, Tellus, let us hear the end.

Tellus. Feeling a continual burning in all my bowels, and a bursting almost in every vein, I could not smother the inward fire, but it must needs be perceived by the outward smoke; and by the flying abroad of divers sparks, divers judged of my scalding flames. Endimion, as full of art as wit, marking mine eyes (in which he might see almost his own), my sighs, by which he might ever hear his name sounded, aimed at my heart, in which was assured his person was imprinted, and by questions wrung out that which was ready to burst out. When he saw the depth of my affections, he swore that mine in respect of his were as fumes to Ætna, valleys to Alps, ants to eagles, and nothing could be compared to my beauty but his love, and eternity. Thus drawing a smooth shoe upon a crooked foot, he made me believe that (which all of our sex willingly acknowledge) I was beautiful. And to wonder (which indeed is a thing miraculous) that any of his sex should be faithful.

Cynth. Endimion, how will you clear yourself?

End. Madam, by mine own accuser.

Cynth. Well, Tellus, proceed, but briefly, lest taking delight in uttering thy love thou offend us with the length of it.

Tellus. I will, madam, quickly make an end of my love and my tale. Finding continual increase of my tormenting thoughts, and that the enjoying of my love made deeper wounds than the entering into it, I could find no means to ease my grief but to follow Endimion, and continually to have him in the object of mine eyes, who had me slave and subject to his love. But in the moment that I feared his falsehood, and fried myself most in mine affections, I found (ah grief, even then I lost myself!) I found him in most melancholy and desperate terms, cursing his stars, his state, the earth, the heavens, the world, and all for the love of—

Cynth. Of whom? Tellus, speak boldly.

Tellus. Madam, I dare not utter for fear to offend.

Cynth. Speak, I say; who dare take offence, if thou be commanded by Cynthia?

Tellus. For the love of Cynthia.

Cynth. For my love, Tellus, that were strange. Endimion, is it true?

End. In all things, madam. Tellus doth not speak false.

Cynth. What will this breed to in the end? Well, Endimion, we shall hear all.

Tellus. I, seeing my hopes turned to mishaps, and a settled dissembling towards me, and an unmovable desire to Cynthia, forgetting both myself and my sex, fell into this unnatural hate; for knowing your virtues, Cynthia, to be immortal, I could not have an imagination to withdraw him. And finding mine own affections unquenchable, I could not carry the mind that any else should possess what I had pursued. For though in majesty, beauty, virtue, and dignity, I always humbled and yielded myself to Cynthia; yet in affections, I esteemed myself equal with the goddesses and all other creatures according to their states with myself. For stars to their bigness have their lights, and the sun hath no more. And little pitchers when they can hold no more are as full as great vessels that run over. Thus, madam, in all truth, have I uttered the unhappiness of my love, and the cause of my hate, yielding wholly to that divine judgment which never erred for want of wisdom, or envied for too much partiality.

Cynth. How say you, my lords, to this matter? But what say you, Endimion, hath Tellus told truth?

End. Madam, in all things, but in that she said I loved her, and swore to honour her.

Cynth. Was there such a time when as for my love thou didst vow thyself to death, and in respect of it loathed thy life? speak, Endimion, I will not revenge it with hate.

End. The time was, madam, and is, and ever shall be, that I honoured your highness above all the world; but to stretch it so far as to call it love, I never durst. There hath none pleased mine eye but Cynthia, none delighted mine ears but Cynthia, none possessed my heart but Cynthia. I have forsaken all other fortunes to follow Cynthia, and here I stand ready to die if it please Cynthia. Such a difference hath the gods set between our states, that all must be duty, loyalty, and reverence, nothing (without it vouchsafe your highness) be termed love. My unspotted thoughts, my languishing body, my discontented life, let them obtain by princely favour, that which to challenge they must not presume, only wishing of impossibilities: with imagination of which, I will spend my spirits, and to myself that no creature may hear, softly call it love. And if any urge to utter what I whisper, then will I name it honour. From this sweet contemplation if I be not driven, I shall live of all men the most content, taking more pleasure in mine aged thoughts than ever I did in my youthful actions.

Cynth. Endimion, this honourable respect of thine shall be

christened love in thee, and my reward for it, favour.
Persevere, Endimion, in loving me, and I account more
strength in a true heart than in a walled city. I have
laboured to win all, and study to keep such as I have won;
but those that neither my favour can move to continue
constant, nor my offered benefits get to be faithful, the gods
shall either reduce to truth or revenge their treacheries
with justice. Endimion, continue as thou hast begun, and
thou shalt find that Cynthia shineth not on thee in vain.

End. Your highness hath blessed me, and your words have
again restored my youth: methinks I feel my joints strong,
and these mouldy hairs to moult, and all by your virtue,
Cynthia, into whose hands the balance that weigheth time
and fortune are committed.

Cynth. What, young again? then it is pity to punish Tellus.

Tellus. Ah, Endimion, now I know thee and ask pardon of thee;
suffer me still to wish thee well.

End. Tellus, Cynthia must command what she will.

Flosc. Endimion, I rejoice to see thee in thy former estate.

End. Good Floscula, to thee also am I in my former affections.

Eum. Endimion, the comfort of my life, how am I ravished with
a joy matchless, saving only the enjoying of my mistress.

Cynth. Endimion, you must now tell who Eumenides shrineth
for his saint.

End. Semele, madam.

Cynth. Semele, Eumenides? is it Semele? the very wasp of all
women, whose tongue stingeth as much as an adder's tooth?

Eum. It is Semele, Cynthia: the possessing of whose love, must
only prolong my life.

Cynth. Nay, sith Endimion is restored, we will have all parties
pleased. Semele, are you content after so long trial of his
faith, such rare secrecy, such unspotted love, to take
Eumenides? Why speak you not? Not a word?

End. Silence, madam, consents: that is most true.

Cynth. It is true, Endimion. Eumenides, take Semele. Take
her, I say.

Eum. Humble thanks, madam, now only do I begin to live.

Sem. A hard choice, madam, either to be married if I say
nothing, or to lose my tongue if I speak a word. Yet do
I rather choose to have my tongue cut out, than my heart
distempered: I will not have him.

Cynth. Speaks the parrot? she shall nod hereafter with signs:

cut off her tongue, nay, her head, that having a servant of honourable birth, honest manners, and true love, will not be persuaded.

Sem. He is no faithful lover, madam, for then would he have asked his mistress.

Ger. Had he not been faithful, he had never seen into the fountain, and so lost his friend and mistress.

Eum. Thine own thoughts, sweet Semele, witness against thy words, for what hast thou found in my life but love? and as yet what have I found in my love but bitterness? Madam, pardon Semele, and let my tongue ransom hers.

Cynth. Thy tongue, Eumenides? what shouldst thou live wanting a tongue to blaze the beauty of Semele? Well, Semele, I will not command love, for it cannot be enforced: let me entreat it.

Sem. I am content your highness shall command, for now only do I think Eumenides faithful, that is willing to lose his tongue for my sake: yet loth, because it should do me better service. Madam, I accept of Eumenides.

Cynth. I thank you, Semele.

Eum. Ah happy Eumenides, that hast a friend so faithful, and a mistress so fair: with what sudden mischief will the gods daunt this excess of joy? Sweet Semele, I live or die as thou wilt.

Cynth. What shall become of Tellus? Tellus, you know Endimion is vowed to a service, from which death cannot remove him. Corsites casteth still a lovely look towards you, how say you? Will you have your Corsites, and so receive pardon for all that is past?

Tellus. Madam, most willingly.

Cynth. But I cannot tell whether Corsites be agreed.

Cors. Ay, madam, more happy to enjoy Tellus than the monarchy of the world.

Eum. Why, she caused you to be pinched with fairies.

Cors. Ay, but her fairness hath pinched my heart more deeply.

Cynth. Well enjoy thy love. But what have you wrought in the castle, Tellus?

Tellus. Only the picture of Endimion.

Cynth. Then so much of Endimion as his picture cometh to, possess and play withal.

Cors. Ah, my sweet Tellus, my love shall be as thy beauty is, matchless.

Cynth. Now it resteth, Dipsas, that if thou wilt forswear that vile art of enchanting, Geron hath promised again to receive thee; otherwise, if thou be wedded to that wickedness, I must and will see it punished to the uttermost.

Dipsas. Madam, I renounce both substance and shadow of that most horrible and hateful trade; vowing to the gods continual penance, and to your highness obedience.

Cynth. How say you, Geron, will you admit her to your wife?

Ger. Ay, with more joy than I did the first day: for nothing could happen to make me happy, but only her forsaking that lewd and detestable course. Dipsas, I embrace thee.

Dipsas. And I thee, Geron, to whom I will hereafter recite the cause of these my first follies.

Cynth. Well, Endimion, nothing resteth now but that we depart. Thou hast my favour. Tellus her friend, Eumenides in Paradise with his Semele, Geron contented with Dipsas.

Top. Nay, soft, I cannot handsomely go to bed without Bagoa.

Cynth. Well, Sir Tophas, it may be there are more virtues in me than myself knoweth of; for I awaked Endimion, and at my words he waxed young; I will try whether I can turn this tree again to thy true love.

Top. Turn her to a true love or false, so she be a wench I care not.

Cynth. Bagoa, Cynthia putteth an end to thy hard fortunes, for being turned to a tree for revealing a truth, I will recover thee again, if in my power be the effect of truth.

Top. Bagoa, a bots upon thee!

Cynth. Come, my lords, let us in. You, Gyptes and Pythagoras, if you cannot content yourselves in our court, to fall from vain follies of philosophers to such virtues as are here practised, you shall be entertained according to your deserts: for Cynthia is no stepmother to strangers.

Pyth. I had rather in Cynthia's court spend ten years, than in Greece one hour.

Gyptes. And I choose rather to live by the sight of Cynthia, than by the possessing of all Egypt.

Cynth. Then follow.

Eum. We all attend.　　　　　　　　　　　　　　[*Exeunt.*

THE EPILOGUE

A MAN walking abroad, the wind and sun strove for sovereignty, the one with his blast, the other with his beams. The wind blew hard, the man wrapped his garment about him harder: it blustered more strongly, he then girt it fast to him: I cannot prevail, said the wind. The sun casting her crystal beams, began to warm the man: he unloosed his gown: yet it shone brighter: he then put it off. I yield, said the wind, for if thou continue shining, he will also put off his coat.

Dread Sovereign, the malicious that seek to overthrow us with threats, do but stiffen our thoughts, and make them sturdier in storms: but if your Highness vouchsafe with your favourable beams to glance upon us, we shall not only stoop, but with all humility, lay both our hand and hearts at your Majesty's feet.

THE OLD WIVES' TALE

The Old Wiues Tale. A pleasant conceited Comedie, played by the Queenes Maiesties players. Written by G. P. Printed at London by John Danter, and are to be sold by Ralph Hancocke, and John Hardie. 1595. 4to. The imprint at the end is:

Printed at London by John Danter, for Ralph Hancocke, and John Hardie, and are to be solde at the shop ouer against Saint Giles his Church without Criplegate. 1595.

The Old Wives' Tale had sunk into complete oblivion, till Steevens (see Wooll's *Life of J. Warton*, p. 398) communicated to Reed the account of it which appeared in the *Biographia Dramatica ;* and it was afterwards more particularly described by T. Warton in his edition of Milton's Minor Poems.

" This very scarce and curious piece exhibits, among other parallel incidents, two Brothers wandering in quest of their Sister, whom an Enchanter had imprisoned. This magician had learned his art from his mother Meroe, as Comus had been instructed by his mother Circe. The Brothers call out on the Lady's name, and Echo replies. The Enchanter had given her a potion which suspends the powers of reason, and super-induces oblivion of herself. The Brothers afterwards meet with an Old Man who is also skilled in magic; and by listening to his soothsayings, they recover their lost Sister. But not till the Enchanter's wreath had been torn from his head, his sword wrested from his hand, a glass broken, and a light extinguished. The names of some of the characters as Sacrapant, Chorebus, and others, are taken from the Orlando Furioso. The history of Meroe a witch, may be seen in ' The xi. Bookes of the Golden Asse, containing the Metamorphosie of Lucius Apuleius interlaced with sundrie pleasant and delectable Tales, etc. Translated out of Latin into English by William Adlington, Lond. 1566.' See Chap. iii. ' How Socrates in his returne from Macedony to Larissa was spoyled and robbed, and how he fell acquainted with one Meroe a witch.' And Chap. iv. ' How Meroe the witch turned divers persons into miserable beasts.' Of this book there were other editions in 1571, 1596, 1600, and 1639. All in quarto and the black letter. The translator was of University College. See also Apuleius in the original. A Meroe is mentioned by Ausonius, Epigr. xix." *T. Warton,—Milton's Poems upon several occasions*, etc., pp. 135-6, ed. 1791. " There is another circumstance in this play taken from the old English Apuleius. It is where the *Old Man* every night is transformed by our magician into a bear, recovering in the daytime his natural shape." *Id.* p. 576. " That Milton had an eye on this ancient drama, which might have been the favourite of his early youth, perhaps it may be at least affirmed with as much credibility, as that he conceived the PARADISE LOST from seeing a Mystery at Florence, written by Andreini a Florentine in 1617, entitled ADAMO." *Id.* p. 136.

An incident similar to that in this play of the two sisters going to the well and meeting with the golden head, is to be found (as Mr. T. Rodd, one of the best-informed of booksellers, observes to me) in a penny history called the *Tales of the Three Kings of Colchester.*

THE OLD WIVES' TALE

DRAMATIS PERSONÆ

SACRAPANT.[1]
First Brother, named CALYPHA.
Second Brother, named THELEA.
EUMENIDES.
ERESTUS.
LAMPRISCUS.
HUANEBANGO.
COREBUS.
WIGGEN.
Churchwarden.
Sexton.
Ghost of JACK.
Friar, Harvest-men, Furies,
    Fiddlers, etc.

DELIA, *sister to Calypha and
    Thelea.*
VENELIA, *betrothed to Erestus.*
ZANTIPPA, } *daughters to Lam-*
CELANTA, } *priscus.*
Hostess.

ANTIC.
FROLIC.
FANTASTIC.
CLUNCH, *a smith.*
MADGE, *his wife.*

Enter ANTIC, FROLIC, *and* FANTASTIC.

Ant. How now, fellow Frolic![2] what, all amort?[3] doth this sad-
    ness become thy madness? What though we have lost our
    way in the woods? yet never hang the head as though thou
    hadst no hope to live till to-morrow; for Fantastic and I
    will warrant thy life to-night for twenty in the hundred.

Fro. Antic, and Fantastic, as I am frolic franion,[4] never in all
    my life was I so dead slain. What, to lose our way in the
    wood, without either fire or candle, so uncomfortable? *O
    cœlum! O terra! O maria!* O Neptune!   9

Fan. Why makes thou it so strange, seeing Cupid hath led our
    young master to the fair lady, and she is the only saint that
    he hath sworn to serve?

Fro. What resteth, then, but we commit him to his wench, and
    each of us take his stand up in a tree, and sing out our ill
    fortune to the tune of "*O man in desperation*"?[5]

[1] So Peele most probably chose to write this name: but the proper
spelling is "Sacripant" (as in Ariosto).
[2] The 4to (and here only) "Franticke."
[3] More properly *alamort, i.e.,* dejected.
[4] *i.e.,* idle fellow: in a subsequent scene Wiggen says that Jack was
"*the frolic'st franion* amongst you."
[5] "By this straw and thrid, I sware you are no gentleman, no proper
man, no honest man, to make me sing, *O man in desperation*." Nash's
Summer's Last Will and Testament, 1600, Sig. E 3.

131

Ant. Desperately spoken, fellow Frolic, in the dark: but seeing
it falls out thus, let us rehearse the old proverb:

> " Three merry men,[1] and three merry men,
> And three merry men be we;
> I in the wood, and thou on the ground,   20
> And Jack sleeps in the tree."

Fan. Hush! a dog in the wood, or a wooden [2] dog! O comfort-
able hearing! I had even as lief the chamberlain of the
White Horse [3] had called me up to bed.

Fro. Either hath this trotting cur gone out of his circuit, or else
are we near some village, which should not be far off, for I
perceive the glimmering of a glow-worm, a candle, or a cat's
eye, my life for a halfpenny!

Enter CLUNCH *with a lantern and candle.*

In the name of my own father, be thou ox or ass that
appearest, tell us what thou art.   30

Clunch. What am I! why, I am Clunch the smith. What are
you? what make you in my territories at this time of the
night?

Ant. What do we make, dost thou ask? why, we make faces for
fear; such as if thy mortal eyes could behold, would make
thee water the long seams of thy side slops,[4] smith.

Fro. And, in faith, sir, unless your hospitality do relieve us, we
are like to wander, with a sorrowful heigh-ho, among the
owlets and hobgoblins of the forest. Good Vulcan, for
Cupid's sake that hath cozened us all, befriend us as thou
mayst; and command us howsoever, wheresoever, when-
soever, in whatsoever, for ever and ever.   42

Clunch. Well, masters, it seems to me you have lost your way
in the wood: in consideration whereof, if you will go with
Clunch to his cottage, you shall have house-room and a
good fire to sit by, although we have no bedding to put
you in.

All. O blessed smith, O bountiful Clunch!   48

---

[1] This ballad is alluded to in Shakespeare's *Twelfth Night*, act ii. sc. 3,
and in other old plays.

[2] *i.e.*, mad.   Let us not fail to observe Fantastic's precious pun, " a dog
in the *wood*, or a wooden [*wood in*] dog."

[3] The White Horse was doubtless well known to our author: " George
was invited one night by certain of his friends to supper at *the White
Horse in Friday Street*," etc.: see among *Peele's Jests*, " *How George helped
his friend to a supper.*"

[4] *i.e.*, long wide breeches or trousers.

Clunch. For your further entertainment, it shall be as it may be,
so and so.   *[A dog barks within.*
Hark! [1] this is Ball my dog, that bids you all welcome in his
own language: come, take heed for stumbling on the thres-
hold.—Open door, Madge; take in guests.

Enter MADGE.

Madge. Welcome, Clunch, and good fellows all, that come with
my good-man: for my good-man's sake, come on, sit down:
here is a piece of cheese, and a pudding of my own making.

Ant. Thanks, gammer: a good example for the wives of our
town.

Fro. Gammer, thou and thy good-man sit lovingly together;
we come to chat, and not to eat.   60

Clunch. Well, masters, if you will eat nothing, take away.
Come, what do we to pass away the time? Lay a crab in
the fire to roast for lamb's-wool.[2] What, shall we have a
game at trump or ruff [3] to drive away the time? how say
you?

Fan. This smith leads a life as merry as a king with Madge his
wife. Sirrah Frolic, I am sure thou art not without some
round or other: no doubt but Clunch can bear his part.

Fro. Else think you me ill brought up: so set to it when you
will.   *[They sing.*

SONG

> Whenas the rye reach to the chin,
> And chopcherry, chopcherry ripe within,
> Strawberries swimming in the cream,
> And school-boys playing in the stream;
> Then, O, then, O, then, O, my true-love said,
> Till that time come again
> She could not live a maid.

[1] Here the audience were to suppose a change of scene—that the stage
now represented the Smith's cottage.

[2] A drink made of strong ale and the pulp of roasted crab-apples.

[3] Mr. Douce and other writers inform us, that *trump* (which greatly
resembled our modern whist) was only a different name for *ruff;* but
several passages, besides that in our text, might be quoted to show that
they were sometimes considered as distinct games: *e.g.*:

> "*Ruffe*, slam, *trump*, noddy, whisk, hole, sant, new cut."
>   Taylor's *Motto, Workes,* 1630, p. 54.

Since I wrote the preceding part of this note, Mr. J. P. Collier has supplied
me with the following illustration:—

"And to confounde all, to amende their badde games, having never a
good carde in their handes, and leaving the ancient game of England
(*Trumpe*), where every coate and sute are sorted in their degree, are running
to *Ruffe*, where the greatest sorte of the sute carrieth away the game."—
Martins Months Minde, 1589—*Epistle to the Reader.*

Ant. This sport does well; but methinks, gammer, a merry
    winter's tale would drive away the time trimly: come, I am
    sure you are not without a score.   80
Fan. I'faith, gammer, a tale of an hour long were as good as an
    hour's sleep.
Fro. Look you, gammer, of the giant and the king's daughter,
    and I know not what: I have seen the day, when I was a
    little one, you might have drawn me a mile after you with
    such a discourse.
Madge. Well, since you be so importunate, my good-man shall
    fill the pot and get him to bed; they that ply their work
    must keep good hours: one of you go lie with him; he is a
    clean-skinned man I tell you, without either spavin or
    wind-gall: so I am content to drive away the time with an
    old wives' winter's tale.   92
Fan. No better hay in Devonshire; o' my word, gammer, I'll
    be one of your audience.
Fro. And I another, that's flat.
Ant. Then must I to bed with the good-man.—*Bona nox*,
    gammer.—Good [1] night, Frolic.
Clunch. Come on, my lad, thou shalt take thy unnatural rest
    with me.   [*Exit with Antic.*
Fro. Yet this vantage shall we have of them in the morning, to
    be ready at the sight thereof extempore.   101
Madge. Now this bargain, my masters, must I make with you,
    that you will say hum and ha to my tale, so shall I know
    you are awake.
Both. Content, gammer, that will we do.
Madge. Once upon a time, there was a king, or a lord, or a duke,
    that had a fair daughter, the fairest that ever was; as
    white as snow and as red as blood: and once upon a time
    his daughter was stolen away: and he sent all his men to
    seek out his daughter; and he sent so long, that he sent all
    his men out of his land.   111
Fro. Who drest his dinner, then?
Madge. Nay, either hear my tale, or kiss my tail.
Fan. Well said! on with your tale, gammer.
Madge. O Lord, I quite forgot! there was a conjurer, and this
    conjurer could do anything, and he turned himself into a
    great dragon, and carried the king's daughter away in his
    mouth to a castle that he made of stone; and there he kept

[1] The 4to " God."

her I know not how long, till at last all the king's men went
out so long that her two brothers went to seek her. O, I
forget! she (he, I would say,) turned a proper [1] young man
to a bear in the night, and a man in the day, and keeps by a
cross [2] that parts three several ways; and he made his lady
run mad,—Gods me bones, who comes here?　　124

Enter the Two Brothers.

Fro. Soft, gammer, here some come to tell your tale for you.
Fan. Let them alone; let us hear what they will say.
First Bro. Upon these chalky cliffs of Albion
　　We are arrivèd now with tedious toil;
　　And compassing the wide world round about,
　　To seek our sister, to seek fair [3] Delia forth,　　130
　　Yet cannot we so much as hear of her.
Second Bro. O fortune cruel, cruel and unkind!
　　Unkind in that we cannot find our sister,
　　Our sister, hapless in her cruel chance.—
　　Soft! who have we here?

Enter ERESTUS [4] *at the Cross, stooping to gather.*

First Bro. Now, father, God be your speed! what do you
　　gather there?
Erest. Hips and haws, and sticks and straws, and things that I
　　gather on the ground, my son.
First Bro. Hips and haws, and sticks and straws! why, is that
　　all your food, father?　　141
Erest. Yea, son.
Second Bro. Father, here is an alms-penny for me; and if I
　　speed in that I go for, I will give thee as good a gown of
　　grey as ever thou didst wear.
First Bro. And, father, here is another alms-penny for me; and
　　if I speed in my journey, I will give thee a palmer's staff of
　　ivory, and a scallop-shell of beaten gold.
Erest. Was she fair? [5]　　149
Second Bro. Ay, the fairest for white, and the purest for red, as
　　the blood of the deer, or the driven snow.

[1] *i.e.,* handsome.
[2] *i.e.* (unless we ought to read " *and keeps* him *by a cross*," etc.), and he
(the transformed young man) keeps by a cross, etc.　Compare *post,* p. 159:
" for, master, this conjurer took the shape of the old man that *kept the
cross,*" etc.
[3] Qy. *dele?*　　　　　　　　　　　　　[4] The 4to " Senex."
[5] Something, which suggested this question, has dropt out.

Erest. Then hark well, and mark well, my old spell:—
      Be not afraid of every stranger;
      Start not aside at every danger;
      Things that seem are not the same;
      Blow a blast at every flame;
      For when one flame of fire goes out,
      Then come your wishes well about:
      If any ask who told you this good,
      Say, the white bear of England's wood.   160
First Bro. Brother, heard you not what the old man said?
      Be not afraid of every stranger;
      Start not aside for every danger;
      Things that seem are not the same;
      Blow a blast at every flame;
      [For when one flame of fire goes out,
      Then come your wishes well about:]
      If any ask who told you this good,
      Say, the white bear of England's wood.
Second Bro. Well, if this do us any good,   170
      Well fare the white bear of England's wood!
                              [*Exeunt the Two Brothers.*
Erest. Now sit thee here, and tell a heavy tale,
      Sad in thy mood, and sober in thy cheer;
      Here sit thee now, and to thyself relate
      The hard mishap of thy most wretched state.
      In Thessaly I liv'd in sweet content,
      Until that fortune wrought my overthrow;
      For there I wedded was unto a dame,
      That liv'd in honour, virtue, love, and fame.
      But Sacrapant, that cursèd sorcerer,   180
      Being besotted with my beauteous love,
      My dearest love, my true betrothèd wife,
      Did seek the means to rid me of my life.
      But worse than this, he with his 'chanting spells
      Did turn me straight unto an ugly bear;
      And when the sun doth settle in the west,
      Then I begin to don my ugly hide:
      And all the day I sit, as now you see,
      And speak in riddles, all inspir'd with rage,
      Seeming an old and miserable man,   190
      And yet I am in April of my age.

Enter VENELIA *mad ; and goes in again.*

See where Venelia, my betrothèd love,
Runs madding, all enrag'd, about the woods,
All by his cursèd and enchanting spells.—
But here comes Lampriscus, my discontented neighbour.

Enter LAMPRISCUS *with a pot of honey.*

How now, neighbour! you look toward the ground as well
as I: you muse on something.

Lamp. Neighbour, on nothing but on the matter I so often
moved to you: if you do anything for charity, help me; if
for neighbourhood or brotherhood, help me: never was one
so cumbered as is poor Lampriscus; and to begin, I pray
receive this pot of honey, to mend your fare.   202

Erest. Thanks, neighbour, set it down; honey is always welcome to the bear. And now, neighbour, let me hear the
cause of your coming.

Lamp. I am, as you know, neighbour, a man unmarried, and
lived so unquietly with my two wives, that I keep every
year holy the day wherein I buried them both: the first
was on Saint Andrew's day, the other on Saint Luke's.

Erest. And now, neighbour, you of this country say, your custom
is out. But on with your tale, neighbour.   211

Lamp. By my first wife, whose tongue wearied me alive, and
sounded in my ears like the clapper of a great bell, whose
talk was a continual torment to all that dwelt by her or
lived nigh her, you have heard me say I had a handsome
daughter.

Erest. True, neighbour.

Lamp. She it is that afflicts me with her continual clamours, and
hangs on me like a bur: poor she is, and proud she is; as
poor as a sheep new-shorn, and as proud of her hopes as a
peacock of her tail well-grown.   221

Erest. Well said, Lampriscus! you speak it like an Englishman.

Lamp. As curst as a wasp, and as froward as a child new-taken
from the mother's teat; she is to my age, as smoke to the
eyes, or as vinegar to the teeth.

Erest. Holily praised, neighbour. As much for the next.

Lamp. By my other wife I had a daughter so hard-favoured, so foul,[1] and ill-faced, that I think a grove full of golden trees, and the leaves of rubies and diamonds, would not be a dowry answerable to her deformity.   230

Erest. Well, neighbour, now you have spoke, hear me speak: send them to the well for the water of life; there shall they find their fortunes unlooked for.   Neighbour, farewell.

Lamp. Farewell, and a thousand.[2] [*Exit Erestus.*] And now goeth poor Lampriscus to put in execution this excellent counsel.   [*Exit.*

Fro. Why, this goes round without a fiddling-stick: but, do you hear, gammer, was this the man that was a bear in the night and a man in the day?   239

Madge. Ay, this is he; and this man that came to him was a beggar, and dwelt upon a green.[3] But soft! who come here? O, these are the harvest-men; ten to one they sing a song of mowing.

Enter the Harvest-men *a-singing, with this song double repeated.*

> All ye that lovely lovers be,
> Pray you for me:
> Lo, here we come a-sowing, a-sowing,
> And sow sweet fruits of love;
> In your sweet hearts well may it prove!

[*Exeunt.*

Enter HUANEBANGO *with his two-hand sword, and* COREBUS.[4]

Fan. Gammer, what is he?

Madge. O, this is one that is going to the conjurer: let him alone, hear what he says.   251

Huan. Now, by Mars and Mercury, Jupiter and Janus, Sol and Saturnus, Venus and Vesta, Pallas and Proserpina, and by the honour of my house, Polimackeroeplacidus, it is a wonder to see what this love will make silly fellows adventure, even in the wane of their wits and infancy of their discretion.   Alas, my friend! what fortune calls thee forth to seek thy fortune among brazen gates, enchanted towers,

---

[1] *i.e.,* ugly.

[2] *i.e.,* a thousand times farewell. So Middleton; " let me hug thee: *farewell, and a thousand.*" *A Trick to catch the old one—Works,* vol. ii. p. 86, ed. Dyce. And S. Rowley; " God ye *god night, and twenty, sir.*" *When you see me, you know me,* Sig. D 3, ed. 1621.

[3] So we read of the Blind Beggar of Bethnal *Green,* etc.

[4] Here the 4to has " Booby; " but in subsequent scenes it names him " Corebus."

fire and brimstone, thunder and lightning? [Her] beauty,
I tell thee, is peerless, and she precious whom thou affectest.
Do off these desires, good countryman: good friend, run
away from thyself; and, so soon as thou canst, forget her,
whom none must inherit but he that can monsters tame,
labours achieve, riddles absolve, loose enchantments,
murder magic, and kill conjuring,—and that is the great
and mighty Huanebango.   266

Cor. Hark you, sir, hark you. First know I have here the
flurting feather, and have given the parish the start for the
long stock:[1] now, sir, if it be no more but running through
a little lightning and thunder, and "riddle me, riddle me
what's this?" I'll have the wench from the conjurer, if he
were ten conjurers.   272

Huan. I have abandoned the court and honourable company, to
do my devoir against this sore sorcerer and mighty magician: if this lady be so fair as she is said to be, she is mine, she
is mine; *meus, mea, meum, in contemptum omnium gram-
maticorum.*

Cor. *O falsum Latinum !*
The fair maid is *minum,*
Cum apurtinantibus gibletis and all.   280

Huan. If she be mine, as I assure myself the heavens will do
somewhat to reward my worthiness, she shall be allied to
none of the meanest gods, but be invested in the most
famous stock[2] of Huanebango,—Polimackeroeplacidus my
grandfather, my father Pergopolineo, my mother Dionora
de Sardinia, famously descended.

Cor. Do you hear, sir? had not you a cousin that was called
Gusteceridis?

Huan. Indeed, I had a cousin that sometime followed the court
infortunately, and his name Bustegusteceridis.   290

Cor. O Lord, I know him well! he is the knight of the neat's-
feet.

Huan. O, he loved no capon better! he hath oftentimes deceived his boy of his dinner; that was his fault, good
Bustegusteceridis.

Cor. Come, shall we go along?

---

[1] *i.e.,* sword, I believe. Corebus means, as it appears to me, that he
has run away from the parish, and become a sort of knight-errant.
[2] Here Peele seems to have had an eye to the hard names in the *Miles
Gloriosus* of Plautus.

Enter ERESTUS *at the Cross.*

Soft! here is an old man at the cross: let us ask him the way thither.—Ho, you gaffer! I pray you tell where the wise man the conjurer dwells.   299

Huan. Where that earthly goddess keepeth her abode, the commander of my thoughts, and fair mistress of my heart.

Erest. Fair enough, and far enough from thy fingering, son.

Huan. I will follow my fortune after mine own fancy, and do according to mine own discretion.

Erest. Yet give something to an old man before you go.

Huan. Father, methinks a piece of this cake might serve your turn.

Erest. Yea, son.   308

Huan. Huanebango giveth no cakes for alms: ask of them that give gifts for poor beggars.—Fair lady, if thou wert once shrined in this bosom, I would buckler thee haratantara.

[*Exit.*

Cor. Father, do you see this man? you little think he'll run a mile or two for such a cake, or pass for [1] a pudding. I tell you, father, he has kept such a begging of me for a piece of this cake! Whoo! he comes upon me with " a superfantial substance, and the foison [2] of the earth," that I know not what he means. If he came to me thus, and said, " My friend Corebus," [3] or so, why, I could spare him a piece with all my heart; but when he tells me how God hath enriched me above other fellows with a cake, why, he makes me blind and deaf at once. Yet, father, here is a piece of cake for you, as hard as the world goes. [4]   [*Gives cake.*

Erest. Thanks, son, but list to me;   323
He shall be deaf when thou shalt not see.
Farewell, my son: things may so hit,
Thou mayst have wealth to mend thy wit.

Cor. Farewell, father, farewell; for I must make haste after my two-hand sword that is gone before.   [*Exeunt severally.*

---

[1] *i.e.*, care for.   [2] *i.e.*, plenty.   [3] The 4to " Booby."

[4] Lest the reader should suppose that Corebus means to say, " his *cake* is as *hard* as the world goes," I subjoin a passage from the *Returne from Pernassus*, 1606, where the expression in the text occurs: " Ile now to Paul's churchyard: meete me, an houre hence, at the signe of the Pegasus in Cheapside; and ile moyst thy temples with a cup of claret *as hard as the world goes.*" Act 1, sc. 2. Sig. B 3.

Enter SACRAPANT *in his study.*

Sac. The day is clear, the welkin bright and grey,
    The lark is merry and records [1] her notes;   330
    Each thing rejoiceth underneath the sky,
    But only I, whom heaven hath in hate,
    Wretched and miserable Sacrapant.
    In Thessaly was I born and brought up;
    My mother Meroe hight,[2] a famous witch,
    And by her cunning I of her did learn
    To change and alter shapes of mortal men.
    There did I turn myself into a dragon,
    And stole away the daughter to the king,
    Fair Delia, the mistress of my heart;   340
    And brought her hither to revive the man,
    That seemeth young and pleasant to behold,
    And yet is agèd, crookèd, weak, and numb.
    Thus by enchanting spells I do deceive
    Those that behold and look upon my face;
    But well may I bid youthful years adieu.
    See where she comes from whence my sorrows grow!

Enter DELIA *with a pot in her hand.*

    How now, fair Delia! where have you been?
Del. At the foot of the rock for running water, and gathering
    roots for your dinner, sir.   350
Sac. Ah, Delia,
    Fairer art thou than the running water,
    Yet harder far than steel or adamant!
Del. Will it please you to sit down, sir?
Sac. Ay, Delia, sit and ask me what thou wilt,
    Thou shalt have it brought into thy lap.
Del. Then, I pray you, sir, let me have the best meat from the
    King of England's table, and the best wine in all France,
    brought in by the veriest knave in all Spain.
Sac. Delia, I am glad to see you so pleasant: 360
    Well, sit thee down.—

---

[1] *i.e.*, sings, tunes. In Coles's *Dict.* we find; " To Record as birds,
Certatim modulari, alternis canere."
[2] *i.e.*, called.

Spread, table, spread,
Meat, drink, and bread,
Ever may I have
What I ever crave,
When I am spread,
Meat for [1] my black cock,
And meat for my red.

Enter a Friar *with a chine of beef and a pot of wine.*

Here, Delia, will ye fall to?
Del. Is this the best meat in England?   370
Sac. Yea.
Del. What is it?
Sac. A chine of English beef, meat for a king and a king's
    followers.
Del. Is this the best wine in France?
Sac. Yea.
Del. What wine is it?
Sac. A cup of neat wine of Orleans, that never came near the
    brewers in England.
Del. Is this the veriest knave in all Spain? [2]   380
Sac. Yea.
Del. What, is he a friar?
Sac. Yea, a friar indefinite, and a knave infinite.
Del. Then, I pray ye, Sir Friar, tell me before you go, which is
    the most greediest Englishman?
Fri. The miserable and most covetous usurer.
Sac. Hold thee there, friar. [*Exit Friar.*] But, soft!
    Who have we here? Delia, away, be gone!

Enter the Two Brothers.

Delia, away! for beset are we.—
But heaven or hell shall rescue her for me.   390
                    [*Exeunt Delia and Sacrapant.*
First Bro. Brother, was not that Delia did appear,
    Or was it but her shadow that was here?
Second Bro. Sister, where art thou? Delia, come again!

[1] The 4to " for *meate for*," etc. Corrected by the Rev. J. Mitford—
Gent. Mag. for Feb. 1833, p. 104.
[2] Perhaps there is an allusion here to the conspiracies of the Catholic
priests against the Queen, encouraged by Philip of Spain.

He calls, that of thy absence doth complain.—
Call out, Calypha, that[1] she may hear,
And cry aloud, for Delia is near.

Echo. Near.

First Bro. Near! O, where? hast thou any tidings?

Echo. Tidings.

Second Bro. Which way is Delia, then? or that, or this?   400

Echo. This.

First Bro. And may we safely come where Delia is?

Echo. Yes.

Second Bro. Brother, remember you the white bear of England's
      wood?
  " Start not aside for every danger,
  Be not afeard of every stranger;
  Things that seem are not the same."

First Bro. Brother,
Why do we not, then, courageously enter?

Second Bro. Then, brother, draw thy sword and follow me.   410

Re-enter SACRAPANT: *it lightens and thunders ; the* Second
              Brother *falls down.*

First Bro. What, brother, dost thou fall?

Sac. Ay, and thou too, Calypha.

                      [*The First Brother falls down.*

  Adeste, dæmones !

Enter Two Furies.

        Away with them:
Go carry them straight to Sacrapanto's cell,
There in despair and torture for to dwell.

        [*Exeunt Furies with the Two Brothers.*
These are Thenores' sons of Thessaly,
That come to seek Delia their sister forth:
But, with a potion I to her have given,
My arts have made her to forget herself.

        [*Removes a turf, and shows a light in a glass.*
See here the thing which doth prolong my life,   420
With this enchantment I do anything;
And till this fade, my skill shall still endure,

    [1] Qy. " *Call out, Calypha,* call, *that,*" etc.?

And never none shall break this little glass,
But she that's neither wife, widow, nor maid:
Then cheer thyself; this is thy destiny,
Never to die but by a dead man's hand.   [*Exit.*

Enter EUMENIDES.

Eum. Tell me, Time,
  Tell me, just Time, when shall I Delia see?
  When shall I see the loadstar of my life?
  When shall my wandering course end with her sight,   430
  Or I but view my hope, my heart's delight?

Enter ERESTUS *at the Cross.*

Father, God speed! if you tell fortunes, I pray, good
  father, tell me mine.
Erest. Son, I do see in thy face
  Thy blessèd fortune work apace:
  I do perceive that thou hast wit;
  Beg of thy fate to govern it,
  For wisdom govern'd by advice,
  Makes many fortunate and wise.
  Bestow thy alms, give more than all,   440
  Till dead men's bones come at thy call.
  Farewell, my son: dream of no rest,
  Till thou repent that thou didst best.   [*Exit.*
Eum. This man hath left me in a labyrinth:
  He biddeth me give more than all,
  Till dead men's bones come at my [1] call;
  He biddeth me dream of no rest,
  Till I repent that I do best.   [*Lies down and sleeps.*

Enter WIGGEN, COREBUS, Churchwarden, *and* Sexton.

Wig. You may be ashamed, you whoreson scald Sexton and
  Churchwarden, if you had any shame in those shameless
  faces of yours, to let a poor man lie so long above ground un-
  buried. A rot on you all, that have no more compassion
  of a good fellow when he is gone!   453
Church.[2] What, would you have us to bury him, and to answer
  it ourselves to the parish?

---

[1] The 4to " thy."
[2] Here, and here only, the 4to has " Simon "—by mistake, I suppose,
for " *Steeven*," which is the name of the Churchwarden.

Sex. Parish me no parishes; pay me my fees, and let the rest
run on in the quarter's accounts, and put it down for one of
your good deeds, o' God's name! for I am not one that
curiously stands upon merits. 459

Cor. You whoreson, sodden-headed sheep's-face, shall a good
fellow do less service and more honesty to the parish, and
will you not, when he is dead, let him have Christmas burial?

Wig. Peace, Corebus! as sure as Jack was Jack, the frolic'st
franion amongst you, and I, Wiggen, his sweet sworn
brother, Jack shall have his funerals, or some of them shall
lie on God's dear earth for it, that's once.

Church. Wiggen, I hope thou wilt do no more than thou darest
answer.

Wig. Sir, sir, dare or dare not, more or less, answer or not
answer, do this, or have this. 470

Sex. Help, help, help!

> [*Wiggen sets upon the parish with a pike-staff:* [1]
> *Eumenides awakes and comes to them.*

Eum. Hold thy hands, good fellow.

Cor. Can you blame him, sir, if he take Jack's part against this
shake-rotten parish that will not bury Jack?

Eum. Why, what was that Jack?

Cor. Who, Jack, sir? who, our Jack, sir? as good a fellow as
ever trod upon neat's-leather.

Wig. Look you, sir; he gave fourscore and nineteen mourning
gowns to the parish, when he died, and because he would
not make them up a full hundred, they would not bury
him: was not this good dealing? 481

Church. O Lord, sir, how he lies! he was not worth a halfpenny,
and drunk out every penny; and now his fellows, his
drunken companions, would have us to bury him at the
charge of the parish. An we make many such matches, we
may pull down the steeple, sell the bells, and thatch the
chancel: he shall lie above ground till he dance a galliard
about the church-yard, for Steeven Loach. 488

Wig. Sic argumentaris, Domine Loach,—An we make many
such matches, we may pull down the steeple, sell the bells,
and thatch the chancel? in good time, sir, and hang yourselves in the bell-ropes, when you have done. *Domine,
opponens præpono tibi hanc quæstionem,* whether will you
have the ground broken or your pates broken first? for

---

[1] Stands in the 4to as a portion of the Sexton's speech.

one of them shall be done presently, and to begin mine,[1] I'll seal it upon your coxcomb.

Eum. Hold thy hands, I pray thee, good fellow; be not too hasty.

Cor. You capon's face, we shall have you turned out of the parish one of these days, with never a tatter to your arse; then you are in worse taking than Jack.   501

Eum. Faith, and he is bad enough. This fellow does but the part of a friend, to seek to bury his friend: how much will bury him?

Wig. Faith, about some fifteen or sixteen shillings will bestow him honestly.

Sex. Ay, even thereabouts, sir.

Eum. Here, hold it, then:—[*aside*] and I have left me but one poor three half-pence: now do I remember the words the old man spake at the cross, "Bestow all thou hast," and this is all, "till dead men's bones come at thy call:"—here, hold it [*gives money*]; and so farewell.   512

Wig. God, and all good, be with you, sir! [*Exit Eumenides.*] Nay, you cormorants, I'll bestow one peal of [2] Jack at mine own proper costs and charges.

Cor. You may thank God the long staff and the bilbo-blade crossed not your coxcomb[s].—Well, we'll to the church-stile and have a pot, and so trill-lill.   [*Exit with Wiggen.*

Church. ⎱
Sex. ⎰ Come, let's go.   [*Exeunt.*

Fan. But, hark you, gammer, methinks this Jack bore a great sway in the parish.   531

Madge. O, this Jack was a marvellous fellow! he was but a poor man, but very well beloved: you shall see anon what this Jack will come to.

Enter the Harvest-men *singing,*[3] *with women in their hands.*

Fro. Soft! who have we here? our amorous harvesters.[4]

Fan. Ay, ay, let us sit still, and let them alone.

---

[1] Some word, or words, wanting here.

[2] *i.e.*, on.

[3] T. Warton (*Milton's Poems upon several occasions*, etc., p. 576, ed. 1791) thinks that to the present scene Shakespeare had an eye in *The Tempest*, act iv. sc. 1. There Iris says, "You sunburn'd sicklemen, of August weary," etc., and where the stage direction is, "*Enter cértain Reapers properly habited: they join with the Nymphs in a graceful dance,*" etc.

[4] The 4to "haruest starres."

Here the Harvest-men *sing, the song doubled.*

> Lo, here we come a-reaping, a-reaping,
> To reap our harvest-fruit!
> And thus we pass the year so long,
> And never be we mute.

[Exeunt the Harvest-men.

Enter HUANEBANGO.

Fro. Soft! who have we here?

Madge. O, this is a choleric gentleman! All you that love your lives, keep out of the smell of his two-hand sword: now goes he to the conjurer.

Fan. Methinks the conjurer should put the fool into a juggling-box.

Huan. Fee, fa, fum,
 Here is the Englishman,—
  Conquer him that can,—
  Come [1] for his lady bright,   540
  To prove himself a knight,
  And win her love in fight.

Enter COREBUS.

Cor. Who-haw, Master Bango, are you here? hear you, you had best sit down here, and beg an alms with me.

Huan. Hence, base cullion! here is he that commandeth ingress and egress with his weapon, and will enter at his voluntary, whosoever saith no.

Voice. No. [*A flame of fire; and Huanebango falls down.*

Madge. So with that they kissed, and spoiled the edge of as good a two-hand sword as ever God put life in. Now goes Corebus in, spite of the conjurer. 551

Enter SACRAPANT *and* Two Furies.[2]

Sac. Away with him into the open fields,
 To be a ravening prey to crows and kites:

[*Huan. is carried out by the Two Furies.*

---

[1] The 4to " Came."

[2] Two Furies are not mentioned here in the 4to: but it afterwards makes Huanebango be brought in by " *two Furies* " and laid beside the Well of Life.

And for this villain, let him wander up and down,
In naught but darkness and eternal night.
                              [*Strikes Corebus blind.*
Cor. Here hast thou slain Huan, a slashing knight,
    And robbèd poor Corebus of his sight.
Sac. Hence, villain, hence!   [*Exit Corebus.*
                  Now I have unto Delia
    Given a potion of forgetfulness,
    That, when she comes, she shall not know her brothers.
    Lo, where they labour, like to country-slaves,   561
    With spade and mattock, on this enchanted ground!
    Now will I call her by another name;
    For never shall she know herself again,
    Until that Sacrapant hath breath'd his last.
    See where she comes.

Enter Delia.

    Come hither, Delia, take this goad; here hard
    At hand two slaves do work and dig for gold:
    Gore them with this, and thou shalt have enough.
                              [*Gives her a goad.*
Del. Good sir, I know not what you mean.   570
Sac. [*aside.*] She hath forgotten to be Delia,
    But not forgot the same she should forget;
    But I will change her name.—
    Fair Berecynthia, so this country calls you,
    Go ply these strangers, wench; they dig for gold.   [*Exit.*
Del. O heavens, how
    Am I beholding [1] to this fair young man!
    But I must ply these strangers to their work:
    See where they come.

Enter the Two Brothers *in their shirts, with spades, digging.*

First Bro. O brother, see where Delia is!   580
Second Bro. O Delia,
    Happy are we to see thee here!
Del. What tell you me of Delia, prating swains?
    I know no Delia, nor know I what you mean.
    Ply you your work, or else you're like to smart.
First Bro. Why, Delia, know'st thou not thy brothers here?
    We come from Thessaly to seek thee forth;

                    [1] *i.e.,* beholden.

And thou deceiv'st thyself, for thou art Delia.

Del. Yet more of Delia? then take this, and smart:

[Pricks them with the goad.

What, feign you shifts for to defer your labour?   590
Work, villains, work; it is for gold you dig.

Second Bro. Peace, brother, peace: this vile [1] enchanter
Hath ravish'd Delia of her senses clean,
And she forgets that she is Delia.

First Bro. Leave, cruel thou, to hurt the miserable.—
Dig, brother, dig, for she is hard as steel.

Here they dig, and descry a light in a glass under a little hill.

Second Bro. Stay, brother; what hast thou descried?

Del. Away, and touch it not; 'tis something that
My lord hath hidden there.   *[Covers the light again.*

Re-enter SACRAPANT.

Sac. Well said! [2] thou plyest these pioners well.—   600
Go get you in, you labouring slaves.

[Exeunt the Two Brothers.

Come, Berecynthia, let us in likewise,
And hear the nightingale record her notes.   *[Exeunt.*

Enter ZANTIPPA,[3] *to the Well of Life, with a pot in her hand.*

Zan. Now for a husband, house, and home: God send a good one
or none, I pray God! My father hath sent me to the well
for the water of life, and tells me, if I give fair words, I shall
have a husband. But here comes Celanta my sweet sister:
I'll stand by and hear what she says.   *[Retires.*

Enter CELANTA,[4] *to the Well of Life, with a pot in her hand.*

Cel. My father hath sent me to the well for water, and he tells
me, if I speak fair, I shall have a husband, and none of the
worst. Well, though I am black, I am sure all the world

[1] The 4to vild.
[2] Equivalent to—*Well done!*—in which sense, as I was the first to observe,
the words are frequently used by our early writers.
[3] The 4to adds, " *the curst Daughter.*"
[4] The 4to " the fowle wench."

will not forsake me; and, as the old proverb is, though I
am black,[1] I am not the devil.   613

Zan. [*coming forward.*] Marry-gup with a murren, I know
  wherefore thou speakest that: but go thy ways home as
  wise as thou camest, or I'll set thee home with a wanion.

*Here she strikes her pitcher against her sister's, and breaks them
    both, and then exit.*

Cel. I think this be the curstest quean in the world: you see
  what she is, a little fair, but as proud as the devil, and the
  veriest vixen that lives upon God's earth.   Well, I'll let her
  alone, and go home, and get another pitcher, and, for all
  this, get me to the well for water.   621
                                                              [*Exit.*

Enter, out of SACRAPANT'S *cell, the* Two Furies *carrying* HUANE-
  BANGO: *they lay him by the Well of Life, and then exeunt.*
  Re-enter ZANTIPPA *with a pitcher to the well.*

Zan. Once again for a husband; and, in faith, Celanta, I have
  got the start of you; belike husbands grow by the well-
  side.   Now my father says I must rule my tongue: why,
  alas, what am I, then? a woman without a tongue is as a
  soldier without his weapon: but I'll have my water, and
  be gone.

Here she offers to dip her pitcher in, and a Head *rises in the well.*

Head. Gently dip, but not too deep,
  For fear you make the golden beard to weep.
  Fair maiden, white and red,   630
  Stroke me smooth, and comb my head,
  And thou shalt have some cockell-bread.[2]

[1] " Marry, quoth hee that lookt like Lucifer, *though I am blacke, I am
not the Divell*, but indeed a Collyer of Croydon."—Greene's *Quip for an
Upstart Courtier*, Sig. E 2, ed. n. d.

[2] After many inquiries on the important subject of *cockell-bread*, I regret
to say I am unable to inform the reader what it was.   A lady tells me that
she perfectly remembers to have heard in her youth the following fragment
of a nursery rhyme:

  " My grandmother is sick, I wish she was dead,
    For she taught me the way to make *cockelly-bread*."

And to " *mould cocklebread* " is noticed as a sport or pastime in Brome's
Jovial Crew: " And then at home here, or wheresoever he comes, our
father is so pensive (what muddy spirit soe'er possesses him, would I could
conjure't out!), that he makes us even sick of his sadness, that were wont
*to see my ghossips cock to day, mould cocklebread, daunce clutterdepouch and
hannykin booby, binde barrels*, or do anything before him, and he would

Zan. What is this?
        " Fair maiden, white and red,

laugh at us." Sig. D 2, ed. 1652.—So I wrote on the present passage in 1828.

The following Article is from Thoms's *Anecdotes and Traditions*, etc., printed for the Camden Society, 1839:—

" Cockle Bread

Young wenches [Aubrey *loquitur*] have a wanton sport which they call moulding of Cockle-bread, viz., they get upon a table-board, and then gather up their knees and their coates with their hands as high as they can, and then they wabble to and fro, as if they were kneading of dowgh, and say these words, viz.:

My dame is sick and gonne to bed,
        And I'le go mould my Cockle-bread.

I did imagine nothing to have been in this but meer wantonesse of youth. But I find in Burchardus, in his ' Methodus Confitendi,' printed at Colon, 1549 (he lived before the Conquest), one of the Articles (on the vii. Commandment) of interrogating a young woman is, ' If she did ever ' subigere panem clunibus,' and then bake it, and give it to one she loved to eate, ' ut in majorem modum exardesceret amor.' So here I find it to be a relique of naturall magick—an unlawful philtrum.

White Kennet adds, in a side note—' In Oxfordshire, the Maids, when they put themselves into the fit posture, sing thus,

My granny is sick, and now is dead,
        And wee'l goe mould some Cockle Bread,
        Up with my heels and down with my head,
        And this is the way to mould Cockle-bread.'

Aubrey, 1232°."

Mr. Thoms subjoins: " The question in Burchardus, and which we here quote at length (from Grimm, xxxix.) fully establishes the correctness of Aubrey's views as to the origin of this game.

' Fecisti quod quædam mulieres facere solent, prosternunt se in faciem, et discoopertibus natibus jubent, ut supra nudas nates conficiatur panis, et eo decocto tradunt maritis suis ad comedendum. Hoc ideo faciunt ut plus exardescant in amorem illorum [illarum].'

The rhyme still heard in our nurseries—

' When I was a little girl, I wash'd my mother's dishes;
        I put my finger in my eye, and pull'd out little fishes—'

is likewise given by Aubrey, with a verbal alteration, and another reference to Burchardus, which seems to establish it as another ' relique of natural magick, an unlawful philtrum.'

From the following passage in another part of the MS. fo. 161, it would seem as if Cockle-Bread derived its name from the peculiar manner in which it was kneaded.

' I have some reason to believe, that the word Cockle is an old antiquated Norman word, which signifies *nates*, from a beastly rustic kind of play, or abuse, which was used when I was a schoolboy by a Norman gardner that lived at Downton near me. So Hott Cockles is as much as to say Hott or Heated Buttocks.'

The name Hot Cockles is derived by Strutt, in his *Sports and Pastimes*, p. 393, ed. 1833 (which contains, however, no allusion to any such Norman word as that to which Aubrey refers), from the ' Hautes Coquilles ' of the French. In the *Memoires de l'Academie Celtique*, tom. iii., we have a description of a curious marriage custom, which may possibly bear some reference to the ' *Cockel Bread* ' or at least to the etymology of the name." pp. 94-6.

Comb me smooth, and stroke my head,
And thou shalt have some cockell-bread "?
"Cockell" callest thou it, boy? faith, I'll give you
cockell-bread.

She breaks her pitcher upon the Head: *then it thunders and
lightens; and* HUANEBANGO, *who is deaf and cannot hear
rises up.*

Huan. Philida, phileridos, pamphilida, florida, flortos:
Dub dub-a-dub, bounce, quoth the guns, with a sulphurous
huff-snuff: [1]   640
Wak'd with a wench, pretty peat, pretty love, and my
sweet pretty pigsnie, [2]
Just by thy side shall sit surnamèd great Huanebango:
Safe in my arms will I keep thee, threat Mars, or thunder
Olympus.

Zan. [*aside.*] Foh, what greasy groom have we here? He looks
as though he crept out of the backside of the well, and
speaks like a drum perished at the west end.

Huan. O, that I might,—but I may not, woe to my destiny
therefore! [3]—
Kiss that I clasp! but I cannot: tell me, my destiny,
wherefore?

Zan. [*aside.*] Whoop! now I have my dream. Did you never
hear so great a wonder as this, three blue beans in a blue
bladder, rattle, bladder, rattle?   651

Huan. [*aside.*] I'll now set my countenance, and to her in prose;
it may be, this rim-ram-ruff [4] is too rude an encounter.—

[1] So Stanyhurst in *The First Fovre Bookes of Virgils Æneis, with other
Poeticall deuises thereto annexed*, 1583:
  " Lowd *dub a dub* tabering with frapping rip rap of Ætna."
                                The Description of Liparen, p. 91.
  " Thee whil'st in the skie seat great *bouncing* rumbelo thundring
Rattleth," etc.   *Æneid* 4, p. 66.
    " Linckt was in wedlock a loftye Thrasonical *huf snuffe.*"
                                Of a cracking Cutter, p. 95.
[2] *i.e.*, little pig. (A term of endearment).
[3] Taken verbatim from Gabriel Harvey's *Encomium Lauri :*
" Faine wod I craue, might I so presume, some farther acquaintaunce:
  O that I might ! but I may not : woe to my destinie therefore ! "
[4] So the copy of the 4to in the British Museum (King's Library,
Pamphlets); while my copy reads " *this* rude *ram ruffe ;* "—the passage
having been corrected before the whole of the impression was struck off.—
Compare Stanyhurst:
    " Of *ruffe* raffe roaring, mens harts with terror agrysing."
                                The Description of Liparen, p. 91.

Let me, fair lady, if you be at leisure, revel with your sweetness, and rail upon that cowardly conjurer, that hath cast
me, or congealed me rather, into an unkind sleep, and
polluted my carcass.

Zan. [*aside.*] Laugh, laugh, Zantippa; thou hast thy fortune,
a fool and a husband under one.

Huan. Truly, sweet-heart, as I seem, about some twenty years,
the very April of mine age.   661

Zan. [*aside.*] Why, what a prating ass is this!

Huan. Her coral lips, her crimson chin,
    Her silver teeth so white within,
    Her golden locks, her rolling eye,
    Her pretty parts, let them go by,
    Heigh-ho, have wounded me,
    That I must die this day to see!

Zan. By Gogs-bones, thou art a flouting knave: "her coral lips,
her crimson chin!" ka, wilshaw!   670

Huan. True, my own, and my own because mine, and mine
because mine, ha, ha! above a thousand pounds in possi-
bility, and things fitting thy desire in possession.

Zan. [*aside.*] The sot thinks I ask of his lands. Lob be your
comfort, and cuckold be your destiny!—Hear you, sir; an
if you will have us, you had best say so betime.

Huan. True, sweet-heart, and will royalise thy progeny with my
pedigree.   [*Exeunt.*

Enter EUMENIDES.

Eum. Wretched Eumenides, still unfortunate,
    Envied by fortune and forlorn by fate,   680
    Here pine and die, wretched Eumenides,
    Die in the spring, the April of thy [1] age!
    Here sit thee down, repent what thou hast done:
    I would to God that it were ne'er begun!

Enter the GHOST OF JACK.

G. of Jack. You are well overtaken, sir.

Eum. Who's that?

G. of Jack. You are heartily well met, sir.

Eum. Forbear, I say: who is that which pincheth me?   688

[1] The 4to "my."

G. of Jack. Trusting in God, good Master Eumenides, that you
are in so good health as all your friends were at the making
hereof,—God give you good morrow, sir! Lack you not a
neat, handsome, and cleanly young lad, about the age of
fifteen or sixteen years, that can run by your horse, and, for
a need, make your mastership's shoes as black as ink?
how say you, sir?

Eum. Alas, pretty lad, I know not how to keep myself, and
much less a servant, my pretty boy; my state is so bad.

G. of Jack. Content yourself, you shall not be so ill a master but
I'll be as bad a servant. Tut, sir, I know you, though you
know not me: are not you the man, sir, deny it if you can,
sir, that came from a strange place in the land of Catita,
where Jack-an-apes [1] flies with his tail in his mouth, to seek
out a lady as white as snow and as red as blood? [2] ha, ha!
have I touched you now?   704

Eum. [*aside.*] I think this boy be a spirit.—How knowest thou
all this?

G. of Jack. Tut, are not you the man, sir, deny it if you can, sir,
that gave all the money you had to the burying of a poor
man, and but one three half-pence left in your purse?
Content you, sir, I'll serve you, that is flat.   710

Eum. Well, my lad, since thou art so impor[tu]nate, I am
content to entertain thee, not as a servant, but a copartner
in my journey. But whither shall we go? for I have not
any money more than one bare three half-pence.

G. of Jack. Well, master, content yourself, for if my divination be
not out, that shall be spent at the next inn or alehouse we
come to; for, master, I know you are passing hungry:
therefore I'll go before and provide dinner until that you
come; no doubt but you'll come fair and softly after.

Eum. Ay, go before; I'll follow thee.   720

G. of Jack. But do you hear, master? do you know my name?

Eum. No, I promise thee, not yet.

G. of Jack. Why, I am Jack.   [*Exit.*[3]

Eum. Jack! why, be it so, then.

---

[1] *i.e.*, monkey, ape.

[2] Compare the third speech of Madge in p. 134.

[3] After Jack's exit, as there was no change of scenery in Peele's days,
the audience were to suppose Eumenides already arrived at the inn.

Enter the Hostess *and* JACK, *setting meat on the table; and
Fiddlers come to play.* EUMENIDES *walks up and down,
and will eat no meat.*

Host. How say you, sir? do you please to sit down?

Eum. Hostess, I thank you, I have no great stomach.

Host. Pray, sir, what is the reason your master is so strange?
doth not this meat please him?

G. of Jack. Yes, hostess, but it is my master's fashion to pay
before he eats; therefore, a reckoning, good hostess.   730

Host. Marry, shall you, sir, presently.   [*Exit.*

Eum. Why, Jack, what dost thou mean? thou knowest I have
not any money; therefore, sweet Jack, tell me what shall
I do?

G. of Jack. Well, master, look in your purse.

Eum. Why, faith, it is a folly, for I have no money.

G. of Jack. Why, look you, master; do so much for me.

Eum. [*looking into his purse.*] Alas, Jack, my purse is full of
money!   739

Jack. "Alas," master! does that word belong to this accident?
why, methinks I should have seen you cast away your cloak,
and in a bravado dance[1] a galliard round about the chamber:
why, master, your man can teach you more wit than this.

Re-enter Hostess.

Come, hostess, cheer up my master.

Host. You are heartily welcome; and if it please you to eat of
a fat capon, a fairer bird, a finer bird, a sweeter bird, a
crisper bird, a neater bird, your worship never eat of.

Eum. Thanks, my fine, eloquent hostess.

G. of Jack. But hear you, master, one word by the way: are
you content I shall be halves in all you get in your journey?

Eum. I am, Jack, here is my hand.   751

G. of Jack. Enough, master, I ask no more.

Eum. Come, hostess, receive your money; and I thank you for
my good entertainment.   [*Gives money.*

Host. You are heartily welcome, sir.

Eum. Come, Jack, whither go we now?

G. of Jack. Marry, master, to the conjurer's presently.

Eum. Content, Jack.—Hostess, farewell.   [*Exeunt.*

[1] The 4to "daunced."

Enter COREBUS, *and* CELANIA,[1] *to the Well of Life for water.*

Cor. Come, my duck, come: I have now got a wife: thou art
    fair, art thou not?[2]   760
Cel. My Corebus, the fairest alive; make no doubt of that.
Cor. Come, wench, are we almost at the well?
Cel. Ay, Corebus, we are almost at the well now. I'll go fetch
    some water: sit down while I dip my pitcher in.

A Head *comes up with ears of corn, which she combs into her lap.*

Head. Gently dip, but not too deep,
    For fear you make the golden beard to weep.
    Fair maiden, white and red,
    Comb me smooth, and stroke my head,
    And thou shalt have some cockell-bread.

A Second Head *comes up full of gold, which she combs into her lap.*

Sec. Head. Gently dip, but not too deep,   770
    For fear thou make the golden beard to weep.
    Fair maid, white and red,
    Comb me smooth, and stroke my head,
    And every hair a sheaf shall be,
    And every sheaf a golden tree.
Cel. O, see, Corebus, I have combed a great deal of gold into my
    lap, and a great deal of corn!
Cor. Well said, wench! now we shall have just[3] enough: God
    send us coiners to coin our gold. But come, shall we go
    home, sweetheart?   780
Cel. Nay, come, Corebus, I will lead you.
Cor. So, Corebus, things have well hit;
    Thou hast gotten wealth to mend thy wit.   [*Exeunt.*

Enter the GHOST OF JACK *and* EUMENIDES.

G. of Jack. Come away, master, come.
Eum. Go along, Jack, I'll follow thee. Jack, they say it is
    good to go cross-legged, and say prayers[4] backward; how
    sayest thou?

[1] Spelt, throughout this scene, in the 4to, " Zelanto."
[2] The reader must not forget that Corebus has been struck blind by
Sacrapant.
[3] So the Museum copy of the 4to; while my copy has " tost."
[4] The 4to " *say* his *prayers.*"

G. of Jack. Tut, never fear, master; let me alone. Here sit you
still; speak not a word; and because you shall not be
enticed with his enchanting speeches, with this same wool
I'll stop your ears [*Puts wool into the ears of Eumenides*]:
and so, master, sit still, for I must to the conjurer.   [*Exit.*

Enter SACRAPANT.

Sac. How now! what man art thou, that sits so sad?   793
Why dost thou gaze upon these stately trees
Without the leave and will of Sacrapant?
What, not a word but mum?   Then, Sacrapant,
Thou art betrayed.

Re-enter the GHOST OF JACK *invisible, and takes* SACRAPANT'S
wreath off from his head, and his sword out of his hand.

What hand invades the head of Sacrapant?
What hateful [1] Fury doth envy my happy state?
Then, Sacrapant, these are thy latest days.   800
Alas, my veins are numb'd, my sinews shrink,
My blood is pierc'd, my breath fleeting away,
And now my timeless date is come to end!
He in whose life his acts have [2] been so foul,
Now in his death to hell decends his soul.   [*Dies.*
G. of Jack. O, sir, are you gone? now I hope we shall have some
other coil.—Now, master, how like you this? the conjurer
he is dead, and vows never to trouble us more: now get you
to your fair lady, and see what you can do with her.—Alas,
he heareth me not all this while! but I will help that. 810
        [*Pulls the wool out of the ears of Eumenides.*
Eum. How now, Jack! what news?
G. of Jack. Here, master, take this sword, and dig with it at
the foot of this hill.   [*Gives sword.*

EUMENIDES *digs, and spies a light in a glass.*

Eum. How now, Jack! what is this?
G. of Jack. Master, without this the conjurer could do nothing;
and so long as this light lasts, so long doth his art endure,
and this being out, then doth his art decay.

[1] Qy. " *What Fury doth* envy *my happy state ?* "
[2] The 4to " *actions hath.*"

Eum. Why, then, Jack, I will soon put out this light.

G. of Jack. Ay, master, how?

Eum. Why, with a stone I'll break the glass, and then blow
it out.   821

G. of Jack. No, master, you may as soon break the smith's
anvil as this little vial: nor the biggest blast that ever
Boreas blew cannot blow out this little light; but she that
is neither maid, wife, nor widow. Master, wind this horn,
and see what will happen.   [*Gives horn.*

EUMENIDES *winds the horn. Enter* VENELIA, *who breaks the
glass, blows out the light, and then exit.*

So, master, how like you this? this is she that ran madding
in the woods, his betrothed love that keeps the cross; and
now, this light being out, all are restored to their former
liberty: and now, master, to the lady that you have so
long looked for.   831

The GHOST OF JACK *draws a curtain, and discovers* DELIA *sitting
asleep.*

Eum. God speed, fair maid, sitting alone,—there is once; God
speed, fair maid,—there is twice; God speed, fair maid,—
that is thrice.

Del. Not so, good sir, for you are by.

G. of Jack. Enough, master, she hath spoke; now I will leave
her with you.   [*Exit.*

Eum. Thou fairest flower of these western parts,
Whose beauty so reflecteth in my sight
As doth a crystal mirror in the sun;   840
For thy sweet sake I have cross'd the frozen Rhine;[1]
Leaving fair Po, I sail'd up Danuby,
As far as Saba, whose enhancing streams
Cut twixt the Tartars and the Russians:
These have I cross'd for thee, fair Delia:
Then grant me that which I have su'd for long.

Del. Thou gentle knight, whose fortune is so good
To find me out and set my brothers free,
My faith, my heart, my hand I give to thee.

[1] This and the next three lines are found, with slight variations, in
Greene's *Orlando Furioso.*

Eum. Thanks, gentle madam: but here comes Jack; thank
him, for he is the best friend that we have. 851

Re-enter the GHOST OF JACK, *with* SACRAPANT'S *head in his hand.*[1]
How now, Jack! what hast thou there?

G. of Jack. Marry, master, the head of the conjurer.

Eum. Why, Jack, that is impossible; he was a young man.

G. of Jack. Ah, master, so he deceived them that beheld him!
but he was a miserable, old, and crooked man, though to
each man's eye he seemed young and fresh; for, master,
this conjurer took the shape of the old man that kept the
cross, and that old man was in the likeness of the conjurer.
But now, master, wind your horn. 860

EUMENIDES *winds his horn. Enter* VENELIA, *the* Two Brothers,
and ERESTUS.

Eum. Welcome, Erestus! welcome, fair Venelia!
Welcome, Thelea and Calypha [2] both!
Now have I her that I so long have sought;
So saith fair Delia, if we have your consent.

First Bro. Valiant Eumenides, thou well deservest
To have our favours; so let us rejoice
That by thy means we are at liberty:
Here may we joy each in other's [3] sight,
And this fair lady have her wandering knight.

G. of Jack. So, master, now ye think you have done; but I must
have a saying to you: you know you and I were partners,
I to have half in all you got. 872

Eum. Why, so thou shalt, Jack.

G. of Jack. Why, then, master, draw your sword, part your lady,
let me have half of her presently.

Eum. Why, I hope, Jack, thou dost but jest: I promised thee
half I got, but not half my lady.

G. of Jack. But what else, master? have you not gotten her?
therefore divide her straight, for I will have half; there
is no remedy. 880

Eum. Well, ere I will falsify my word unto my friend, take her
all: here, Jack, I'll give her thee.

[1] But where did the decapitation take place? Perhaps when " the
Ghost of Jack drew a curtain, and discovered Delia "—the curtain was
at the same time so drawn as to conceal the body of the conjurer.
[2] Spelt here in the 4to " Kalepha."
[3] Qy. " *in* the *other's* "? (unless " *joy* " be a dissyllable here).

G. of Jack. Nay, neither more nor less, master, but even just half.

Eum. Before I will falsify my faith unto my friend, I will divide her: Jack, thou shalt have half.

First Bro. Be not so cruel unto our sister, gentle knight.

Second Bro. O, spare fair Delia! she deserves no death.

Eum. Content yourselves; my word is passed to him.—Therefore prepare thyself, Delia, for thou must die. 890

Del. Then farewell, world! adieu, Eumenides!

EUMENIDES *offers to strike, and the* GHOST OF JACK *stays him.*

G. of Jack. Stay, master; it is sufficient I have tried your constancy. Do you now remember since you paid for the burying of a poor fellow?

Eum. Ay, very well, Jack.

G. of Jack. Then, master, thank that good deed for this good turn: and so God be with you all!

[*Leaps down in* [1] *the ground.*

Eum. Jack, what, art thou gone? then farewell, Jack!—
Come, brothers, and my beauteous Delia,
Erestus, and thy dear Venelia, 900
We will to Thessaly with joyful hearts.

All. Agreed: we follow thee and Delia.

[*Exeunt all except Frolic, Fantastic, and Madge.*

Fan. What, gammer, asleep?

Madge. By the mass, son, 'tis almost day; and my windows shut at the cock's-crow.

Fro. Do you hear, gammer? methinks this Jack bore a great sway amongst them.

Madge. O, man, this was the ghost of the poor man that they kept such a coil to bury; and that makes him to help the wandering knight so much. But come, let us in: we will have a cup of ale and a toast this morning, and so depart. [2]

Fan. Then you have made an end of your tale, gammer? 912

Mage. Yes, faith: when this was done, I took a piece of bread and cheese, and came my way; and so shall you have, too, before you go, to your breakfast. [*Exeunt.*

[1] *i.e.*, into.   [2] *i.e.*, part.

FRIAR BACON AND FRIAR BUNGAY

The Honorable Historie of frier Bacon, and frier Bongay.   As it was plaid by her Maiesties seruants.   Made by Robert Greene, Maister of Arts.   London, Printed for Edward White, and are to be sold at his shop, at the little North dore of Poules, at the signe of the Gun. 1594, 4to.

This play was reprinted in 1599, 1630, and 1655; and forms a part of the viiith vol. of the new edition of Dodsley's *Old Plays*.

THE HONOURABLE HISTORY OF
FRIAR BACON AND FRIAR BUNGAY

DRAMATIS PERSONÆ

KING HENRY THE THIRD.
EDWARD, Prince of Wales, *his son.*
EMPEROR OF GERMANY.
KING OF CASTILE.
LACY, Earl of Lincoln.
WARREN, Earl of Sussex.
ERMSBY, *a gentleman.*
RALPH SIMNELL, *the King's Fool.*[1]
FRIAR BACON.
MILES, *Friar Bacon's poor scholar.*
FRIAR BUNGAY.
JAQUES VANDERMAST.
BURDEN,
MASON, } *Doctors of Oxford.*
CLEMENT,
LAMBERT, } *gentlemen.*
SERLSBY,

Two Scholars, *their sons.*
Keeper.
THOMAS,
RICHARD, } *clowns.*
Constable.
A Post.
Lords, Clowns, etc.

ELINOR, *daughter to the King of Castile.*
MARGARET, *the Keeper's daughter.*
JOAN, *a country wench.*
Hostess of the Bell at Henley.

A DEVIL.
Spirit in the shape of HERCULES.

Enter PRINCE EDWARD *malcontented, with* LACY, WARREN, ERMSBY, *and* RALPH SIMNELL.

Lacy. Why looks my lord like to a troubled sky
    When heaven's bright shine is shadow'd with a fog?
    Alate we ran the deer, and through the lawnds [2]
    Stripp'd [3] with our nags the lofty frolic bucks
    That scudded 'fore the teasers [4] like the wind:
    Ne'er was the deer of merry Fressingfield
    So lustily pull'd down by jolly mates,
    Nor shar'd the farmers such fat venison,
    So frankly dealt, this hundred years before;
    Nor have   10
    I seen my lord more frolic in the chase,
    And now chang'd to a melancholy dump.

---

[1] Not the Prince's.   [2] *i.e.,* lawns.   [3] *i.e.,* Outstripped.
[4] " But these *Teazers*, rather to rouze then pinch the game, onely made Whitaker find his spirits. The fiercest *dog* is behind, even Bellarmine himself," etc.   Fuller's *Holy State*, p. 66, ed. 1642.

War. After the prince got to the Keeper's lodge,
 And had been jocund in the house awhile,
 Tossing off ale and milk in country cans,
 Whether it was the country's sweet content,
 Or else the bonny damsel fill'd us drink
 That seem'd so stately in her stammel red,[1]
 Or that a qualm did cross his stomach then,
 But straight he tell into his passions.   20

Erms. Sirrah Ralph, what say you to your master,
 Shall he thus all amort [2] live malcontent?

Ralph. Hearest thou, Ned?—Nay, look if he will speak to me!

P. Edw. What say'st thou to me, fool?

Ralph. I prithee, tell me, Ned, art thou in love with the Keeper's
 daughter?

P. Edw. How if I be, what then?

Ralph. Why, then, sirrah, I'll teach thee how to deceive Love.

P. Edw. How, Ralph?

Ralph. Marry, Sirrah Ned, thou shalt put on my cap and my
 coat and my dagger, and I will put on thy clothes and thy
 sword; and so thou shalt be my fool.   32

P. Edw. And what of this?

Ralph. Why, so thou shalt beguile Love; for Love is such a
 proud scab, that he will never meddle with fools nor children.
 Is not Ralph's counsel good, Ned?

P. Edw. Tell me, Ned Lacy, didst thou mark the maid,
 How lovely [3] in her country-weeds she look'd?
 A bonnier wench all Suffolk cannot yield:—
 All Suffolk! nay, all England holds none such.   40

Ralph. Sirrah Will Ermsby, Ned is deceived.

Erms. Why, Ralph?

Ralph. He says all England hath no such, and I say, and I'll
 stand to it, there is one better in Warwickshire.

War. How provest thou that, Ralph?

Ralph. Why, is not the abbot a learned man, and hath read
 many books, and thinkest thou he hath not more learning
 than thou to choose a bonny wench? yes, warrant I thee,
 by his whole grammar.

---

[1] *Stammel* was a kind of woollen cloth. The words "red" and
"stammel" were, I believe, seldom used together, the former being the
understood colour of the latter. ("*Stammel-colour*, Spadex, Spadiceus."
Coles's *Dict.*)

[2] More properly *alamort, i.e.*, dejected.

[3] The 4tos "lively."

Erms. A good reason, Ralph.   50
P. Edw. I tell thee, Lacy, that her sparkling eyes
    Do lighten forth sweet love's alluring fire;
    And in her tresses she doth fold the looks
    Of such as gaze upon her golden hair:
    Her bashful white, mix'd with the morning's red,
    Luna doth boast upon her lovely cheeks;
    Her front is beauty's table, where she paints
    The glories of her gorgeous excellence;
    Her teeth are shelves of precious margarites,[1]
    Richly enclos'd with ruddy coral cleeves.[2]   60
    Tush, Lacy, she is beauty's over-match,
    If thou survey'st her curious imagery.
Lacy. I grant, my lord, the damsel is as fair
    As simple Suffolk's homely towns can yield;
    But in the court be quainter dames than she,
    Whose faces are enrich'd with honour's taint,[3]
    Whose beauties stand upon the stage of fame,
    And vaunt their trophies in the courts of love.
P. Edw. Ah, Ned, but hadst thou watch'd her as myself,
    And seen the secret beauties of the maid,   70
    Their courtly coyness were but foolery.
Erms. Why, how watch'd you her, my lord?
P. Edw. Whenas she swept like Venus through the house,
    And in her shape fast folded up my thoughts,
    Into the milk-house went I with the maid,
    And there amongst the cream-bowls she did shine
    As Pallas 'mongst her princely huswifery:
    She turn'd her smock over her lily arms,
    And div'd them into milk to run her cheese;
    But whiter than the milk her crystal skin,   80
    Checkèd with lines of azure, made her blush [4]
    That art or nature durst bring for compare.
    Ermsby,
    If thou hadst seen, as I did note it well,
    How beauty play'd the huswife, how this girl,
    Like Lucrece, laid her fingers to the work,
    Thou wouldst, with Tarquin, hazard Rome and all

[1] *i.e.,* pearls.
[2] *i.e.,* cliffs: Drayton uses the singular, *cleeve.*
[3] Equivalent to *tint.*
[4] Means, I suppose—made (would have made) that woman blush
whom art, etc.

To win the lovely maid of Fressingfield.

Ralph. Sirrah Ned, wouldst fain have her?

P. Edw. Ay, Ralph.   90

Ralph. Why, Ned, I have laid the plot in my head; thou shalt have her already.

P. Edw. I'll give thee a new coat, an learn me that.

Ralph. Why, Sirrah Ned, we'll ride to Oxford to Friar Bacon: O, he is a brave scholar, sirrah; they say he is a brave necromancer, that he can make women of devils, and he can juggle cats into costermongers.

P. Edw. And how then, Ralph?

Ralph. Marry, sirrah, thou shalt go to him: and because thy father Harry shall not miss thee, he shall turn me into thee; and I'll to the court, and I'll prince it out; and he shall make thee either a silken purse full of gold, or else a fine wrought smock.   103

P. Edw. But how shall I have the maid?

Ralph. Marry, sirrah, if thou be'st a silken purse full of gold, then on Sundays she'll hang thee by her side, and you must not say a word. Now, sir, when she comes into a great prease[1] of people, for fear of the cutpurse, on a sudden she'll swap thee into her plackerd;[2] then, sirrah, being there, you may plead for yourself.   110

Erms. Excellent policy!

P. Edw. But how if I be a wrought smock?

Ralph. Then she'll put thee into her chest and lay thee into lavender, and upon some good day she'll put thee on; and at night when you go to bed, then being turned from a smock to a man, you may make up the match.

Lacy. Wonderfully wisely counselled, Ralph.

P. Edw. Ralph shall have a new coat.

Ralph. God thank you when I have it on my back, Ned.

P. Edw. Lacy, the fool hath laid a perfect plot;   120
     For why[3] our country Margaret is so coy,
     And stands so much upon her honest points,
     That marriage or no market with the maid.
     Ermsby, it must be necromantic spells

---

    [1] *i.e.,* press.

    [2] Plackerd, commonly written *placket*, is equivalent here to *pocket.* (Concerning the various significations of this word see Amner's [*i.e.,* Steevens's] note on *King Lear*, act iii. sc. 4, Halliwell's *Dict. of Arch. and Prov. Words*, and *A Few Notes on Shakespeare*, p. 53.)

    [3] *i.e.,* Because.

And charms of art that must enchain her love,
Or else shall Edward never win the girl.
Therefore, my wags, we'll horse us in the morn,
And post to Oxford to this jolly friar:
Bacon shall by his magic do this deed.

War. Content, my lord; and that's a speedy way   130
To wean these headstrong puppies from the teat.

P. Edw. I am unknown, not taken for the prince;
They only deem us frolic courtiers,
That revel thus among our liege's game:
Therefore I have devis'd a policy.
Lacy, thou know'st next Friday is Saint James',
And then the country flocks to Harleston fair:
Then will the Keeper's daughter frolic there,
And over-shine the troop of all the maids
That come to see and to be seen that day.   140
Haunt thee disguis'd among the country-swains,
Feign thou'rt a farmer's son, not far from thence,
Espy her loves, and who she liketh best;
Cote [1] him, and court her to control the clown;
Say that the courtier 'tirèd all in green,
That help'd her handsomely to run her cheese,
And fill'd her father's lodge with venison,
Commends him, and sends fairings to herself.
Buy something worthy of her parentage,
Not worth her beauty; for, Lacy, then the fair   150
Affords no jewel fitting for the maid:
And when thou talk'st of me, note if she blush:
O, then she loves; but if her cheeks wax pale,
Disdain it is.   Lacy, send how she fares,
And spare no time nor cost to win her loves.

Lacy. I will, my lord, so execute this charge
As if that Lacy were in love with her.

P. Edw. Send letters speedily to Oxford of the news.

Ralph. And, Sirrah Lacy, buy me a thousand thousand million
of fine bells.   160

Lacy. What wilt thou do with them, Ralph?

Ralph. Marry, every time that Ned sighs for the Keeper's
daughter, I'll tie a bell about him: and so within three or
four days I will send word to his father Harry, that his son,
and my master Ned, is become Love's morris-dance[r].

---

[1] *i.e.*, Keep along side of.   Fr. *cotoyer*.

P. Edw. Well, Lacy, look with care unto thy charge,
  And I will haste to Oxford to the friar,
  That he by art and thou by secret gifts
  Mayst make me lord of merry Fressingfield.   169
Lacy. God send your honour your heart's desire.[1]   [*Exeunt.*

Enter FRIAR BACON, *and* MILES *with books under his arm;*
  BURDEN, MASON, *and* CLEMENT.

Bacon. Miles, where are you?
Miles. *Hic sum, doctissime et reverendissime doctor.*
Bacon. *Attulisti nos libros meos de necromantia?*
Miles. *Ecce quam bonum et quam jucundum habitare libros in
  unum !*
Bacon. Now, masters of our academic state,
  That rule in Oxford, viceroys in your place,
  Whose heads contain maps of the liberal arts,
  Spending your time in depth of learnèd skill,
  Why flock you thus to Bacon's secret cell,   180
  A friar newly stall'd in Brazen-nose?
  Say what's your mind, that I may make reply.
Burd. Bacon, we hear that long we have suspect,
  That thou art read in magic's mystery;
  In pyromancy, to divine by flames;
  To tell, by hydromatic, ebbs and tides;
  By aeromancy to discover doubts,
  To plain out questions, as Apollo did.
Bacon. Well, Master Burden, what of all this?   189
Miles. Marry, sir, he doth but fulfil, by rehearsing of these
  names, the fable of the Fox and the Grapes; that which is
  above us pertains nothing to us.
Burd. I tell thee, Bacon, Oxford makes report,
  Nay, England, and the court of Henry says,
  Thou'rt making of a brazen head by art,
  Which shall unfold strange doubts and aphorisms,
  And read a lecture in philosophy;
  And, by the help of devils and ghastly fiends,
  Thou mean'st, ere many years or days be past,
  To compass England with a wall of brass.   200
Bacon. And what of this?
Miles. What of this, master! why, he doth speak mystically;

---

[1] Qy. " all *your heart's desire* " ?

for he knows, if your skill fail to make a brazen head, yet
Mother Waters' strong ale will fit his turn to make him
have a copper nose.

Clem. Bacon, we come not grieving at thy skill,
But joying that our académy yields
A man suppos'd the wonder of the world;
For if thy cunning work these miracles,
England and Europe shall admire thy fame,   210
And Oxford shall in characters of brass,
And statues, such as were built up in Rome,
Etérnise Friar Bacon for his art.

Mason. Then, gentle friar, tell us thy intent.

Bacon. Seeing you come as friends unto the friar,
Resolve you,[1] doctors, Bacon can by books
Make storming Boreas thunder from his cave,
And dim fair Luna to a dark eclipse.
The great arch-ruler, potentate of hell,
Trembles when Bacon bids him, or his fiends,   220
Bow to the force of his pentageron.
What art can work, the frolic friar knows;
And therefore will I turn my magic books,
And strain out necromancy to the deep.
I have contriv'd and fram'd a head of brass
(I made Belcephon hammer out the stuff),
And that by art shall read philosophy:
And I will strengthen England by my skill,
That if ten Cæsars liv'd and reign'd in Rome,
With all the legions Europe doth contain,   230
They should not touch a grass of English ground:
The work that Ninus rear'd at Babylon,
The brazen walls fram'd by Semiramis,
Carv'd out like to the portal of the sun,
Shall not be such as rings the English strand
From Dover to the market-place of Rye.

Burd. Is this possible?

Miles. I'll bring ye two or three witnesses.

Burd. What be those?   239

Miles. Marry, sir, three or four as honest devils and good companions as any be in hell.

Mason. No doubt but magic may do much in this;
For he that reads but mathematic rules

[1] *i.e.*, Be you assured.

Shall find conclusions that avail to work
Wonders that pass the common sense of men.

Burd. But Bacon roves a bow beyond his reach,[1]
And tells of more than magic can perform;
Thinking to get a fame by fooleries.
Have I not pass'd as far in state of schools,
And read of many secrets? yet to think   250
That heads of brass can utter any voice,
Or more, to tell of deep philosophy,
This is a fable Æsop had forgot.

Bacon. Burden, thou wrong'st me in detracting thus,
Bacon loves not to stuff himself with lies.
But tell me 'fore these doctors, if thou dare,
Of certain questions I shall move to thee.

Burd. I will: ask what thou can.

Miles. Marry, sir, he'll straight be on your pick-back, to know
whether the feminine or the masculine gender be most
worthy.   261

Bacon. Were you not yesterday, Master Burden, at Henley upon
the Thames?

Burd. I was: what then?

Bacon. What book studied you thereon all night?

Burd. I! none at all; I read not there a line.

Bacon. Then, doctors, Friar Bacon's art knows naught.

Clem. What say you to this, Master Burden? doth he not touch
you?

Burd. I pass not of [2] his frivolous speeches.   270

Miles. Nay, Master Burden, my master, ere he hath done with
you, will turn you from a doctor to a dunce, and shake you
so small, that he will leave no more learning in you than is
in Balaam's ass.

Bacon. Masters, for that learn'd Burden's skill is deep,
And sore he doubts of Bacon's cabalism,
I'll show you why he haunts to Henley oft:
Not, doctors, for to taste the fragrant air,
But there to spend the night in alchemy,
To multiply with secret spells of art;   280
Thus private steals he learning from us all.

---

[1] "To *rove a bow beyond his reach* is equivalent to the proverbial phrase
of shooting with a long bow: the bow is too long for the stretch of his
arms."—*Editor of Dodsley's Old Plays.*

[2] *i.e.*, care not for. "Since he hath let them passe, I greatly *passe* not."
—Chettle's *Kind-harts Dream*, n. d. [1592], Sig. D 3.

To prove my sayings true, I'll show you straight
The book he keeps at Henley for himself.

Miles. Nay, now my master goes to conjuration, take heed.

Bacon. Masters,
    Stand still, fear not, I'll show you but his book. [*Conjures.*
    Per omnes deos infernales, Belcephon!

Enter Hostess *with a shoulder of mutton on a spit, and a* Devil.

Miles. O, master, cease your conjuration, or you spoil all; for
here's a she-devil come with a shoulder of mutton on a spit:
you have marred the devil's supper; but no doubt he thinks
our college fare is slender, and so hath sent you his cook
with a shoulder of mutton, to make it exceed.   292

Hostess. O, where am I, or what's become of me?

Bacon. What art thou?

Hostess. Hostess at Henley, mistress of the Bell.

Bacon. How cam'st thou here?

Hostess. As I was in the kitchen 'mongst the maids,
    Spitting the meat 'gainst supper for my guess,[1]
    A motion mov'd me to look forth of door:
    No sooner had I pried into the yard,   300
    But straight a whirlwind hoisted me from thence,
    And mounted me aloft unto the clouds.
    As in a trance I thought nor feared naught,
    Nor know I where or whither I was ta'en,
    Nor where I am nor what these persons be.

Bacon. No? know you not Master Burden?

Hostess. O, yes, good sir, he is my daily guest.—
    What, Master Burden! 'twas but yesternight
    That you and I at Henley play'd at cards.   309

Burd. I know not what we did.—A pox of all conjuring friars!

Clem. Now, jolly friar, tell us, is this the book
    That Burden is so careful to look on?

Bacon. It is.—But, Burden, tell me now,
    Think'st thou that Bacon's necromatic skill
    Cannot perform his head and wall of brass,
    When he can fetch thine hostess in such post?

---

[1] Frequently used for *guests* by our early writers: so Chamberlayne:

    " The empty tables stood, for never *guess*
      Came there, except the bankrupts whom distress
      Spurr'd on," etc.—*Pharonnida,* 1659, B. IV. C. iii. p. 53.

Miles. I'll warrant you, master, if Master Burden could conjure
    as well as you, he would have his book every night from
    Henley to study on at Oxford.

Mason. Burden,   320
    What, are you mated [1] by this frolic friar?—
    Look how he droops; his guilty conscience
    Drives him to 'bash, and makes his hostess blush.

Bacon. Well, mistress, for I will not have you miss'd,
    You shall to Henley to cheer up your guests
    'Fore supper gin.—Burden, bid her adieu;
    Say farewell to your hostess 'fore she goes.—
    Sirrah, away, and set her safe at home.

Hostess. Master Burden, when shall we see you at Henley?

Burd. The devil take thee and Henley too.   330

                                    [*Exeunt Hostess and Devil.*

Miles. Master, shall I make a good motion?

Bacon. What's that?

Miles. Marry, sir, now that my hostess is gone to provide supper,
    conjure up another spirit, and send Doctor Burden flying
    after.

Bacon. Thus, rulers of our academic state,
    You have seen the friar frame his art by proof;
    And as the college callèd Brazen-nose
    Is under him, and he the master there,
    So surely shall this head of brass be fram'd,   340
    And yield forth strange and uncouth aphorisms;
    And hell and Hecate shall fail the friar,
    But I will circle England round with brass

Miles. So be it *et nunc et semper ;* amen.   [*Exeunt.*

Enter MARGARET *and* JOAN; THOMAS, RICHARD, *and other*
    Clowns; *and* LACY *disguised in country apparel.*

Thom. By my troth, Margaret, here's a weather is able to make
    a man call his father "whoreson": if this weather hold,
    we shall have hay good cheap, and butter and cheese at
    Harleston will bear no price.

Mar. Thomas, maids when they come to see the fair
    Count not to make a cope for dearth of hay: 350
    When we have turn'd our butter to the salt,

                        [1] *i.e.,* confounded.

And set our cheese safely upon the racks,
Then let our fathers prize it as they please.
We country sluts of merry Fressingfield
Come to buy needless naughts to make us fine,
And look that young men should be frank this day,
And court us with such fairings as they can.
Phœbus is blithe, and frolic looks from heaven,
As when he courted lovely Semele,
Swearing the pedlers shall have empty packs,   360
If that fair weather may make chapmen buy.

Lacy. But, lovely Peggy, Semele is dead,
And therefore Phœbus from his palace pries,
And, seeing such a sweet and seemly saint,
Shows all his glories for to court yourself.

Mar. This is a fairing, gentle sir, indeed,
To soothe me up with such smooth flattery;
But learn of me, your scoff's too broad before.—
Well, Joan, our beauties must abide their jests;
We serve the turn in jolly Fressingfield.   370

Joan. Margaret,
A farmer's daughter for a farmer's son:
I warrant you, the meanest of us both
Shall have a mate to lead us from the church.
                    [*Lacy whispers Margaret in the ear.*
But, Thomas, what's the news? what, in a dump?
Give me your hand, we are near a pedler's shop;
Out with your purse, we must have fairings now.

Thom. Faith, Joan, and shall: I'll bestow a fairing on you, and
then we will to the tavern, and snap off a pint of wine or two.

Mar. Whence are you, sir? of Suffolk? for your terms   380
Are finer than the common sort of men.

Lacy. Faith, lovely girl, I am of Beccles by,
Your neighbour, not above six miles from hence,
A farmer's son, that never was so quaint
But that he could do courtesy to such dames.
But trust me, Margaret, I am sent in charge
From him that revell'd in your father's house,
And fill'd his lodge with cheer and venison,
'Tirèd in green: he sent you this rich purse,
His token that he help'd you run your cheese,   390
And in the milkhouse chatted with yourself.

Mar. To me?

Lacy. You forget yourself:[1]
   Women are often weak in memory.
Mar. O, pardon, sir, I call to mind the man:
   'Twere little manners to refuse his gift,
   And yet I hope he sends it not for love;
   For we have little leisure to debate of that.   398
Joan. What, Margaret! blush not: maids must have their loves.
Thom. Nay, by the mass, she looks pale as if she were angry.
Rich. Sirrah, are you of Beccles? I pray, how doth Good-
   man Cob? my father bought a horse of him.—I'll tell
   you, Margaret, 'a were good to be a gentleman's jade, for
   of all things the foul hilding[2] could not abide a dung-cart.
Mar. [*aside.*] How different is this farmer from the rest
   That erst as yet have pleas'd my wandering sight!
   His words are witty, quicken'd with a smile,
   His courtesy gentle, smelling of the court;
   Facile and debonair in all his deeds;
   Proportion'd as was Paris, when, in grey,[3]   410
   He courted Œnon in the vale by Troy.
   Great lords have come and pleaded for my love:
   Who but the Keeper's lass of Fressingfield?
   And yet methinks this farmer's jolly son
   Passeth the proudest that hath pleas'd mine eye.
   But, Peg, disclose not that thou art in love,
   And show as yet no sign of love to him,
   Although thou well wouldst wish him for thy love:
   Keep that to thee till time doth serve thy turn,

[1] The 4tos give these words to Margaret.
[2] *i.e.*, low creature—a common term of contempt in our old authors.
[3] That this "was the phrase for a homely shepherd's garb" is observed
by the Rev. J. Mitford (*Gent. Mag.* for March 1833, p. 216), who cites from
Greene's *Shepherd's Ode* in his *Ciceronis Amor*—

> "A *cloak of grey* fenc'd the rain;
> Thus 'tired was this lovely swain;
>
> Such was *Paris*, shepherds say,
> When with Œnone he did play."

and from Peele's *War of Troy*—

> "So couth he [*Paris*] sing . . .
>
> And wear his coat *of grey* and lusty green," etc.

Mr. Mitford might also have quoted from our author's *Orlando Furioso*—

> "As *Paris*, when Œnone lov'd him well,
>
> All *clad in grey*, sat piping on a reed," etc.

To show the grief wherein thy heart doth burn.— 420
Come, Joan and Thomas, shall we to the fair?—
You, Beccles man, will not forsake us now?

Lacy. Not whilst I may have such quaint girls as you.

Mar. Well, if you chance to come by Fressingfield,
Make but a step into the Keeper's lodge,
And such poor fare as woodmen can afford,
Butter and cheese, cream and fat venison,
You shall have store, and welcome therewithal.

Lacy. Gramercies, Peggy; look for me ere long.   [*Exeunt.*

Enter KING HENRY THE THIRD, *the* EMPEROR, *the* KING OF
CASTILE, ELINOR, *and* VANDERMAST.

K. Hen. Great men of Europe, monarchs of the west, 430
Ring'd with the walls of old Oceanus,
Whose lofty surge is [1] like the battlements
That compass'd high-built Babel in with towers,
Welcome, my lords, welcome, brave western kings,
To England's shore, whose promontory-cleeves
Show Albion is another little world;
Welcome says English Henry to you all;
Chiefly unto the lovely Elinor,
Who dar'd for Edward's sake cut through the seas,
And venture as Agenor's damsel through the deep, [2] 440
To get the love of Henry's wanton son.

K. of Cast. England's rich monarch, brave Plantagenet,
The Pyren Mounts swelling above the clouds,
That ward the wealthy Castile in with walls,
Could not detain the beauteous Elinor;
But hearing of the fame of Edward's youth,
She dar'd to brook Neptunus' haughty pride,
And bide the brunt of froward Æolus:
Then may fair England welcome her the more.

Elin. After that English Henry by his lords 450
Had sent Prince Edward's lovely counterfeit, [3]

---

[1] The 4tos " surges."
[2] A corrupted line. Qy. " *And venture as Agenor's damsel did* "? (Greene would hardly have written here " through the deep " when the preceding line ended with " through the seas.")
[3] *i.e.*, portrait: " so that if a painter were to draw any of their *counterfeits* on table, he needs no more but wet his pencil, and dab it on their cheeks, and he shall haue vermillion and white enough to furnish out his worke." —Nash's *Pierce Pennilesse*, etc., ed. 1595, Sig. C 4.

A present to the Castile Elinor,
The comely portrait of so brave a man,
The virtuous fame discoursèd of his deeds,
Edward's courageous resolution,
Done [1] at the Holy Land 'fore Damas' walls,
Led both mine eye and thoughts in equal links,
To like so of the English monarch's son,
That I attempted perils for his sake.

Emp. Where is the prince, my lord?　　　　　　　　460

K. Hen. He posted down, not long since, from the court,
To Suffolk side, to merry Framlingham,
To sport himself amongst my fallow deer:
From thence, by packets sent to Hampton-house,
We hear the prince is ridden, with his lords,
To Oxford, in the acadèmy there
To hear dispute amongst the learnèd men.
But we will send forth letters for my son,
To will him come from Oxford to the court.

Emp. Nay, rather, Henry, let us, as we be,　　　　470
Ride for to visit Oxford with our train.
Fain would I see your universities,
And what learn'd men your acadèmy yields.
From Hapsburg have I brought a learnèd clerk
To hold dispute with English orators:
This doctor, surnam'd Jaques Vandermast,
A German born, pass'd into Padua,
To Florence and to fair Bologna,
To Paris, Rheims, and stately Orleans,
And, talking there with men of art, put down　　　480
The chiefest of them all in aphorisms,
In magic, and the mathematic rules:
Now let us, Henry, try him in your schools.

K. Hen. He shall, my lord; this motion likes me well.
We'll progress straight to Oxford with our trains,
And see what men our acadèmy brings.—
And, wonder [2] Vandermast, welcome to me:
In Oxford shalt thou find a jolly friar,
Call'd Friar Bacon, England's only flower:
Set him but nonplus in his magic spells,　　　　490
And make him yield in mathematic rules,
And for thy glory I will bind thy brows,

---

[1] Qy. " Shown "?　　　　　　　　[2] Qy. " wondrous "?

Not with a poet's garland made of bays,
But with a coronet of choicest gold.
Whilst [1] then we set [2] to Oxford with our troops,
Let's in and banquet in our English court.   [*Exeunt.*

Enter RALPH SIMNELL *in* PRINCE EDWARD'S *apparel; and*
   PRINCE EDWARD, WARREN, *and* ERMSBY, *disguised.*

Ralph. Where be these vagabond knaves, that they attend no
   better on their master?

P. Edw. If it please your honour, we are all ready at an inch.

Ralph. Sirrah Ned, I'll have no more post-horse to ride on: I'll
   have another fetch.   501

Erms. I pray you, how is that, my lord?

Ralph. Marry, sir, I'll send to the Isle of Ely for four or five
   dozen of geese, and I'll have them tied six and six together
   with whip-cord: now upon their backs will I have a fair
   field-bed with a canopy; and so, when it is my pleasure,
   I'll flee into what place I please. This will be easy.

War. Your honour hath said well: but shall we to Brazen-nose
   College before we pull off our boots?

Erms. Warren, well motion'd; we will to the friar   510
   Before we revel it within the town.—
   Ralph, see you keep your countenance like a prince.

Ralph. Wherefore have I such a company of cutting [3] knaves
   to wait upon me, but to keep and defend my countenance
   against all mine enemies? have you not good swords and
   bucklers?

Erms. Stay, who comes here?

War. Some scholar; and we'll ask him where Friar Bacon is.

Enter FRIAR BACON *and* MILES.

Bacon. Why, thou arrant dunce, shall I never make thee a good
   scholar? doth not all the town cry out and say, Friar Bacon's
   subsizer is the greatest blockhead in all Oxford? why, thou
   canst not speak one word of true Latin.   522

Miles. No, sir? yet,[4] what is this else? *Ego sum tuus homo,*
   "I am your man": I warrant you, sir, as good Tully's
   phrase as any is in Oxford.

---

[1] *i.e.*, Until.   [2] The 4to of 1594 "fit."   [3] *i.e.*, swaggering.
[4] The earlier 4tos "yes;" which the latest 4to omits.

Bacon. Come on, sirrah; what part of speech is *Ego ?*
Miles. *Ego,* that is " I "; marry, *nomen substantivo.*
Bacon. How prove you that?
Miles. Why, sir, let him prove himself an 'a will; I can be heard,
　　felt, and understood.　　　　　　　　　　　　530
Bacon. O gross dunce!　　　　　　　　　　　*[Beats him.*
P. Edw. Come, let us break off this dispute between these two.—
　　Sirrah, where is Brazen-nose College?
Miles. Not far from Coppersmith's Hall.
P. Edw. What, dost thou mock me?
Miles. Not I, sir: but what would you at Brazen-nose?
Erms. Marry, we would speak with Friar Bacon.
Miles. Whose men be you?
Erms. Marry, scholar, here's our master.　　　　　　539
Ralph. Sirrah, I am the master of these good fellows; mayst
　　thou not know me to be a lord by my reparrel?
Miles. Then here's good game for the hawk; for here's the
　　master-fool and a covey of coxcombs: one wise man, I
　　think, would spring you all.
P. Edw. Gog's wounds! Warren, kill him.
War. Why, Ned, I think the devil be in my sheath; I cannot
　　get out my dagger.
Erms. Nor I mine: swones, Ned, I think I am bewitched.
Miles. A company of scabs! the proudest of you all draw your
　　weapon, if he can.—*[Aside.]*　See how boldly I speak, now
　　my master is by.　　　　　　　　　　　　551
P. Edw. I strive in vain; but if my sword be shut
　　And conjur'd fast by magic in my sheath,
　　Villain, here is my fist.　　　*[Strikes Miles a box on the ear.*
Miles. O, I beseech you conjure his hands too, that he may not
　　lift his arms to his head, for he is light-fingered!
Ralph. Ned, strike him; I'll warrant thee by mine honour.
Bacon. What means the English prince to wrong my man?
P. Edw. To whom speak'st thou?
Bacon. To thee.　　　　　　　　　　　　560
P. Edw. Who art thou?
Bacon. Could you not judge when all your swords grew fast,
　　That Friar Bacon was not far from hence?
　　Edward, King Henry's son and Prince of Wales,
　　Thy fool disguis'd cannot conceal thyself:
　　I know both Ermsby and the Sussex Earl,
　　Else Friar Bacon had but little skill.

Thou com'st in post from merry Fressingfield,
Fast-fancied [1] to the Keeper's bonny lass,
To crave some succour of the jolly friar: 570
And Lacy, Earl of Lincoln, hast thou left
To treat [2] fair Margaret to allow thy loves;
But friends are men, and love can baffle lords;
The earl both woos and courts her for himself.

War. Ned, this is strange; the friar knoweth all.

Erms. Apollo could not utter more than this.

P. Edw. I stand amaz'd to hear this jolly friar
Tell even the very secrets of my thoughts.—
But, learnèd Bacon, since thou know'st the cause
Why I did post so fast from Fressingfield,   580
Help, friar, at a pinch, that I may have
The love of lovely Margaret to myself,
And, as I am true Prince of Wales, I'll give
Living and lands to strength thy college-state.[3]

War. Good friar, help the prince in this.

Ralph. Why, servant Ned, will not the friar do it? Were not
my sword glued to my scabbard by conjuration, I would cut
off his head, and make him do it by force.

Miles. In faith, my lord, your manhood and your sword is all
alike; they are so fast conjured that we shall never see them.

Erms. What, doctor, in a dump! tush, help the prince,   591
And thou shalt see how liberal he will prove.

Bacon. Crave not such actions greater dumps than these?
I will, my lord, strain out my magic spells;
For this day comes the earl to Fressingfield,
And 'fore that night shuts in the day with dark,
They'll be betrothèd each to other fast.
But come with me; we'll to my study straight,
And in a glass prospective I will show
What's done this day in merry Fressingfield.   600

P. Edw. Gramercies, Bacon; I will quite thy pain.

Bacon. But send your train, my lord, into the town:
My scholar shall go bring them to their inn;
Meanwhile we'll see the knavery of the earl.

P. Edw. Warren, leave me:—and, Ermsby, take the fool;

---

[1] Tied by fancy (love).   [2] *i.e.*, entreat.
[3] Here Walker (*Shakespeare's Versification*, etc., p. 257), considering
"college" as a genitive, would print " thy *college'* state " (*the state or
estate of thy college*).

Let him be master, and go revel it,
Till I and Friar Bacon talk awhile.
War. We will, my lord.
Ralph. Faith, Ned, and I'll lord it out till thou comest: I'll be
Prince of Wales over all the black-pots in Oxford.   610
              [*Exeunt Warren, Ermsby, Ralph Simnell, and Miles.*

FRIAR BACON *and* PRINCE EDWARD *go into the study* [1]

Bacon. Now, frolic Edward, welcome to my cell;
Here tempers Friar Bacon many toys,
And holds this place his consistory-court,
Wherein the devils plead homage to his words.
Within this glass prospective thou shalt see
This day what's done in merry Fressingfield
'Twixt lovely Peggy and the Lincoln Earl.
P. Edw. Friar, thou glad'st me: now shall Edward try
How Lacy meaneth to his sovereign Lord.
Bacon. Stand there and look directly in the glass.   620

Enter MARGARET *and* FRIAR BUNGAY.[2]

What sees my lord?
P. Edw. I see the Keeper's lovely lass appear,
As brightsome [3] as the paramour of Mars,
Only attended by a jolly friar.
Bacon. Sit still, and keep the crystal in your eye.
Mar. But tell me, Friar Bungay, is it true
That this fair courteous [4] country swain,
Who says his father is a farmer nigh,
Can be Lord Lacy, Earl of Lincolnshire?
Bun. Peggy, 'tis true, 'tis Lacy for my life,   630
Or else mine art and cunning both do fail,
Left by Prince Edward to procure his loves;

[1] Here, after the exit of Warren, Ermsby, etc., and after Bacon and
Edward had walked a few paces about (or perhaps towards the back of)
the stage, the audience were to suppose that the scene was changed to the
interior of Bacon's cell.
[2] Perhaps the curtain which concealed the upper-stage (*i.e.*, the balcony
at the back of the stage) was withdrawn, discovering Margaret and Bungay
standing there, and when the representation in the glass was supposed to
be over, the curtain was drawn back again.
[3] The 4tos "*bright*-sunne."
[4] Qy. "*That this fair*, witty, *courteous*," etc.? See before, Margaret's
first speech in p. 174, and her second speech on next page.

For he in green, that holp you run your cheese,
Is son to Henry and the Prince of Wales.
Mar. Be what he will, his lure is but for lust:
But did Lord Lacy like poor Margaret,
Or would he deign to wed a country lass,
Friar, I would his humble handmaid be,
And for great wealth quite him with courtesy.
Bun. Why, Margaret, dost thou love him?   640
Mar. His personage, like the pride of vaunting Troy,
Might well avouch to shadow Helen's rape: [1]
His wit is quick and ready in conceit,
As Greece afforded in her chiefest prime:
Courteous, ah friar, full of pleasing smiles!
Trust me, I love too much to tell thee more;
Suffice to me he's England's paramour.
Bun. Hath not each eye that view'd thy pleasing face
Surnamèd thee Fair Maid of Fressingfield?
Mar. Yes, Bungay; and would God the lovely earl   650
Had that in *esse* that so many sought.
Bun. Fear not, the friar will not be behind
To show his cunning to entangle love.
P. Edw. I think the friar courts the bonny wench:
Bacon, methinks he is a lusty churl.
Bacon. Now look, my lord.

Enter LACY *disguised as before.*

P. Edw. Gog's wounds, Bacon, here comes Lacy!
Bacon. Sit still, my lord, and mark the comedy.
Bun. Here's Lacy, Margaret; step aside awhile.
                                    [*Retires with Margaret.*
Lacy. Daphne, the damsel that caught Phœbus fast,   660
And lock'd him in the brightness of her looks,
Was not so beauteous in Apollo's eyes
As is fair Margaret to the Lincoln Earl.
Recant thee, Lacy, thou art put in trust:
Edward, thy sovereign's son, hath chosen thee,
A secret friend, to court her for himself,
And dar'st thou wrong thy prince with treachery?
Lacy, love makes no exception [2] of a friend,
Nor deems it of a prince but as a man.

---

[1] The 4tos " cape."   [2] The 4to of 1594 " acception."

Honour bids thee control him in his lust;   670
His wooing is not for to wed the girl,
But to entrap her and beguile the lass.
Lacy, thou lov'st, then brook not such abuse,
But wed her, and abide thy prince's frown;
For better die than see her live disgrac'd.

Mar. Come, friar, I will shake him from his dumps.—
                                        [*Comes forward.*

How cheer you, sir? a penny for your thought:
You're early up, pray God it be the near.[1]
What, come from Beccles in a morn so soon?

Lacy. Thus watchful are such men as live in love,   680
Whose eyes brook broken slumbers for their sleep.
I tell thee, Peggy, since last Harleston fair
My mind hath felt a heap of passions.

Mar. A trusty man, that court it for your friend:
Woo you still for the courtier all in green?
I marvel that he sues not for himself.

Lacy. Peggy,
I pleaded first to get your grace for him;
But when mine eyes survey'd your beauteous looks,
Love, like a wag, straight div'd into my heart,   690
And there did shrine the idea of yourself.
Pity me, though I be a farmer's son,
And measure not my riches, but my love.

Mar. You are very hasty; for to garden well,
Seeds must have time to sprout before they spring:
Love ought to creep as doth the dial's shade,
For timely [2] ripe is rotten too-too soon.

Bun. [*coming forward.*] *Deus hic;* room for a merry friar!
What, youth of Beccles, with the Keeper's lass?
'Tis well; but tell me, hear you any news?   700

Lacy.[3] No, friar: what news?

---

[1] *Near, i.e.,* nearer. An allusion to the proverb, "Early up and never the
nearer."

> "In you, yfaith, the proverb's verified,—
> Y'are *earely up, and yet are nere the neare.*"
>   Munday and Chettle's *Death of the Earle of Huntington,*
>   1601, Sig. F 4.

"In this perplexity," says that mendacious woman, Mrs. Elizabeth
Thomas, speaking of herself, " she languished for some time, when hearing
Bishop Burnet's Exposition of the XXXIX. Articles was in the press, she
waited the publication with the utmost impatience. But alas! *never the
near,"* etc. *Pylades and Corinna,* etc., 1731, vol. i. p. 15.

[2] *i.e.,* early.   [3] The 4tos " Mar."

Bun. Hear you not how the pursuivants do post
    With proclamations through each country-town?
Lacy. For what, gentle friar? tell the news.
Bun. Dwell'st thou in Beccles, and hear'st not of these news?
    Lacy, the Earl of Lincoln, is late fled
    From Windsor court, disguisèd like a swain,
    And lurks about the country here unknown.
    Henry suspects him of some treachery,
    And therefore doth proclaim in every way,   710
    That who can take the Lincoln Earl shall have,
    Paid in the Exchequer, twenty thousand crowns.
Lacy. The Earl of Lincoln! Friar, thou art mad:
    It was some other; thou mistak'st the man.
    The Earl of Lincoln! why, it cannot be.
Mar. Yes, very well, my lord, for you are he:
    The Keeper's daughter took you prisoner.
    Lord Lacy, yield, I'll be your gaoler once.
P. Edw. How familiar they be, Bacon!
Bacon. Sit still, and mark the sequel of their loves.   720
Lacy. Then am I double prisoner to thyself:
    Peggy, I yield. But are these news in jest?
Mar. In jest with you, but earnest unto me;
    For why [1] these wrongs do wring me at the heart.
    Ah, how these earls and noblemen of birth
    Flatter and feign to forge poor women's ill!
Lacy. Believe me, lass, I am the Lincoln Earl:
    I not deny but, 'tirèd thus in rags,
    I liv'd disguis'd to win fair Peggy's love.
Mar. What love is there where wedding ends not love?   730
Lacy. I mean,[2] fair girl, to make thee Lacy's wife.
Mar. I little think that earls will stoop so low.
Lacy. Say shall I make thee countess ere I sleep?
Mar. Handmaid unto the earl, so please himself:
    A wife in name, but servant in obedience.
Lacy. The Lincoln Countess, for it shall be so:
    I'll plight the bands, and seal it with a kiss.
P. Edw. Gog's wounds, Bacon, they kiss! I'll stab them.
Bacon. O, hold your hands, my lord, it is the glass!
P. Edw. Choler to see the traitors gree so well   740
    Made me [to] think the shadows substances.

---

[1] *i.e.*, Because.   [2] The earlier 4tos " meant."

Bacon. 'Twere a long poniard,[1] my lord, to reach between
　　Oxford and Fressingfield; but sit still and see more.
Bun. Well, Lord of Lincoln, if your loves be knit,
　　And that your tongues and thoughts do both agree,
　　To avoid ensuing jars, I'll hamper up the match.
　　I'll take my portace [2] forth and wed you here:
　　Then go to bed and seal up your desires.
Lacy. Friar, content.—Peggy, how like you this?
Mar. What likes my lord is pleasing unto me.　　　　　　750
Bun. Then hand-fast hand, and I will to my book.
Bacon. What sees my lord now?
P. Edw. Bacon, I see the lovers hand in hand,
　　The friar ready with his portace there
　　To wed them both: then am I quite undone.
　　Bacon, help now, if e'er thy magic serv'd;
　　Help, Bacon; [3] stop the marriage now,
　　If devils or necromancy may suffice,
　　And I will give thee forty thousand crowns.
Bacon. Fear not, my lord, I'll stop the jolly friar　　　760
　　For mumbling up his orisons this day.
Lacy. Why speak'st not, Bungay? Friar, to thy book.
　　　　　　　　[*Bungay is mute, crying,*" Hud, hud."
Mar. How look'st thou, friar, as a man distraught?
　　Reft of thy senses, Bungay? show by signs,
　　If thou be dumb, what passion [4] holdeth thee.
Lacy. He's dumb indeed. Bacon hath with his devils
　　Enchanted him, or else some strange disease
　　Or apoplexy hath possess'd his lungs:
　　But, Peggy, what he cannot with his book,
　　We'll 'twixt us both unite it up in heart.　　　　　　770
Mar. Else let me die, my lord, a miscreant.
P. Edw. Why stands Friar Bungay [5] so amaz'd?
Bacon. I have struck [6] him dumb, my lord; and, if your honour
　　please,
　　I'll fetch this Bungay straightway from Fressingfield,
　　And he shall dine with us in Oxford here.

---

[1] Is this a prose-speech, or corrupted verse?
[2] *i.e.*, breviary, *portable* prayer-book.
[3] Some word, or words, wanting here.
[4] The 4to of 1594 " passions."　　　　The 4tos " Bacon."
[5] Qy.—
　　" *I have struck him dumb, my lord : and, if you please,
　　I'll fetch this Bungay straight from Fressingfield,
　　And he,*" etc.?

P. Edw. Bacon, do that, and thou contentest me.
Lacy. Of courtesy, Margaret, let us lead the friar
      Unto thy father's lodge, to comfort him
      With broths, to bring him from this hapless trance.
Mar. Or else, my lord, we were passing unkind [1]   780
      To leave the friar so in his distress.

Enter a Devil, *who carries off* BUNGAY *on his back.*

      O, help, my lord! a devil, a devil, my lord!
      Look how he carries Bungay on his back!
      Let's hence, for Bacon's spirits be abroad. [*Exit with Lacy.*
P. Edw. Bacon, I laugh to see the jolly friar
      Mounted upon the devil, and how the earl
      Flees with his bonny lass for fear.[2]
      As soon as Bungay is at Brazen-nose,
      And I have chatted with the merry friar,
      I will in post hie me to Fressingfield,   790
      And quite these wrongs on Lacy ere 't be long.
Bacon. So be it, my lord: but let us to our dinner;
      For ere we have taken our repast awhile,
      We shall have Bungay brought to Brazen-nose.   [*Exeunt.*

Enter BURDEN, MASON, *and* CLEMENT.

Mason. Now that we are gather'd in the Regent-house,
      It fits us talk about the king's repair,
      For he, troopèd with all the western kings,
      That lie alongst the Dantzic seas by east,
      North by the clime of frosty Germany,
      The Almain monarch, and the Saxon [3] duke,   800
      Castile and lovely Elinor with him,
      Have in their jests resolv'd for Oxford town.
Bard. We must lay plots of stately tragedies,
      Strange comic shows, such as proud Roscius
      Vaunted before the Roman emperors,
      To welcome all the western potentates.[4]
Clem. But more; the king by letters hath foretold
      That Frederick, the Almain emperor,

---

[1] Qy. " passing unkind we were "?
[2] Some word or words wanting.
[3] The 4tos " Scocon."   [4] The 4tos give this line to Clement.

Hath brought with him a German of esteem,
Whose surname is Don Jaques Vandermast,   810
Skilful in magic and those secret arts.
Mason. Then must we all make suit unto the friar,
To Friar Bacon, that he vouch this task,
And undertake to countervail in skill
The German; else there's none in Oxford can
Match and dispute with learnèd Vandermast.
Burd. Bacon, if he will hold the German play,
Will teach him what an English friar can do:
The devil, I think, dare not dispute with him.
Clem. Indeed, Mas doctor, he [dis]pleasur'd you,   820
In that he brought your hostess with her spit,
From Henley, posting unto Brazen-nose.
Burd. A vengeance on the friar for his pains!
But leaving that, let's hie to Bacon straight,
To see if he will take this task in hand.
Clem. Stay, what rumour is this?   The town is up in a mutiny:
what hurly-burly is this?

Enter a Constable, *with* RALPH SIMNELL, WARREN, ERMSBY,
    all three disguised as before, and MILES.

Cons. Nay, masters, if you were ne'er so good, you shall before
the doctors to answer your misdemeanour.
Burd. What's the matter, fellow?   830
Cons. Marry, sir, here's a company of rufflers, that, drinking in
the tavern, have made a great brawl and almost killed the
vintner.
Miles. Salve, Doctor Burden!
This lubberly lurden
Ill-shap'd and ill-fac'd,
Disdain'd and disgrac'd,
What he tells unto *vobis*
Mentitur de nobis.
Burd. Who is the master and chief of this crew?   840
Miles. Ecce asinum mundi
    Figura rotundi,
Neat, sheat, and fine,
As brisk as a cup of wine.
Burd. What are you?
Ralph. I am, father doctor, as a man would say, the bell-wether

of this company: these are my lords, and I the Prince of Wales.

Clem. Are you Edward, the king's son?

Ralph. Sirrah Miles, bring hither the tapster that drew the wine, and, I warrant, when they see how soundly I have broke his head, they'll say 'twas done by no less man than a prince.

Mason. I cannot believe that this is the Prince of Wales.   853

War. And why so, sir?

Mason. For they say the prince is a brave and a wise gentleman.

War. Why, and think'st thou, doctor, that he is not so?
   Dar'st thou detract and derogate from him,
   Being so lovely and so brave a youth?

Erms. Whose face, shining with many a sugar'd smile,
   Bewrays that he is bred of princely race.   860

Miles. And yet, master doctor,
   To speak like a proctor,
   And tell unto you
   What is veriment and true;
   To cease of this quarrel,
   Look but on his apparel;
   Then mark but my talis,
   He is great Prince of Walis,
   The chief of our *gregis*,
   And *filius regis :*   870
   Then 'ware what is done,
   For he is Henry's white son.

Ralph. Doctors, whose doting night-caps are not capable of my ingenious dignity, know that I am Edward Plantagenet, whom if you displease, [I] will make a ship that shall hold all your colleges, and so carry away the niniversity with a fair wind to the Bankside in Southwark —How sayest thou, Ned Warren, shall I not do it?

War. Yes, my good lord; and, if it please your lordship, I will gather up all your old pantofles,[1] and with the cork make you a pinnace of five-hundred ton, that shall serve the turn marvellous well, my lord.   882

Erms. And I, my lord, will have pioners [2] to undermine the town, that the very gardens and orchards be carried away for your summer-walks.

---

[1] *i.e.*, slippers.

[2] So (not " pioneers ") the word is usually, if not always, spelt by our early writers.

Miles. And I, with *scientia*.
        And great *diligentia*,
        Will conjure and charm,
        To keep you from harm;
        That *utrum horum mavis*,   890
        Your very great *navis*,
        Like Barclay's ship,[1]
        From Oxford do skip
        With colleges and schools,
        Full-loaden with fools.
        Quid dicis ad hoc,
        Worshipful *Domine* Dawcock? [2]
Clem. Why, hare-brain'd courtiers, are you drunk or mad,
        To taunt us up with such scurrility?
        Deem you us men of base and light esteem,   900
        To bring us such a fop for Henry's son?—
        Call out the beadles and convey them hence
        Straight to Bocardo: [3] let the roisters [4] lie
        Close clapt in bolts, until their wits be tame.
Erms. Why, shall we to prison, my lord?
Ralph. What sayest, Miles, shall I honour the prison with my
        presence?
Miles. No, no: out with your blades,
        And hamper these jades;
        Have a flurt and a crash,   910
        Now play revel-dash,
        And teach these sacerdos
        That the Bocardos,
        Like peasants and elves,
        Are meet for themselves.
Mason. To the prison with them, constable.

---

[1] The 4tos " Bartlets *ship* " (a mistake perhaps of the original compositor, the MS. having had " *Barcleis ship* ").—Miles alludes to *The shyp of Folys of the Worlde, translated out of Laten Frenche and Doche into Englysshe Tonge, by Alexander Barclay Preste.   London by Richarde Pynson.* 1509, folio.

[2] An expression borrowed from the author whose style is here imitated:

> " *Construas hoc,*
> *Domine* Dawcocke! "
> *Ware the Hauke*—Skelton's *Works*, i. 163, ed. Dyce.

[3] *i.e.*, the old north gate of Oxford, which was used as a prison; so called, we may certainly presume, from some allusion to the Aristotelian syllogism in *Bocardo*.   It was taken down in 1771.

[4] *i.e.*, wild fellows, rioters.

War. Well, doctors, seeing I have sported me
    With laughing at these mad and merry wags,
    Know that Prince Edward is at Brazen-nose,
    And this, attirèd like the Prince of Wales,   920
    Is Ralph, King Henry's only lovèd fool;
    I, Earl of Sussex,[1] and this Ermsby,[2]
    One of the privy-chamber to the king;
    Who, while the prince with Friar Bacon stays,
    Have revell'd it in Oxford as you see.
Mason. My lord, pardon us, we knew not what you were:
    But courtiers may make greater scapes than these.
    Wilt please your honour dine with me to-day?
War. I will, Master doctor, and satisfy the vintner for his hurt;
    only I must desire you to imagine him all this forenoon the
    Prince of Wales.   931
Mason. I will, sir.
Ralph. And upon that I will lead the way; only I will have
    Miles go before me, because I have heard Henry say that
    wisdom must go before majesty.   *[Exeunt.*

Enter PRINCE EDWARD *with his poniard in his hand,* LACY,
    and MARGARET.

P. Edw. Lacy, thou canst not shroud thy traitorous thoughts,
    Nor cover, as did Cassius, all thy [3] wiles;
    For Edward hath an eye that looks as far
    As Lynceus from the shores of Græcia.
    Did not I sit in Oxford by the friar,   940
    And see thee court the maid of Fressingfield,
    Sealing thy flattering fancies with a kiss?
    Did not proud Bungay draw his portace forth,
    And joining hand in hand had married you,
    If Friar Bacon had not struck him dumb,
    And mounted him upon a spirit's back,
    That we might chat at Oxford with the friar?
    Traitor, what answer'st? is not all this true?
Lacy. Truth all, my lord; and thus I make reply.
    At Harleston fair, there courting for your grace,   950
    Whenas mine eye survey'd her curious shape,
    And drew the beauteous glory of her looks

---

[1] The 4tos " Essex."
[2] A trisyllable here, I believe.   [3] The 4tos " his."

To dive into the centre of my heart,
Love taught me that your honour did but jest,
That princes were in fancy but as men;
How that the lovely maid of Fressingfield
Was fitter to be Lacy's wedded wife
Than concubine unto the Prince of Wales.

P. Edw. Injurious Lacy, did I love thee more
Than Alexander his Hephæstion?   960
Did I unfold the passions [1] of my love,
And lock them in the closet of thy thoughts?
Wert thou to Edward second to himself,
Sole friend, and partner of his secret loves?
And could a glance of fading beauty break
Th' enchainèd fetters of such private friends?
Base coward, false, and too effeminate
To be corrival with a prince in thoughts!
From Oxford have I posted since I din'd,
To quite a traitor 'fore that Edward sleep.   970

Mar. 'Twas I, my lord, not Lacy stept awry:
For oft he su'd and courted for yourself,
And still woo'd for the courtier all in green;
But I, whom fancy made but over-fond,
Pleaded myself with looks as if I lov'd;
I fed mine eye with gazing on his face,
And still bewitch'd lov'd Lacy with my looks;
My heart with sighs, mine eyes pleaded with tears,
My face held pity and content at once,
And more I could not cipher-out by signs,   980
But that I lov'd Lord Lacy with my heart.
Then, worthy Edward, measure with thy mind
If women's favours will not force men fall,
If beauty, and if darts of piercing love,
Are not of force to bury thoughts of friends.

P. Edw. I tell thee, Peggy, I will have thy loves:
Edward or none shall conquer Margaret.
In frigates bottom'd with rich Sethin planks,
Topt with the lofty firs of Lebanon,
Stemm'd and incas'd with burnish'd ivory,   990
And over-laid with plates of Persian wealth,
Like Thetis shalt thou wanton on the waves,
And draw the dolphins to thy lovely eyes,

[1] The 4to of 1594 " passion."

To dance lavoltas in the purple streams:
Sirens, with harps and silver psalteries,
Shall wait with music at thy frigate's stem,
And entertain fair Margaret with their [1] lays.
England and England's wealth shall wait on thee;
Britain shall bend unto her prince's love,
And do due homage to thine excellence,   1000
If thou wilt be but Edward's Margaret.

Mar. Pardon, my lord: if Jove's great royalty
Sent me such presents as to Danaë;
If Phœbus, 'tirèd [2] in Latona's webs,
Came [3] courting from the beauty of his lodge; [4]
The dulcet tunes of frolic Mercury,
Nor all the wealth heaven's treasury affords,
Should make me leave Lord Lacy or his love.

P. Edw. I have learn'd at Oxford, then, this point of schools,—
Ablata causa, tollitur effectus: 1010
Lacy, the cause that Margaret cannot love
Nor fix her liking on the English prince,
Take him away, and then th' effects will fail.
Villain, prepare thyself; for I will bathe
My poniard in the bosom of an earl.

Lacy. Rather than live, and miss fair Margaret's love,
Prince Edward, stop not at the fatal doom,
But stab it home: end both my loves and life.

Mar. Brave Prince of Wales, honour'd for royal deeds,
'Twere sin to stain fair Venus' courts with blood;   1020
Love's conquest [5] ends, my lord, in courtesy:
Spare Lacy, gentle Edward; let me die,
For so both you and he do cease your loves.

P. Edw. Lacy shall die as traitor to his lord.

Lacy. I have deserv'd it, Edward; act it well.

---

[1] The 4tos " her."

[2] The 4tos " tied " and " try."—We have already had in this play—

> " Say that the courtier *'tired* all in green,"

and

> " I not deny, but *'tired* thus in rags."

[3] The 4tos " Come."

[4] So Shakespeare (according to the first folio):

> " Gallop apace, you fiery-footed steeds,
>   Towards *Phœbus' lodging*," etc.
>
> *Romeo and Juliet*, act iii. sc. 2.

[5] The 4to of 1594 " conquests."

Mar. What hopes the prince to gain by Lacy's death?
P. Edw. To end the loves 'twixt him and Margaret.
Mar. Why, thinks King Henry's son that Margaret's love
    Hangs in th' uncertain balance of proud time?
    That death shall make a discord of our thoughts?   1030
    No, stab the earl, and, 'fore the morning sun
    Shall vaunt him thrice over the lofty east,
    Margaret will meet her Lacy in the heavens.
Lacy. If aught betides to lovely Margaret
    That wrongs or wrings her honour from content,
    Europe's rich wealth nor England's monarchy
    Should not allure Lacy to over-live.
    Then, Edward, short my life, and end her [1] loves.
Mar. Rid [2] me, and keep a friend worth many loves.
Lacy. Nay, Edward, keep a love worth many friends.   1040
Mar. An if thy mind be such as fame hath blaz'd,
    Then, princely Edward, let us both abide
    The fatal resolution of thy rage:
    Banish thou fancy,[3] and embrace revenge,
    And in one tomb knit both our carcases,
    Whose hearts were linkèd in one perfect love.
P. Edw. [*aside.*] Edward, art thou that famous Prince of Wales,
    Who at Damasco beat the Saracens,
    And brought'st home triumph on thy lance's point?
    And shall thy plumes be pull'd by Venus down?   1050
    Is't princely to dissever lovers' leagues,
    To part such friends as glory in their loves? [4]
    Leave, Ned, and make a virtue of this fault,
    And further Peg and Lacy in their loves:
    So in subduing fancy's passion,
    Conquering thyself, thou gett'st the richest spoil.—
    Lacy, rise up.   Fair Peggy, here's my hand:
    The Prince of Wales hath conquer'd all his thoughts,
    And all his loves he yields unto the earl.
    Lacy, enjoy the maid of Fressingfield;   1060
    Make her thy Lincoln Countess at the church,
    And Ned, as he is true Plantagenet,
    Will give her to thee frankly for thy wife.
Lacy. Humbly I take her of my sovereign,
    As if that Edward gave me England's right,

---

[1] Qy. " our "?   [2] *i.e.*, Get rid of, destroy.
[3] *i.e.*, love.   [4] Not in the later 4tos.

And rich'd me with the Albion diadem.

Mar. And doth [1] the English prince mean true?
Will he vouchsafe to cease his former loves,
And yield the title of a country maid
Unto Lord Lacy?   1070

P. Edw. I will, fair Peggy, as I am true lord.

Mar. Then, lordly sir, whose conquest is as great,
In conquering love, as Cæsar's victories,
Margaret, as mild and humble in her thoughts
As was Aspasia unto Cyrus self,
Yields thanks, and, next Lord Lacy, doth enshrine
Edward the second secret in her heart.

P. Edw. Gramercy, Peggy:—now that vows are past,
And that your loves are not to be revolt,
Once, Lacy, friends again. Come, we will post   1080
To Oxford; for this day the king is there,
And brings for Edward Castile Elinor.
Peggy, I must go see and view my wife:
I pray God [2] I like her as I lovèd thee.
Beside, Lord Lincoln, we shall hear dispute
'Twixt Friar Bacon and learn'd Vandermast.
Peggy, we'll leave you for a week or two.

Mar. As it please Lord Lacy: but love's foolish looks [3]
Think footsteps miles and minutes to be hours.

Lacy. I'll hasten, Peggy, to make short return.—   1090
But please your honour go unto the lodge,
We shall have butter, cheese, and venison;
And yesterday I brought for Margaret
A lusty bottle of neat claret-wine:
Thus can we feast and entertain your grace.

P. Edw. 'Tis cheer, Lord Lacy, for an emperor,
If he respect the person and the place.
Come, let us in; for I will all this night
Ride post until I come to Bacon's cell.   *[Exeunt.*

Enter KING HENRY, *the* EMPEROR, *the* KING OF CASTILE,
ELINOR, VANDERMAST, *and* BUNGAY.

Emp. Trust me, Plantagenet, these Oxford schools   1100
Are richly seated near the river-side:

---

[1] Qy. "*And doth the English prince* indeed *mean true?*"
[2] "Read for harmony's sake, '*Pray God*, and pronounce *lovèd*." Walker's
Crit. Exam. of the text of Shakespeare, etc., i. 77.
[3] Can this be the right word?

Friar Bacon and Friar Bungay

The mountains full of fat and fallow deer,
The battling [1] pastures lade with kine and flocks,
The town gorgeous with high-built colleges,
And scholars seemly in their grave attire,
Learnèd in searching principles of art.—
What is thy judgment, Jaques Vandermast?

Van. That lordly are the buildings of the town,
Spacious the rooms, and full of pleasant walks;
But for the doctors, how that they be learnèd,   1110
It may be meanly, for aught I can hear.

Bun. I tell thee, German, Hapsburg holds none such,
None read so deep as Oxenford contains:
There are within our academic state
Men that may lecture it in Germany
To all the doctors of your Belgic schools.

K. Hen. Stand to him, Bungay, charm this Vandermast,
And I will use thee as a royal king.

Van. Wherein dar'st thou dispute with me?

Bun. In what a doctor and a friar can.   1120

Van. Before rich Europe's worthies put thou forth
The doubtful question unto Vandermast.

Bun. Let it be this,—Whether the spirits of pyromancy or geomancy be most predominant in magic?

Van. I say, of pyromancy.

Bun. And I, of geomancy.

Van. The cabalists that write of magic spells,
As Hermes, Melchie,[2] and Pythagoras,
Affirm that, 'mongst the quadruplicity
Of elemental essence, *terra* is but thought   1130
To be a *punctum* squarèd to the rest;
And that the compass of ascending elements
Exceed in bigness as they do in height;
Judging the concave circle of the sun
To hold the rest in his circumference.
If, then, as Hermes says, the fire be greatest,
Purest, and only giveth shape to spirits,
Then must these dæmones that haunt that place
Be every way superior to the rest.

Bun. I reason not of elemental shapes,   1140
Nor tell I of the concave latitudes,

---

[1] *i.e.*, causing to increase, or to grow fat.
[2] Meant, I suppose, for Malchus (Melech), *i.e.*, Porphyrius.

Noting their essence nor their quality,
But of the spirits that pyromancy calls,
And of the vigour of the geomantic fiends
I tell thee, German, magic haunts the ground,[1]
And those strange [2] necromantic spells,
That work such shows and wondering in the world,
Are acted by those geomantic spirits
That Hermes calleth *terræ filii*.
The fiery spirits are but transparent shades,   1150
That lightly pass as heralds to bear news;
But earthly fiends, clos'd in the lowest deep,
Dissever mountains, if they be but charg'd,
Being more gross and massy in their power.

Van. Rather these earthly geomantic spirits
Are dull and like the place where they remain;
For when proud Lucifer fell from the heavens,
The spirits and angels that did sin with him,
Retain'd their local essence as their faults,
All subject under Luna's continent: 1160
They which offended less hung [3] in the fire,
And second faults did rest within the air;
But Lucifer and his proud-hearted fiends
Were thrown into the centre of the earth,
Having less understanding than the rest,
As having greater sin and lesser grace.
Therefore such gross and earthly spirits do serve
For jugglers, witches, and vile [4] sorcerers;
Whereas the pyromantic genii
Are mighty, swift, and of far-reaching power.   1170
But grant that geomancy hath most force;
Bungay, to please these mighty potentates,
Prove by some instance what thy art can do.

Bun. I will.

Emp. Now, English Harry, here begins the game;
We shall see sport between these learnèd men.

Van. What wilt thou do?

Bun. Show thee the tree, leav'd with refinèd gold,

---

[1] The 4tos " grounds."
[2] Something dropt out here.   [3] The 4tos " hang."
[4] The 4tos " vild "—as the word was often written formerly: but in our
author's *Orlando Furioso* the old copies have " a truthless *vile* circumference," and in his *James the Fourth*, the 4to has " more *vile*," and " *vile*
lust," see pp. 188 and 191.

Whereon the fearful dragon held his seat,
That watch'd the garden call'd Hesperides,   1180
Subdu'd and won by conquering Hercules.

Here BUNGAY *conjures, and the tree appears with the dragon*
shooting fire.

Van. Well done!

K. Hen. What say you, royal lordings, to my friar?
    Hath he not done a point of cunning skill?

Van. Each scholar in the necromantic spells
    Can do as much as Bungay hath perform'd
    But as Alcmena's bastard raz'd this tree,
    So will I raise him up as when he liv'd,
    And cause him pull the dragon from his seat,
    And tear the branches piecemeal from the root.—   1190
    Hercules! *Prodi, prodi,* Hercules!

HERCULES *appears in his lion's skin.*

Her. Quis me vult?

Van. Jove's bastard son, thou Libyan Hercules,
    Pull off the sprigs from off th' Hesperian tree,
    As once thou didst to win the golden fruit.

Her. Fiat.   [*Begins to break the branches.*

Van. Now, Bungay, if thou canst by magic charm
    The fiend, appearing like great Hercules,
    From pulling down the branches of the tree,
    Then art thou worthy to be counted learnèd.   1200

Bun. I cannot.

Van. Cease, Hercules, until I give thee charge.—
    Mighty commander of this English isle,
    Henry, come from the stout Plantagenets,
    Bungay is learn'd enough to be a friar;
    But to compare with Jaques Vandermast,
    Oxford and Cambridge must go seek their cells
    To find a man to match him in his art.
    I have given non-plus to the Paduans,
    To them of Sien, Florence, and Bologna,   1210
    Rheims, Louvain, and fair Rotterdam,
    Frankfort, Utrecht,[1] and Orleans:

[1] The 4tos "Lutrech."—This line is certainly mutilated; and so
perhaps is the preceding line: from the Emperor's speech, p. 159, it would
seem that "Paris" ought to be one of the places mentioned here.

And now must Henry, if he do me right,
Crown me with laurel, as they all have done.

Enter BACON.

Bacon. All hail to this royal company,
    That sit to hear and see this strange dispute!—
    Bungay, how stand'st thou as a man amaz'd?
    What, hath the German acted more than thou?
Van. What art thou that question'st thus?
Bacon. Men call me Bacon.   ·   1220
Van. Lordly thou look'st, as if that thou wert learn'd:
    Thy countenance as if science held her seat
    Between the circled arches of thy brows.
K. Hen. Now, monarchs, hath the German found his match.
Emp. Bestir thee, Jaques, take not now the foil,
    Lest thou dost lose what foretime thou didst gain.
Van. Bacon, wilt thou dispute?
Bacon. No,
    Unless he were more learn'd than Vandermast:
    For yet, tell me, what hast thou done?   1230
Van. Rais'd Hercules to ruinate that tree
    That Bungay mounted by his magic spells.
Bacon. Set Hercules to work.
Van. Now, Hercules, I charge thee to thy task;
    Pull off the golden branches from the root.
Her. I dare not.   See'st thou not great Bacon here,
    Whose frown doth act more than thy magic can?
Van. By all the thrones, and dominations,
    Virtues, powers, and mighty hierarchies,
    I charge thee to obey to Vandermast.   1240
Her. Bacon, that bridles headstrong Belcephon,
    And rules Asmenoth guider of the north,
    Binds me from yielding unto Vandermast.
K. Hen. How now, Vandermast! have you met with your
    match?
Van. Never before was't known to Vandermast
    That men held devils in such obedient awe.
    Bacon doth more than art, or else I fail.
Emp. Why, Vandermast, art thou overcome?—
    Bacon, dispute with him, and try his skill.   1250

Bacon. I came [1] not, monarchs, for to hold dispute
    With such a novice as is Vandermast;
    I came to have your royalties to dine
    With Friar Bacon here in Brazen-nose:
    And, for this German troubles but the place,
    And holds this audience with a long suspence,
    I'll send him to his acadèmy hence.—
    Thou Hercules, whom Vandermast did raise,
    Transport the German unto Hapsburg straight,
    That he may learn by travail, 'gainst the spring,[2]   1260
    More secret dooms and aphorisms of art.
    Vanish the tree, and thou away with him!
                    [*Exit Hercules with Vandermast and the tree.*
Emp. Why, Bacon, whither dost thou send him?
Bacon. To Hapsburg: there your highness at return
    Shall find the German in his study safe.
K. Hen. Bacon, thou hast honour'd England with thy skill,
    And made fair Oxford famous by thine art:
    I will be English Henry to thyself.[3]
    But tell me, shall we dine with thee to-day?
Bacon. With me, my lord; and while I fit my cheer,   1270
    See where Prince Edward comes to welcome you,
    Gracious as the morning-star of heaven.   [*Exit.*

Enter PRINCE EDWARD, LACY, WARREN, ERMSBY.

Emp. Is this Prince Edward, Henry's royal son?
    How martial is the figure of his face!
    Yet lovely and beset with amorets.[4]
K. Hen. Ned, where hast thou been?
P. Edw. At Framlingham, my lord, to try your bucks
    If they could scape the teasers or the toil.
    But hearing of these lordly potentates
    Landed, and progress'd up to Oxford town,   1280

[1] The 4tos " come " (but see what follows).
[2] The 4tos " springs."   [3] Something wanting here.
[4] So afterwards, p. 210—
            " those piercing *amorets.*
    That Daphne glancèd at his deity,"—
whence it is plain that Greene uses the word as equivalent to—love-kindling looks. (Cotgrave has " *Amourettes.* Loue-tricks, wanton loue-toyes, tickling, ticklings, daliances," etc).

I posted to give entertain to them:
Chief to the Almain monarch; next to him,
And joint with him, Castile and Saxony
Are welcome as they may be to the English court.
Thus for the men: but see, Venus appears,
Or one
That overmatcheth Venus in her shape!
Sweet Elinor, beauty's high-swelling pride,
Rich nature's glory and her wealth at once,
Fair of all fairs, welcome to Albion;   1290
Welcome to me, and welcome to thine own,
If that thou deign'st the welcome from myself.

Elin. Martial Plantagenet, Henry's high-minded son,
The mark that Elinor did count her aim,
I lik'd thee 'fore I saw thee: now I love,
And so as in so short a time I may;
Yet so as time shall never break that so,
And therefore so accept of Elinor.

K. of Cast. Fear not, my lord, this couple will agree,
If love may creep into their wanton eyes:—   1300
And therefore, Edward, I accept thee here,
Without suspence, as my adopted son.

K. Hen. Let me that joy in these consorting greets,
And glory in these honours done to Ned,
Yield thanks for all these favours to my son,
And rest a true Plantagenet to all.

Enter MILES *with a cloth and trenchers and salt.*

Miles. Salvete, omnes reges,
    That govern your *greges*
    In Saxony and Spain,
    In England and in Almain!   1310
    For all this frolic rabble
    Must I cover the table
    With trenchers, salt, and cloth;
    And then look for your broth

Emp. What pleasant fellow is this?

K. Hen. 'Tis, my lord, Doctor Bacon's poor scholar.

Miles. [aside.] My master hath made me sewer of these great
    lords; and, God knows, I am as serviceable at a table as
    a sow is under an apple-tree: 'tis no matter; their cheer

shall not be great, and therefore what skills where the salt
    stand,[1] before or behind?   *[Exit.*

K. of Cast. These scholars know more skill in axioms,   1322
    How to use quips and sleights of sophistry,
    Than for to cover courtly for a king.

Re-enter MILES *with a mess of pottage and broth ; and, after*
him, BACON.

Miles. Spill, sir? why, do you think I never carried twopenny
    chop before in my life?—
    By your leave, *nobile decus,*
    For here comes Doctor Bacon's *pecus,*
    Being in his full age
    To carry a mess of pottage.

Bacon. Lordings, admire not if your cheer be this,   1330
    For we must keep our academic fare;
    No riot where philosophy doth reign:
    And therefore, Henry, place these potentates,
    And bid them fall unto their frugal cates.

Emp. Presumptuous friar! what, scoff'st thou at a king?
    What, dost thou taunt us with thy peasants' fare,
    And give us cates fit for country swains?—
    Henry, proceeds this jest of thy consent,
    To twit us with a [2] pittance of such price?
    Tell me, and Frederick will not grieve thee long.   1340

K. Hen. By Henry's honour, and the royal faith
    The English monarch beareth to his friend,
    I knew not of the friar's feeble fare,
    Nor am I pleas'd he entertains you thus.

Bacon. Content thee, Frederick, for I show'd these [3] cates,
    To let thee see how scholars use to feed;
    How little meat refines our English wits.—
    Miles, take away, and let it be thy dinner.

Miles. Marry, sir, I will.
    This day shall be a festival-day with me;   1350
    For I shall exceed in the highest degree.   *[Exit.*

Bacon. I tell thee, monarch, all the German peers
    Could not afford thy entertainment such,

---

[1] *Skills, i.e.,* signifies.—The seats at table above the salt-cellar (which
used to be placed about the middle) were assigned to the more distinguished
guests; the seats below it, to those of inferior rank.
    [2] The 4to of 1594 " *with* such *a.*"   [3] The 4tos " thee."

So royal and so full of majesty,
As Bacon will present to Frederick.
The basest waiter that attends thy cups
Shall be in honours greater than thyself;
And for thy cates, rich Alexandria drugs,
Fetch'd by carvels from Ægypt's richest [1] streights,
Found in the wealthy strand of Africa,   1360
Shall royalise the table of my king;
Wines richer than th' Ægyptian courtesan
Quaff'd to Augustus' kingly countermatch,
Shall be carous'd in English Henry's feast;
Candy shall yield the richest of her canes;
Persia, down her Volga [2] by canoes,
Send down the secrets of her spicery;
The Afric dates, mirabolans [3] of Spain,
Conserves and suckets from Tiberias,
Cates from Judæa, choicer than the lamp   1370
That firèd Rome with sparks of gluttony,[4]
Shall beautify the board for Frederick:
And therefore grudge not at a friar's feast   [*Exeunt.*

Enter LAMBERT *and* SERLSBY *with the* Keeper.

Lam. Come, frolic Keeper of our liege's game,
Whose table spread hath ever venison
And jacks of wine to welcome passengers,
Know I'm in love with jolly Margaret,
That overshines our damsels as the moon
Darkeneth the brightest sparkles of the night.
In Laxfield here my land and living lies: 1380
I'll make thy daughter jointer of it all,
So thou consent to give her to my wife;
And I can spend five hundred marks a-year.

---

[1] An error. (In the preceding line we have had " rich," and just after this we have " richer " and " richest! ")

[2] " This," observes my friend, Mr. W. N. Lettsom, " is much as if France were to send claret and burgundy down her Thames."

[3] *i.e.*, dried plums. The 4tos " *mirabiles* " in italics. " I have eaten Spanishe *mirabolanes*, and yet am nothing the more metamorphosed."—Greene's *Notable Discouery of Coosnage*, 1591, Sig. A 2.

[4] A corrupted or rather (as I think) a mutilated passage. The Rev. J. Mitford (*Gent. Mag.* for March 1833, p. 217) alters " *lamp* " to " balm;" which, he feels confident, restores the true reading: " Balm," he says, " or the exudation of the Balsamum, was the *only export* of Judea to Rome; and the balm was peculiar to Judæa." But the correction " balm " does not suit what immediately follows.

Ser. I am the lands-lord, Keeper, of thy holds,
        By copy all thy living lies in me;
        Laxfield did never see me raise my due:
        I will enfeoff fair Margaret in all,
        So she will take her to a lusty squire.
Keep. Now, courteous gentles, if the Keeper's girl
        Hath pleas'd the liking fancy of you both,   1390
        And with her beauty hath subdu'd your thoughts,
        'Tis doubtful to decide the question.
        It joys me [1] that such men of great esteem
        Should lay their liking on this base estate,
        And that her state should grow so fortunate
        To be a wife to meaner men than you:
        But sith such squires will stoop to keeper's fee,
        I will, to avoid displeasure of you both,
        Call Margaret forth, and she shall make her choice.
Lam. Content, Keeper; send her unto us.   [*Exit Keeper.*
        Why, Serlsby, is thy wife so lately dead,   1401
        Are all thy loves so lightly passèd over,
        As thou canst wed before the year be out?
Ser. I live not, Lambert, to content the dead,
        Nor was I wedded but for life to her:
        The grave [2] ends and begins a married state.

                    Enter MARGARET.

Lam. Peggy, the lovely flower of all towns,
        Suffolk's fair Helen, and rich England's star,
        Whose beauty, temper'd with her huswifery,
        Makes England talk of merry Fressingfield!   1410
Ser. I cannot trick it up with posies,
        Nor paint my passions with comparisons,
        Nor tell a tale of Phœbus and his loves:
        But this believe me,—Laxfield here is mine,
        Of ancient rent seven hundred pounds a-year,
        And if thou canst but love a country squire,
        I will enfeoff thee, Margaret, in all:
        I cannot flatter; try me, if thou please.
Mar. Brave neighbouring squires, the stay of Suffolk's clime,
        A keeper's daughter is too base in gree [3]   1420

---

[1] If this be what the author wrote, it is at least very obscurely expressed.
[2] The 4to of 1594 " graves."   [3] *i.e.*, degree.

To match with men accounted of such worth:
But might I not displease, I would reply.

Lam. Say, Peggy; naught shall make us discontent.

Mar. Then, gentles, note that love hath little stay,
 Nor can the flames that Venus sets on fire
 Be kindled but by fancy's motion:
 Then pardon, gentles, if a maid's reply
 Be doubtful, while [1] I have debated with myself,[2]
 Who, or of whom, love shall constrain me like.

Ser. Let it be me; and trust me, Margaret,   1430
 The meads environ'd with the silver streams,
 Whose battling pastures fatten [3] all my flocks,
 Yielding forth fleeces stapled with such wool
 As Lemnster cannot yield more finer stuff,
 And forty kine with fair and burnish'd [4] heads,
 With strouting dugs that paggle to the ground,
 Shall serve thy dairy, if thou wed with me.

Lam. Let pass the country wealth, as flocks and kine,
 And lands that wave with Ceres' golden sheaves,
 Filling my barns with plenty of the fields;   1440
 But, Peggy, if thou wed thyself to me,
 Thou shalt have garments of embroider'd silk,
 Lawns, and rich net-works for thy head-attire:
 Costly shall be thy fair habiliments,
 If thou wilt be but Lambert's loving wife.

Mar. Content you, gentles, you have proffer'd fair,
 And more than fits a country maid's degree:
 But give me leave to counsel me a time,
 For fancy blooms not at the first assault;
 Give me [5] but ten days' respite, and I will reply,   1450
 Which or to whom myself affectionates.

Ser. Lambert, I tell thee, thou'rt importunate;
 Such beauty fits not such a base esquire:
 It is for Serlsby to have Margaret.

Lam. Think'st thou with wealth to overreach me?
 Serlsby, I scorn to brook thy country braves:

[1] *i.e.,* until.   [2] Qy. " I've with myself debated "?
[3] The 4to of 1594 " fatneth."
[4] The editor of the last ed. of Dodsley's *Old Plays* alters this word into
" furnish'd," which, he says, " in reference to their horns, seems to be the
true reading: besides Greene rather ' affected the letter,' and the change
affords an alliteration." I can perceive no necessity for rejecting the
reading of the 4tos.
[5] Qy. ought these words to be omitted?

I dare thee, coward, to maintain this wrong,
At dint of rapier, single in the field.

Ser. I'll answer, Lambert, what I have avouch'd.—   1459
Margaret, farewell; another time shall serve.   [*Exit.*

Lam. I'll follow.—Peggy, farewell to thyself;
Listen how well I'll answer for thy love.   [*Exit.*

Mar. How fortune tempers lucky haps with frowns,
And wrongs [1] me with the sweets of my delight!
Love is my bliss, and love is now my bale.
Shall I be Helen in my froward fates,
As I am Helen in my matchless hue,
And set rich Suffolk with my face afire?
If lovely Lacy were but with his Peggy,
The cloudy darkness of his bitter frown   1470
Would check the pride of these aspiring squires.
Before the term of ten days be expir'd,
Whenas they look for answer of their loves,
My lord will come to merry Fressingfield,
And end their fancies and their follies both:
Till when, Peggy, be blithe and of good cheer.

Enter a Post *with a letter and a bag of gold.*

Post. Fair lovely damsel, which way leads this path?
How might I post me unto Fressingfield?
Which footpath leadeth to the Keeper's lodge?

Mar. Your way is ready, and this path is right: 1480
Myself do dwell hereby in Fressingfield;
And if the Keeper be the man you seek,
I am his daughter: may I know the cause?

Post. Lovely, and once belovèd of my lord,—
No marvel if his eye was lodg'd so low,
When brighter beauty is not in the heavens,—
The Lincoln Earl hath sent you letters here,
And, with them, just an hundred pounds in gold.
    [*Gives letter and bag.*
Sweet, bonny wench, read them, and make reply.

Mar. The scrolls that Jove sent Danaë,   1490
Wrapt in rich closures of fine burnish'd gold,
Were not more welcome than these lines to me.
Tell me, whilst that I do unrip the seals,

[1] Qy. " wrings "?

Lives Lacy well? how fares my lovely lord?

Post. Well, if that wealth may make men to live well.

Mar. [reads.] *The blooms of the almond-tree grow in a night, and vanish in a morn; the flies hæmeræ, fair Peggy, take life with the sun, and die with the dew; fancy that slippeth in with a gaze, goeth out with a wink; and too timely* [1] *loves have ever the shortest length. I write this as thy grief, and my folly, who at Fressingfield loved that which time hath taught me to be but mean dainties: eyes are dissemblers, and fancy is but queasy; therefore know, Margaret, I have chosen a Spanish lady to be my wife, chief waiting-woman to the Princess Elinor; a lady fair, and no less fair than thyself, honourable and wealthy. In that I forsake thee, I leave thee to thine own liking; and for thy dowry I have sent thee an hundred pounds; and ever assure thee of my favour, which shall avail thee and thine much.*   1509

　　　　Farewell.   *Not thine, nor his own,*
　　　　　　　　　　　　　　　EDWARD LACY.

Fond Ate, doomer of bad-boding fates,
That wrapp'st proud fortune in thy snaky locks,
Didst thou enchant my birth-day with such stars
As lighten'd mischief from their infancy?
If heavens had vow'd, if stars had made decree,
To show on me their froward influence,
If Lacy had but lov'd, heavens, hell, and all,
Could not have wrong'd the patience of my mind.

Post. It grieves me, damsel; but the earl is forc'd   1520
To love the lady by the king's command.

Mar. The wealth combin'd within the English shelves,
Europe's commander, nor the English king,
Should not have mov'd the love of Peggy from her lord. [2]

Post. What answer shall I return to my lord?

Mar. First, for thou cam'st from Lacy whom I lov'd,—
Ah, give me leave to sigh at very [3] thought!—
Take thou, my friend, the hundred pound he sent;
For Margaret's resolution craves no dower:
The world shall be to her as vanity;   1530

---

[1] *i.e.*, early.
[2] Qy. "*from* him"?　But the earlier part of the speech is also evidently corrupted.
[3] The 4tos "euery."

Wealth, trash;[1] love, hate; pleasure, despair:
For I will straight to stately Framlingham,
And in the abbey there be shorn a nun,
And yield my loves and liberty to God.
Fellow, I give thee this, not for the news,
For those be hateful unto Margaret,
But for thou'rt Lacy's man, once Margaret's love.

Post. What I have heard, what passions I have seen,
I'll make report of them unto the earl.

Mar. Say that she joys his fancies be at rest,   1540
And prays that his misfortunes may be hers.   [*Exeunt.*

FRIAR BACON *is discovered in his cell, lying on a bed, with a white
stick in one hand, a book in the other, and a lamp lighted beside
him ; and the* Brazen Head, *and* MILES *with weapons by him.*

Bacon. Miles, where are you?

Miles. Here, sir.

Bacon. How chance you tarry so long?

Miles. Think you that the watching of the Brazen Head craves
no furniture?   I warrant you, sir, I have so armed myself
that if all your devils come, I will not fear them an inch.

Bacon. Miles,
Thou know'st that I have divèd into hell,
And sought the darkest palaces of fiends;   1550
That with my magic spells great Belcephon
Hath left his lodge and kneelèd at my cell;
The rafters of the earth rent from the poles,
And three-form'd Luna hid her silver looks,
Trembling upon her concave continent,
When Bacon read upon his magic book.
With seven years' tossing necromantic charms,
Poring upon dark Hecat's principles,
I have fram'd out a monstrous head of brass,
That, by the enchanting forces of the devil,   1560
Shall tell out strange and uncouth aphorisms,
And girt fair England with a wall of brass.
Bungay and I have watch'd these threescore days,
And now our vital spirits crave some rest:
If Argus liv'd, and had his hundred eyes,
They could not over-watch Phobetor's night.

[1] Qy. " *Wealth* shall be *trash*," etc.?

Now, Miles, in thee rests Friar Bacon's weal:
The honour and renown of all his life
Hangs in the watching of this Brazen Head;
Therefore I charge thee by the immortal God,   1570
That holds the souls of men within his fist,
This night thou watch; for ere the morning-star
Sends out his glorious glister on the north,
The head will speak: then, Miles, upon thy life,
Wake me; for then by magic art I'll work
To end my seven years' task with excellence.
If that a wink but shut thy watchful eye,
Then farewell Bacon's glory and his fame!
Draw close the curtains, Miles: now, for thy life,   1579
Be watchful, and—   [*Falls asleep.*

Miles. So; I thought you would talk yourself asleep anon; and
'tis no marvel, for Bungay on the days, and he on the nights,
have watched just these ten and fifty days: now this is the
night, and 'tis my task, and no more.   Now, Jesus bless me,
what a goodly head it is! and a nose! you talk of *nos autem
glorificare;* but here's a nose that I warrant may be called
nos autem populare for the people of the parish.   Well, I
am furnished with weapons: now, sir, I will set me down
by a post, and make it as good as a watchman to wake me,
if I chance to slumber.   I thought, Goodman Head, I would
call you out of your *memento.*   Passion o' God, I have almost
broke my pate!   [*A great noise.*]   Up, Miles, to your task;
take your brown-bill [1] in your hand; here's some of your
master's hobgoblins abroad.   1594

The Brazen Head. Time is.

Miles. Time is!   Why, Master Brazen-head, have you such a
capital nose, and answer you with syllables, "Time is"?
is this all my master's cunning, to spend seven years' study
about "Time is"?   Well, sir, it may be we shall have some
better orations of it anon: well, I'll watch you as narrowly
as ever you were watched, and I'll play with you as the
nightingale with the slow-worm; I'll set a prick against
my breast.   Now rest there, Miles.   Lord have mercy upon
me, I have almost killed myself!   [*A great noise.*]   Up,
Miles; list how they rumble.   1605

The Brazen Head. Time was.

---

[1] A weapon formerly borne by our foot-soldiers, and afterwards by
watchmen: it was a sort of pike or halbert, with a hooked point.

Miles. Well, Friar Bacon, you have spent your seven-years'
study well, that can make your head speak but two words
at once, "Time was." Yea, marry, time was when my
master was a wise man, but that was before he began to
make the Brazen Head. You shall lie while [1] your arse
ache, an your head speak no better. Well, I will watch,
and walk up and down, and be a peripatetian and a philo-
sopher of Aristotle's stamp. [*A great noise.*] What, a fresh
noise? Take thy pistols in hand, Miles. 1615

The Brazen Head. Time is past.
　　　　　　[*A lightning flashes forth, and a hand appears
　　　　　　　　　that breaks down the Head with a hammer.*

Miles. Master, master, up! hell's broken loose; your head
speaks; and there's such a thunder and lightning, that I
warrant all Oxford is up in arms. Out of your bed, and take
a brown-bill in your hand; the latter day is come. 1620

Bacon. Miles, I come. [*Rises and comes forward.*] O, passing
　　　warily watched!
Bacon will make thee next himself in love.
When spake the head?

Miles. When spake the head! did not you say that he should
tell strange principles of philosophy? Why, sir, it speaks
but two words at a time.

Bacon. Why, villain, hath it spoken oft?

Miles. Oft! ay, marry, hath it, thrice; but in all those three
times it hath uttered but seven words.

Bacon. As how? 1630

Miles. Marry, sir, the first time he said "Time is," as if Fabius
Commentator should have pronounced a sentence; [the
second time] he said "Time was;" and the third time, with
thunder and lightning, as in great choler, he said, "Time
is past."

Bacon. 'Tis past indeed. Ah, villain! time is past:
My life, my fame, my glory, all are past.—
Bacon,
The turrets of thy hope are ruin'd down,
Thy seven years' study lieth in the dust: 1640
Thy Brazen Head lies broken through a slave,
That watch'd, and would not when the head did will.—
What said the head first?

Miles. Even, sir, "Time is."
　　　　　　　　　[1] *i.e.*, until.

Bacon. Villain, if thou hadst call'd to Bacon then,
    If thou hadst watch'd, and wak'd the sleepy friar,
    The Brazen Head had utter'd aphorisms,
    And England had been circled round with brass:
    But proud Asmenoth, ruler of the north,
    And Demogorgon, master of the fates,   1650
    Grudge that a mortal man should work so much.
    Hell trembled at my deep-commanding spells,
    Fiends frown'd to see a man their over-match;
    Bacon might boast more than a man might boast
    But now the braves of Bacon have an end,
    Europe's conceit of Bacon hath an end,
    His seven years' practice sorteth to ill end:
    And, villain, sith my glory hath an end,
    I will appoint thee to some fatal end.[1]
    Villain, avoid! get thee from Bacon's sight!   1660
    Vagrant, go roam and range about the world,
    And perish as a vagabond on earth!
Miles. Why, then, sir, you forbid me your service?
Bacon. My service, villain! with a fatal curse,
    That direful plagues and mischief fall on thee.
Miles. 'Tis no matter, I am against you with the old proverb,—
    The more the fox is cursed, the better he fares. God be
    with you, sir; I'll take but a book in my hand, a wide-
    sleeved gown on my back, and a crowned cap on my head,
    and see if I can want promotion.   1670
Bacon. Some fiend or ghost haunt on thy weary steps,
    Until they do transport thee quick to hell:
    For Bacon shall have never merry day,
    To lose the fame and honour of his head.   [*Exeunt.*

Enter the EMPEROR, *the* KING OF CASTILE, KING HENRY, ELINOR,
    PRINCE EDWARD, LACY, *and* RALPH SIMNELL.

Emp. Now, lovely prince, the prime [2] of Albion's wealth,
    How fare the Lady Elinor and you?
    What, have you courted and found Castile fit
    To answer England in equivalence?
    Will't be a match 'twixt bonny Nell and thee?
P. Edw. Should Paris enter in the courts of Greece,   1680
    And not lie fetter'd in fair Helen's looks?

---

[1] The 4tos " fatall to some *end.*"   [2] The 4tos " prince."
    II—H 49²

Or Phœbus scape those piercing amorets
That Daphne glancèd at his deity?
Can Edward, then, sit by a flame and freeze,
Whose heat puts Helen and fair Daphne down?
Now, monarchs, ask the lady if we gree.

K. Hen. What, madam, hath my son found grace or no?

Elin. Seeing, my lord, his lovely counterfeit,[1]
And hearing how his mind and shape agreed,
I came not, troop'd with all this warlike train,   1690
Doubting of love, but so affectionate,
As Edward hath in England what he won in Spain.[2]

K. of Cast. A match, my lord; these wantons needs must love:
Men must have wives, and women will be wed:
Let's haste the day to honour up the rites.

Ralph. Sirrah Harry, shall Ned marry Nell?

K. Hen. Ay, Ralph: how then?

Ralph. Marry, Harry, follow my counsel: send for Friar Bacon
to marry them, for he'll so conjure him and her with his
necromancy, that they shall love together like pig and lamb
whilst they live.   1701

K. of Cast. But hearest thou, Ralph, art thou content to have
Elinor to thy lady?

Ralph. Ay, so she will promise me two things.

K. of Cast. What's that, Ralph?

Ralph. That she will never scold with Ned, nor fight with me.—
Sirrah Harry, I have put her down with a thing unpossible.

K. Hen. What's that, Ralph?

Ralph. Why, Harry, didst thou ever see that a woman could
both hold her tongue and her hands? no: but when egg-
pies grow on apple-trees, then will thy grey mare prove a
bag-piper.   1712

Emp. What say the Lord of Castile and the Earl of Lincoln, that
they are in such earnest and secret talk?

K. of Cast. I stand, my lord, amazèd at his talk,
How he discourseth of the constancy
Of one surnam'd, for beauty's excellence,
The Fair Maid of merry Fressingfield.[3]

K. Hen. 'Tis true, my lord, 'tis wondrous for to hear;
Her beauty passing Mars's paramour,   1720

---

[1] *i.e.*, portrait.   [2] Corrupted.
[3] Here " fair " is a dissyllable: see Walker's *Shakespeare's Versification*,
etc., p. 146.

Her virgin's right as rich as Vesta's was.
Lacy and Ned have told me miracles.

K. of Cast. What says Lord Lacy? shall she be his wife?

Lacy. Or else Lord Lacy is unfit to live.—
May it please your highness give me leave to post
To Fressingfield, I'll fetch the bonny girl,
And prove, in true appearance at the court,
What I have vouchèd often with my tongue.

K. Hen. Lacy, go to the 'querry of my stable,
And take such coursers as shall fit thy turn: 1730
Hie thee to Fressingfield, and bring home the lass;
And, for her fame flies through the English coast,
If it may please the Lady Elinor,
One day shall match your excellence and her.

Elin. We Castile ladies are not very coy;
Your highness may command a greater boon:
And glad were I to grace the Lincoln Earl
With being partner of his marriage-day.

P. Edw. Gramercy, Nell, for I do love the lord,
As he that's second to thyself [1] in love.   1740

Ralph. You love her?—Madam Nell, never believe him you,
though he swears he loves you.

Elin. Why, Ralph?

Ralph. Why, his love is like unto a tapster's glass that is broken
with every touch; for he loved the fair maid of Fressingfield
once out of all ho [2]—Nay, Ned, never wink upon me; I care
not, I.

K. Hen. Ralph tells all; you shall have a good secretary of
him.—
But, Lacy, haste thee post to Fressingfield;   1750
For ere thou hast fitted all things for her state,
The solemn marriage-day will be at hand.

Lacy. I go, my lord.   [*Exit.*

Emp. How shall we pass this day, my lord?

K. Hen. To horse, my lord; the day is passing fair,
We'll fly the partridge, or go rouse the deer.
Follow, my lords; you shall not want for sport.   [*Exeunt.*

Enter, to Friar Bacon *in his cell,* Friar Bungay.

Bun. What means the friar that frolick'd it of late,

---

[1] The 4tos "myselfe."
[2] *i.e.,* out of measure. (" *Out of all ho,* Immodicè." Coles's *Dict.*)

To sit as melancholy in his cell [1]
As if he had neither lost nor won to-day?   1760
Bacon. Ah, Bungay, my [2] Brazen Head is spoil'd,
My glory gone, my seven years' study lost!
The fame of Bacon, bruited through the world,
Shall end and perish with this deep disgrace.
Bun. Bacon hath built foundation of his fame
So surely on the wings of true report,
With acting strange and uncouth miracles,
As this cannot infringe what he deserves.
Bacon. Bungay, sit down, for by prospective skill
I find this day shall fall out ominous: 1770
Some deadly act shall 'tide me ere I sleep;
But what and wherein little can I guess.
Bun. My mind is heavy, whatsoe'er shall hap.

                                     [*Knocking within.*

Bacon. Who's that knocks?
Bun. Two scholars that desire to speak with you.
Bacon. Bid them come in.

                Enter two Scholars.

Now, my youths, what would you have?
First Schol. Sir, we are Suffolk-men and neighbouring friends;
Our fathers in their countries lusty squires;
Their lands adjoin: in Cratfield mine doth dwell,   1780
And his in Laxfield.   We are college-mates,
Sworn brothers, as our fathers live as friends.
Bacon. To what end is all this?
Second Schol. Hearing your worship kept within your cell
A glass prospective, wherein men might see
Whatso their thoughts or hearts' desire could wish,
We come to know how that our fathers fare.
Bacon. My glass is free for every honest man.
Sit down, and you shall see ere long, how [3]
Or in what state your friendly fathers live. [4]   1790
Meanwhile, tell me your names.
First Schol. Mine Lambert.

        [1] This line is printed twice over in the 4to of 1594.
        [2] Qy. "*Ah, Bungay, ah, my,*" etc.?
        [3] Qy. "*ere long, sirs, how*"?
        [4] The 4to of 1594 "father liues."

Second Schol. And mine Serlsby.

Bacon. Bungay, I smell there will be a tragedy.

Enter LAMBERT *and* SERLSBY *with rapiers and daggers.*

Lam. Serlsby, thou hast kept thine hour like a man:[1]
Thou'rt worthy of the title of a squire,
That durst, for proof of thy affection
And for thy mistress' favour, prize[2] thy blood.
Thou know'st what words did pass at Fressingfield,
Such shameless braves as manhood cannot brook: 1800
Ay, for I scorn to bear such piercing taunts,
Prepare thee, Serlsby; one of us will die.

Ser. Thou see'st I single [meet] thee [in] the field,
And what I spake, I'll maintain with my sword:
Stand on thy guard, I cannot scold it out.
An if thou kill me, think I have a son,
That lives in Oxford in the Broadgates-hall,
Who will revenge his father's blood with blood.

Lam. And, Serlsby, I have there a lusty boy,
That dares at weapon buckle with thy son,   1810
And lives in Broadgates too, as well as thine:
But draw thy rapier, for we'll have a bout.

Bacon. Now, lusty younkers, look within the glass,
And tell me if you can discern your sires.

First Schol. Serlsby, 'tis hard; thy father offers wrong,
To combat with my father in the field.

Second Schol. Lambert, thou liest, my father's is th' abuse,
And thou shalt find it, if my father harm.

Bun. How goes it, sirs?

First Schol. Our fathers are in combat hard by Fressingfield.

Bacon. Sit still, my friends, and see the event.   1821

Lam. Why stand'st thou, Serlsby? doubt'st thou of thy life?
A veney,[3] man! fair Margaret craves so much.

Ser. Then this for her.

First Schol. Ah, well thrust!

Second Schol. But mark the ward.

> [*Lambert and Serlsby stab each other.*

Lam. O, I am slain!   [*Dies.*

---

[1] I may just notice that the author intended this line to be read thus—
   " Serlsby, *thou'st* kept thine *hower* like a man.''

[2] *i.e.*, venture, risk, in combat.   [3] *i.e.*, A bout.

Ser. And, I,—Lord have mercy on me!   [*Dies.*
First Schol. My father slain!—Serlsby, ward that.
Second Schol. And so is mine!—Lambert, I'll quite thee well.
              [*The two Scholars stab each other, and die.*
Bun. O strange stratagem!   1831
Bacon. See, friar, where the fathers [1] both lie dead!—
    Bacon, thy magic doth effect this massacre:
    This glass prospective worketh many woes;
    And therefore seeing these brave lusty Brutes,
    These friendly youths, did perish by thine art,
    End all thy magic and thine art at once.
    The poniard that did end their [2] fatal lives,
    Shall break the cause efficiat of their woes.
    So fade the glass, and end with it the shows   1840
    That necromancy did infuse the crystal with.
                 [*Breaks the glass.*
Bun. What means learn'd Bacon thus to break his glass?
Bacon. I tell thee, Bungay, it repents me sore
    That ever Bacon meddled in this art.
    The hours I have spent in pyromantic spells,
    The fearful tossing in the latest night
    Of papers full of necromantic charms,
    Conjuring and abjuring devils and fiends,
    With stole and alb and strong [3] pentageron;
    The wresting of the holy name of God,   1850
    As Sother, Eloim, and Adonai,
    Alpha, Manoth, and Tetragrammaton,
    With praying to the five-fold powers of heaven,
    Are instances that Bacon must be damn'd
    For using devils to countervail his God.—
    Yet, Bacon, cheer thee, drown not in despair:
    Sins have their salves, repentance can do much:
    Think Mercy sits where Justice holds her seat,
    And from those wounds those bloody Jews did pierce,
    Which by thy magic oft did bleed afresh,   1860
    From thence for thee the dew of mercy drops,
    To wash the wrath of high Jehovah's ire,
    And make thee as a new-born babe from sin.—
    Bungay, I'll spend the remnant of my life

---

[1] Qy. " scholars "?   [2] The 4tos " the."
[3] The 4tos " strange." But compare, in p. 155, " Bow to the force
of his pentageron."

In pure devotion, praying to my God
That he would save what Bacon vainly lost.   [*Exeunt.*

Enter MARGARET *in nun's apparel, the* Keeper, *and their*
Friend.

Keeper. Margaret, be not so headstrong in these vows:
O, bury not such beauty in a cell,
That England hath held famous for the hue!
Thy father's hair, like to the silver blooms   1870
That beautify the shrubs of Africa,
Shall fall before the dated time of death,
Thus to forego his lovely Margaret.
Mar. Ah, father, when the harmony of heaven
Soundeth the measures of a lively faith,
The vain illusions of this flattering world
Seem odious to the thoughts of Margaret.
I lovèd once,—Lord Lacy was my love;
And now I hate myself for that I lov'd,
And doted more on him than on my God,—   1880
For this I scourge myself with sharp repents.
But now the touch of such aspiring sins
Tells me all love is lust but love of heavens;
That beauty used for love is vanity:
The world contains naught but alluring baits,
Pride,[1] flattery, and inconstant thoughts.
To shun the pricks of death, I leave the world,
And vow to meditate on heavenly bliss,
To live in Framlingham a holy nun,
Holy and pure in conscience and in deed;   1890
And for to wish all maids to learn of me
To seek heaven's joy before earth's vanity.
Friend. And will you, then, Margaret, be shorn a nun, and so
leave us all?
Mar. Now farewell world, the engine of all woe!
Farewell to friends and father!   Welcome Christ!
Adieu to dainty robes! this base attire
Better befits an humble mind to God
Than all the show of rich habiliments.
Farewell, O love![2] and, with fond love, farewell   1900
Sweet Lacy, whom I lovèd once so dear!

---

[1] A slightly mutilated line.   [2] The 4tos " Loue, *O loue.*"

Ever be well, but never in my thoughts,
Lest I offend to think on Lacy's love:
But even to that, as to the rest, farewell!

Enter LACY, WARREN, *and* ERMSBY, *booted and spurrèd.*

Lacy. Come on, my wags, we're near the Keeper's lodge.
　　Here have I oft walk'd in the watery meads,
　　And chatted with my lovely Margaret.
War. Sirrah Ned, is not this the Keeper?
Lacy. 'Tis the same.
Erms. The old lecher hath gotten holy mutton[1] to him; a nun,
　　my lord.   1911
Lacy. Keeper, how far'st thou? holla, man, what cheer?
　　How doth Peggy, thy daughter and my love?
Keeper. Ah, good my lord! O, woe is me for Peggy!
　　See where she stands clad in her nun's attire,
　　Ready for to be shorn in Framlingham:
　　She leaves the world because she left your love.
　　O, good my lord, persuade her if you can!
Lacy. Why, how now, Margaret! what, a malcontent?
　　A nun? what holy father taught you this,   1920
　　To task yourself to such a tedious life
　　As die a maid? 'twere injury to me,
　　To smother up such beauty in a cell.
Mar. Lord Lacy, thinking of my[2] former 'miss,[3]
　　How fond[4] the prime of wanton years were spent[5]
　　In love (O, fie upon that fond conceit,
　　Whose hap and essence hangeth in the eye!),
　　I leave both love and love's content at once,
　　Betaking me to him that is true love,
　　And leaving all the world for love of him.   1930
Lacy. Whence, Peggy, comes this metamorphosis?
　　What, shorn a nun, and I have from the court
　　Posted with coursers to convey thee hence
　　To Windsor, where our marriage shall be kept!
　　Thy wedding-robes are in the tailor's hands.
　　Come, Peggy, leave these peremptory vows.

[1] A cant term for a prostitute.　　　　[2] The earlier 4tos " thy "
[3] For *amiss, i.e.,* fault.　　　　　　[4] *i.e., fondly*—foolishly, vainly.
[5] In almost all our early writers (Shakespeare included) are similar
instances of a nominative singular being followed by a verb plural when a
genitive plural intervenes.

Mar. Did not my lord resign his interest,
 And make divorce 'twixt Margaret and him?
Lacy. 'Twas but to try sweet Peggy's constancy.
 But will fair Margaret leave her love and lord?   1940
Mar. Is not heaven's joy before earth's fading bliss,
 And life above sweeter than life in love?
Lacy. Why, then, Margaret, will be shorn a nun?
Mar. Margaret
 Hath made a vow which may not be revok'd.
War. We cannot stay, my lord;[1] an if she be so strict,
 Our leisure grants us not to woo afresh.
Erms. Choose you, fair damsel, yet the choice is yours,—
 Either a solemn nunnery or the court,
 God or Lord Lacy: which contents you best,   1950
 To be a nun or else Lord Lacy's wife?
Lacy. A good motion.—Peggy, your answer must be short.
Mar. The flesh is frail: my lord doth know it well,
 That when he comes with his enchanting face,
 Whate'er[2] betide, I cannot say him nay.
 Off goes the habit of a maiden's heart,
 And, seeing fortune will, fair Framlingham,
 And all the show of holy nuns, farewell!
 Lacy for me, if he will be my lord.
Lacy. Peggy, thy lord, thy love, thy husband.[3]   1960
 Trust me, by truth of knighthood, that the king
 Stays for to marry matchless Elinor,
 Until I bring thee richly to the court,
 That one day may both marry her and thee.—
 How say'st thou, Keeper? art thou glad of this?
Keep. As if[4] the English king had given
 The park and deer of Fressingfield to me.
Erms. I pray thee, my Lord of Sussex, why art thou in a brown
 study?
War. To see the nature of women; that be they never so near
 God, yet they love to die in a man's arms.   1971
Lacy. What have you fit for breakfast? We have hied
 And posted all this night to Fressingfield.

---

[1] Most probably an addition by some transcriber; which not only
injures the metre, but is out of place in the mouth of Warren, who is
himself a "lord," and who, when he last addressed Lacy, called him
"Sirrah Ned."
[2] The 4tos "Whatsoe'er."   [3] Qy. "*thy husband,* I"?
[4] Qy. "*As* glad as *if*"?

Mar. Butter and cheese, and umbles[1] of a deer,
      Such as poor keepers have within their lodge.
Lacy. And not a bottle of wine?
Mar. We'll find one for my lord.
Lacy. Come, Sussex, let us in: we shall have more,
      For she speaks least, to hold her promise sure.   [*Exeunt.*

Enter a Devil.

Devil. How restless are the ghosts of hellish sprites,[2]   1980
      When every charmer with his magic spells
      Calls us from nine-fold-trenchèd Phlegethon,
      To scud and over-scour the earth in post
      Upon the speedy wings of swiftest winds!
      Now Bacon hath rais'd me from the darkest deep,
      To search about the world for Miles his man,
      For Miles, and to torment his lazy bones
      For careless watching of his Brazen Head.
      See where he comes: O, he is mine.   1989

Enter MILES *in a gown and a corner-cap.*

Miles. A scholar, quoth you! marry, sir, I would I had been a
      bottle-maker when I was made a scholar; for I can get
      neither to be a deacon, reader, nor schoolmaster, no, not
      the clerk of a parish. Some call me a dunce; another saith,
      my head is as full of Latin as an egg's full of oatmeal: thus
      I am tormented, that the devil and Friar Bacon haunt me.—
      Good Lord, here's one of my master's devils! I'll go speak
      to him.—What, Master Plutus, how cheer you?
Dev. Dost thou know me?
Miles. Know you, sir! why, are not you one of my master's
      devils, that were wont to come to my master, Doctor Bacon,
      at Brazen-nose?   2001
Dev. Yes, marry, am I.
Miles. Good Lord, Master Plutus, I have seen you a thousand
      times at my master's, and yet I had never the manners to
      make you drink. But, sir, I am glad to see how conform-
      able you are to the statute.—I warrant you, he's as yeomanly
      a man as you shall see: mark you, masters, here's a plain

---

[1] *i.e.*, the inward parts.
[2] The 4to of 1594 " spirits."

honest man, without welt or guard.[1]—But I pray you, sir, do you come lately from hell?

Dev. Ay, marry: how then? 2010

Miles. Faith, 'tis a place I have desired long to see: have you not good tippling-houses there? may not a man have a lusty fire there, a pot of good ale, a pair [2] of cards, a swinging piece of chalk, and a brown toast that will clap a white waistcoat on a cup of good drink?

Dev. All this you may have there.

Miles. You are for me, friend, and I am for you. But I pray you, may I not have an office there?

Dev. Yes, a thousand: what wouldst thou be? 2019

Miles. By my troth, sir, in a place where I may profit myself. I know hell is a hot place, and men are marvellous dry, and much drink is spent there; I would be a tapster.

Dev. Thou shalt.

Miles. There's nothing lets me from going with you, but that 'tis a long journey, and I have never a horse.

Dev. Thou shalt ride on my back.

Miles. Now surely here's a courteous devil, that, for to pleasure his friend, will not stick to make a jade of himself.—But I pray you, goodman friend, let me move a question to you.

Dev. What's that? 2030

Miles. I pray you, whether is your pace a trot or an amble?

Dev. An amble.

Miles. 'Tis well; but take heed it be not a trot: but 'tis no matter, I'll prevent it. [*Puts on spurs.*

Dev. What dost?

Miles. Marry, friend, I put on my spurs; for if I find your pace either a trot or else uneasy, I'll put you to a false gallop; I'll make you feel the benefit of my spurs.

Dev. Get up upon my back. [*Miles mounts on the Devil's back.*

Miles. O Lord, here's even a goodly marvel, when a man rides to hell on the devil's back! [*Exeunt, the Devil roaring.*

---

[1] Or *gard*—*i.e.*, facing, trimming.
[2] *i.e.*, paek: "out commeth an old *paire* of cardes, whereat the Barnard teacheth the Verser a new game," etc. Greene's *Notable Discouery of Coosnage*, 1591, Sig. A 4.

Enter the EMPEROR *with a pointless sword; next the* KING OF
CASTILE *carrying a sword with a point;* LACY *carrying the
globe;* PRINCE EDWARD; WARREN *carrying a rod of gold with
a dove on it;* ERMSBY *with a crown and sceptre;* PRINCESS
ELINOR *with* MARGARET *Countess of Lincoln on her left hand;*
KING HENRY; BACON; *and* Lords *attending.*

P. Edw. Great potentates, earth's miracles for state,   2042
　　　Think that Prince Edward humbles at your feet,
　　　And, for these favours, on his martial sword
　　　He vows perpetual homage to yourselves,
　　　Yielding these honours unto Elinor.
K. Hen. Gramercies, lordings; old Plantagenet,
　　　That rules and sways the Albion diadem,
　　　With tears discovers these conceivèd joys,
　　　And vows requital, if his men-at-arms,   2050
　　　The wealth of England, or due honours done
　　　To Elinor, may quite his favourites.[1]
　　　But all this while what say you to the dames
　　　That shine like to the crystal lamps of heaven?
Emp. If but a third were added to these two,
　　　They did surpass those gorgeous images
　　　That gloried Ida with rich beauty's wealth.
Mar. 'Tis I, my lords, who humbly on my knee
　　　Must yield her orisons to mighty Jove
　　　For lifting up his handmaid to this state;   2060
　　　Brought from her homely cottage to the court,
　　　And grac'd with kings, princes, and emperors,
　　　To whom (next to the noble Lincoln Earl)
　　　I vow obedience, and such humble love
　　　As may a handmaid to such mighty men.
P. Elin. Thou martial man that wears the Almain crown,
　　　And you the western potentates of might,
　　　The Albion princess, English Edward's wife,
　　　Proud that the lovely star of Fressingfield,
　　　Fair Margaret, Countess to the Lincoln Earl,   2070
　　　Attends on Elinor,—gramercies, lord, for her,—
　　　'Tis I give thanks for Margaret to you all,
　　　And rest for her due bounden to yourselves.
K. Hen. Seeing the marriage is solémnizèd,
　　　　　　　　　[1] Qy. " favourers "?

Let's march in triumph to the royal feast.—
But why stands Friar Bacon here so mute?

Bacon. Repentant for the follies of my youth,
That magic's secret mysteries misled,
And joyful that this royal marriage
Portends such bliss unto this matchless realm.   2080

K. Hen. Why, Bacon,
What strange event shall happen to this land?
Or what shall grow from Edward and his queen?

Bacon. I find [1] by deep prescience of mine art,
Which once I temper'd in my secret cell,
That here where Brute did build his Troynovant,
From forth the royal garden of a king
Shall flourish out so rich and fair a bud,
Whose brightness shall deface proud Phœbus' flower,
And over-shadow Albion with her leaves.   2090
Till then Mars shall be master of the field,
But then the stormy threats of wars shall cease:
The horse shall stamp as careless of the pike,
Drums shall be turn'd to timbrels of delight;
With wealthy favours plenty shall enrich
The strand that gladded wandering Brute to see,
And peace from heaven shall harbour in these [2] leaves
That gorgeous beautify this matchless flower:
Apollo's heliotropion then shall stoop,
And Venus' hyacinth shall vail [3] her top;   2100
Juno shall shut her gilliflowers up,
And Pallas' bay shall 'bash her brightest green;
Ceres' carnation, in consort with those,
Shall stoop and wonder at Diana's rose.

K. Hen. This prophecy is mystical.—
But, glorious [4] commanders of Europa's love,
That make fair England like that wealthy isle
Circled with Gihon and swift Euphrates,[5]
In royalizing Henry's Albion

---

[1] One of those compliments to Queen Elizabeth which frequently occur at the conclusion of dramas acted during her lifetime.
[2] Qy. " those "? but our early writers did not always make the distinction between " *these* " and " those " which is made at the present day.
[3] *i.e.*, lower.
[4] Some corruption here. Qy. " *But, glorious* comrades *of*," etc.?
[5] The 4tos " first *Euphrates*."—That I have rightly corrected the text is proved by the following line of our author's *Orlando Furioso*—
  " From whence floweth Gihon and *swift Euphrates*."

With presence of your princely mightiness,—   2110
Let's march:[1] the tables all are spread,
And viands, such as England's wealth affords,
Are ready set to furnish out the boards.
You shall have welcome, mighty potentates:
It rests to furnish up this royal feast,
Only your hearts be frolic; for the time
Craves that we taste of naught but jouissance.
Thus glories England over all the west.   [*Exeunt omnes.*

Omne tulit[2] *punctum qui miscuit utile dulci.*

The Famous Historie of Fryer Bacon, on which Greene founded
his drama, has been already noticed. A specimen of it is now
subjoined:—

" How Fryer Bacon made a Brasen Head to speake, by the which
       hee would have walled England about with brasse.

"FRYER BACON, reading one day of the many conquests of
England, bethought himselfe how he might keepe it hereafter
from the like conquests, and so make himselfe famous hereafter
to all posterities. This, after great study, hee found could be
no way so well done as one; which was to make a head of brasse,
and if he could make this head to speake, and heare it when it
speakes, then might hee be able to wall all England about with
brasse. To this purpose hee got one Fryer Bungey to assist
him, who was a great scholler and a magician, but not to bee
compared to Fryer Bacon: these two with great study and
paines so framed a head of brasse, that in the inward parts
thereof there was all things like as in a naturall man's head.
This being done, they were as farre from perfection of the worke
as they were before, for they knew not how to give those parts
that they had made motion, without which it was impossible
that it should speake: many bookes they read, but yet could
not finde out any hope of what they sought, that at the last they
concluded to raise a spirit, and to know of him that which they
could not attaine to by their owne studies. To do this they
prepared all things ready, and went one evening to a wood
thereby, and after many ceremonies used, they spake the words

---

[1] Qy. " *Let* us *march* hence "?
[2] Greene's favourite motto: see the titles of his prose-works in the List
appended to the *Account of his life.*

of coniuration; which the Devill straight obeyed, and appeared
unto them, asking what they would? 'Know,' said Fryer
Bacon, 'that wee have made an artificiall head of brasse, which
we would have to speake, to the furtherance of which wee have
raised thee; and being raised, wee will here keepe thee, unlesse
thou tell to us the way and manner how to make this head to
speake.' The Devill told him that he had not that power of
himselfe. 'Beginner of lyes,' said Fryer Bacon, 'I know that
thou dost dissemble, and therefore tell it us quickly, or else wee
will here bind thee to remaine during our pleasures.' At these
threatnings the Devill consented to doe it, and told them, that
with a continuel fume of the six hotest simples it should have
motion, and in one month space speak; the time of the moneth
or day hee knew not: also hee told them, that if they heard it
not before it had done speaking, all their labour should be lost.
They being satisfied, licensed the spirit for to depart.

"Then went these two learned fryers home againe, and prepared the simples ready, and made the fume, and with continuall
watching attended when this brasen head would speake. Thus
watched they for three weekes without any rest, so that they
were so weary and sleepy that they could not any longer refraine
from rest: then called Fryer Bacon his man Miles, and told him,
that it was not unknown to him what paines Fryer Bungey and
himselfe had taken for three weekes space, onely to make, and
to heare the Brazen-head speake, which if they did not, then had
they lost all their labour, and all England had a great losse
thereby; therefore hee intreated Miles that he would watch
whilst that they slept, and call them if the head speake. 'Feare
not, good master,' said Miles, 'I will not sleepe, but harken and
attend upon the head, and if it doe chance to speake, I will call
you; therefore I pray take you both your rests and let mee alone
for watching this head.' After Fryer Bacon had given him a
great charge the second time, Fryer Bungey and he went to sleepe,
and Miles, alone to watch the brasen head. Miles, to keepe him
from sleeping, got a tabor and pipe, and being merry disposed,
sung this song to a northren tune of

'CAM'ST THOU NOT FROM NEWCASTLE?'

> To couple is a custome,
>   all things thereto agree:
> Why should not I, then, love?
> since love to all is free.

But Ile have one that's pretty,
   her cheekes of scarlet die,
For to breed my delight,
   When that I ligge [1] her by.

Though vertue be a dowry,
   yet Ile chuse money store:
If my love prove untrue,
   with that I can get more.

The faire is oft unconstant,
   the blacke is often proud:
Ile chuse a lovely browne;——
   come, fidler, scrape thy crowd.[2]

Come, fidler, scrape thy crowd,
   for Peggie the browne is she
Must be my bride: God guide
   that Peggy and I agree !

"With his owne musicke and such songs as these spent he
his time, and kept from sleeping at last. After some noyse the
head spake these two words, TIME IS. Miles, hearing it to speake
no more, thought his master would be angry if hee waked him
for that, and therefore he let them both sleepe, and began to
mocke the head in this manner; ' Thou brazen-faced head, hath
my master tooke all this paines about thee, and now dost thou
requite him with two words, TIME IS? Had hee watched with
a lawyer so long as he hath watched with thee, he would have
given him more and better words then thou hast yet. If thou
canst speake no wiser, they shal sleepe till doomes day for me:
TIME IS! I know Time is, and that you shall heare, Goodman
Brazen-face:——

TO THE TUNE OF 'DAINTIE, COME THOU TO ME.'

Time is for some to plant,
Time is for some to sowe,
Time is for some to graft
The horne, as some doe knowe.

Time is for some to eate,
Time is for some to sleepe,
Time is for some to laugh,
Time is for some to weepe.

Time is for some to sing,
Time is for some to pray,
Time is for some to creepe,
That have drunke all the day.

[1] *i.e.*, lie.   [2] *i.e.*, fiddle.

Time is to cart a bawd,
Time is to whip a whore,
Time is to hang a theefe,
And time is for much more.

"'Do you tell us, copper-nose, when TIME IS? I hope we schollers know our times, when to drinke drunke, when to kisse our hostes, when to goe on her score, and when to pay it,—that time comes seldome.' After halfe an houre had passed, the head did speake againe, two words, which were these, TIME WAS. Miles respected these words as little as he did the former, and would not wake them, but still scoffed at the brazen head, that it had learned no better words, and have such a tutor as his master: and in scorne of it sung this song:—

TO THE TUNE OF 'A RICH MERCHANT-MAN.'

Time was when thou, a kettle,
    wert fill'd with better matter;
But Fryer Bacon did thee spoyle
    when he thy sides did batter.

Time was when conscience dwellèd
    with men of occupation;
Time was when lawyers did not thrive
    so well by mens vexation.

Time was when kings and beggars
    of one poore stuffe had being;
Time was when office kept no knaves,——
    that time it was worth seeing.

Time was a bowle of water
    did give the face reflection;
Time was when women knew no paint,
    Which now they call complexion.

"'TIME WAS! I know that, brazen-face, without your telling, I know Time was, and I know what things there was when Time was; and if you speake no wiser, no master shall be waked for mee.' Thus Miles talked and sung till another halfe-houre was gone: then the brazen head spake again these words, TIME IS PAST; and therewith fell downe, and presently followed a terrible noyse, with strange flashes of fire, so that Miles was halfe dead with feare. At this noyse the two Fryers awaked, and wondred to see the whole roome so full of smoake; but that being vanished they might perceive the brazen head broken and lying on the ground. At this sight they grieved, and called Miles to know

how this came.   Miles, halfe dead with feare, said that it fell
downe of itselfe, and that with the noyse and fire that followed
he was almost frighted out of his wits.   Fryer Bacon asked him
if hee did not speake?   'Yes,' quoth Miles, 'it spake, but to
no purpose: Ile have a parret speake better in that time that
you have been teaching this brazen head.'   'Out on thee,
villaine!' said Fryer Bacon; 'thou hast undone us both: hadst
thou but called us when it did speake, all England had been
walled round about with brasse, to its glory and our eternal
fames.   What were the wordes it spake?'   'Very few,' said
Miles, 'and those were none of the wisest that I have heard
neither: first he said, TIME IS.'   'Hadst thou call'd us then,'
said Fryer Bacon, 'we had been made for ever.'   'Then,' said
Miles, 'half-an-houre after it spake againe and said, TIME WAS.'
'And wouldst thou not call us then?' said Bungey.   'Alas,'
said Miles, 'I thought he would have told me some long tale,
and then I purposed to have called you: then half-an-houre
after he cried, TIME IS PAST, and made such a noyse that hee hath
waked you himselfe, mee thinkes.'   At this Fryer Bacon was in
such a rage that hee would have beaten his man, but he was
restrained by Bungey: but neverthelesse, for his punishment,
he with his art struck him dumbe for one whole months space.
Thus the greate worke of these learned fryers was overthrown,
to their great griefes, by this simple fellow."

JAMES THE FOURTH

The Scottish Historie of Iames the fourth, slaine at Flodden. Entermixed with a pleasant Comedie, presented by Oboram King of Fayeries : As it hath bene sundrie times publikely plaide. Written by Robert Greene, Maister of Arts. Omne tulit punctum. London Printed by Thomas Creede, 1598, 4to.

JAMES THE FOURTH

DRAMATIS PERSONÆ

KING OF ENGLAND.	SLIPPER,
LORD PERCY.	NANO, *a dwarf,* } *sons to Bohan.*
SAMLES.	ANDREW.
KING OF SCOTS.	Purveyor, Herald, Scout, Hunts-
LORD DOUGLAS.	men, Soldiers, Revellers, etc.
LORD MORTON.	
LORD ROSS.	DOROTHEA, *Queen of Scots.*
BISHOP OF ST. ANDREWS.	COUNTESS OF ARRAN.
LORD EUSTACE.	IDA, *her daughter.*
SIR BARTRAM.	LADY ANDERSON.
SIR CUTHBERT ANDERSON.	Ladies, etc.
ATEUKIN.	
JAQUES.	OBERON, *King of Fairies.*
A Lawyer.	BOHAN.
A Merchant.	Antics, Fairies, etc.
A Divine.	

Music playing within, enter ASTER OBERON, *King of Fairies ; and* Antics, *who dance about a tomb placed conveniently on the stage ; out of the which suddenly starts up, as they dance,* BOHAN, *a Scot, attired like a ridstall* [1] *man, from whom the* Antics *fly.* OBERON *manet.*

Boh. Ay say, what's thou?

Ober. Thy friend, Bohan.

Boh. What wot I or reck I that? Whay, guid man, I reck no friend nor ay reck no foe; als ene to me. Git thee ganging, and trouble not may whayet,[2] or ays gar [3] thee recon me nene of thay friend, by the Mary mass, sall I.

Ober. Why, angry Scot,[4] I visit thee for love; then what moves thee to wrath?   8

Boh. The deil a whit reck I thy love; for I know too well that

---

[1] A mis-spelling, if not a corruption.

[2] *i.e.,* I suppose, my quiet.

[3] *i.e.,* I'll make. (Bohan, the reader will observe, sometimes says " Ay " and sometimes " I ": nor in several other words does he always adhere to the Scottish dialect.)

[4] Walker (*Shakespeare's Versification*, etc., p. 167) would make this speech verse—

> " Why, angry Scot, I visit thee for love;
> Then what moves thee to wrath? "

true love took her flight twenty winter sence to heaven, whither till ay can, weel I wot, ay sal ne'er find love: an thou lovest me, leave me to myself. But what were those puppets that hopped and skipped about me year whayle? [1]

Ober. My subjects.

Boh. Thay subjects! whay, art thou a king?

Ober. I am.

Boh. The deil thou art! whay, thou lookest not so big as the King of Clubs, nor so sharp as the King of Spades, nor so fain as the King o' Daymonds: be the mass, ay take thee to be the king of false hearts; therefore I rid [2] thee away, or ayse so curry your kingdom that you's be glad to run to save your life.   22

Ober. Why, stoical Scot, [3] do what thou darest to me: here is my breast, strike.

Boh. Thou wilt not threap me, [4] this whinyard has gard many better men to lope than thou? [*Tries to draw his sword.*] But how now! Gos sayds, what, will't not out? Whay, thou witch, thou deil! Gad's fute, may whinyard!

Ober. Why, pull, man: but what an 'twere out, how then?   29

Boh. This, then,—thou weart best be gone first; for ay'l so lop thy limbs that thou's go with half a knave's carcass to the deil.

Ober. Draw it out: now strike, fool, canst thou not?

Boh. Bread ay gad, what deil is in me? Whay, tell me, thou skipjack, what art thou?

Ober. Nay, first tell me what thou wast from thy birth, what thou hast passed hitherto, why thou dwellest in a tomb and leavest the world? and then I will release thee of these bonds; before, not.   39

Boh. And not before! then needs must, needs sall. I was born a gentleman of the best blood in all Scotland, except the king. When time brought me to age, and death took my parents, I became a courtier; where, though ay list not praise myself, ay engraved the memory of Bohan [5] on the skin-coat of some of them, and revelled with the proudest.

---

[1] *i.e.,* erewhile.   [2] *i.e., rede*—advise.

[3] Here again Walker (*ubi supra*) would arrange as verse—

      " Why, stoical Scot, do what thou dar'st to me:
        Here is my breast, strike."

[4] *i.e.,* obstinately contradict me, that this sword has made many better men to leap, etc.

[5] Here the 4to " *Boughon.*"

Ober. But why, living in such reputation, didst thou leave to be
    a courtier? 47

Boh. Because my pride was vanity, my expense loss, my reward
    fair words and large promises, and my hopes spilt, for that
    after many years' service one outran me; and what the
    deil should I then do there? No, no; flattering knaves,
    that can cog and prate fastest, speed best in the court.

Ober. To what life didst thou then betake thee?

Boh. I then changed the court for the country, and the wars
    for a wife: but I found the craft of swains more vile than
    the knavery of courtiers, the charge of children more heavy
    than servants, and wives' tongues worse than the wars
    itself; and therefore I gave o'er that, and went to the city
    to dwell; and there I kept a great house with small cheer,
    but all was ne'er the near.[1] 60

Ober. And why?

Boh. Because, in seeking friends, I found table-guests to eat
    me and my meat, my wife's gossips to bewray the secrets of
    my heart, kindred to betray the effect of my life: which
    when I noted, the court ill, the country worse, and the city
    worst of all, in good time my wife died—ay would she had
    died twenty winter sooner, by the mass!—leaving [2] my two
    sons to the world, and shutting myself into this tomb, where
    if I die I am sure I am safe from wild beasts, but whilst I
    live cannot be free from ill company. Besides, now I am
    sure, gif all my friends fail me, I sall have a grave of mine
    own providing. This is all. Now, what art thou? 72

Ober. Oberon, King of Fairies, that loves thee because thou
    hatest the world; and to gratulate thee, I brought these
    antics to show thee some sport in dancing, which thou hast
    loved well.

Boh. Ha, ha, ha! Thinkest thou those puppets can please me?
    whay, I have two sons, that with one Scottish jig shall
    break the neck of thy antics.

Ober. That would I fain see. 80

Boh. Why, thou shalt.—Ho,[3] boys!

---

[1] See note [1], p. 182.   [2] Some words are wanting here.

[3] The 4to "Howe"—which, as innumerable passages in early books
prove, was frequently the spelling of "Ho:" so in the folio *Shakespeare*,
1623:

    "Ware pensals. *How?*" ["Ware pencils, *ho!*"]
                        Love's Labour's Lost, act v. sc. 2.

    "*How?* Let the doore be lock'd."

                            Hamlet, last scene.

Enter SLIPPER *and* NANO.

Haud your clacks, lads,[1] trattle not for thy life, but gather
up your legs, and dance me forthwith a jig worth the sight.

Slip. Why, I must talk, an[2] I die for't: wherefore was my
tongue made?

Boh. Prattle, an thou darest, ene word more, and ais dib this
whinyard in thy wemb.

Ober. Be quiet, Bohan. I'll strike him dumb, and his brother
too: their talk shall not hinder our jig.—Fall to it; dance,
I say, man.   90

Boh. Dance Humer,[3] dance, ay rid[4] thee.

[*The two dance a jig devised for the nonst.*[5]
Now get you to the wide world with more than my father
gave me, that's learning enough both kinds, knavery and
honesty; and that I gave you, spend at pleasure.

Ober. Nay, for their sport I will give them this gift: to the
dwarf I give a quick wit, pretty[6] of body, and awarrant[7]
his preferment to a prince's service, where by his wisdom
he shall gain more love than common; and to loggerhead
your son I give a wandering life, and promise he shall never
lack, and avow,[8] if in all distresses he call upon me, to help
him. Now let them go.   101

[*Exeunt Slipper and Nano with courtesies.*
Boh. Now, king, if thou be a king, I will show thee whay I hate
the world by demonstration. In the year fifteen hundred
and twenty, was in Scotland a king, over-ruled with
parasites, misled by lust, and many circumstances too long
to trattle on now, much like our court of Scotland this day.
That story have I set down. Gang with me to the gallery,
and I'll show thee the same in action by guid fellows of our
countrymen; and then when thou see'st that, judge if any
wise man would not leave the world if he could.   110

Ober. That will I see: lead, and I'll follow thee.   [*Exeunt.*

---

[1] *i.e.*, Hold you your chattering.   [2] The 4to "on."

[3] In my former edition I gave "Heimore," because I found that reading
in the only copy of the 4to (Mr. Mitford's) which I was then able to see:
*but in that copy the leaf containing the present passage was a very modern
reprint.* After all, the alteration "Heimore" may be right.

[4] *i.e.*, *I rede*, I advise.   [5] Or *nonce* —*i.e.*, occasion.

[6] The substantive to which this epithet belongs has dropt out (unless
Greene wrote "prettiness.")

[7] *i.e.*, warrant.   [8] The 4to "auow that."

Laus Deo detur in æternum.

ACT I

SCENE I

Enter the KING OF ENGLAND, *the* KING OF SCOTS, QUEEN DOROTHEA, *the* COUNTESS OF ARRAN, IDA, *and* Lords; *and* ATEUKIN *aloof.*

K. of Scots. Brother of England, since our neighbouring land[s]
And near alliance do invite our loves,
The more I think upon our last accord,
The more I grieve your sudden parting hence.
First, laws of friendship did confirm our peace,
Now both the seal of faith and marriage-bed,
The name of father, and the style of friend;
These force in me affection full confirm'd;
So that I grieve—and this my hearty grief
The heavens record, the world may witness well—　　10
To lose your presence, who are now to me
A father, brother, and a vow'd friend.

K. of Eng. Link all these lovely [1] styles, good king, in one:
And since thy grief exceeds in my depart,
I leave my Dorothea to enjoy
Thy whole compact [of] loves and plighted vows.
Brother of Scotland, this is my joy,[2] my life,
Her father's honour, and her country's hope,
Her mother's comfort, and her husband's bliss:
I tell thee, king, in loving of my Doll,　　20
Thou bind'st her father's heart, and all his friends,

---

[1] Mr. Collier somewhere pronounces this to be a misprint for "loving." But compare Shakespeare:

"And seal the title with a *lovely* kiss."
　　　　　　Taming of the Shrew, act iii. sc. 2.

"Two *lovely* berries moulded on one stem," etc.
　　　　　　Midsummer-Night's Dream, act ii. sc. 3.
and Peele;

"And I will give thee many a *lovely* kiss," etc.
　　　　　　The Arraignment of Paris, act ii.

[2] Walker (*Shakespeare's Versification,* etc., p. 88) would read "*this*' [contraction for "this is"] my joy," etc.

233

In bands of love that death can not dissolve.

K. of Scots. Nor can her father love her like to me,
My life's light, and the comfort of my soul.—
Fair Dorothea, that wast England's pride,
Welcome to Scotland; and, in sign of love,
Lo, I invest thee with the Scottish crown.—
Nobles and ladies, stoop unto your queen,
And trumpets sound, that heralds may proclaim
Fair Dorothea peerless Queen of Scots.   30

All. Long live and prosper our fair Queen of Scots!

          [*They install and crown her.*

Q. Dor. Thanks to the king of kings for my dignity;
Thanks to my father that provides so carefully;
Thanks to my lord and husband for this honour;
And thanks to all that love their king and me.

All. Long live fair Dorothea, our true queen!

K. of Eng. Long shine the sun of Scotland in her pride,
Her father's comfort, and fair Scotland's bride!
But, Dorothea, since I must depart,
And leave thee from thy tender mother's charge,   40
Let me advise my lovely daughter first
What best befits her in a foreign land.
Live, Doll, for many eyes shall look on thee,
With [1] care of honour and the present state;
For she that steps to height of majesty
Is even the mark whereat the enemy aims:
Thy virtues shall be construèd to vice,
Thine affable discourse to abject mind;
If, coy, detracting tongues will call thee proud.
Be therefore wary in this slippery state: 50
Honour thy husband, love him as thy life,
Make choice of friends, as eagles of their young,
Who soothe no vice, who flatter not for gain,
But love such friends as do the truth maintain.
Think on these lessons when thou art alone,
And thou shalt live in health when I am gone.

Q. Dor. I will engrave these precepts in my heart:
And as the wind with calmness wooes you hence,
Even so I wish the heavens in all mishaps
May bless my father with continual grace.   60

K. of Eng. Then, son, farewell:

              [1] The 4to " Haue."

The favouring winds invite us to depart.
Long circumstance in taking princely leaves
Is more officious than convenient.
Brother of Scotland, love me in my child;
You greet me well, if so you will her good.
K. of Scots. Then, lovely Doll, and all that favour me,
Attend to see our English friends at sea:
Let all their charge depend upon my purse:
They are our neighbours, by whose kind accord   70
We dare attempt the proudest potentate.
Only, fair countess, and your daughter, stay;
With you I have some other thing to say.

> [*Exeunt, in all royalty, the King of England, Queen
> Dorothea, and Lords.*

[*Aside.*] So let them triumph that have cause to joy:
But, wretched king, thy nuptial knot is death,
Thy bride the breeder of thy country's ill;
For thy false heart dissenting from thy hand,
Misled by love, hath [1] made another choice,
Another choice, even when thou vow'd'st thy soul
To Dorothea, England's choicest pride: 80
O, then thy wandering eyes bewitch'd thy heart!
Even in the chapel did thy fancy change,
When, perjur'd man, though fair Doll had thy hand,
The Scottish Ida's beauty stale thy heart:
Yet fear and love have tied thy ready tongue
From blabbing forth the passions of thy mind,
'Less [2] fearful silence have in subtle looks
Bewray'd the treason of my new-vow'd love.
Be fair and lovely, Doll; but here's the prize,
That lodgeth here, and enter'd through mine eyes: 90
Yet, howsoe'er I love, I must be wise.—
Now, lovely countess, what reward or grace
May I employ [3] on you for this your zeal,
And humble honours, done us in our court,

---

[1] The 4to " hast."   [2] The 4to " lest."
[3] In my former edition I altered this word to " impose; " but I have
since met with several passages in our early writers which forbid the
alteration: *e.g.*—

> " Princes may pick their suffering nobles out,
>   And one by one *employ* 'em to the block," etc.

Fletcher and ——*'s Bloody Brother*, act iv. sc. 1 (where, according to Mr.
Collier in one of his notes on Shakespeare, " *employ* " is a misprint).

In entertainment of the English king?

Count. of A. It was of duty, prince, that I have done;
 And what in favour may content me most,
 Is, that it please your grace to give me leave
 For to return unto my country-home.

K. of Scots. But, lovely Ida, is your mind the same? 100

Ida. I count of court, my lord, as wise men do,
 'Tis fit for those that know what 'longs thereto:
 Each person to his place; the wise to art,
 The cobbler to his clout, the swain to cart.

K. of Scots. But, Ida, you are fair, and beauty shines,
 And seemeth best, where pomp her pride refines.

Ida. If beauty, as I know there's none in me,
 Were sworn my love, and I his life should be,
 The farther from the court I were remov'd,
 The more, I think, of heaven I were belov'd. 110

K. of Scots. And why?

Ida. Because the court is counted Venus' net,
 Where gifts and vows for stales[1] are often set:
 None, be she chaste as Vesta, but shall meet
 A curious tongue to charm her ears with sweet.

K. of Scots. Why, Ida, then I see you set at naught
 The force of love.

Ida. In sooth, this is my thought,
 Most gracious king,—that they that little prove,
 Are mickle blest from bitter sweets of love. 120
 And weel I wot, I heard a shepherd sing,
 That, like a bee, Love hath a little sting:
 He lurks in flowers, he percheth on the trees,
 He on kings' pillows bends his pretty knees;
 The boy is blind, but when he will not spy,
 He hath a leaden foot and wings to fly:
 Beshrew me yet, for all these strange effects,
 If I would like the lad that so infects.

K. of Scots. [*aside.*] Rare wit, fair face, what heart could more
  desire?
 But Doll is fair and doth concern thee near: 13c
 Let Doll be fair, she is won; but I must woo
 And win fair Ida, there's some choice in two.—
 But, Ida, thou art coy.

Ida. And why, dread king?

      [1] *i.e.*, decoys.

K. of Scots. In that you will dispraise so sweet a thing
　　As love.   Had I my wish——

Ida. What then?

K. of Scots. Then would I place
　　His arrow here, his beauty in that face.

Ida. And were Apollo mov'd and rul'd by me,　　　140
　　His wisdom should be yours, and mine his tree.

K. of Scots. But here returns our train.

Re-enter Queen Dorothea *and* Lords.

　　　　　　　　　　　　　Welcome, fair Doll:
　　How fares our father? is he shipp'd and gone?

Q. Dor. My royal father is both shipp'd and gone:
　　God and fair winds direct him to his home!

K. of Scots. Amen, say I.—[*Aside.*] Would thou wert with him
　　　too!
　　Then might I have a fitter time to woo.—
　　But, countess, you would be gone, therefore, farewell,—
　　Yet, Ida, if thou wilt, stay thou behind
　　To accompany my queen:　　　　　　　　　150
　　But if thou like the pleasures of the court,—
　　Or if she lik'd me, though she left the court,—
　　What should I say?   I know not what to say.—
　　You may depart:—and you, my courteous queen,
　　Leave me a space; I have a weighty cause
　　To think upon:—Ida, it nips me near;
　　It came from thence, I feel it burning here.
　　　　　　　[*Exeunt all except the King of Scots and Ateukin.*
　　Now am I free from sight of common eye,
　　Where to myself I may disclose the grief
　　That hath too great a part in mine affects.　　　160

Ateu. [*aside.*] And now is my time by wiles and words to rise,
　　Greater than those that think themselves more wise.

K. of Scots. And first, fond king, thy honour doth engrave
　　Upon thy brows the drift of thy disgrace.
　　Thy new-vow'd love, in sight of God and men,
　　Links [1] thee to Dorothea during life;
　　For who more fair and virtuous than thy wife?
　　Deceitful murderer of a quiet mind,
　　Fond love, vile lust, that thus misleads us men,

　　　　　　　　　[1] The 4to " Linke."

To vow our faiths, and fall to sin again!   170
But kings stoop not to every common thought:
Ida is fair and wise, fit for a king;
And for fair Ida will I hazard life,
Venture my kingdom, country, and my crown:
Such fire hath love to burn a kingdom down.
Say Doll dislikes that I estrange my love;
Am I obedient to a woman's look?
Nay, say her father frown when he shall hear
That I do hold fair Ida's love so dear;
Let father frown and fret, and fret and die,   180
Nor earth nor heaven shall part my love and I.
Yea, they shall part us, but we first must meet,
And woo and win, and yet the world not see't.
Yea, there's the wound, and wounded with that thought,
So let me die, for all my drift is naught.

Ateu. [*coming forward.*] Most gracious and imperial majesty,—
    [*Aside.*] A little [1] flattery more were but too much.
K. of Scots. Villain, what art thou
    That thus dar'st interrupt a prince's secrets?
Ateu. Dread king, thy vassal is a man of art,   190
    Who knows, by constellation of the stars,
    By oppositions and by dry aspécts,
    The things are past and those that are to come.
K. of Scots. But where's thy warrant to approach my presence?
Ateu. My zeal, and ruth to see your grace's wrong,
    Make me lament I did detract [2] so long.
K. of Scots. If thou know'st thoughts, tell me, what mean I now?
Ateu. I'll calculate the cause
    Of those your highness' smiles, and tell your thoughts.
K. of Scots. But lest thou spend thy time in idleness,   200
    And miss the matter that my mind aims at,
    Tell me,
    What star was opposite when that was thought?
                              [*Strikes him on the ear.*
Ateu. 'Tis inconvenient,[3] mighty potentate,
    Whose looks resemble Jove in majesty,
    To scorn the sooth of science with contempt.
    I see in those imperial looks of yours
    The whole discourse of love: Saturn combust,

---

[1] This line the 4to gives to the king.
[2] *i.e.,* avoid, forbear.   [3] *i.e.,* unbecoming, improper.

    With direful looks, at you nativity,
    Beheld fair Venus in her silver orb: 210
    I know, by certain axioms I have read,
    Your grace's griefs, and further can express
    Her name that holds you thus in fancy's bands.
K. of Scots. Thou talkest wonders.
Ateu. Naught but truth, O king.
    'Tis Ida is the mistress of your heart,
    Whose youth must take impression of affects;
    For tender twigs will bow, and milder minds
    Will yield to fancy, be they follow'd well.
K. of Scots. What god art thou, compos'd in human shape, 220
    Or bold Trophonius, to decide our doubts?
    How know'st thou this?
Ateu. Even as I know the means
    To work your grace's freedom and your love.
    Had I the mind, as many courtiers have,
    To creep into your bosom for your coin,
    And beg rewards for every cap and knee,
    I then would say, "If that your grace would give
    This lease, this manor, or this patent seal'd,
    For this or that I would effect your love:"   230
    But Ateukin is no parasite, O prince.
    I know your grace knows scholars are but poor;
    And therefore, as I blush to beg a fee,
    Your mightiness is so magnificent,
    You cannot choose but cast some gift apart,
    To ease my bashful need that cannot beg.
    As for your love, O, might I be employ'd,
    How faithfully would Ateukin compass it!
    But princes rather trust a smoothing tongue,
    Than men of art that can accept the time.   240
K. of Scots. Ateukin, if so thy name, for so thou say'st,
    Thine art appears in entrance of my love;
    And since I deem thy wisdom match'd with truth,
    I will exalt thee, and thyself alone
    Shalt be the agent to dissolve my grief.
    Sooth is, I love, and Ida is my love;
    But my new marriage nips me near, Ateukin,
    For Dorothea may not brook th' abuse.
Ateu. These lets are but as motes against the sun,
    Yet not so great; like dust before the wind,   250

Yet not so light.   Tut, pacify your grace:
You have the sword and sceptre in your hand;
You are the king, the state depends on you;
Your will is law.   Say that the case were mine:
Were she my sister whom your highness loves,
She should consent, for that our lives, our goods,
Depend on you; and if your queen repine,
Although my nature cannot brook of blood,
And scholars grieve to hear of murderous deeds,
But if the lamb should let the lion's way,   260
By my advice the lamb should lose her life.
Thus am I bold to speak unto your grace,
Who am too base to kiss your royal feet,
For I am poor, nor have I land nor rent,
Nor countenance here in court, but for my love,
Your grace shall find none such within the realm.

K. of Scots. Wilt thou effect my love? shall she be mine?
Ateu. I'll gather moly, crocus,[1] and the herbs
That heal the wounds of body and the mind;
I'll set out charms and spells, naught [2] shall be left   270
To tame the wanton if she shall rebel:
Give me but tokens of your highness' trust.

K. of Scots. Thou shalt have gold, honour, and wealth enough;
Win my love,[3] and I will make thee great.
Ateu. These words do make me rich, most noble prince;
I am more proud of them than any wealth.
Did not your grace suppose I flatter you,
Believe me, I would boldly publish this;—
Was never eye that saw a sweeter face,
Nor never ear that heard a deeper wit: 280
O God, how I am ravish'd in your worth!

K. of Scots. Ateukin, follow me; love must have ease.
Ateu. I'll kiss your highness' feet, march when you please.
                                                    [*Exeunt.*

---

[1] Corrected by the Rev. J. Mitford, *Gent. Mag.* for March 1833, p. 217.—
The 4to " *Moly*-rocus."
[2] The 4to " *nought* else."
[3] Qy. " *Win* thou *my love,*" etc., or " *Win* but *my love,*" etc.?

SCENE II

Enter SLIPPER, NANO, *and* ANDREW, *with their bills,
ready written, in their hand.*

And. Stand back, sir; mine shall stand highest.

Slip. Come under mine arm, sir, or get a footstool; or else, by
the light of the moon, I must come to it.

Nano. Agree, my masters; every man to his height: though I
stand lowest, I hope to get the best master.

And. Ere I will stoop to a thistle, I will change turns; as good
luck comes on the right hand as the left: here's for me,
and me, and mine. [*They set up their bills.*] But tell me,
fellows, till better occasion come, do you seek masters? 292

Slip. }
Nano. } We do.

And. But what can you do worthy preferment?

Nano. Marry, I can smell a knave from a rat.

Slip. And I can lick a dish before a cat.

And. And, I can find two fools unsought,—how like you that?
But, in earnest, now tell me of what trades are you two?

Slip. How mean you that, sir, of what trade? Marry, I'll tell
you, I have many trades: the honest trade when I needs
must; the filching trade when time serves; the cozening
trade as I find occasion. And I have more qualities: I
cannot abide a full cup unkissed, a fat capon uncarved, a
full purse unpicked, nor a fool to prove a justice as you do.

And. Why, sot, why callest thou me fool?

Nano. For examining wiser than thyself.

And. So do many more than I in Scotland.

Nano. Yea, those are such as have more authority than wit,
and more wealth than honesty.   309

Slip. This is my little brother with the great wit; 'ware him!—
But what canst thou do, tell me, that art so inquisitive of us?

And. Any thing that concerns a gentleman to do, that can I do.

Slip. So you are of the gentle trade?

And. True.

Slip. Then, gentle sir, leave us to ourselves, for here comes one
as if he would lack a servant ere he went.

[*Andrew stands aside.*

Enter ATEUKIN.

Ateu. Why, so, Ateukin this becomes thee best,
        Wealth, honour, ease, and angels in thy chest:
        Now may I say, as many often sing,
        " No fishing to ¹ the sea, nor service to a king."   320
        Unto this high promotion ² doth belong
        Means to be talk'd of in the thickest throng.
        And first, to fit the humours of my lord,
        Sweet lays and lines of love I must record;
        And such sweet lines and love-lays I'll indite,
        As men may wish for, and my liege ³ delight:
        And next a train of gallants at my heels,
        That men may say, the world doth run on wheels;
        For men of art, that rise by indirection
        To honour and the favour of their king,   330
        Must use all means to save what they have got,
        And win their favours whom they ⁴ never knew.
        If any frown to see my fortunes such,
        A man must bear a little, not too much.
        But, in good time, these bills portend, I think,
        That some good fellows do for service seek.   [*Reads.*
            *If any gentleman, spiritual or temporal, will entertain out of
        his service a young stripling of the age of thirty years, that
        can sleep with the soundest, eat with the hungriest, work with
        the sickest,⁵ lie with the loudest, face with the proudest, etc.,
        that can wait in a gentleman's chamber when his master is a
        mile off, keep his stable when 'tis empty, and his purse when
        'tis full, and hath many qualities worse than all these,—let him
        write his name and go his way, and attendance shall be given.*
        By my faith, a good servant: which is he?*   345
Slip. Truly, sir, that am I.
Ateu. And why dost thou write such a bill? are all these
        qualities in thee?
Slip. O Lord, ay, sir, and a great many more, some better, some
        worse, some richer, some poorer. Why, sir, do you look
        so? do they not please you?   351
Ateu. Truly, no, for they are naught, and so art thou: if thou
        hast no better qualities, stand by.

¹ *i.e.*, compared with.   ² The 4to " promotions."
³ The 4to " leech."   ⁴ The 4to " he."
⁵ A friend conjectures " sickerest."—Qy. " stoutest "?

Slip. O, sir, I tell the worst first; but, an you lack a man, I am for you: I'll tell you the best qualities I have.

Ateu. Be brief, then.

Slip. If you need me in your chamber, I can keep the door at a whistle; in your kitchen, turn the spit, and lick the pan, and make the fire burn; but if in the stable,—

Ateu. Yea, there would I use thee. 360

Slip. Why, there you kill me, there am I,[1] and turn me to a horse and a wench, and I have no peer.

Ateu. Art thou so good in keeping a horse? I pray thee tell me how many good qualities hath a horse?

Slip. Why, so, sir: a horse hath two properties of a man, that is, a proud heart and a hardy stomach; four properties of a lion, a broad breast, a stiff docket,—hold your nose, master,—a wild countenance, and four good legs; nine properties of a fox, nine of a hare, nine of an ass, and ten of a woman. 370

Ateu. A woman! why, what properties of a woman hath a horse?

Slip. O, master, know you not that? draw your tables,[2] and write what wise I speak. First, a merry countenance; second, a soft pace; third, a broad forehead; fourth, broad buttocks; fifth, hard of ward; sixth, easy to leap upon; seventh, good at long journey; eighth, moving under a man; ninth, alway busy with the mouth; tenth, ever chewing on the bridle.

Ateu. Thou art a man for me: what's thy name?

Slip. An ancient name, sir, belonging to the chamber and the night-gown: guess you that. 371

Ateu. What's that? Slipper?

Slip. By my faith, well guessed; and so 'tis indeed. You'll be my master?

Ateu. I mean so.

Slip. Read this first.

Ateu. [*reads.*] *Pleaseth it any gentleman to entertain a servant of more wit than stature, let them subscribe, and attendance shall be given.*
     What of this? 380

Slip. He is my brother, sir; and we two were born together,

---

[1] A corrupted passage.—The Rev. J. Mitford (*Gent. Mag.* for March, 1833, p. 217) suggests " *am I a per se, turn me to a horse and a wench, and I have no peer.*"

[2] *i.e.*, take out your memorandum book.

must serve together, and will die together, though we be
both hanged.

Ateu. What's thy name?

Nano. Nano.

Ateu. The etymology of which word is a dwarf.　Art not thou
the old stoic's son that dwells in his tomb?

Slip. ⎱
Nano. ⎰ We are.

Ateu. Thou art welcome to me.　Wilt thou give thyself wholly
to be at my disposition?　　　　　　　　　　　　　390

Nano. In all humility I submit myself.

Ateu. Then will I deck thee princely, instruct thee courtly, and
present thee to the queen as my gift: art thou content?

Nano. Yes, and thank your honour too.

Slip. Then welcome, brother, and fellow now.

And. [*coming forward.*]　May it please your honour to abase
your eye so low as to look either on my bill or myself?

Ateu. What are you?　　　　　　　　　　　　　　398

And. By birth a gentleman; in profession a scholar; and one
that knew your honour in Edinburgh, before your worthiness called you to this reputation: by me, Andrew Snoord.

Ateu. Andrew, I remember thee: follow me, and we will confer
further, for my weighty affairs for the king command me
to be brief at this time.—Come on, Nano.—Slipper, follow.
　　　　　　　　　　　　　　　　　　　　　　[*Exeunt.*

SCENE III

Enter Sir Bartram, *with* Eustace, *and others, booted.*

Sir Bar. But tell me, lovely Eustace, as thou lov'st me,
　Among the many pleasures we have pass'd,
　Which is the rifest in thy memory,
　To draw thee over to thine ancient friend?

Eust. What makes Sir Bartram thus inquisitive?
　Tell me, good knight, am I welcóme or no?　　　410

Sir Bar. By sweet Saint Andrew and may sale [1] I swear,
　As welcome is my honest Dick to me
　As morning's sun, or as the watery moon
　In merkest [2] night, when we the borders track.

---

[1] *i.e.*, my soul—the author thinking it necessary to interlard the dialogue
with Scottish forms of words.

[2] *i.e.*, murkiest, darkest.

I tell thee, Dick, thy sight hath clear'd my thoughts
Of many baneful troubles that there woon'd [1]:
Welcome to [2] Sir Bartram as his life!
Tell me, bonny Dick, hast got a wife?

Eust. A wife! God shield, Sir Bartram, that were ill,
To leave my wife and wander thus astray: 　　　420
But time and good advice, ere many years,
May chance to make my fancy bend that way.
What news in Scotland? therefore came I hither,
To see your country and to chat together.

Sir Bar. Why, man, our country's blithe, our king is well,
Our queen so-so, the nobles well and worse,
And weel are they that are [3] about the king,
But better are the country gentlemen:
And I may tell thee, Eustace, in our lives
We old men never saw so wondrous change. 　　　430
But leave this trattle, and tell me what news
In lovely England with our honest friends?

Eust. The king, the court, and all our noble friends
Are well; and God in mercy keep them so!
The northern lords and ladies hereabouts,
That know I come [4] to see your queen and court,
Commend them to my honest friend Sir Bartram,
And many others that I have not seen.
Amongst the rest, the Countess Elinor,
From Carlisle, where we merry oft have been, 　　　440
Greets well my lord, and hath directed me
By message this fair lady's face to see.

　　　　　　　　　　　　　　[Shows a portrait.

Sir Bar. I tell thee, Eustace, 'less [5] mine old eyes daze,
This is our Scottish moon and evening's pride;
This is the blemish of your English bride.
Who sail by her are sure of wrack at will;
Her face is dangerous, her sight is ill;
And yet, in sooth, sweet Dick, it may be said,
The king hath folly, there's virtue in the maid.

Eust. But knows my friend this portrait? be advis'd. 　　　450
Sir Bar. Is it not Ida, the Countess of Arran's daughter's?

[1] *i.e.*, dwelt.
[2] Qy.—

　　　　" As *welcome to Sir Bartram as his life!*
　　　　　　But *tell me*," etc.?
[3] The 4to " were."　　　[4] The 4to " came."　　　[5] The 4to " lest."

Eust. So was I told by Elinor of Carlisle:
    But tell me, lovely Bartram, is the maid
    Evil-inclin'd, misled, or concubine
    Unto the king or any other lord?
Sir Bar. Should I be brief and true, then thus, my Dick.
    All England's grounds yield not a blither lass,
    Nor Europe can surpass [1] her for her gifts
    Of virtue, honour, beauty, and the rest:
    But our fond king, not knowing sin in lust,
    Makes love by endless means and precious gifts;   460
    And men that see it dare not say't, my friend,
    But we may wish that it were otherwise.
    But I rid [2] thee to view the picture still,
    For by the person's sight [3] there hangs some ill.
Eust. O, good Sir Bartram,[4] you suspect I love
    (Then were I mad) her [5] whom I never saw.
    But howsoe'er, I fear not enticings;
    Desire will give no place unto a king:
    I'll see her whom the world admires so much,
    That I may say with them, " There lives none such."   470
Sir Bar. Be gad, and sall [6] both see and talk with her;
    And when thou'st done, whate'er her beauty be,
    I'll warrant thee her virtues may compare
    With the proudest she that waits upon your queen.

Enter Servant.

Serv. My lady [7] entreats your worship in to supper.
Sir Bar. Guid, bonny Dick, my wife will tell thee more:
    Was never no man in her book before;
    Be gad, she's blithe, fair, lewely,[8] bonny, etc.[9]   [*Exeunt.*

---

[1] The 4to " art."   [2] *i.e., rede*—advise (as before).
[3] The 4to " sights."
[4] The 4to gives these six lines to Sir Bartram.
[5] The 4to " hee."   [6] *i.e.,* By God, and shalt.
[7] The 4to gives this line to Eustace, and does not mark the entrance of the Servant.
[8] *i.e.,* I suppose, lovely.—The Rev. J. Mitford (*Gent. Mag.* for March 1833, p. 218), speaking of the present passage, says: " This word [*lewely*] we find in the old romance of *Havelok*, ed. Madden, v. 2921:

    ' So the rose in roser,
      Hwan it is fayr sprad ut newe
      Ageyn the sunne, brith, and *lewe.*' "

But was Mr. Mitford aware that in the lines just quoted "*lewe*" means *warm ?*
[9] Was the player here to speak extempore whatever he chose?

Enter BOHAN *and* OBERON *after the first act ; to them a round
of* Fairies, *or some pretty dance.*

Boh. Be gad, gramercies, little king, for this;
  This sport is better in my exile life   48₇
  Than ever the deceitful werld could yield.
Ober. I tell thee, Bohan, Oberon is king
  Of quiet, pleasure, profit, and content,
  Of wealth, of honour, and of all the world;
  Tied to no place, yet all are tied to me.[1]
  Live thou this life,[2] exil'd from world and men,
  And I will show thee wonders ere we part.
Boh. Then mark my story,[3] and the strange doubts [4]
  That follow flatterers, lust, and lawless will,
  And then say I have reason to forsake   490
  The world and all that are within the same.
  Go shroud us in our harbour, where we'll see
  The pride [5] of folly, as it ought to be.   *[Exeunt.*

     After the first Act.

Ober. Here see I good fond actions in thy jig,
  And means to paint the world's inconstant ways:
  But turn thine ene, see what [6] I can command.

Enter two battles, strongly fighting, the one led by SEMIRAMIS,[7] *the
other by* STABROBATES [8]: *she flies, and her crown is taken, and
she hurt.*

Boh. What gars this din of mirk and baleful harm,
  Where every wean is all betaint with blood?
Ober. This shows thee, Bohan, what is worldly pomp:
  Semiramis, the proud Assyrian queen,   500
  When Ninus died, did levy [9] in her wars
  Three millions of footmen to the fight,
  Five hundred thousand horse, of armèd cars
  A hundred thousand more, yet in her pride

---

[1] The 4to " one."   [2] The 4to " in *this life.*"
[3] The 4to " stay."
[4] Qy. " debates " (in the sense of—strifes)?
[5] Qy. " prize " (*i.e.*, reward)?—The whole of what follows, till the
beginning of the next act, is a mass of confusion and corruption.
[6] The 4to " which for."
[7] Here the 4to " Simi Ranus," and afterwards " Simeranus."
[8] Here the 4to " Staurobates," and afterwards " S. Taurobates."
[9] The 4to " tene."

Was hurt and conquer'd by Stabrobates.
 Then what is pomp?
Boh. I see thou art thine ene,
 Thou bonny king, if princes fall from high:
 My fall is past, until I fall to die.
 Now mark my talk, and prosecute my jig.   510

2.

Ober. How should these crafts withdraw thee from the world!
 But look, my Bohan, pomp allureth.[1]

Enter Cyrus, *kings humbling themselves ; himself crowned by
Olive Pat* [2] *: at last dying, laid in a marble tomb with this
inscription :*

 " Whoso thou be that passest [by],
  For I know one shall pass, know I
  Am Cyrus of Persia,[3] and I pray
  Leave me not thus like a clod of clay
  Wherewith my body is cover'd."

         [All exeunt.

Enter the King *in great pomp, who reads it, and issueth,
crying " Ver meum."* [4]

Boh. What meaneth this?
Ober. Cyrus of Persia,
 Mighty in life, within a marble grave   520
 Was laid to rot; whom Alexander once
 Beheld entomb'd, and weeping did confess,
 Nothing in life could scape from wretchedness:
 Why, then, boast men?

---

[1] A quadrisyllable: see Walker's *Shakespeare's Versification*, etc., p. 146.
[2] I cannot even conjecture what the author wrote here.
[3] The 4to:

  " I *am Cirus of Persia,*
   And I prithee *leave me not thus,*" etc.

But all this is stark nonsense. See the inscription on the tomb of Cyrus
in Plutarch, *Alex.* 69.

[4] The 4to " vermeum:" qy. if a misprint for " *vermium,*" the first word
of some Latin sentence on the vanity of earthly grandeur?—" We think
with him [the editor of the present volume] that it is an introduction to a
moral reflection; but that it is ' Ver meum,' my spring hath passed away,
etc. The king probably quoted the two first words of some moral sentence,
and *Vermium* was not likely to be the common by-word." *Rev. J. Mitford*
—*Gent. Mag.* for March 1833, p. 217.

Boh. What reck I, then, of life,
    Who make [1] the grave my home,[2] the earth my wife?
Ober. But mark me more.[3]

3.

Boh. I can no more; my patience will not warp
    To see these flatterers [4] how they scorn and carp.
Ober. Turn but thy head.   530

*Enter [f]our Kings carrying crowns, Ladies presenting odours to
    Potentate [5] enthroned, who suddenly is slain by his Servants
    and thrust out ; and so they eat.*   [*Exeunt.*

Boh.[6] Sike is the werld; but whilk is he I saw?
Ober. Sesostris, who was conqueror of the world,
    Slain at the last and stamp'd on by his slaves.
Boh. How blest are peur men, then, that know their graves! [7]
    Now mark the sequel of my jig;
    An he weel meet ends.   The mirk and sable night
    Doth leave the peering morn to pry abroad;
    Thou nill me stay: hail, then, thou pride of kings!
    I ken the world, and wot well worldly things.
    Mark thou my jig, in mirkest terms that tells   540
    The loath of sins and where corruption dwells.
    Hail me ne mere with shows of guidly sights;
    My grave is mine, that rids me from despites;
    Accept my jig, guid king, and let me rest;
    The grave with guid men is a gay-built nest.
Ober. The rising sun doth call me hence away;
    Thanks for thy jig, I may no longer stay:
    But if my train did wake thee from thy rest,
    So shall they sing thy lullaby to nest.   [*Exeunt.*

---

[1] The 4to " makes."
[2] The 4to " tomb." Corrected by Mr. Collier, Introd. to *The Tempest*,
p. 11, *Shakespeare*, ed. 1858.
[3] The 4to gives this to Bohan.
[4] The 4to " flatteries."   [5] The 4to " Potentates."
[6] Not in the 4to.   [7] The 4to " graue."

ACT II

SCENE I

The COUNTESS OF ARRAN *and* IDA *discovered in their porch, sitting at work : a* Servant *attending.*

A Song.[1]

Count. of A. Fair Ida, might you choose the greatest good,
    Midst all the world in blessings that abound,
    Wherein, my daughter, should your liking be?
Ida. Not in delights, or pomp, or majesty.
Count. of A. And why?
Ida. Since these are means to draw the mind
    From perfect good, and make true judgment blind.
Count. of A. Might you have wealth and Fortune's richest store?
Ida. Yet would I, might I choose, be honest-poor;
    For she that sits at Fortune's feet a-low   10
    Is sure she shall not taste a further woe,
    But those that prank on top of Fortune's ball
    Still fear a change, and, fearing, catch a fall.
Count. of A. Tut, foolish maid, each one contemneth need.
Ida. Good reason why, they know not good indeed.
Count. of A. Many, marry, then, on whom distress doth lour.
Ida. Yes, they that virtue deem an honest dower.
    Madam, by right this world I may compare
    Unto my work, wherein with heedful care
    The heavenly workman plants with curious hand,   20
    As I with needle draw each thing on land,
    Even as he list: some men like to the rose
    Are fashion'd fresh; some in their stalks do close,
    And, born, do sudden die; some are but weeds,
    And yet from them a secret good proceeds:
    I with my needle, if I please, may blot
    The fairest rose within my cambric plot;
    God with a beck can change each worldly thing,

---

[1] In the printed copies of our early plays the " Songs " are frequently omitted.

The poor to rich,[1] the beggar to the king.
What, then, hath man wherein he well may boast,   30
Since by a beck he lives, a lour [2] is lost?

Count. of A. Peace, Ida, here are strangers near at hand.

Enter EUSTACE *with letters.*

Eust. Madam, God speed!

Count. of A. I thank you, gentle squire.

Eust. The country Countess of Northumberland
Doth greet you well, and hath requested me
To bring these letters to your ladyship. [*Delivers the letters.*

Count. of A. I thank her honour, and yourself, my friend.
                                                  [*Peruses them.*
I see she means you good, brave gentleman.—
Daughter, the Lady Elinor salutes   40
Yourself as well as me: then for her sake
'Twere good you entertain'd that courtier well.

Ida. As much salute as may become my sex,
And he in virtue can vouchsafe to think,
I yield him for the courteous countess' sake.—
Good sir, sit down: my mother here and I
Count time misspent an endless vanity.

Eust. [*aside.*] Beyond report, the wit, the fair,[3] the shape!—
What work you here, fair mistress? may I see it?

Ida. Good sir, look on: how like you this compáct?   50

Eust. Methinks in this I see true love in act:
The woodbines with their leaves do sweetly spread,
The roses blushing prank them in their red;
No flower but boasts the beauties of the spring;
This bird hath life indeed, if it could sing.
What means, fair mistress, had you in this work?

Ida. My needle, sir.

Eust. In needles, then, there lurk [4]
Some hidden grace, I deem, beyond my reach.

Ida. Not grace in them, good sir, but those that teach.   60

Eust. Say that your needle now were Cupid's sting,—

---

[1] The 4to " earth."

[2] *i.e.,* frown.—The 4to " louer."—The Rev. J. Mitford (*Gent. Mag.* for March 1833, p. 217) strangely enough would read " flower."

[3] *i.e.,* beauty.

[4] The 4to " lurkes "—which destroys the rhyme. (The construction is— " I deem there *lurk* "=*lurks*.)

[*Aside.*] But, ah, her eye must be no less,
　In which is heaven and heavenliness,
　In which the food of God is shut,
　Whose powers the purest minds do glut!
Ida. What if it were?
Eust. Then see a wondrous thing;
　I fear me you would paint in Tereus'[1] heart
　Affection in his power and chiefest part.[2]
Ida. Good Lord, sir, no! for hearts but prickèd soft　　　70
　Are wounded sore, for so I hear it oft.
Eust. What recks the wound,[3] where but your happy eye
　May make him live whom Jove hath judg'd to die?
Ida. Should life and death within this needle lurk,
　I'll prick no hearts, I'll prick upon my work.
Count. of A. Peace, Ida, I perceive the fox at hand.
Eust. The fox! why, fetch your hounds, and chase him hence.
Count. of A. O, sir, these great men bark at small offence.
　Come,[4] will it please you to enter, gentle sir?
　　　　　　　　　　　　　　　[*They offer to go out.*

Enter ATEUKIN *and* SLIPPER.

Ateu. Stay, courteous ladies; favour me so much　　　80
　As to discourse a word or two apart.
Count. of A. Good sir, my daughter learns this rule of me,
　To shun resort and strangers' company;
　For some are shifting mates that carry letters,
　Some, such as you, too good because our betters.
Slip. Now, I pray you, sir, what akin are you to a pickerel?[5]
Ateu. Why, knave?
Slip. By my troth, sir, because I never knew a proper situation
　fellow of your pitch fitter to swallow a gudgeon.
Ateu. What meanest thou by this?　　　90
Slip. Shifting fellow, sir,—these be thy words;[6] shifting fellow:
　this gentlewoman, I fear me, knew your bringing up.
Ateu. How so?
Slip. Why, sir, your father was a miller, that could shift for a

---

[1] The 4to "Teneus."　　　[2] The 4to "parts."　　　[3] The 4to "second."
[4] The 4to gives to Ateukin this line; in which "*to*" seems to be an
interpolation.
[5] A small or young pike.
[6] *i.e.*, the words which describe you.

peck of grist in a bushel, and you['re] a fair-spoken gentleman, that can get more land by a lie than an honest man by
his ready money.

Ateu. Caitiff, what sayest thou?

Slip. I say, sir, that if she call you shifting knave, you shall not
put her to the proof.   100

Ateu. And why?

Slip. Because, sir, living by your wit as you do, shifting is your
letters-patents: [1] it were a hard matter for me to get my
dinner that day wherein my master had not sold a dozen of
devices, a case of cogs, and a suit of shifts, in the morning.
I speak this in your commendation, sir, and, I pray you, so
take it.

Ateu. If I live, knave, I will be revenged. What gentleman
would entertain a rascal thus to derogate from his honour?

Ida. My lord, why are you thus impatient?   110

Ateu. Not angry, Ida; but I teach this knave
How to behave himself among his betters.—
Behold, fair countess, to assure your stay,
I here present the signet of the king,
Who now by me, fair Ida, doth salute you:
And since in secret I have certain things
In his behalf, good madam, to impart,
I crave your daughter to discourse apart.

Count. of A. She shall in humble duty be addrest.[2]
To do his highness' will in what she may.   120

Ida. Now, gentle sir, what would his grace with me?

Ateu. Fair, comely nymph, the beauty of your face,
Sufficient to bewitch the heavenly powers,
Hath wrought so much in him that now of late
He finds himself made captive unto love;
And though his power and majesty require
A straight command before an humble suit,
Yet he his mightiness doth so abase
As to entreat your favour, honest maid.

Ida. Is he not married, sir, unto our queen?   130

Ateu. He is.

Ida. And are not they by God accurs'd,

---

[1] Such was the phraseology of the time (not, as we now say, " letters
patent "). So in Shakespeare's *Henry VIII.* act iii. sc. 2. "Tied it by
letters-patents; " and in his *Richard II.* act ii. sc. 1., "Call in the *letters-
patents*," etc.

[2] *i.e.*, prepared, ready.

That sever them whom he hath knit in one?
Ateu. They be: what then? we seek not to displace
 The princess from her seat, but, since by love
 The king is made your own, he [1] is resolv'd
 In private to accept your dalliance,
 In spite of war, watch,[2] or worldly eye.
Ida. O, how he talks, as if he should not die!
 As if that God in justice once could wink   140
 Upon that fault I am asham'd to think!
Ateu. Tut, mistress, man at first was born to err;
 Women are all not formèd to be saints:
 'Tis impious for to kill our native king,
 Whom by a little favour we may save.
Ida. Better, than live unchaste, to lie [3] in grave.
Ateu. He shall erect your state, and wed you well.
Ida. But can his warrant keep my soul from hell?
Ateu. He will enforce, if you resist his suit.
Ida. What tho [4]? the world may shame to him account, 150
 To be a king of men and worldly pelf,
 Yet hath [5] no power to rule and guide himself.
Ateu. I know you, gentle lady, and the care
 Both of your honour and his grace's health
 Makes me confusèd in this dangerous state.
Ida. So counsel him, but soothe thou not his sin:
 'Tis vain allurement that doth make him love:
 I shame to hear, be you asham'd to move.
Count. of A. I see my daughter grows impatient:
 I fear me, he pretends some bad intent.   160
Ateu. Will you despise the king and scorn him so?
Ida. In all allegiance I will serve his grace,
 But not in lust: O, how I blush to name it!
Ateu. [*aside.*] An endless work is this: how should I frame it?
         [*They discourse privately.*
Slip. O, mistress, may I turn a word upon you?
Count. of A.[6] Friend, what wilt thou?
Slip. O, what a happy gentlewoman be you truly! the world
 reports this of you, mistress, that a man can no sooner come
 to your house but the butler comes with a black-jack and

---

[1] The 4to " shee."
[2] Qy. " or *watch* "?
[3] The 4to " liue."
[4] *i.e.,* then.
[5] The 4to gives this line to Ateukin, and reads " *Yet hath* to *power* no *rule,*" etc.
[6] The 4to " Ateu."

says, "Welcome, friend, here's a cup of the best for you":
verily, mistress, you are said to have the best ale in all
Scotland.   172

Count. of A. Sirrah, go fetch him drink.   [*Servant brings drink.*
How lik'st thou this?

Slip. Like it, mistress! why, this is quincy quarie pepper de
watchet, single goby, of all that ever I tasted.   I'll prove
in this ale and toast the compass of the whole world.   First,
this is the earth,—it lies [1] in the middle, a fair brown toast,
a goodly country for hungry teeth to dwell upon; next,
this is the sea, a fair pool for a dry tongue to fish in: now
come I, and seeing the world is naught, I divide it thus;
and because the sea cannot stand without the earth, as
Aristotle saith, I put them both into their first chaos, which
is my belly: and so, mistress, you may see your ale is
become a miracle.   185

Eust. A merry mate, madam, I promise you.

Count. of A. Why sigh you, sirrah?

Slip. Truly, madam, to think upon the world, which, since I
denounced it, keeps such a rumbling in my stomach that,
unless your cook give it a counterbuff with some of your
roasted capons of beef, I fear me I shall become a loose
body, so dainty, I think, I shall neither hold fast before nor
behind.   193

Count. of A. Go take him in, and feast this merry swain.—
Sirrah, my cook is your physician;
He hath a purge for to digest the [2] world.
                                              [*Exeunt Slipper and Servant.*

Ateu. Will you not, Ida, grant his highness this?

Ida. As I have said, in duty I am his:
For other lawless lusts that ill beseem him,
I cannot like, and good I will not deem him.[3]   200

Count. of A. Ida, come in:—and, sir, if so you please,
Come, take a homely widow's entertain.

Ida. If he have no great haste, he may come nigh;
If haste, though he be gone, I will not cry.
                                [*Exeunt the Countess of Arran, Ida, and Eustace.*

Ateu. I see this labour lost, my hope in vain;
Yet will I try another drift again.   [*Exit.*

[1] The 4to " ties."
[2] The 4to " disiest "—a spelling which (as well as " disgest ") occurs
frequently in our old writers.
[3] Qy. " 'em "?

SCENE II

Enter, one by one, the Bishop of St. Andrews, Douglas, Morton,
and others, one way ; Queen Dorothea *with* Nano,[1] *another
way.*

Bp. of St. And. [*aside.*] O wreck of commonweal, O wretched
    state !
Doug. [*aside.*] O hapless flock whereas [2] the guide is blind !
Mort. [*aside.*] O heedless youth where counsel is despis'd ! 210
                              [*They all are in a muse.*
Q. Dor. Come, pretty knave, and prank it by my side;
    Let's see your best attendance out of hand.
Nano. Madam, although my limbs are very small,
    My heart is good; I'll serve you therewithal.
Q. Dor. How, if I were assail'd, what couldst thou do?
Nano. Madam, call help, and boldly fight it too:
    Although a bee be but a little thing,
    You know, fair queen, it hath a bitter sting.
Q. Dor. How couldst thou do me good, were I in grief?
Nano. Counsel, dear princess, is a choice relief: 220
    Though Nestor wanted force, great was his wit,
    And though I am but weak, my words are fit.
Bp. of St. And. [*aside.*] Like to a ship upon the ocean-seas,
    Tost in the doubtful stream, without a helm,
    Such is a monarch without good advice.
    I am o'erheard: cast rein upon thy tongue;
    Andrews, beware; reproof will breed a scar.
Mor. Good day, my lord.
Bp. of St. And. Lord Morton, well y-met.—
    Whereon deems [3] Lord Douglas all this while? 230
Doug. Of that which yours and my poor heart doth break,
    Although fear shuts our mouths, we dare not speak.
Q. Dor. [*aside.*] What mean these princes sadly to consult?
    Somewhat, I fear, betideth them amiss,
    They are so pale in looks, so vex'd in mind.—
    In happy hour, ye [4] noble Scottish peers,

---

[1] The 4to " Dwarfes: " but there is only one such diminutive person in
the play—Nano, whom Ateukin has presented to the Queen.   See first
speech, p. 194.
[2] *i.e.*, where.   [3] Qy. " dreams " ?   [4] The 4to " the."

Have I encounter'd you: what makes you mourn?

Bp. of St. And. If we with patience may attention [1] gain,
    Your grace shall know the cause of all our grief.

Q. Dor. Speak on, good father; come and sit by me: 240
    I know thy care is for the common good.

Bp. of St. And. As fortune, mighty princess, reareth some
    To high estate and place in commonweal,
    So by divine bequest to them is lent
    A riper judgment and more searching eye,
    Whereby they may discern the common harm;
    For where our fortunes [2] in the world are most,
    Where all our profits rise and still encrease,
    There is our mind, thereon we meditate,
    And what we do partake of good advice,   250
    That we employ for to concern the same.
    To this intent, these nobles and myself,
    That are, or should be, eyes of commonweal,
    Seeing his highness' reckless course of youth,
    His lawless and unbridled vein in love,
    His too intentive trust to flatterers,
    His abject care of counsel and his friends,
    Cannot but grieve; and since we cannot draw
    His eye or judgment to discern his faults,
    Since we have spoke [3] and counsel is not heard,   260
    I, for my part,—let others as they list,—
    Will leave the court, and leave him to his will,
    Lest with a ruthful eye I should behold
    His overthrow, which, sore I fear, is nigh.

Q. Dor. Ah father, are you so estrang'd from love,
    From due allegiance to your prince and land,
    To leave your king when most he needs your help?
    The thrifty husbandmen are never wont,
    That see their lands unfruitful, to forsake them;
    But when the mould is barren and unapt,   270
    They toil, they plough, and make the fallow fat:
    The pilot in the dangerous seas is known;
    In calmer waves the silly sailor strives,
    Are you not members, lords, of commonweal,
    And can your head, your dear anointed king,

---

[1] The 4to " attentiue."

[2] Mr. Collier's conjecture, Introd. to the *Tempest*, p. 11, *Shakespeare*, ed. 1858.—The 4to " importunes."

[3] The 4to " spake."

Default, ye lords, except yourselves do fail?
O, stay your steps, return, and counsel him!
Doug. Men seek not moss upon a rolling stone,
    Or water from the sieve, or fire from ice,
    Or comfort from a reckless monarch's hands.   280
    Madam, he sets us light that serv'd in court,
    In place of credit, in his father's days:
    If we but enter presence of his grace,
    Our payment is a frown, a scoff, a frump;[1]
    Whilst flattering Gnatho[2] pranks it by his side,
    Soothing the careless king in his misdeeds:
    And if your grace consider your estate,
    His life should urge you too, if all be true.
Q. Dor. Why, Douglas, why?
Doug. As if you have not heard   290
    His lawless love to Ida grown of late,
    His careless estimate of your estate.
Q. Dor. Ah Douglas, thou misconstru'st[3] his intent!
    He doth but tempt his wife, he tries my love:
    This injury pertains to me, not you.[4]
    The king is young; and if he step awry,
    He may amend, and I will love him still.
    Should we disdain our vines because they sprout
    Before their time? or young men, if they strain
    Beyond their reach? No; vines that bloom and spread 300
    Do promise fruits, and young men that are wild
    In age grow wise. My friends and Scottish peers,
    If that an English princess may prevail,
    Stay, stay with him: lo, how my zealous prayer
    Is plead with tears! fie, peers, will you hence?
Bp. of St. And. Madam, 'tis virtue in your grace to plead;
    But we, that see his vain untoward course,
    Cannot but fly the fire before it burn,

---

[1] *i.e.*, flout.

[2] *i.e.*, Ateukin: our author appears to have wavered between these two names; see *post*. (*Gnatho* is the parasite in the *Eunuchus* of Terence.)

[3] The 4to " misconstrest "—our early authors frequently writing *conster* and *misconster*: but they are seldom consistent, writing in other places *construe* and *misconstrue*: compare, in the present play, p. 189:
    " Thy virtues shall be *construed* to vice; "
and, in *Pandosto*, as cited in the *Account of Greene and his Writings*, p. 41, " He then began to measure all their actions, and to *misconstrue* of their too priuate familiaritie," etc.

[4] The 4to " *not* to you."

    And shun the court before we see his fall.

Q. Dor. Will you not stay? then, lordings, fare you well.   310
    Though you forsake your king, the heavens, I hope,
    Will favour him through mine incessant prayer.

Nano. Content you, madam; thus old Ovid sings,
    'Tis foolish to bewail recureless [1] things.

Q. Dor. Peace, dwarf; [2] these words my patience move.

Nano. Although you charm my speech, charm not my love.

                          [*Exeunt Queen and Nano.*

    Enter the KING OF SCOTS; *the* Nobles,[3] *spying him as they
                are about to go off, return.*

K. of Scots. Douglas, how now! why changest thou thy cheer?

Doug. My private troubles are so great, my liege,
    As I must crave your license for a while,
    For to intend mine own affairs at home.   320

K. of Scots. You may depart.   [*Exit Douglas.*
                   But why is Morton sad?

Mor. The like occasion doth import me too,
    So I desire your grace to give me leave.

K. of Scots. Well, sir, you may betake you to your ease.

                           [*Exit Morton.*

    [*Aside.*] When such grim sirs are gone, I see no let
    To work my will.

Bp. of St. And.[4] What, like the eagle, then,
    With often flight wilt thou thy feathers lose?
    O king, canst thou endure to see thy court   330
    Of finest wits and judgments dispossess'd,
    Whilst cloaking craft with soothing climbs so high
    As each bewails ambition is so bad?
    Thy father left thee with estate and crown,
    A learnèd council to direct thy course: [5]
    These carelessly, O king, thou castest off
    To entertain a train of sycophants.
    Thou well mayst see, although thou wilt not see,
    That every eye and ear both sees and hears

---

[1] *i.e.,* irrecoverable.

[2] An epithet belonging to this word would seem to have dropt out.

[3] The 4to " *Enter the King of Scots,* Arius, *the nobles spying him, returnes.*"

[4] The 4to " 8. Atten.;" but it is plain, from the King's reply, that the Bishop of St. Andrews is the speaker.

[5] The 4to " court."

The certain signs of thine incontinence.   340
Thou art allied unto the English king
By marriage; a happy friend indeed,
If usèd well, if not, a mighty foe.
Thinketh your grace, he can endure and brook
To have a partner in his daughter's love?
Thinketh your grace, the grudge of privy wrongs
Will not procure him change his smiles to threats?
O, be not blind to good! call home your lords,
Displace these flattering Gnathoes, drive them hence;
Love and with kindness take your wedlock wife;   350
Or else, which God forbid, I fear a change:
Sin cannot thrive in courts without a plague.

K. of Scots. Go pack thou too, unless thou mend thy talk:
On pain of death, proud bishop, get you gone
Unless you headless mean to hop away.

Bp. of St. And.[1] Thou God of heaven prevent my country's fall!
                              [*Exit with other Nobles.*

K. of Scots. These stays and lets to pleasure plague my thoughts,
Forcing my grievous wounds anew to bleed:
But care that hath transported me so far,
Fair Ida, is dispers'd in thought of thee,   360
Whose answer yields me life or breeds my death.
Yond comes the messenger of weal or woe.

Enter ATEUKIN.[2]

Ateukin, what news?

Ateu. The adamant, O king, will not be fil'd
But by itself, and beauty that exceeds
By some exceeding favour must be wrought.
Ida is coy as yet, and doth repine,
Objecting marriage, honour, fear, and death:
She's holy-wise and too precise for me.

K. of Scots. Are these thy fruits of wit,[3] thy sight in art,   370
Thine eloquence, thy policy, thy drift,—
To mock thy prince? Then, caitiff, pack thee hence,
And let me die devourèd in my love.

Ateu. Good Lord, how rage gainsayeth reason's power!
My dear, my gracious, and belovèd prince,

---

[1] The 4to " 8. Atten."   [2] The 4to " Gnato."
              [3] The 4to " wits."

The essence of my soul,[1] my god on earth,
Sit down and rest yourself: appease your wrath,
Lest with a frown ye wound me to the death.
O, that I were included in my grave,
That either now, to save my prince's life,   380
Must counsel cruelty, or lose my king!

K. of Scots. Why, sirrah, is there means to move her mind?
Ateu. O, should I not offend my royal liege,—
K. of Scots. Tell all, spare naught, so I may gain my love.
Ateu. Alas, my soul, why art thou torn in twain,
For fear thou talk a thing that should displease!
K. of Scots. Tut, speak whatso thou wilt, I pardon thee.
Ateu. How kind a word, how courteous is his grace!
Who would not die to succour such a king?
My liege, this lovely maid of modest mind   390
Could well incline to love, but that she fears
Fair Dorothea's power: your grace doth know,
Your wedlock is a mighty let to love.
Were Ida sure to be your wedded wife,
That then the twig would bow you might command:
Ladies love presents, pomp, and high estate.
K. of Scots. Ah Ateukin, how should we displace [2] this let?
Ateu. Tut, mighty prince,—O, that I might be whist! [3]
K. of Scots. Why dalliest thou?
Ateu. I will not move my prince;   400
I will prefer his safety 'fore my life.
Hear me, O king! 'tis Dorothea's death
Must do you good.
K. of Scots. What, murder of my queen!
Yet, to enjoy my love, what is my queen?
O, but my vow and promise to my queen!
Ay, but my hope to gain a fairer queen:
With how contrarious thoughts am I withdrawn!
Why linger I twixt hope and doubtful fear?
If Dorothea die, will Ida love?   410
Ateu. She will, my lord.
K. of Scots. Then let her die: devise, advise the means;
All likes me well that lends me hope in love.
Ateu. What, will your grace consent? then let me work.

---

[1] The 4to " sute."—Corrected by Mr. Collier, Introd. to *The Tempest* p. 11. *Shakespeare,* ed. 1858.
[2] The 4to " display."   [3] *i.e.,* silent.

There's here in court a Frenchman, Jaques call'd,
A fit performer of our enterprise,
Whom I by gifts and promise will corrupt
To slay the queen, so that your grace will seal
A warrant for the man, to save his life.

K. of Scots. Naught shall he want; write thou, and I will sign:
And, gentle Gnatho, if my Ida yield,   421
Thou shalt have what thou wilt; I'll give thee straight
A barony, an earldom for reward.

Ateu. Frolic, young king, the lass shall be your own:
I'll make her blithe and wanton by my wit.   [*Exeunt.*

Enter BOHAN *with* OBERON.

Boh. So, Oberon, now it begins [1] to work in kind.
The ancient lords by leaving him alone,[2]
Disliking of his humours and despite,[3]
Let him run headlong, till his flatterers,
Soliciting [4] his thoughts of lawless [5] lust   430
With vile persuasions and alluring words,
Make him make way by murder to his will.
Judge, fairy king, hast heard a greater ill?

Ober. Nor seen [6] more virtue in a country maid.
I tell thee, Bohan, it doth make me sorry,[7]
To think the deed the king means to perform.

Boh. To change that humour, stand and see the rest:
I trow my son Slipper will show's a jest.

Enter SLIPPER *with a companion,* boy *or* wench, *dancing a
hornpipe, and dance out again.*

Now after this beguiling of our thoughts,
And changing them from sad to better glee,   440
Let's to our cell, and sit and see the rest,
For, I believe, this jig will prove no jest.   [*Exeunt.*

---

[1] Qy. " gins "?   [2] The 4to " aliue."   [3] The 4to " respight."
[4] The excellent correction of Walker, *Crit. Exam. of the text of Shakespeare*, etc., ii. 349: " read," he says, " *Soliciting* (in the old Latin sense, as
frequent in the writers of that age)."—The 4to " Sweeting; " which Mr.
Collier (Preface to *Coleridge's Seven Lectures on Shakespeare and Milton*, etc.,
p. cxvi.) " has no doubt " is a misprint for " *Suiting.*"
[5] Mr. Collier's correction, *ubi supra.*—The 4to " lucklesse."
[6] The 4to " send."   [7] The 4to " merrie."

ACT III

SCENE I

Enter SLIPPER *one way, and* SIR BARTRAM *another way.*

Sir Bar. Ho, fellow! stay, and let me speak with thee.

Slip. Fellow! friend, thou dost abuse [1] me; I am a gentleman.

Sir Bar. A gentleman! how so?

Slip. Why, I rub horses, sir.

Sir Bar. And what of that?

Slip. O simple-witted! mark my reason. They that do good service in the commonweal are gentlemen; but such as rub horses do good service in the commonweal, ergo, tarbox, master courtier, a horse-keeper is a gentleman.

Sir Bar. Here is overmuch wit, in good earnest.　　　　10
But, sirrah, where is thy master?

Slip. Neither above ground nor under ground, drawing out red into white, swallowing that down without chawing that was never made without treading.

Sir Bar. Why, where is he, then?

Slip. Why, in his cellar, drinking a cup of neat and brisk claret in a bowl of silver. O, sir, the wine runs trillill down his throat, which cost the poor vintner many a stamp before it was made. But I must hence, sir, I have haste.

Sir Bar. Why, whither now, I prithee?　　　　20

Slip. Faith, sir, to Sir Silvester, a knight, hard by, upon my master's errand, whom I must certify this, that the lease of East Spring shall be confirmed: and therefore must I bid him provide trash, for my master is no friend without money.

Sir Bar. [*aside.*] This is the thing for which I su'd so long,
This is the lease which I, by Gnatho's means,
Sought to possess by patent from the king;
But he, injurious man, who lives by crafts,
And sells king's favours for who will give most,　　　　30
Hath taken bribes of me, yet covertly

[1] The 4to " disbuse."

263

Will sell away the thing pertains to me:
But I have found a present help, I hope,
For to prevent his purpose and deceit.—
Stay, gentle friend.

Slip. A good word; thou hast won me: this word is like a warm
caudle [1] to a cold stomach.

Sir Bar. Sirrah, wilt thou, for money and reward,
Convey me certain letters, out of hand,
From out thy master's pocket?   40

Slip. Will I, sir? why, were it to rob my father, hang my
mother, or any such like trifles, I am at your commandment, sir. What will you give me, sir?

Sir Bar. A hundred pounds.

Slip. I am your man: give me earnest. I am dead at a pocket,
sir; why, I am a lifter, master, by my occupation.

Sir Bar. A lifter! what is that?

Slip. Why, sir, I can lift a pot as well as any man, and pick a
purse as soon as any thief in my country.

Sir Bar. Why, fellow, hold; here is earnest, ten pound to assure
thee. [*Gives money.*] Go, despatch, and bring it me to
yonder tavern thou seest; and assure thyself, thou shalt
both have thy skin full of wine and the rest of thy money.

Slip. I will, sir.—Now room for a gentleman, my masters! who
gives me money for a fair new angel, a trim new angel? 55
                                        [*Exeunt severally.*

SCENE II

Enter ANDREW *and* Purveyor.

Pur. Sirrah, I must needs have your master's horses: the king
cannot be unserved.

And. Sirrah, you must needs go without them, because my
master must be served.

Pur. Why, I am the king's purveyor, and I tell thee I will have
them.   61

And. I am Ateukin's servant, Signior Andrew, and I say, thou
shalt not have them.

Pur. Here's my ticket, deny it if thou darest.

And. There is the stable, fetch them out if thou darest.

Pur. Sirrah, sirrah, tame your tongue, lest I make you.

---

[1] The 4to " candle."

And. Sirrah, sirrah, hold your hand, lest I bum [1] you.

Pur. I tell thee, thy master's geldings are good, and therefore
   fit for the king.   69

And. I tell thee, my master's horses have galled backs, and
   therefore cannot fit the king. Purveyor, purveyor, purvey
   thee of more wit: darest thou presume to wrong my Lord
   Ateukin, being the chiefest man in court?

Pur. The more unhappy commonweal where flatterers are chief
   in court.

And. What sayest thou?

Pur. I say thou art too presumptuous, and the officers shall school
   thee.

And. A fig for them and thee, purveyor! they seek a knot in a
   ring that would wrong my master or his servants in this
   court.   81

Enter Jaques.

Pur. The world is at a wise pass when nobility is afraid of a
   flatterer.

Jaq. Sirrah, what be you that parley *contre* Monsieur my Lord
   Ateukin? *en bonne foi,* prate you against Sir *Altesse,* me
   maka your *tête* to leap from your shoulders, *par ma foi c'y
   ferai-je.*

And. O, signior captain, you show yourself a forward and
   friendly gentleman in my master's behalf: I will cause him
   to thank you.   90

Jaq. *Poltron,* speak me one parola against *bon gentilhomme,* I
   shall estramp your guts, and thump your backa, that you
   no point manage this ten ours.

Pur. Sirrah, come open me the stable, and let me have the
   horses:—and, fellow, for all your French brags, I will do my
   duty.

And. I'll make garters of thy guts, thou villain, if thou enter this
   office.

Jaq. *Mort Dieu,* take me that cappa *pour votre labeur :* be gone,
   villain, in the *mort.*   [*Exit.*

Pur. What, will you resist me, then? well, the council, fellow,
   shall know of your insolency.   102

And. Tell them what thou wilt, and eat that I can best spare
   from my back parts, and get you gone with a vengeance.
                                                       [*Exit Purveyor.*

---

[1] *i.e.,* strike, beat.

Enter ATEUKIN.[1]

Ateu. Andrew.

And. Sir.

Ateu. Where be my writings I put in my pocket last night?

And. Which, sir? your annotations upon Machiavel?

Ateu. No, sir; the letters-patents for East Spring.   109

And. Why, sir, you talk wonders to me, if you ask that question.

Ateu. Yea, sir, and will work wonders too with [2] you, unless
you find them out: villain, search me them out, and bring
them me, or thou art but dead.

And. A terrible word in the latter end of a sessions. Master,
were you in your right wits yesternight?

Ateu. Dost thou doubt it?

And. Ay, and why not, sir? for the greatest clerks are not the
wisest, and a fool may dance in a hood, as well as a wise
man in a bare frock: besides, such as give themselves to
philautia,[3] as you do, master, are so choleric of complexion
that that which they burn in fire over night they seek for
with fury the next morning. Ah, I take care of your
worship! this commonweal should have a great loss of so
good a member as you are.

Ateu. Thou flatterest me.

And. Is it flattery in me, sir, to speak you fair? what is it,
then, in you to dally with the king?

Ateu. Are you prating, knave? I will teach you better nurture.
Is this the care you have of my wardrobe, of my accounts,
and matters of trust?   130

And. Why, alas, sir, in times past your garments have been so
well inhabited as your tenants would give no place to a
moth to mangle them; but since you are grown greater,
and your garments more fine and gay, if your garments are
not fit for hospitality, blame your pride and commend my
cleanliness: as for your writings, I am not for them, nor
they for me.

Ateu. Villain, go fly, find them out: if thou losest them, thou
losest my credit.

---

[1] The 4to " Gnato."   [2] The 4to " which."
[3] *i.e.,* φιλαυτία, self-love.—The 4to " Plulantia."—Corrected by Mr.
Collier, Preface to *Coleridge's Seven Lectures on Shakespeare and Milton*,
p. cxvii.

And. Alas, sir, can I lose that you never had?		140
Ateu. Say you so? then hold, feel you that you never felt.

[*Beats him.*

Re-enter JAQUES.

Jaq. O *monsieur, ayez patience;* pardon your *pauvre valet:* me be at your commandment.

Ateu. Signior Jaques, well met; you shall command me.— Sirrah, go cause my writings be proclaimed in the market-place; promise a great reward to them that find them: look where I supped and everywhere.

And. I will, sir.—Now are two knaves well met, and three well parted: if you conceive mine enigma, gentlemen,[1] what shall I be, then? faith, a plain harp-shilling.[2]		[*Exit.*

Ateu. Sieur Jaques, this our happy meeting hinders [3]		151
Your friends and me of care and grievous toil;
For I that look into deserts of men,
And see among the soldiers in this court
A noble forward mind, and judge thereof,
Cannot but seek the means to raise them up
Who merit credit in the commonweal.
To this intent, friend Jaques, I have found
A means to make you great, and well esteem'd
Both with the king and with the best in court;		160
For I espy in you a valiant mind,
Which makes me love, admire, and honour you.
To this intent, if so your trust, and faith,
Your secrecy be equal with your force,
I will impart a service to thyself,
Which if thou dost effect, the king, myself,

[1] So, again, in the next act, the same speaker, *when alone on the stage,* says, " is not this a wily accord, *gentlemen?* " nor would it be difficult to cite passages from various early dramas, in which, with similar impropriety, the audience is addressed.

[2] The harp-shilling, so called from having a *harp* on it, was coined for the use of Ireland, and was not worth more than nine-pence English money:

> " Lyke to an other Orpheus can she play
> Vpon her *treble harpe,* whose siluer sound
> Inchaunts the eare, and steales the hart away;
> Nor hardly can deceit therein be found.
> Although such musique some a shilling cost,
> Yet is it worth but *nine-pence* at the most."
> Barnfield's *Encomion of the Lady Pecunia,* 1598, Sig. C 2.

[3] The 4to " hides."

And what or he, and I with him, can work,
Shall be employ'd in what thou wilt desire.   168

Jaq. Me sweara by my ten bones, my signior, to be loyal to your
lordship's intents, affairs: yea, my *monseigneur, que non
ferai-je pour* your pleasure?[1] By my sworda, me be no
babillard.[2]

Ateu. Then hoping on thy truth, I prithee see
How kind Ateukin is to forward thee.[3]
Hold [*giving money*] take this earnest penny of my love,
And mark my words: the king, by me, requires
No slender service, Jaques, at thy hands.
Thou must by privy practice make away
The queen, fair Dorothea, as she sleeps,
Or how thou wilt, so she be done to death: 180
Thou shalt not want promotion here in court.

Jaq. Stabba the woman! *par ma foi, monseigneur*, me thrusta
my weapon into her belly, so me may be guard *par le roi.*
Me de your service: but me no be hanged *pour* my labour?

Ateu. Thou shalt have warrant, Jaques, from the king:
None shall outface, gainsay, and wrong my friend.
Do not I love thee, Jaques? fear not then:
I tell thee, whoso toucheth thee in aught
Shall injure me: I love, I tender thee:
Thou art a subject fit to serve his grace.   190
Jaques, I had a written warrant once,
But that by great misfortune late is lost.
Come, wend we to Saint Andrews, where his grace
Is now in progress, where he shall assure
Thy safety, and confirm thee to the act.

Jaq. We will attend your nobleness.   [*Exeunt.*

SCENE III

Enter Queen Dorothea, Sir Bartram, Nano, Ross,
Ladies, Attendants.

Q. Dor. Thy credit, Bartram, in the Scottish court,
Thy reverend years, the strictness of thy vows,
All these are means sufficient to persuade;

---

[1] The 4to " *ye my monsignieur, qui non fera* ic *pour.   Yea pleasure?* "
[2] The 4to " *babie Lords.*"   [3] The 4to " *mee.*"

But love, the faithful link of loyal hearts,   200
That hath possession of my constant mind,
Exiles all dread, subdueth vain suspect.
Methinks no craft should harbour in that breast
Where majesty and virtue are install'd:
Methink[s] my beauty should not cause my death.

Sir Bar. How gladly, sovereign princess, would I err,
And bind [1] my shame to save your royal life!
'Tis princely in yourself to think the best,
To hope his grace is guiltless of this crime:
But if in due prevention you default,   210
How blind are you that were forewarn'd before!

Q. Dor. Suspicion without cause deserveth blame.

Sir Bar. Who see, and shun not, harms, deserve the same.
Behold the tenor of this traitorous plot.   [*Gives warrant.*

Q. Dor. What should I read? perhaps he wrote it not.

Sir Bar. Here is his warrant, under seal and sign,
To Jaques, born in France, to murder you.

Q. Dor. Ah, careless king, would God this were not thine!
What though I read? ah, should I think it true?

Ross. The hand and seal confirm the deed is his.   220

Q. Dor. What know I though, if now he thinketh this?

Nano. Madam, Lucretius saith that to repent
Is childish, wisdom to prevent.

Q. Dor. What tho? [2]

Nano. Then cease your tears that have dismay'd you,
And cross the foe before he have betray'd you.

Sir Bar. What need these [3] long suggestions in this cause,
When every circumstance confirmeth truth?
First, let the hidden mercy from above
Confirm your grace, since by a wondrous means   230
The practice of your dangers came to light:
Next, let the tokens of approved truth
Govern and stay your thoughts too much seduc'd,
And mark the sooth and listen the intent.
Your highness knows, and these my noble lords
Can witness this, that whilst your husband's sire
In happy peace possess'd the Scottish crown,
I was his sworn attendant here in court;
In dangerous fight I never fail'd my lord,

---

[1] Qy. " find "?   [2] *i.e.,* then.
          [3] The 4to " needes this."

And since his death, and this your husband's reign,   240
No labour, duty, have I left undone,
To testify my zeal unto the crown,
But now my limbs are weak, mine eyes are dim,
Mine age unwieldy and unmeet for toil,
I came to court, in hope, for service past,
To gain some lease to keep me, being old.
There found I all was upsy-turvy turn'd,
My friends displac'd, the nobles loth to crave:
Then sought I to the minion of the king,
Ateukin, who, allured by a bribe,   250
Assur'd me of the lease for which I sought.
But see the craft! when he had got the grant,
He wrought to sell it to Sir Silvester,
In hope of greater earnings from his hands.
In brief, I learn'd his craft, and wrought the means,
By one his needy servant [1] for reward,
To steal from out his pocket all the briefs;
Which he perform'd, and with reward resign'd.
Them when I read,—now mark the power of God,—
I found this warrant seal'd among the rest.   260
To kill your grace, whom God long keep alive!
Thus, in effect, by wonder are you sav'd:
Trifle not, but seek a speedy flight;
God will conduct your steps and shield the right.

Q. Dor. What should I do? ah poor unhappy queen,
Born to endure what fortune can contain!
Alas, the deed is too apparent now!
But, O mine eyes, were you as bent to hide
As my poor heart is forward to forgive,
Ah cruel king, my love would thee acquit!   270
O, what avails to be allied and match'd
With high estates, that marry but in show!
Were I baser [2] born, my mean estate
Could warrant me from this impendent harm:
But to be great and happy, these are twain.
Ah, Ross, what shall I do? how shall I work?

Ross. With speedy letters to your father send,
Who will revenge you and defend your right.

---

[1] The 4to " seruants."
[2] Qy. " If *I* were *baser*," or (according to the phraseology of our author's time) " *Were I* more *baser* " ?

Q. Dor. As if they kill not me, who with him fight!
    As if his breast be touch'd, I am not wounded!   280
    As if he wail'd, my joys were not confounded!
    We are one heart, though rent by hate in twain;
    One soul, one essence doth our weal contain:
    What, then, can conquer him, that kills not me?
Ross. If this advice displease, then, madam, flee.
Q. Dor. Where may I wend or travel without fear?
Nano. Where not, in changing this attire you wear?
Q. Dor. What, shall I clad [1] me like a country maid?
Nano. The policy is base, I am afraid.
Q. Dor. Why, Nano?   290
Nano. Ask you why? What, may a queen
    March forth in homely weed, and be not seen?
    The rose, although in thorny shrubs she spread,
    Is still the rose, her beauties wax not dead;
    And noble minds, although the coat be bare,
    Are by their semblance known, how great they are.
Sir Bar. The dwarf saith true.
Q. Dor. What garments lik'st thou, than? [2]
Nano. Such as may make you seem a proper man.
Q. Dor. He makes me blush and smile, though I am sad.   300
Nano. The meanest coat for safety is not bad.
Q. Dor. What, shall I jet [3] in breeches like a squire?
    Alas, poor dwarf, thy mistress is unmeet! [4]
Nano. Tut, go me thus, your cloak before your face,
    Your sword uprear'd with quaint and comely grace:
    If any come and question what you be,
    Say you, " A man," and call for witness me.
Q. Dor. What should I wear a sword, to what intent?
Nano. Madam, for show; it is an ornament:
    If any wrong you, draw: a shining blade   310
    Withdraws a coward thief that would invade.
Q. Dor. But if I strike, and he should strike again,
    What should I do? I fear I should be slain.
Nano. No, take it single on your dagger so:
    I'll teach you, madam, how to ward a blow.
Q. Dor. How little shapes much substance may include!—

---

[1] *i.e.,* clothe.
[2] A form of *then :* used here for the sake of the rhyme.
[3] *i.e.,* strut.
[4] Corrupted. This line ought to rhyme with the preceding one.

Sir Bartram, Ross, ye ladies, and my friends,
Since presence yields me death, and absence life,
Hence will I fly disguisèd like a squire,
As one that seeks to live in Irish wars: 320
You, gentle Ross, shall furnish my depart.
Ross. Yea, prince, and die with you with all my heart:
Vouchsafe me, then, in all extremest states
To wait on you and serve you with my best.
Q. Dor. To me pertains the woe: live thou [1] in rest.
Friends, fare you well; keep secret my depart:
Nano alone shall my attendant be.
Nano. Then, madam, are you mann'd, I warrant ye:
Give me a sword, and if there grow debate,
I'll come behind, and break your enemy's pate.   330
Ross. How sore we grieve to part so soon away!
Q. Dor. Grieve not for those that perish if they stay.
Nano. The time in words mispent is little worth;
Madam, walk on, and let them bring us forth.   [*Exeunt.*

Chorus. Enter BOHAN.

Boh. So, these sad motions make the fairy sleep;
And sleep he shall in quiet and content:
For it would make a marble melt and weep,
To see these treasons 'gainst the innocent.
But since she scapes by flight to save her life,
The king may chance repent she was his wife.   340
The rest is ruthful; yet, to beguile the time,
'Tis interlac'd with merriment and rhyme.   [*Exit.*

[1] The 4to " then."

ACT IV

SCENE I

After a noise of horns and shoutings, enter certain Huntsmen
(if you please, singing) one way ; another way ATEUKIN *and*
JAQUES.[1]

Ateu. Say, gentlemen, where may we find the king?
First Hunts. Even here at hand, on hunting;[2]
    And at this hour he taken hath a stand,
    To kill a deer.
Ateu. A pleasant work in hand.
    Follow your sport, and we will seek his grace.
First Hunts. When such him seek, it is a woeful case.
    [*Exeunt Huntsmen one way, Ateukin and Jaques another.*

SCENE II

Enter the COUNTESS OF ARRAN, IDA, *and* EUSTACE.

Count. of A. Lord Eustace, as your youth and virtuous life
    Deserve a far[3] more fair and richer wife,
    So, since I am a mother, and do wit   10
    What wedlock is and that which 'longs to it,
    Before I mean my daughter to bestow,
    'Twere meet that she and I your state did know.
Eust. Madam, if I consider Ida's worth,
    I know my portion merits[4] none so fair,
    And yet I hold in farm and yearly rent
    A thousand pound, which may her state content.
Count. of A. But what estate, my lord, shall she possess?
Eust. All that is mine, grave countess, and no less.—
    But, Ida, will you love?   20
Ida. I cannot hate.
Eust. But will you wed?

---

[1] The 4to adds " *Gnato* ; " but *Gnatho* is only another name for Ateukin.
[2] A mutilated line.   [3] The 4to " faire."
[4] The 4to " portions merrit."

Ida. 'Tis Greek to me, my lord:
    I'll wish you well, and thereon take my word.
Eust. Shall I some sign of favour, then, receive?
Ida. Ay, if her ladyship will give me leave.
Count. of A. Do what thou wilt.
Ida.   Then, noble English peer,
    Accept this ring, wherein my heart [1] is set,
    A constant heart with burning flames be fret,   30
    But under written this, *O morte dura :*
    Hereon whenso you look with eyes pura,
    The maid you fancy most will favour you.
Eust. I'll try this heart, in hope to find it true.

       Enter certain Huntsmen *and* Ladies.

First Hunts. Widow Countess, well y-met;
      Ever may thy joys be many;—
    Gentle Ida, sair beset,[2]
      Fair and wise, not fairer any;
    Frolic huntsmen of the game
      Will you well and give you greeting.   40
Ida. Thanks, good woodman, for the same,
    And our sport, and merry meeting.
First Hunts. Unto thee we do present
    Silver hart with arrow wounded.
Eust. [*aside*]. This doth shadow my lament,
    Both [with] fear and love confounded.
First Lady. To the mother of the maid,
      Fair as the lilies, red as roses,
    Even so many goods are said,
      As herself in heart supposes.   50
Count. of A. What are you, friends, that thus do wish us well?
First Hunts. Your neighbours nigh, that have on hunting been,
    Who, understanding of your walking forth,
    Prepar'd this train to entertain you with:
    This Lady Douglas, this Sir Egmond is.
Count. of A. Welcome, ye ladies, and thousand thanks for this:
    Come, enter you a homely widow's house,

---

    [1] " *Qu. ' a heart ' ?* " Walker's *Crit. Exam. of the text of Shakespeare,* etc.
ii. 329.
    [2] So Walker, who adds, " *Scoticè, ut passim.*" *Crit. Exam. of the text of
Shakespeare,* etc., ii. 293.—The 4to " faire *beset.*"

And if mine entertainment please you, let us [1] feast.
First Hunts. A lovely lady never wants a guest.

> [*Exeunt Countess of Arran, Huntsmen, and Ladies.*

Eust. Stay, gentle Ida, tell me what you deem,   60
    What doth this hart,[2] this tender hart beseem?
Ida. Why not, my lord, since nature teacheth art
    To senseless beasts to cure their grievous smart;
    Dictamnum [3] serves to close the wound again.
Eust. What help for those that love?
Ida. Why, love again.
Eust. Were I the hart,——
Ida. Then I the herb would be: 68
    You shall not die for help; come, follow me.   [*Exeunt.*

SCENE III

Enter Andrew *and* Jaques.

Jaq. *Mon dieu,* what *malheur* be this! Me comea the chamber, Signior Andrew, *mon dieu ;* taka my poniard *en ma main* to give the *estocade* to the damoisella: *par ma foi,* there was no person; *elle s'est en allée.*
And. The worse luck, Jaques: but because I am thy friend, I will advise thee somewhat towards the attainment of the gallows.
Jaq. Gallows! what be that?
And. Marry, sir, a place of great promotion, where thou shalt by one turn above ground rid the world of a knave, and make a goodly ensample for all bloody villains of thy profession.   81

[1] Qy. if an interpolation?
[2] The 4to "hast."—Is there not something wrong in the next speech?
[3] Or *dictamnus,* is the herb *dittany*.

> " Hic Venus, indigno nati concussa dolore,
>   *Dictamnum* genetrix Cretæa carpit ab Ida,
>   Puberibus caulem foliis et flore comantem
>   Purpureo: *non illa feris incognita capris*
>   *Gramina, cum tergo volucres hæsere sagittæ.*"
>
>   Virgil—*Æn.* **xii.** 411.

Our author in one of his tracts says: " *The deare being strooken,* though neuer so deep, *feedeth on the hearb Dictamnum, and forthwith is healed.*" *Carde of Fancie,* Sig. E 4, ed. 1608.   But in another tract, being at a loss for a simile, he tells us: " *Weomen, poore soules, are like to the harts* in Calabria, that *knowing Dictamnum to bee deadly, yet browse on it with greedinesse.*"   *Neuer too late, Part First,* Sig. D 2, n. d.

Jaq. *Que dites vous, Monsieur Andrew ?*

And. I say, Jaques, thou must keep this path, and hie thee;
for the queen, as I am certified, is departed with her dwarf,
apparelled like a squire.　Overtake her, Frenchman, stab
her : I'll promise thee, this doublet shall be happy.

Jaq. *Pourquoi ?*

And. It shall serve a jolly gentleman, Sir Dominus Monseigneur
Hangman.　　　　　　　　　　　　　　　　　　89

Jaq. *C'est tout un ;* me will rama *pour la monnoie.*　　　[*Exit.*

And. Go, and the rot consume thee !—O, what a trim world
is this !　My master lives by cozening the king, I by flattering him ; Slipper, my fellow, by stealing, and I by lying :
is not this a wily accord, gentlemen ?　This last night, our
jolly horsekeeper, being well steeped in liquor, confessed to
me the stealing of my master's writings and his great reward :
now dare I not bewray him, lest he discover my knavery ;
but thus have I wrought.　I understand he will pass this
way, to provide him necessaries ; but if I and my fellows
fail not, we will teach him such a lesson as shall cost him a
chief place on Pennyless Bench for his labour.　But yonder
he comes.　　　　　　　　　　　　　　　　　　102

Enter SLIPPER, *with a* Tailor, *a* Shoemaker, *and a* Cutler.

Slip. Tailor.

Tai. Sir ?

Slip. Let my doublet be white northern, five groats the yard :
I tell thee, I will be brave.[1]

Tai. It shall, sir.

Slip. Now, sir, cut it me like the battlements of a custard, full
of round holes : edge me the sleeves with Coventry blue,
and let the linings be of tenpenny lockram.　　　　　110

Tai. Very good, sir.

Slip. Make it the amorous cut, a flap before.

Tai. And why so ? that fashion is stale.

Slip. O, friend, thou art a simple fellow.　I tell thee a flap is a
great friend to a storrie,[2] it stands him instead of clean
napery ; and if a man's shirt be torn, it is a present pent-
house to defend him from a clean huswife's scoff.

Tai. You say sooth, sir.

---

[1] *i.e.*, fine.

[2] A word, if it be not a misprint, with which I am unacquainted.

Slip. [*Giving money.*] Hold, take thy money; there is seven
shillings for the doublet, and eight for the breeches: seven
and eight; by'rlady,[1] thirty-six is a fair deal of money. 121

Tai. Farewell, sir.

Slip. Nay, but stay, tailor.

Tai. Why, sir?

Slip. Forget not this special make,[2] let my back-parts be well
lined, for there come many winter-storms from a windy
belly, I tell thee. [*Exit Tailor.*] Shoemaker.

Shoe. Gentleman, what shoe will it please you to have?

Slip. A fine neat calves'-leather, my friend.

Shoe. O, sir, that is too thin, it will not last you. 130

Slip. I tell thee, it is my near kinsman, for I am Slipper, which
hath his best grace in summer to be suited in Jack-ass'
skins. Goodwife Calf[3] was my grandmother, and good-
man Netherleather mine uncle; but my mother, good
woman, alas, she was a Spaniard, and being well tanned
and dressed by a goodfellow, an Englishman, is grown
to some wealth: as when I have but my upper-parts clad
in her husband's costly Spanish leather, I may be bold to
kiss the fairest lady's foot in this country.

Shoe. You are of high birth, sir: but have you all your mother's
marks on you? 141

Slip. Why, knave?

Shoe. Because if thou come of the blood of the Slippers, you
should have a shoemaker's awl thrust through your ear.

Slip. [*Giving money.*] Take your earnest, friend, and be packing,
and meddle not with my progenitors. [*Exit Shoemaker.*]
Cutler.

Cut. Here, sir.

Slip. I must have a reaper and digger.[4]

Cut. A rapier and dagger, you mean, sir. 150

Slip. Thou sayest true; but it must have a very fair edge.

Cut. Why so, sir?

Slip. Because it may cut by himself, for truly, my friend, I
am a man of peace, and wear weapons but for fashion.

[1] *i.e.,* by our Lady. [2] The 4to "mate."

[3] Mr. Collier's conjecture (which I adopt with some hesitation), note on
Shakespeare, ed. 1858, vol. v. p. 600.—The 4to "lakus *skins, Guidwife*
Clarke," etc.

[4] The 4to "*a* Rapier *and* Dagger;" which I retained in my former
edition with the remark, "from the Cutler's reply it seems that Slipper
miscalled the weapons." I now give Mr. Collier's emendation, note on
Shakespeare, ed. 1858, vol. v. p. 599.

Cut. Well, sir, give me earnest, I will fit you.

Slip. [*Giving money.*] Hold, take it: I betrust thee, friend; let me be well armed.

Cut. You shall.   [*Exit.*

Slip. Now what remains? there's twenty crowns for a house, three crowns for household-stuff, sixpence to buy a constable's staff; nay, I will be the chief of my parish. There wants nothing but a wench, a cat, a dog, a wife, and a servant, to make an whole family. Shall I marry with Alice, Good-man Grimshawe's daughter? she is fair, but indeed her tongue is like clocks on Shrovetuesday, always out of temper. Shall I wed Sisley of the Whighton? O, no; she is like a frog in a parsley-bed; as skittish as an eel: if I seek to hamper her, she will horn me. But a wench must be had, Master Slipper; yea, and shall be, dear friend.

And. [*aside.*] I now will drive him from his contemplations.— O, my mates, come forward: the lamb is unpent, the fox shall prevail.   172

Enter three Antics, *who dance round, and take* SLIPPER *with them.*

Slip. I will, my friend[s], and I thank you heartily: pray, keep your courtesy: I am yours in the way of an hornpipe.— [*Aside.*] They are strangers, I see, they understand not my language: wee, wee.—[1] Nay, but, my friends, one hornpipe further, a refluence back, and two doubles forward: what, not one cross-point against Sundays? What, ho, sirrah, you gome,[2] you with the nose like an eagle, an you be a right Greek, one turn more.   180

[*Whilst they are dancing, Andrew takes away Slipper's money, and then he and the Antics depart.*

Thieves, thieves! I am robbed! thieves! Is this the knavery of fiddlers? Well, I will then bind the whole credit of their occupation on a bag-piper, and he for my money. But I will after, and teach them to caper in a halter, that have cozened me of my money.   [*Exit.*

[1] I know not what this means. (In the fifth scene of the present act the 4to has " Wee " as the spelling of the Fr. " Oui.")
[2] *i.e.*, fellow.—The 4to " gone."

SCENE IV

Enter Queen Dorothea *in man's apparel, and* Nano.

Q. Dor. Ah Nano, I am weary of these weeds,
　　Weary to wield this weapon that I bear,
　　Weary of love from whom my woe proceeds,
　　Weary of toil, since I have lost my dear!
　　O weary life, where wanteth [1] no distress,   190
　　But every thought is paid with heaviness!
Nano. Too much of weary, madam: if you please,
　　Sit down, let weary die, and take your ease.
Q. Dor. How look I, Nano? like a man or no?
Nano. If not a man, yet like a manly shrow. [2]
Q. Dor. If any come and meet us on the way,
　　What should we do, if they enforce us stay?
Nano. Set cap a-huff, and challenge him the field:
　　Suppose the worst, the weak may fight to yield.
Q. Dor. The battle, Nano, in this troubled mind   200
　　Is far more fierce than ever we may find.
　　The body's [3] wounds by medicines may be eas'd,
　　But griefs of mind by salves are not appeas'd.
Nano. Say, madam, will you hear your Nano sing?
Q. Dor. Of woe, good boy, but of no other thing.
Nano. What, if I sing of fancy,[4] will it please?
Q. Dor. To such as hope success such notes breed ease.
Nano. What, if I sing, like Damon, to my sheep?
Q. Dor. Like Phillis, I will sit me down to weep.
Nano. Nay, since my songs afford such pleasure small,   210
　　I'll sit me down, and sing you none at all.
Q. Dor. O, be not angry, Nano!
Nano, Nay, you loathe
　　To think on that which doth content us both.
Q. Dor. And [5] how?
Nano. You scorn disport when you are weary,
　　And loathe my mirth, who live to make you merry.
Q. Dor. Danger and fear withdraw me from delight.
Nano. 'Tis virtue to contemn false fortune's spite.

---

[1] The 4to " wanted."　　　　　　　　　　[2] *i.e.*, shrew.
[3] The 4to has " bodies," and, in the next line, " mindes."
[4] *i.e.*, love.　　　　　　　　　　　　[5] Qy. " As"?

Q. Dor. What should I do to please thee, friendly squire?   220
Nano. A smile a-day is all I will require;
    And if you pay me well the smiles you owe me,
    I'll kill this cursèd care, or else beshrow me.
Q. Dor. We are descried; O, Nano, we are dead!

Enter JAQUES, *his sword drawn.*

Nano. Tut, yet you walk, you are not dead indeed.
    Draw me your sword, if he your way withstand,
    And I will seek for rescue out of hand.[1]
Q. Dor. Run, Nano, run, prevent thy princess' death.
Nano. Fear not, I'll run all danger out of breath.   [*Exit.*
Jaq. Ah, you calleta,[2] you strumpet! ta Maitressa Doretie,
    êtes vous surprise ? Come, say your paternoster, *car vous*
    êtes morte, par ma foi.   232
Q. Dor. Callet,[2] me strumpet! caitiff as thou art!
    But even a princess born, who scorn thy threats:
    Shall never Frenchman say, an English maid
    Of threats of foreign force will be afraid.
Jaq. You no *dire votres prières ? morbleu, mechante femme,*
    guarda your breasta there: me make you die on my
    Morglay.[3]
Q. Dor. God shield me, hapless princess and a wife,   240
    And save my soul, although I lose my life!
                  [*They fight, and she is sore wounded.*
    Ah, I am slain! some piteous power repay
    This murderer's cursèd deed, that doth me slay!
Jaq. *Elle est tout morte :* me will run *pour* a wager, for fear me
    be *surpris* and *pendu* for my labour. *Bien, je m'en allerai*
    au roi lui dire[4] *mes affaires. Je serai un chevalier* for this
    day's travail.   [*Exit.*

---

[1] The 4to gives this line to Dorothea.
[2] *i.e.,* drab, trull.—But qy. " Callest *me strumpet,*" etc.?
[3] The name of the sword of Sir Bevis of Southampton:

    " And how fair Josian gave him Arundel his steed,
      And *Morglay* his good sword."
                         Drayton's *Poly-Olbion, Song Second.*

[4] The 4to " auy cits."

Re-enter Nano, *with* Sir Cuthbert Anderson, *his sword drawn, and* Servants.

Sir Cuth. Where is this poor distressèd gentleman?
Nano. Here laid on ground, and wounded to the death,
    Ah, gentle heart, how are these beauteous looks   250
    Dimm'd by the tyrant cruelties of death!
    O weary soul, break thou from forth my breast,
    And join thee with the soul I honour'd most!
Sir Cuth. Leave mourning, friend, the man is yet alive.
    Some help me to convey him to my house:
    There will I see him carefully recur'd,[1]
    And send [out] privy search to catch the murderer.
Nano. The God of heaven reward thee, courteous knight!
                [Exeunt, bearing out Dorothea.

SCENE V

Enter the King of Scots, Jaques, Ateukin, Andrew; Jaques
running with his sword one way, the King *with his train
another way.*

K. of Scots. Stay, Jaques, fear not, sheath thy murdering blade.
    Lo, here thy king and friends are come abroad   260
    To save thee from the terrors of pursuit.
    What, is she dead?
Jaq. *Oui, Monsieur, elle est blessée par la tête* over *les épaules:* [2]
    I warrant, she no trouble you.
Ateu. O, then, my liege, how happy art thou grown,
    How favour'd of the heavens, and blest by love!
    Methinks I see fair Ida in thine arms,
    Craving remission for her late contempt! [3]
    Methink[s] I see her blushing steal a kiss,
    Uniting both your souls by such a sweet,   270
    And you, my king, suck nectar from her lips.
    Why, then, delays your grace to gain the rest
    You long desir'd? why lose we forward time?

---

[1] *i.e.*, recovered.
[2] I know not if this be what the author intended. The 4to has "*per lake teste, oues les espanes.*"
[3] The 4to "attempt."

Write, make me spokesman now, vow marriage:
If she deny you favour,[1] let me die.

And. Mighty and magnificent potentate, give credence to mine
honourable good lord, for I heard the midwife swear at his
nativity that the fairies gave him the propetry of the
Thracian stone; for who toucheth it is exempted from
grief, and he that heareth my master's counsel is already
possessed of happiness; nay, which is more miraculous, as
the nobleman in his infancy lay in his cradle, a swarm of
bees laid honey on his lips in token of his eloquence, for
melle dulcior fluit oratio.   284

Ateu. Your grace must bear with imperfections:
This is exceeding love that makes him speak.

K. of Scots. Ateukin, I am ravish'd in conceit,
And yet depress'd again with earnest thoughts.
Methinks, this murder soundeth in mine ear
A threatening noise of dire and sharp revenge: 290
I am incens'd with grief, yet fain would joy.
What may I do to end me of these doubts?

Ateu. Why, prince, it is no murder in a king,
To end another's life to save his own:
For you are not as common people be,
Who die and perish with a few men's [2] tears;
But if you fail, the state doth whole default,
The realm is rent in twain in such a loss.
And Aristotle holdeth this for true,
Of evil needs [3] we must choose the least: 300
Then better were it that a woman died
Than all the help of Scotland should be blent.
'Tis policy, my liege, in every state,
To cut off members that disturb the head:
And [4] by corruption generation grows,
And contraries maintain the world and state.

K. of Scots. Enough, I am confirm'd. Ateukin, come,
Rid me of love, and rid me of my grief;
Drive thou the tyrant from this tainted breast,
Then may I triumph in the height of joy.   310
Go to mine Ida, tell her that I vow
To raise her head, and make her honours great:
Go to mine Ida, tell her that her hairs

---

[1] The 4to " your *fauour.*"   (Compare line 13, p. 254.)
[2] The 4to " mans."   [3] Qy. " needeth "?   [4] Qy. " As "?

Shall be embellishèd with orient pearls,
And crowns of sapphire,[1] compassing her brows,
Shall war[2] with those sweet beauties of her eyes:
Go to mine Ida, tell her that my soul
Shall keep her semblance closèd in my breast;
And I, in touching of her milkwhite mould,
Will think me deified in such a grace.   320
I like no stay; go write, and I will sign:
Reward me Jaques; give him store of crown[s].
And, Sirrah Andrew, scout thou here in court,
And bring me tidings, if thou canst perceive
The least intent of muttering in my train;
For either those that wrong thy lord or thee
Shall suffer death.

Ateu.   How much, O mighty king,
Is thy Ateukin bound to honour thee!—
Bow thee, Andrew, bend thine sturdy knees;   330
Seest thou not here thine only God on earth?

                                    [*Exit the King.*

Jaq.   *Mais ou est mon argent, seigneur ?*

Ateu.   Come, follow me.—[*Aside.*]   His grave, I see, is made,
That thus on sudden he hath left us here.—
Come, Jaques: we will have our packet soon despatch'd,
And you shall be my mate upon the way.

Jaq.   *Comme vous plaira, monsieur.*

                        [*Exeunt Ateukin and Jaques.*

And.   Was never such a world, I think, before,
When sinners seem to dance within a net;
The flatterer and the murderer, they grow big;   340
By hook or crook promotion now is sought.
In such a world, where men are so misled,
What should I do, but, as the proverb saith,
Run with the hare, and hunt with the hound?
To have two means beseems a witty man.
Now here in court I may aspire and climb
By subtlety, for[3] my master's death:
And if that fail, well fare another drift;
I will, in secret, certain letters send
Unto the English king, and let him know   350
The order of his daughter's overthrow,
That if my master crack his credit here,

---

[1] The 4to " sapphires."   [2] The 4to " weare."   [3] Qy. " before " ?

As I am sure long flattery cannot hold,
I may have means within the English court
To scape the scourge that waits on bad advice.   [*Exit.*

Chorus. Enter Bohan *and* Oberon.

Ober. Believe me, bonny Scot, these strange events
    Are passing pleasing, may they end as well.
Boh. Else say that Bohan hath a barren skull,
    If better motions yet than any past
    Do not more glee to make the fairy greet.   360
    But my small son made pretty handsome shift
    To save the queen his mistress, by his speed.
Ober. Yea, and yon laddy, for the sport [1] he made,
    Shall see, when least he hopes, I'll stand his friend,
    Or else he capers in a halter's end.
Boh. What, hang my son! I trow not, Oberon:
    I'll rather die than see him woebegone.

Enter a round, or some dance at pleasure.

Ober. Bohan, be pleas'd, for, do they what they will,
    Here is my hand, I'll save thy son from ill.   [*Exeunt.*

---

[1] The 4to has " *Yea,* you Ladie *for* his *sport*," etc.—Oberon alludes to Slipper.

ACT V

SCENE I

Enter QUEEN DOROTHEA *in man's apparel and in a nightgown,* LADY ANDERSON, *and* NANO; *and* SIR CUTHBERT ANDERSON *behind.*

Lady An. My gentle friend, beware, in taking air,
    Your walks grow not offensive to your wounds.
Q. Dor. Madam, I thank you of your courteous care:
    My wounds are well nigh clos'd, though sore they are.
Lady An. Methinks these closèd wounds should breed more grief,
    Since open wounds have cure and find relief.
Q. Dor. Madam, if undiscover'd wounds you mean,
    They are not cur'd, because they are not seen.
Lady An. I mean the wounds which do the heart subdue.
Nano. O, that is love: madam, speak I not true?   10
                                       [*Lady Anderson overhears.*
Lady An. Say it were true, what salve for such a sore?
Nano. Be wise, and shut such neighbours out of door.
Lady An. How if I cannot drive him from my breast?
Nano. Then chain him well, and let him do his best.
Sir Cuth. [*aside.*] In ripping up their wounds, I see their wit;
    But if these wounds be cur'd, I sorrow it.
Q. Dor. Why are you so intentive to behold
    My pale and woeful looks, by care controll'd?
Lady An. Because in them a ready way is found
    To cure my care and heal my hidden wound.   20
Nano. Good master, shut your eyes, keep that conceit;
    Surgeons give coin to get a good receipt.
Q. Dor. Peace, wanton son: this lady did amend
    My wounds; mine eyes her hidden grief shall end:
    Look not too much, it is a weighty case.
Nano. Whereas a man puts on a maiden's face,
    For many times, if ladies 'ware them not,
    A nine months' wound with little work is got.
Sir Cuth. [*aside.*] I'll break off their dispute, lest love proceed
    From covert smiles to perfect love indeed.   [*Comes forward.*

Nano. The cat's abroad, stir not, the mice be still.   31
Lady An. Tut, we can fly such cats, when so we will.
Sir Cuth. How fares my guest? take cheer, naught shall default,
        That either doth concern your health or joy:
        Use me, my house, and what is mine as [1] yours.
Q. Dor. Thanks, gentle knight; and if all hopes be true,
        I hope ere long to do as much for you.
Sir Cuth. Your virtue doth acquit me of that doubt:
        But, courteous sir, since troubles call me hence,
        I must to Edinburgh, unto the king,   40
        There to take charge and wait him in his wars.—
        Meanwhile, good madam, take this squire in charge,
        And use him so as if it were myself.
Lady An. Sir Cuthbert, doubt not of my diligence:
        Meanwhile, till your return, God send you health.
Q. Dor. God bless his grace, and, if his cause be just,
        Prosper his wars: if not, he'll mend, I trust.
        Good sir, what moves the king to fall to arms?
Sir Cuth. The King of England forageth his land,
        And hath besieg'd Dunbar [2] with mighty force.   50
Q. Dor. What other news [3] are common in the court?
Sir Cuth. [*giving letters to Lady Anderson.*] Read you these
        letters, madam; tell the squire
        The whole affairs of state, for I must hence.
Q. Dor. God prosper you, and bring you back from thence!
                                [*Exit Sir Cuthbert Anderson.*
        Madam, what news?
Lady An. They say the queen is slain.
Q. Dor. Tut, such reports more false than truth contain.
Lady An. But these reports have made his nobles leave him.
Q. Dor. Ah, careless men, and would they so deceive him?   60
Lady An. The land is spoil'd, the commons fear the cross;
        All cry against the king, their cause of loss:
        The English king subdues and conquers all.
Q. Dor. Alas, this war grows great on causes small!
Lady An. Our court is desolate, our prince alone,
        Still dreading death.
Q. Dor. Woes me, for him I moan!
        Help, now help,[4] a sudden qualm

---

[1] The 4to "is."   [2] The 4to "Dambac."
[3] The 4to gives this line to Sir Cuthbert.
[4] Something is wanting here.

    Assails my heart!

Nano. Good madam, stand his [1] friend: 70
    Give us some liquor to refresh his [1] heart.

Lady An. Daw thou him up,[2] and I will fetch thee forth
    Potions of comfort, to repress his pain.   [*Exit.*

Nano. Fie, princess, faint on every fond [3] report!
    How well nigh had you open'd your estate!
    Cover these sorrows with the veil of joy,
    And hope the best; for why [4] this war will cause
    A great repentance in your husband's mind.

Q. Dor. Ah, Nano, trees live not without their sap,
    And Clytie cannot blush but on the sun;   80
    The thirsty earth is broke with many a gap,
    And lands are lean where rivers do not run:
    Where soul is reft from that it loveth best,
    How can it thrive or boast of quiet rest?
    Thou know'st the prince's loss must be my death,
    His grief, my grief; his mischief must be mine.
    O, if thou love me, Nano, hie to court!
    Tell Ross, tell Bartram, that I am alive;
    Conceal thou yet the place of my abode:
    Will them,[5] even as they love their queen,   90
    As they are chary of my soul and joy,
    To guard the king, to serve him as my lord.
    Haste thee, good Nano, for my husband's care
    Consumeth me, and wounds me to the heart.

Nano. Madam, I go, yet loth to leave you here.

Q. Dor. Go thou with speed: even as thou hold'st me dear,
    Return in haste.   [*Exit Nano.*

    Re-enter Lady Anderson *with broth.*

Lady An. Now, sir, what cheer? come taste this broth I bring.

Q. Dor. My grief is past, I feel no further sting.

Lady An. Where is your dwarf? why hath he left you, sir? 100

Q. Dor. For some affairs: he is not travell'd far.

---

[1] The 4to " her "—the transcriber perhaps having forgot that Dorothea is disguised as a man.

[2] *Daw,* *i.e.,* revive, resuscitate.—The 4to " *Daw thou* her *up* ; " and in the next line " her *paine.*"

[3] *i.e.,* foolish, idle.

[4] *i.e.,* because.

[5] Qy. " But *will them,*" or " And *will them* "—*Will them, i.e.,* Desire them.

Lady An. If so you please, come in and take your rest.
Q. Dor. Fear keeps awake a discontented breast.   [*Exeunt.*

SCENE II

After a solemn service,[1] *enter, from the* COUNTESS OF ARRAN'S
house, a band of Revellers: *to them* ATEUKIN *and* JAQUES.

Ateu. What means this triumph, friend? why are these feasts?
First Revel. Fair Ida, sir, was married yesterday
    Unto Sir Eustace, and for that intent
    We feast and sport it thus to honour them:
    An if you please, come in and take your part;
    My lady is no niggard of her cheer.
                                [*Exit with other Revellers.*

Jaq. Monseigneur, why be you so sadda? *faites bonne chere:
    foutre de ce monde !*
Ateu. What, was I born to be the scorn of kin?   111
    To gather feathers like to a [2] hopper-crow,
    And lose them in the height of all my pomp?
    Accursèd man, now is my credit lost!
    Where are my vows I made unto the king?
    What shall become of me, if he shall hear
    That I have caus'd him kill a virtuous queen,
    And hope in vain for that which now is lost?
    Where shall I hide my head? I know the heavens   120
    Are just and will revenge; I know my sins
    Exceed compare.   Should I proceed in this,
    This Eustace must amain [3] be made away.
    O, were I dead, how happy should I be!
Jaq. Est ce donc à tel point votre etat ? faith, then, adieu,
    Scotland, adieu, Signior Ateukin: me will homa to France,
    and no be hanged in a strange country.   [*Exit.*
Ateu. Thou dost me good to leave me thus alone,
    That galling grief and I may yoke in one.
    O, what are subtle means to climb on high,   130
    When every fall swarms with exceeding shame?
    I promis'd Ida's love unto the prince,

---

[1] The 4to " *After a solemne seruice, enter from the* widdowes *house* a
seruice, musical songs of marriages, or a maske, or what prettie triumph
you list, *to them, Ateukin and* Gnato."
    [2] Qy. dele?   [3] The 4to " a man."

But she is lost, and I am false forsworn.
I practis'd Dorothea's hapless death,
And by this practice have commenc'd a war.
O cursèd race of men, that traffic guile,
And in the end themselves and kings beguile!
Asham'd to look upon my prince again,
Asham'd of my suggestions and advice,
Asham'd of life, asham'd that I have err'd,   140
I'll hide myself, expecting [1] for my shame.
Thus God doth work with those that purchase fame
By flattery, and make their prince their game.[2]   [Exit

SCENE III

Enter the KING OF ENGLAND, PERCY, SAMLES, *and others.*

K. of Eng.[3] Thus far, ye [4] English peers, have we display'd
    Our waving ensigns with a happy war;
    Thus nearly hath our furious rage reveng'd
    My daughter's death upon the traitorous Scot.
    And now before Dunbar our camp is pitch'd;
    Which, if it yield not to our compromise,
    The plough [5] shall furrow where the palace stood,   150
    And fury shall enjoy [6] so high a power
    That mercy shall be banish'd from our swords.

Enter DOUGLAS *and others on the walls.*

Doug. What seeks the English king?
K. of Eng. Scot, open those gates, and let me enter in:
    Submit thyself and thine unto my grace,
    Or I will put each mother's son to death,

---

[1] Qy. if the right word (in the sense of—waiting for)?
[2] The 4to " gaine."
[3] To the speeches of the King of England throughout this scene is prefixed " Arius."—" It is a singular circumstance," says Mr. Collier, " that the King of England, who forms one of the characters in this play, is called *Arius*, as if Greene at the time he wrote had some scruple in naming Henry VIII., on account of the danger of giving offence to the Queen and court." *Hist. of Engl. Dram. Poet.* iii. 161.   But it is only in the present scene that the King of England " is called *Arius* ; " and in a stage-direction to an earlier scene (p. 259,) the 4to gives the name " *Arius* " when the King of England cannot be meant.
[4] The 4to " the."   [5] The 4to " place."   [6] The 4to " enuy."

And lay this city level with the ground.

Doug. For what offence, for what default of ours,
Art thou incens'd so sore against our state?
Can generous hearts in nature be so stern　　　　160
To prey on those that never did offend?
What though the lion, king of brutish race,
Through outrage sin, shall lambs be therefore slain?
Or is it lawful that the humble die
Because the mighty do gainsay the right?
O English king, thou bearest in thy crest[1]
The king of beasts, that harms not yielding ones:
The roseal cross is spread within thy field,
A sign of peace, not of revenging war.
Be gracious, then, unto this little town;　　　　170
And, though we have withstood thee for a while
To show allegiance to our liefest liege,
Yet since we know no hope of any help,
Take us to mercy, for we yield ourselves.

K. of Eng. What, shall I enter, then, and be your lord?

Doug. We will submit us to the English king.
　　[They descend down, open the gates, and humble themselves.

K. of Eng. Now life and death dependeth on my sword:
This hand now rear'd, my Douglas, if I list,
Could part thy head and shoulders both in twain;
But since I see thee wise and old in years,　　　　180
True to thy king, and faithful in his wars,
Live thou and thine.　Dunbar is too-too small
To give an entrance to the English king:
I, eagle like, disdain these little fowls,
And look on none but those that dare resist.
Enter your town, as those that live by me:
For others that resist, kill, forage, spoil.
Mine English soldiers, as you love your king,
Revenge his daughter's death, and do me right.　　*[Exeunt.*

SCENE IV

Enter a Lawyer, *a* Merchant, *and a* Divine.

Law. My friends, what think you of this present state?　　190
Were ever seen such changes in a time?
The manners and the fashions of this age

---

¹ The 4to " brest."

Are, like the ermine['s] skin, so full of spots,
As soone[r] may the Moor be washèd white
Than these corruptions banish'd from this realm.
Merch. What sees Mas Lawyer in this state amiss?
Law. A wresting power that makes a nose of wax
    Of grounded law, a damn'd and subtle drift
    In all estates to climb by other's loss,
    An eager thirst [1] of wealth, forgetting truth: 200
    Might I ascend unto the highest states,
    And by descent discover every crime,
    My friends, I should lament, and you would grieve
    To see the hapless ruins of this realm.
Div. O lawyer, thou hast curious eyes to pry
    Into the secret maims of their estate;
    But if thy veil of error were unmask'd,
    Thyself should see your sect do maim her most.
    Are you not those that should maintain the peace,
    Yet only are the patrons of our strife?   210
    If your profession have his ground and spring
    First from the laws of God, then country's right,
    Not any ways inverting nature's power,
    Why thrive you by contentions? why devise you
    Clauses and subtle reasons to except?
    Our state was first, before you grew so great,
    A lantern to the world for unity:
    Now they that are befriended and are rich
    Oppress [2] the poor: come Homer without coin,
    He is not heard.   What shall we term this drift?   220
    To say the poor man's cause is good and just,
    And yet the rich man gains the best in law.
    It is your guise (the more the world laments)
    To coin provisos to beguile your laws,
    To make a gay pretext of due proceeding,
    When you delay your common pleas for years.
    Mark what these dealings lately here have wrought:
    The crafty men have purchas'd great men's lands;
    They powl,[3] they pinch, their tenants are undone;
    If these complain, by you they are undone;   230
    You fleece them of their coin, their children beg,
    And many want, because you may be rich:

---

[1] The 4to " thrift."
[2] The 4to " Or presse."   [3] *i.e.*, poll.

This scar is mighty, Master Lawyer.[1]
Now war [2] hath gotten head within this land,
Mark but the guise.　The poor man that is wrong'd
Is ready to rebel; he spoils, he pills;
We need no foes to forage that we have:
The law, say they, in peace consumèd us,
And now in war we will consume the law.
Look to this mischief, lawyers: conscience knows　　　240
You live amiss; amend it, lest you end.

Law.　Good Lord, that these [3] divines should see so far
In others' faults, without amending theirs!
Sir, sir, the general defaults in state
(If you would read before you did correct)
Are, by a hidden working from above,
By their successive changes still remov'd.[4]
Were not the law by contraries maintain'd,
How could the truth from falsehood be discern'd?
Did we not taste the bitterness of war,　　　250
How could we know the sweet effects of peace?
Did we not feel the nipping winter-frosts,
How should we know the sweetness of the spring?
Should all things still remain in one estate,
Should not in greatest arts some scars be found,
Were all upright nor [5] chang'd, what world were this?
A chaos, made of quiet, yet no world,
Because the parts thereof did still accord:
This matter craves a variance, not a speech.
But, Sir Divine, to you: look on your maims,　　　260
Divisions, sects, your simonies, and bribes.
Your cloaking with the great for fear to fall,
You shall perceive you are the cause of all.
Did each man know there were a storm at hand,
Who would not clothe him well, to shun the wet?
Did prince and peer, the lawyer and the least,
Know what were sin without a partial gloss,
We'd need no long discoursing [6] then of crimes,
For each would mend, advis'd by holy men.
Thus [I] but slightly shadow out your sins;　　　270

---

[1] Here "*Lawyer*" is a trisyllable: see Walker's *Shakespeare's Versification*, etc., p. 177.
[2] The 4to "man."　　　　　　　　　　[3] The 4to "their."
[4] The 4to "remainde."　　　　　　　　[5] The 4to "and."
[6] The 4to "*Wee need no long discouery.*"

But if they were depainted out for life,
Alas, we both had wounds enough to heal!
Merch. None of you both, I see, but are in fault;
Thus simple men, as I, do swallow flies.
This grave divine can tell us what to do;
But we may say, " Physician, mend thyself."
This lawyer hath a pregnant wit to talk;
But all are words, I see no deeds of worth.
Law. Good merchant, lay your fingers on your mouth;
Be not a blab, for fear you bite yourself.   280
What should I term your state, but even the way
To every ruin in this commonweal?
You bring us in the means of all excess,
You rate it and retail [1] it as you please;
You swear, forswear, and all to compass wealth;
Your money is your god, your hoard your heaven;
You are the ground-work of contention.
First heedless youth by you is over-reach'd
We are corrupted by your many crowns:
The gentlemen, whose titles you have bought,   290
Lose all their fathers' toil within a day,
Whilst Hob your son, and Sib your nutbrown child,
Are gentlefolks, and gentles are beguil'd.
This makes so many noble minds [2] to stray,
And take sinister courses in the state.

Enter a Scout.

Scout. My friends, be gone, an if you love your lives;
The King of England marcheth here at hand:
Enter the camp, for fear you be surpris'd.
Div. Thanks, gentle scout.—God mend that is amiss,
And place true zeal whereas [3] corruption is!   [*Exeunt.*

SCENE V

Enter Queen Dorothea *in man's apparel*, Lady Anderson,
and Nano.

Q. Dor. What news in court, Nano? let us know it.   301
Nano. If so you please, my lord, I straight will show it:
The English King hath all the borders spoil'd,
Hath taken Morton prisoner, and hath slain

---

[1] The 4to " retalde."   [2] The 4to " maides."   [3] *i.e.,* where.

Seven thousand Scottish lads [1] not far from Tweed.

Q. Dor. A woeful murder and a bloody deed!

Nano. The king,[2] our liege, hath sought by many means
    For to appease his enemy by prayers:
    Naught will prevail unless he can restore
    Fair Dorothea, long supposèd dead;   310
    To this intent he hath proclaimèd late,
    That whosoe'er return the queen to court
    Shall have a thousand marks for his reward.

Lady An. He loves her, then, I see, although enforc'd,
    That would bestow such gifts for to regain her.
    Why sit you sad, good sir? be not dismay'd.

Nano. I'll lay my life, this man would be a maid.

Q. Dor. [*aside.*] Fain would I show myself, and change my tire.

Lady An. Whereon divine you, sir?

Nano. Upon desire.   320
    Madam, make but my skill, I'll lay my life,
    My master here will prove a married wife.

Q. Dor. [*aside to N.*] Wilt thou bewray me, Nano?

Nano. [*aside to Q. D.*] Madam, no:
    You are a man, and like a man you go:
    But I that am in speculation seen [3]
    Know you would change your state and be a queen.

Q. Dor. [*aside to N.*] Thou art not, dwarf, to learn thy mistress'
    mind:
    Fain would I with [4] thyself disclose my kind,
    But yet I blush.   330

Nano. [*aside to Q. D.*] What blush you, madam, than,[5]
    To be yourself, who are a feignèd man?
    Let me alone.

Lady An. Deceitful beauty, hast thou scorn'd me so?

Nano. Nay, muse not, madam, for he [6] tells you true.

Lady An. Beauty bred love, and love hath bred my shame.

Nano. And women's faces work more wrongs than these:
    Take comfort, madam, to cure your [7] disease.
    And yet he loves a man as well as you,

---

[1] The 4to " Lords."   Corrected by Mr. Collier, Introd. to *The Tempest*,
p. 11, *Shakespeare*, ed. 1858.

[2] The 4to " Thinking."   [3] *i.e.*, skilled.

[4] Qy. " wish? "   [5] *i.e.*, then.

[6] The 4to " maiden, *for* she."—I hardly understand this; and perhaps
the text here is somewhat mutilated: but it is evident that Lady Anderson
has not yet learned the sex of her guest.

[7] The 4to " our."

Only this difference, he [1] cannot fancy two.   340
Lady An. Blush, grieve, and die in thine insatiate lust.
Q. Dor. Nay, live, and joy that thou hast won a friend,
    That loves thee as his life by good desert.
Lady An. I joy, my lord, more than my tongue can tell:
    Though [2] not as I desir'd, I love you well.
    But modesty, that never blush'd before,
    Discover my false heart: I say no more.
    Let me alone.
Q. Dor. Good Nano, stay awhile.
    Were I not sad, how kindly could I smile,   350
    To see how fain I am to leave this weed!
    And yet I faint to show myself indeed:
    But danger hates delay, I will be bold.—
    Fair lady, I am not [as you] suppose,
    A man, but even that queen, more hapless I,
    Whom Scottish King appointed hath to die;
    I am the hapless princess for whose right
    These kings in bloody wars revenge despite;
    I am that Dorothea whom they seek,
    Yours bounden for your kindness and relief;   360
    And since you are the means that save my life,
    Yourself and I will to the camp repair,
    Whereas [3] your husband shall enjoy reward,
    And bring me to his highness once again.
Lady An. Pardon, most gracious princess, if you please,
    My rude discourse and homely entertain;
    And if my words may savour any worth,
    Vouchsafe my counsel in this weighty cause:
    Since that our liege hath so unkindly dealt,
    Give him no trust, return unto your sire;   370
    There may you safely live in spite of him.
Q. Dor. Ah lady, so would worldly counsel work;
    But constancy, obedience, and my love,
    In that my husband is my lord and chief,
    These call me to compassion of his state: [4]
    Dissuade me not, for virtue will not change.
Lady An. What wondrous constancy is this I hear!
    If English dames their husbands love so dear,
    I fear me, in the world they have no peer.

---

[1] The 4to " she."   [2] The 4to " Alhough."
[3] *i.e.*, Where.   [4] The 4to " estate."

Nano. Come, princess, wend, and let us change your weed: 380
    I long to see you now a queen indeed.   *[Exeunt.*

SCENE VI

Enter the KING OF SCOTS, *the* English Herald, *and* Lords.

K. of Scots. He would have parley, lords:—herald, say he shall,
    And get thee gone: go, leave me to myself.
                      [Exit Herald.—Lords retire.
    'Twixt love and fear continual are the wars;
    The one assures me of my Ida's love,
    The other moves me for my murder'd queen:
    Thus find I grief of that whereon I joy,
    And doubt in greatest hope, and death in weal.
    Alas, what hell may be compar'd with mine,
    Since in extremes my comforts do consist!   39
    War then will cease when dead ones are reviv'd;
    Some then will yield when I am dead for hope.—
    Who doth disturb me? Andrew?

Enter ANDREW *and* SLIPPER.

And. Ay, my liege.
K. of Scots. What news?
And. I think my mouth was made at first
    To tell these tragic tales, my liefest lord.
K. of Scots. What, is Ateukin dead? tell me the worst.
And. No, but your Ida—shall I tell him all?—
    Is married late—ah, shall I say to whom?—   400
    My master sad—for why [1] he shames the court—
    Is fled away; ah most unhappy flight!
    Only myself—ah, who can love you more!—
    To show my duty, duty past belief,
    Am come unto your grace, O gracious liege,
    To let you know—O, would it were not thus!—
    That love is vain and maids soon lost and won.
K. of Scots. How have the partial heavens, then, dealt with me,
    Boding my weal for to abase my power!
    Alas, what thronging thoughts do me oppress!   410
    Injurious love is partial in my right,
    And flattering tongues, by whom I was misled,

                [1] *i.e.,* because.

Have laid a snare to spoil my state and me.
Methinks I hear my Dorothea's ghost
Howling revenge for my accursèd hate:
The ghosts [1] of those my subjects that are slain
Pursue me, crying out, " Woe, woe to lust! "
The foe pursues me at my palace door,
He breaks my rest, and spoils me in my camp.
Ah, flattering brood of sycophants, my foes!   420
First shall my dire revenge begin on you.
I will reward thee, Andrew.

Slip. Nay, sir, if you be in your deeds of charity, remember
me. I rubbed Master Ateukin's horse-heels when he rid
to the meadows.

K. of Scots. And thou shalt have thy recompense for that.—
Lords, bear them to the prison, chain them fast,
Until we take some order for their deaths.

And. If so your grace in such sort give rewards,
Let me have naught; I am content to want.   430

Slip. Then, I pray, sir, give me all; I am as ready for a reward
as an oyster for a fresh tide; spare not me, sir.

K. of Scots. Then hang them both as traitors to the king.

Slip. The case is altered, sir: I'll none of your gifts. What,
I take a reward at your hands, master! faith, sir, no; I
am a man of a better conscience.

K. of Scots. Why dally you? go draw them hence away.

Slip. Why, alas, sir, I will go away.—I thank you, gentle
friends; I pray you spare your pains: I will not trouble
his honour's mastership; I'll run away.   440

K. of Scots. Why stay you? move me not.   Let search be made
For vile Ateukin: whoso finds him out
Shall have five hundred marks for his reward.
Away with them! [2]

---

[1] The 4to " gifts."
[2] The 4to has:
          " *Away with* the Lords troupes *about my tent;* "
and it makes Oberon and the Antics enter too soon (the stage-directions
in our old dramas—which were generally printed from prompters' copies—
being often prematurely marked in order to give the players notice to be
in readiness).
Oberon (see **p. 284**) had told Bohan that he would save his son on this
critical occasion:
          " *Ober.* Yea, and yon laddy, for the sport he made,
     Shall see, when least he hopes, I'll stand his friend,
     Or else he capers in a halter's end.
          Boh. What, hang my son," etc.

Enter OBERON [1] *and* Antics, *and carry away* SLIPPER; *he makes*
mops,[2] *and sports, and scorns.* ANDREW *is removed.*

> Lords, troop about my tent:
> Let all our soldiers stand in battle 'ray,
> For, lo, the English to their parley come.

March over bravely, first the English host, the sword carried before
the King *by* PERCY; *the Scottish on the other side, with all*
their pomp, bravely.

> What seeks the King of England in this land?

K. of Eng. False, traitorous Scot, I come for to revenge
My daughter's death; I come to spoil thy wealth,   450
Since thou hast spoil'd me of my marriage-joy;
I come to heap thy land with carcases,
That this thy thirsty soil, chok'd up with blood,
May thunder forth revenge upon thy head;
I come to quit thy lawless love [3] with death:
In brief, no means of peace shall e'er be found,
Except I have my daughter or thy head.

K. of Scots. My head, proud king! abase thy pranking plumes: [4]
So striving fondly mayst thou catch thy grave.
But if true judgment do direct thy course,   460
These lawful reasons should divide the war: [5]
Faith, not by my consent thy daughter died.

K. of Eng. Thou liest, false Scot! thy agents have confess'd it.
These are but fond delays: thou canst not think
A means to [6] reconcile me for thy friend.
I have thy parasite's confession penn'd;
What, then, canst thou allege in thy excuse?

K. of Scots. I will repay the ransom for her blood.

K. of Eng. What, think'st thou, caitiff, I will sell my child?

---

[1] The 4to " Adam."
[2] *i.e.,* grimaces.—The 4to " pots."—I once conjectured " pouts."
[3] *Quit, i.e.,* requite.—The 4to " *quit thy* louelesse *loue.*"—Corrected by
Mr. Collier, Preface to *Coleridge's Seven Lectures on Shakespeare and Milton,*
etc., p. cxvi.
[4] The 4to " plaines."
[5] Qy. " This *lawful* reason *should* divert *the war*"?
[6] The 4to " for *io.*"

No, if thou be a prince and man-at-arms,   470
   In single combat come and try thy right,
   Else will I prove thee recreant to thy face.
K. of Scots. I brook [1] no combat, false injurious king.
   But since thou needless art inclin'd to war,
   Do what thou dar'st; we are in open field;
   Arming my battle,[2] I will fight with thee.
K. of Eng. Agreed.—Now, trumpets, sound a dreadful charge.
   Fight for your princess, [my] brave Englishmen!
K. of Scots. Now [3] for your lands, your children, and your wives.
   My Scottish peers, and lastly for your king!   480

*Alarm sounded; both the batiles offer to meet, and, just as they
   are joining, enter* SIR CUTHBERT ANDERSON *and* LADY
   ANDERSON, *with* QUEEN DOROTHEA *richly attired, and* NANO.

Sir Cuth. Stay, princes, wage not war: a privy grudge
   'Twixt such as you, most high in majesty,
   Afflicts both nocent and the innocent.
   How many swords, dear princes, see I drawn!
   The friend against his friend, a deadly fiend; [4]
   A desperate division in those lands
   Which, if they join in one, command the world.
   O, stay, with reason mitigate your rage;
   And let an old man, humbled on his knees,
   Entreat a boon, good princes, of you both.   490
K. of Eng. I condescend, for why [5] thy reverend years
   Import some news of truth and consequence.
K. of Scots. I am content [6] for, Anderson, I know
   Thou art my subject and dost mean me good.
Sir Cuth. But by your gracious favours grant me this,
   To swear upon your sword[s] to do me right.
K. of Eng. See, by my sword and a prince's faith,
   In every lawful sort I am thine own.
K. of Scots. And, by my sceptre and the Scottish crown,
   I am resolv'd to grant thee thy request.   500
Sir Cuth. I see you trust me, princes, who repose

---

[1] The 4to " tooke."   [2] The 4to " thy battles."
[3] The 4to gives these two lines to the King of England.
[4] The 4to " friend."   [5] *i.e.,* because.
[6] The 4to gives this line to the King of England.

The weight of such a war upon my will.
Now mark my suit.   A tender lion's whelp,
This other day, came straggling in the woods,
Attended by a young and tender hind,
In courage haught,[1] yet 'tirèd like a lamb.
The prince of beasts had left this young in keep,
To foster up as love-mate and compeer,
Unto the lion's mate, a [2] neighbour-friend:
This stately guide, seducèd by the fox,   510
Sent forth an eager wolf, bred up in France,
That grip'd the tender whelp and wounded it.
By chance, as I was hunting in the woods,
I heard the moan the hind made for the whelp:
I took them both and brought them to my house.
With chary care I have recur'd [3] the one;
And since I know the lions are at strife
About the loss and damage of the young,
I bring her home; make claim to her who list.
        [*Discovers Queen Dorothea.*

Q. Dor. I am the whelp, bred by this lion up, 520
This royal English King, my happy sire:
Poor Nano is the hind that tended me.
My father, Scottish King, gave me to thee,
A hapless wife: thou, quite misled by youth,
Hast sought sinister loves and foreign joys.
The fox Ateukin, cursèd parasite,
Incens'd your grace to send the wolf abroad,
The French-born Jaques, for to end my days:
He, traitorous man, pursu'd me in the woods,
And left me wounded; where this noble knight 530
Both rescu'd me and mine, and sav'd my life.
Now keep thy promise: Dorothea lives;
Give Anderson his due and just reward:
And since, you kings, your wars began by me,
Since I am safe, return, surcease your fight.

K. of Scots. Durst I presume to look upon those eyes
Which I have tirèd with a world of woes,
Or did I think submission were enough,
Or sighs might make an entrance to my soul,
You heavens, you know how willing I would weep; 540
You heavens can tell how glad I would submit;

---

[1] The 4to " hautie." [2] Qy. " and "? [3] *i.e.*, recovered.

You heavens can say how firmly I would sigh.
Q. Dor. Shame me not, prince, companion in thy bed:
    Youth hath misled,—tut, but a little fault:
    'Tis kingly to amend what is amiss.
    Might I with twice as many pains as these
    Unite our hearts, then should my wedded lord
    See how incessant labours I would take.—
    My gracious father, govern your affects:
    Give me that hand, that oft hath blest this head,   550
    And clasp thine arms, that have embrac'd this [neck],
    About the shoulders of my wedded spouse.
    Ah, mighty prince, this king and I am one!
    Spoil thou his subjects, thou despoilest me;
    Touch thou his breast, thou dost attaint this heart:
    O, be my father, then, in loving him!
K. of Eng. Thou provident kind mother of increase,
    Thou must prevail, ah, Nature, thou must rule!
    Hold, daughter, join my hand and his in one;
    I will embrace him for to favour thee: 560
    I call him friend, and take him for my son.
Q. Dor. Ah, royal husband, see what God hath wrought!
    Thy foe is now thy friend.—Good men-at-arms,
    Do you the like.—These nations if they join,
    What monarch, with his liege-men, in this world,
    Dare but encounter you in open field?
K. of Scots. All wisdom, join'd with godly piety!—
    Thou English king, pardon my former youth;
    And pardon, courteous queen, my great misdeed;
    And, for assurance of mine after-life,   570
    I take religious vows before my God,
    To honour thee for father,[1] her for wife.
Sir Cuth. But yet [2] my boons, good princes, are not pass'd.
    First, English king, I humbly do request,
    That by your means our princess may unite
    Her love unto mine aldertruest [3] love,
    Now you will love, maintain, and help them both.
K. of Eng. Good Anderson, I grant thee thy request.

---

[1] The 4to " fauour."
[2] The 4to gives to Lady Anderson this and the next speech of Sir
Cuthbert Anderson.
[3] *i.e.,* truest of all—*alder* being used as the genitive of *all.* So Chaucer
has " *alderfirst ;* " and Shakespeare, and our author in a poem in his
Mourning Garment, have " *alderliefest.*"

Sir Cuth. But you, my prince, must yield me mickle more.
　　You know your nobles are your chiefest stays,　　　580
　　And long time have been banish'd from your court:
　　Embrace and reconcile them to yourself;
　　They are your hands, whereby you ought to work.
　　As for Ateukin and his lewd compeers,
　　That sooth'd you in your sins and youthly pomp,
　　Exile, torment, and punish such as they;
　　For greater vipers never may be found
　　Within a state than such aspiring heads,
　　That reck not how they climb, so that they climb.

K. of Scots. Guid knight, I grant thy suit.—First I submit, 590
　　And humbly [1] crave a pardon of your grace.—
　　Next, courteous queen, I pray thee by thy loves
　　Forgive mine errors past and pardon me.—
　　My lords and princes, if I have misdone
　　(As I have wrong'd indeed both you and yours),
　　Hereafter, trust me, you are dear to me.
　　As for Ateukin, whoso finds the man,
　　Let him have martial law, and straight be hang'd,
　　As all his vain abettors now are dead.[2]
　　And Anderson our treasurer shall pay　　　600
　　Three thousand marks for friendly recompense.

Nano.[3] But, princes, whilst you friend it thus in one,
　　Methinks of friendship Nano shall have none.

Q. Dor. What would my dwarf, that I will not bestow?

Nano. My boon, fair queen, is this,—that you would go:
　　Although my body is but small and neat,
　　My stomach, after toil, requireth meat:
　　An easy suit, dread princess; will you wend

K. of Scots. Art thou a pigmy-born, my pretty friend?

Nano. Not so, great king, but nature, when she fram'd me, 610
　　Was scant of earth, and Nano therefore nam'd me;
　　And, when she saw my body was so small,
　　She gave me wit to make it big withal.

K. of Scots. Till time when.[4]

Q. Dor. Eat, then.

---

[1] The 4to " humble."
[2] The 4to:
　　" As (*all his vaine* arbetters *now are* diuided)."
[3] The 4to " L. Andr."
[4] To this and the next speech of the King of Scots the 4to prefixes
merely " *K.*" Part of the text appears to be wanting here.

K. of Scots. My friend, it stands with wit,
    To take repast when stomach serveth it.
Q. Dor. Thy policy, my Nano, shall prevail.—
    Come, royal father, enter we my tent:—
    And, soldiers, feast it, frolic it, like friends:—   620
    My princes, bid this kind and courteous train
    Partake some favours of our late accord.
    Thus wars have end, and, after dreadful hate,
    Men learn at last to know their good estate.
                               [Exeunt omnes.

GLOSSARY

ABIDE, suffer

ABUSE (DISBUSE), dishonour, insult

ABYE, atone, suffer for

ACCOMPT, account

ADAMANT, loadstone

ADDICTED, devoted, bound by vow

ADDREST, prepared

ADMIRE, wonder

ADVISED, well-considered, deliberate, cautious

AFFECT, affection, desire

AFFECT, love

A-HUFF, in a huff (Oxford Dict.)

ALDER, of all, " alder truest "

ALIE LAND, ? holy, or kindred, neighbouring (see ed. by Farmer, *Early English Dramatists*)

ALLOW, approve

ALMAIN, German

AMAZED, bewildered, perplexed

AMORETS, love-kindling looks (Dyce), or love tricks

AMORT (À LA MORT), dejected

ANATOMY, dissected body

ANGEL, gold coin worth ten shillings, stamped with the figure of the Archangel Michael

ANON, straightway, presently

ANSWER, answer for

ANTIC, ANTIQUE, buffoon

APPLY, comply, consent; fit, suit; " — pastimes," take them as representing real events and persons

APPOSE, pose with hard question

ASLAKED, abated

AVOID, 'VOID, begone, stand away

AVOUCH, sanction, justify

AY, I

BABY, doll

" BACKARE, etc.," Baccare, a cant word meaning " go back," used in allusion to this proverbial saying; probably made in ridicule of some man who affected a knowlede of Latin, etc. (Nares)

BALE, evil, sorrow, injury

BANDOG, band-dog, dog tied or chained up

BARTLET, Barclay, author of the English version of *The Ship of Fools*

BASH, be abashed, ashamed; confound, put out of countenance

BATTEN, grow fat with ease and plenty

BATTLING, battening, fattening

BEHOLDING, beholden

BERY, berry, mound, hillock

BESEEM, seem, appear

BEWRAY, betray, reveal

BIE, bye (*see* abye)

BILBO, Spanish blade

BILL, kind of pike or halbert (combined axe and spear), the usual weapon of watchmen

BILLIMENT, some kind of gold or jewelled ornament of attire

BIND, " — my shame," find (Dyce), bide (Grosart); perhaps binde, technical phrase in hawking for tiring or seizing (Collins)

BLAZE, proclaim

BLEND, render turbid, agitate, trouble (*see* Oxford Dict.)

BOCARDO, a prison so-called situated at the old north gate of Oxford

BODKIN, short pointed weapon of some kind

BOLT, arrow

BONNET, cap

BORD, joke, jest

BORROW, " Saint George to —," defend

BOTTOM, valley

BOTS, a worm disease

BRAVE, bragging, bravado

BRAVE, fine, gay

BRAVERY, finery

BRAWN, muscle; " brawn fallen," with lost strength and nerve

BRIM, fierce, fiercely

BROOK, suffer, endure, put up with

BROTHS, decoctions

BRUIT, report

BRUTE, the Trojan Brut, legendary first King of Britain; hence a noble, or prince, a hero

BUCKLE, grapple, meet in close combat

BUM, strike, beat

BUNTING, name of a group of birds

BURBOLT, birdbolt, blunt-headed arrow for shooting at birds

BUSK, bush or copse

BY AND BY, immediately, at once

CALEYS, Calais

CALLETA, callet, drat

CAMMOCK, crooked stick

CAN, know, be able; "can (con) thanks," give, express thanks

CARRIAGE, burden

CARVEL, light vessel

CASSOCK, loose dress or coat

CAST, "a stroke, a touch" (Johnson), specimen, "taste" (Oxford Dict.). ("Show a cast"; "cast of mine office")

CAST, forecast, anticipate; design, plan

CATES, provisions, dainties

CENSURE, criticise, pass judgment

CHAD, chotte, chwas, chwine, I had, I wot, I was, I ween

CHAFE, state of anger and fret

CHARM, hold in check by magic

CHEAP, "good —," at a low price

CHEER, countenance, expression, mood; entertainment

CHERRY, chirr, chirrup

CHICKEN-PEEPER, chick peeping from its shell

CHIP, cheep, chirp

CHOP-CHERRY, game of bob-cheery (trying to seize a floating cherry with the mouth)

CIRCUMSTANCE, circumlocution, details

CLEVE (CLEEVE), cliff

CLIME, region

CLOUT, cloth, handkerchief, patch, piece of leather, etc., for mending

COAT, cote, outstrip

COCK, corrupt form of God

COCKELL-BREAD, reference to "a wanton sport" played by "young wenches" . . . "a relique of natural magic—an unlawful philtrum" (Dyce)

COG, cheat

COIL, tumult, fuss, confusion

COIL, beat

COLLOCAVIT, some kind of kitchen utensil

COLOUR, pretext, excuse; "in colours," in feigning

COMBUST, said of a planet in such near conjunction with the sun that its light is extinguished

COMPACT, composition, combination

COMPLETE, equipped with necessary accomplishments

CONCEIT, fancy, idea, witty notion or expression, etc.; opinion

CONCEITED, of intelligence, understanding, hence "base conceited"

CONSENT, harmony

CONSUMPTION, act of consuming, waste

CONTEMN, scorn, dispise

CONVEY, steal

CONVEYANCE, juggling, trickery

COPE, purchase, barter

CORIVAL, one having equal rights, etc.

COSTARD, head

COTSOLD, Cotswold; "cotsold lion," sheep

COUNSEL, counsellor

COUNTENANCE, patronage, favour

COUNTERFEIT, image, portrait

COUNTERVAIL, balance, outweigh; prevail against

COURTESY, "keep your —," this and similar expressions refer to the covering or uncovering the head

COUSTRELING, groom, squire, knave

COVER, spread, set the table

COXCOMB, fool's cap, head

CRAKE, crack, boast; ("facing and craking")

CROSS, thwart

CROSS-POINT, name of a step in dancing (Oxford Dict.)

CROWD, fiddle

CULL, coll, hug, embrace; ("kill by culling")

CULLION, low fellow, rascal

CUNNING, skill, knowledge

CURIOUS(LY), elegant, dainty; scrupulous(ly), particular(ly)

CURRY, beat

CURST, shrewish

CUTTING, bullying, swaggering

DAUNT, abate, check, subdue

DAW, simpleton, fool

DAW, awaken, rouse, revive

DAWCOCK, male jackdaw, dolt

DAZE, become dazed

DECEIT, deception, evil wile or device

DEEM, judge, think

DEPART, departure

DESERT, deserter

DESPITE, spite, malice, hate, contempt

DETRACT, forbear, hold back

DICTAMNUS, dittany

DISCOVER, reveal; uncover

DISGRACE, misfortune

DISTEMPERED, vexed, put out, troubled

DOCKET, ? dock

DOOM, sentence, judgment

DOTAGE, extreme fondness

DOTING, senile, foolish

DOTTRELL, plover; simpleton, dolt, from the fact that the silly bird easily lets itself be caught

DRIFT, purpose, aim, intention

DUMP, mournful, plaintive melody; fit of musing, reverie

EARNEST, money in advance

EARST, erst, formerly

EFFECT, fulfilment

EKE, also, moreover

EMPLOY (ON), bestow

ENCHANTING, charming by magic means

ENE, eyen, eyes

ENGIN(E), agent

ENTERTAIN, take into service

ENTWITE, twit, reproach

ESSAY (ASSAY), trial, attempt; " at all —s," ready for anything

FACE, brag, bully; (" facing and craking ")

FACT, feat, deed

FAIN, well pleased or disposed

FAIR, beauty

FANCY, love; " fast fancied," bound by love

FASHION, figure, shape

FATAL, ill-fated, doomed

FAVOUR, features; appearance, charm, etc.

FEARFUL, full of fear

FERDEGEW, ? farthingale, hooped petticoat

FET, fetch

FETCH, stratagem, trick

FEY, FAY, faith

FILED, polished, neatly finished

FIST, handwriting

FIT, division of a song, song

FIT, to be suitable, meet

FLURT, set, start

FLURT, sudden jerk or movement, quick throw or cast (Oxford Dict.)

FODGE, trudge, jog along (Oxford Dict.)

FOIL, repulse, check

FOIL, soil, pollute

FOISON, plenty

FOND, foolish

FOOT, step to music, dance

FORCE, " no force," no matter; " of force," possessing the power

FORDO, undo

FOUL, ugly

FRANION, gay, idle fellow

FROM, away from

FRUMP, flout

GAINST, against, in anticipation of

GALLIARD, lively dance in triple time

GAR, make, force

GARB, manner, fashion

GARD (GUARD), facing, or trimming, ornament

GEAR, matter, business; dress

GEOMANTICK, pertaining to geomancy, divination by lines and figures

GIF, if

GIGLOT, wanton

GILLYFLOWER, clove

GIRDLE, " by your —," alluding to practise of wearing keys hung at the girdle (Oxford Dict.)

GITTERN, kind of guitar

GLAD, make glad

GLASS PROSPECTIVE, magic glass, showing things distant and to come

GLOMING, glumness

GLORY, bestow glory on, glorify

GOME, man, this is suggested by Dyce for " gone," but the Oxford Dict. gives 1515 as latest use of the word

GOOD, " a good," in good earnest

GRACE (" gracing "), adorn, embellish

GRATULATE, gratify, please, welcome

GREE, grade, degree

GREE, agree

GREETS, greetings

GRIEF, grievance; " take with me no —," bear me no grudge

GRISTLE, one of young and tender age

GRUDGE, grumble

GUESSE, guests

HADROMATICK, hydromancy, divination by water

HAMPER (UP), fetter, restrain; tie up, make fast

HAND-FAST, betroth

HAP, chance, fortune

HAPPILY, haply, perchance

HARD-FAVOURED, harsh featured

HARDILY, HARDLY, by all means

HASTE, "no — but good" (prov.). *See* proverb, Act iii. 3, "good hap is not hasty"

HARP-SHILLING, Irish coin with harp stamped on it, worth ninepence

HATEFUL, full of hate

HAZE, have us

HEAL, health

HEIDEGYES, hay-de-guy, — guise, particular kind of "hay," a dance of the nature of a reel (Oxford Dict.)

HELLITROPIAN, heliotrope

HIGHT, called, named

HILDING, base good-for-nothing

HOB, country bumpkin, clown

HOBALL, fool, clown

HOBBY, species of falcon

HOE, "out of all —," out of all bounds or measure (from the interjection Ho! originally a call, afterward rather like a stop or limit, as in the phrase above. *See* Nares)

HOLD, take

HOMELY, familiarly

HORISONS, orisons, prayers

HUFF-SNUFF, fierce, bullying person; from *huff*, and *snuff*, both denoting anger (Nares)

HUMBLE, do obeisance

HUMER, uncertain meaning

IMP, engraft feathers in the wing of a hawk, to supply the loss or deficiency

IMPENDENT, threatening

IMPORT, concern

INCAST, throw in, add

INCH, "at an —," in the nick of time

INCONVENIENT, unbecoming

INDIRECTION, indirect means

INFEOFFE, invest with estate, property

INJURIOUS, pernicious, hurtful, insulting

INTEND, attend to

INTEND, intention

INTENTIVE, attentive, intent

INTREAT (ENTREAT), treat

I WIS, YWIS, indeed, certainly

JACK, BLACK-JACK, jug, tankard, pitcher made of leather

JACK-AN-APES, ape, monkey

JET, strut

JIG, short lively performance, act, or interlude

JOY, rejoice

JUST, joust, distinguished from the tourney, in which many knights engaged, by being a combat between two only (*see* Strutt, *Sports and Pastimes*)

JUT, jostle

KA, quotha

KEN, know

KNOT, company

KO, quoth

LAID, laden

LADE, load, laden

LAMB'S-WOOL, strong ale mixed with pulp of roasted crab-apples

LAMP, ? lampreys (*see* ed. Dr. Ward, Clarendon Press)

LATE, lately, recently

LAWND, open space or glade

LAVOLTA, lively dance

LEAVE, leave off, let be

LEAVE, LEFT, leave, left off

LEECH (LECH), liege

LESE (LEESE), lose

LEST, unless

LET, hindrance, impediment

LET, hinder

LEVEL, aim

LEWD, low, ignorant

LEWELY, ? lovely

LIFTER, thief

LIGGE, lie

LIKE, the like, similarly

LILBURN, heavy, stupid fellow (Halliwell)

LILY, white, pure

LIST, like, choose

LIVELY, true to life

LOBCOCKE, lubber

LOB'S POUND, jail, any tight place or difficulty, "thraldom of hen-pecked husband" (Bullen)

LOCKRAM, coarse linen

LONG, belong

LOPE, leap

Glossary

LOUR, frown

LOUT, mock at for a lout

LOVELY, loving

LOW (see allow)

LOZEL, worthless fellow

LUMPE, lump fish, a thick, clumsy shaped fish

LUNARY, moonwort

LURCHER, robber

LURDEN, heavy, dull fellow

LYTHERNESS, listlessness, lack of energy

M, for Master (see girdle)

MAIDENHEAD, maidenhood

MAINTAIN, uphold, encourage

MALKIN, term of contempt

MALLARD, drake

MANKINE, mankind, masculine, fierce as a man

MARGARITES, pearls

MARRY-GUP, corruption of Mary of Egypt

MASHIP, mastership

MATCH, bargain

MATE, confound

MATTE, " by the —," mass

MEAN, moderation; means, measure; middle part in a musical composition

MEDICINE, poison

MERK(MIRK)EST, dark(est), mirkiest

METELY, fitly

MINION, darling, pet

MIRABILES, mirabolanes, dried plums

MISCHIEF, harm, evil

MISS, fault, error

Mo, more

MOLY, Homer's magic herb has been identified with various plants, among them the wild garlic

MOME, blockhead

MOP, grimace

MORGLAY, name of Bevis of Southampton's sword

MORRIS (MOORISH) DANCE, dance in which different personages were represented; the dancer (Morisco) was hung with bells

MOTION, proposal; puppet-show

MUTTON, woman of ill repute

NEAR, nearer; the old proverb runs " early up and never the nearer "

NEAT, larger horned cattle

NEAT, dainty, spruce; unmixed

NICE, fastidious, particular, coy

NIGHTGOWN, dressing-gown, wrapper

NILL, not will

NOCENT, guilty

NOISE, music, or company of musicians

NONES, nonce, occasion, time being

NONST (see Nones)

NOTABLE, remarkable, egregious

NOWN, short for " mine own "

ONCE, once for all

OPPOSITE, OPPOSITION, astronomical terms applied to heavenly bodies when directly opposite one another

OUT, fallen out

OVERTHWART, contention, repartee, sharp retort or speech

OVERWATCH, watch out, watch through

PAGGLE, hang loosely, like a bag

PAIR (OF CARDS), pack

PAISHE, PASHE, passion

PANTABLES (see Pantofles)

PANTOFLES (PANTOPHLES), ornamented slippers or other rich footgear

PARAGE, lineage, birth

PARDIE, par Dieu

PART, depart

PASS, care, trouble about; exceed bounds or belief

PASSING, exceedingly

PASTANCE, pastime

PATCH, fool, in reference to his motley dress

PEAT, pet

PEEVISH(NESS), perverse, capricious, childish, foolish(ness)

PELTING, paltry

PENTAGERON, a mystic five-pointed figure of the magicians

PEREMPTORY, fixed, determined

PEZZANT, peasant

PHILAUTIA, self-love

PHOBETER, god of sleep

PICKEREL, young pike

PICKPACK, pick-a-back

PIGSNIE, little pig, term of endearment

PIROMANCY, divination by fire

PITCH, fix

PLACKERD, placket-hole, pocket

PLAIN, explain

POLL, plunder

PORTACE, portable breviary

POSY, motto

POTGUN, mocking term for some inefficient weapon, popgun

POWL (see poll)

POWTING (POUTING), kind of small fish; small kind of whiting, a whiting-pout (Oxford Dict.)

PRACTICE, treacherous device, intrigue, stratagem

PREASE, press

PRESENT(LY), immediate, instant(ly)

PRETEND, intend

PRIZE, stake

PROCURE, induce, persuade

PROPER, handsome

PROSECUTE, pursue

PROSPECTIVE, able to forecast (see glass)

PSALTERY, ancient stringed instrument of the zither type

PUG, puck, term of endearment

PURSUIVANT (PERSEVANT), king's messenger, herald

PURSY, short winded

QUAINT, fine, dainty, elegant

QUEAN, hussy

QUILLER, bird not fully fledged

QUIRIE, equerry

QUITE, requite, repay

QUOD, quoth

RABBIT-SUCKER, sucking rabbit

RACE, erase, obliterate

RAIL, one of the Rallidæ family of birds

RATHER, earlier

RECEIPT, " at —," hunting term; to be at stand to await driven game

RECK, heed, care

RECORD, tune, warble

RECORDER, kind of flageolet

RECURE, recovery, restoration

RECURED, healed, recovered

RECURELESS, beyond cure

REFLUENCE, flowing back

REMOVE, move; (" whose hearts are removed ")

RENTED, rent, torn

REPAIR, coming, arrival

REPINE, show displeasure, dissatisfaction

REPRIEF, reproof

RESOLVE YOU, be assured, make up your mind

RESORT, act of visiting

REVOLT, overthrown

RID, destroy, do away; rede, advise

RIDSTALL MAN, stable cleaner, from rid or red to cleanse, etc. (Collins, after Skeat)

RIM-RAM-RUFFE, expressive of something high-flown and swaggering

ROIL, roam, romp

ROUND(ING), whisper(ing)

ROUT, assemble

ROVE, to shoot with rovers, arrows used by archers when aiming at a random mark

RUFF, old game of cards

RUFFLERS, brawlers, swaggerers

RUTH, pity

SAD(LY), sober, grave, serious(ly)

SADNESS, seriousness

SAID SAW, proverb (Halliwell)

SALAMICH, salamander

SALE, " by my —," soul

SALL, shalt

SAUNCE, santis, sanctus, a hymn to St. Satan

SAVOUR, scent

SCAB, term of contempt

SCALD, word of contempt, implying poverty, disease, etc.

SCALLOP-SHELL, the badge of the pilgrim

SCAPE (SKAPE), escapade

SCAPE, escape

SCONCE, head

SECOND, secondary

SECRETARY, confidant, one to whom secrets are confided

SECTOUR, executor

SECURE, confident

SEEN, skilled, proved

SENS (see since)

SENSE, feeling, perception

SENSELESS, devoid of sensation or feeling

SEWER, officer who served the dishes at table

SHADOW, screen, excuse (" — Helen's rape "), or foreshadow, " justify us in anticipating, etc." (Collins); depict in painting, pourtray

SHAMEFAST, shamefaced

SHEAT, apparently, trim, or some such sense (Whitney)

SHELF, reef, shoal, rock

SHENT, blamed, scolded

SHIFT, cheat, cog, cozen

SHOOT-ANCHOR, sheet-anchor, chief hope or resource

SHORT, snappish, cross

SHREW, beshrew, curse

SHREWDNESS, shrewishness

SHROUD, shelter, hide

SHROW, shrew

SIB, some one of kin, relative

SIDE SLOPS, wide breeches

SILLY, simple, plain

SIMPLENESS, simplicity, sincerity

SIMPLES, herbs

SINCE, already

SITH, since

SKILL, have understanding, comprehend; matter, signify

SKRINE (SCRINE), chest, or case of some kind

SLIGHT, sleight, artifice

SLUT, young woman of lower class

SMOOTH, flatter, cajole

SMOOTH, soft, mild

SOOTH, truth, true; " for sooth," in truth

SOOTH(E), assent to, confirm; humour, flatter

SORE, fierce, terrible, mighty

SORRY, sad

SORT, company

SORT, turn out, fall out, come to pass

SPAVIN, disease of horses, causing lameness

SPED, done for

SPEED, cause to succeed, prosper

SPEEDER, one who is successful, who speeds

SPILL, destroy

SPIGHT, spite

SPITE, vex, mortify

SQUARE, measure, compare with

STALE, lure, decoy

STAMMELL, coarse woollen cloth

STAPLED, with fleece of a certain staple or quality

STAY, support; check

STAY, detain, hold back, etc.

STEM, stern

STOCK, sword (Dyce); " long stock," fashionable stocking fastened high above the knee (Bullen)

STOMACH, courage, resolution

STOMACH, resent

STORRIE (unexplained)

STOUND, grief, bewilderment, alarm, or blow, attack

STOUT, proud, stubborn

STOUTNESS, obstinacy

STRANGE, cold, distant, like a stranger

STRIP, outstrip

STROND, strand, shore

STROUTING, swelling

STYLE (STILE), title

SUBSISER, under sizar or student

SUCCESS, result, issue

SUCKET, sweetmeat

SUPERSTITIOUS, scrupulous

SUSPECT, suspicion

SUSPENCE, pause, hesitation

SWATHE, swadling

TABLES, note book, tablets

TAINT, tint

TAKE ME WITH YOU, " let me understand you," " let me go along with you "; or " don't leave me out of consideration " (Bond)

TARBOX, shepherd, who carried tar with him for dressing his sheep's sores

TEISER, teaser, hound

TEMPER, prepare, bring by mixing, etc., to required state; qualify

TENDER, cherish, care for

THEN, than

THO, " what —," then

THREAP, contradict

TICKLING, exciting to any kind of feeling, emotion

TIMELY, early

TIRED, attired

TOIL, net, snare

TOUCH, touchstone

TOWARD, in preparation, at hand

TRASH, money

TRATTLE, tattle

TRAVICE, traverse

TREAT, entreat

TREY, three

TRICK, smart

TRICK UP, adorn

TRIM, " fine," " capital "

TROW, think, believe, know

TRUMP, old game of cards

TURKIS, turquoise

TWAY, two

UMBLES (HUMBLES), the inward parts

UNACQUAINTED, unknown, unheard of

UNAPT, unfit

UNCOUTH, strange, unknown

UNEQUAL, unjust

UNETH, scarcely, not easily

UNKEMBD, uncombed

UNSMOOTHED, unmoved by flattery or blandishments

UNTEWED, undressed, uncombed (*see* Nares)

UNTOWARD, perverse

UNTRUSS, undo, untie the "points" (tagged laces) that fastened different parts of the dress together

USE, to be used or accustomed

VAIL, lower

VENIE, venue, bout, hit, or thrust in fencing

VILD, vile

VOUCH, answer for, guarantee

WAGPASTY, young rascal, jackanapes

WAKE-ROBIN, any species of arum; cuckoo-pint (Webster)

WAMBLE, rumble

WANION, "with a —," with a vengeance, with a plague (Nares)

WARD, guard in fencing

WATCHET, pale blue

WEALTH, welfare

WEAN, perhaps for "whean," a northern English form of "quean," woman (Collins)

WELKIN, sky

WELT, trimming, border (*see* Gard)

WHAYET, quiet

WHEREAS, where

WHILST, until

WHINIARD, short sword or dagger

WHIPPET, frisk about

WHIST, silent

WHIT, jot

"WHITE SON," term of endearment

WHUR, hurry, scurry

WIDE, wide of the mark

WILL, command

WINDGALL, disease of horses

WIT, know

WITHDRAW, cause to retire

WONDER, miracle

WONDER, marvel and admire

WONDER, used as adjective, wondrous

WOODCOCK, simpleton

WOODEN, mad

WOOND, wonned, dwelt

YEAR WHAYLE, erewhile

EVERYMAN'S LIBRARY

A LIST OF THE 990 VOLUMES
ARRANGED UNDER AUTHORS

Anonymous works are given under titles
Anthologies, Composite Volumes, Dictionaries, etc., are
arranged at the end of the list

January 1951.   *The Publishers regret that some of the volumes are out of print.*
A Selected List is available showing volumes in stock.

LONDON: J. M. DENT & SONS LTD.
NEW YORK: E. P. DUTTON & CO. INC.